# CONTROLLING THE ADMINISTRATIVE STATE

This book discusses some of the most important issues facing administrative law and related doctrines.

Leading public law scholars from across the common law world have contributed chapters to recognise the exceptional scholarship and career of Matthew Groves, Distinguished Professor at Deakin University, Australia.

Over the last century, the power of the administrative state has grown immensely and the scope of administrative law as a field of inquiry has grown with it. This collection of essays provides an up-to-date analysis of some of the most important issues in administrative law in the 2020s, including: access to justice issues; the role, purpose and future of ombuds institutions and tribunals; government liability within and beyond judicial review; integrity bodies; 'lawfare'; the role of policies in government decisionmaking; and the tension between military and civilian systems of justice. These topics have been central to the work and career of Matthew Groves.

Readers interested in public law – whether practitioners, researchers or students – will discover a wealth of engaging and thought-provoking considerations of the most topical current issues in administrative law by a selection of prominent academics.

# Controlling the Administrative State

## *Essays in Honour of Matthew Groves*

Edited by
Mark Aronson
and
Greg Weeks

•HART•
OXFORD • LONDON • NEW YORK • NEW DELHI • SYDNEY

HART PUBLISHING
Bloomsbury Publishing Plc
Kemp House, Chawley Park, Cumnor Hill, Oxford, OX2 9PH, UK
1385 Broadway, New York, NY 10018, USA
Bloomsbury Publishing Ireland Limited, 29 Earlsfort Terrace, Dublin 2, D02 AY28, Ireland

HART PUBLISHING, the Hart/Stag logo, BLOOMSBURY and the Diana logo are trademarks of Bloomsbury Publishing Plc

First published in Great Britain 2025



A catalogue record for this book is available from the British Library.

A catalogue record for this book is available from the Library of Congress.

Library of Congress Control Number: 2025945745

ISBN: HB: 978-1-50997-550-1
ePDF: 978-1-50997-552-5
ePub: 978-1-50997-551-8

Typeset by Compuscript Ltd, Shannon

# FOREWORD

Only a novice in the administrative law community would not know of Matthew Groves. Matthew's name is stamped on modern Australian administrative law (and, not surprisingly, he has edited a book by that title). His name pops up everywhere – as an author of several books, an untiring article writer, journal editor, scholarly commentator, seminar organiser and participant, member of government advisory bodies, and in professional associations.

It is fitting, indeed, that Matthew's comprehensive and unique contribution to public law should be recognised in a standalone publication in his honour. It is equally fitting that the contributors range broadly across established and maturing scholars from Australia and abroad. They comment on Matthew's influence on their thinking and careers, and laud his ability to link administrative law scholarship to other social trends. Footnote references to his prodigious output abound.

Comments by contributors that capture those sentiments are that Matthew 'imbues his work with authenticity and intellectual sincerity' and that he has an 'enduring interest in public perception of the legitimacy and impartiality of government decision-making'.

We, too, have been fortunate to work alongside Matthew over a couple of decades in research, writing, editing, presenting, advising and planning. We have seen first-hand Matthew's energy and knowledge, and benefit greatly from his friendship and intellect.

The extraordinary range of Matthew's work is brought out in Greg Weeks' masterly Introduction to this book. Dipping into only a selection of Matthew's 160 or more publications, Greg lists the many core public law topics on which Matthew is an acknowledged expert and is frequently cited – among them, natural justice doctrine, the fairness principle, standing, *habeas corpus*, the ombudsman, tribunals, the judiciary and rights protection.

Matthew's writing typically draws out relevant international comparisons (his fascination with English jurisprudence has not dimmed). Mingled with his serious scholarship is a common deviation into story-telling, providing both a human context and a humorous flair in his analysis. The tapestry of his life and events seems to be expansive and still emerging!

Another laudable aspect of Matthew's career that the Introduction draws out is the support, encouragement and platform he consistently provides to newer scholars. He frequently invites them to contribute to his edited collections and symposia, and includes discussion of their views in his own writing. Likewise, he is assiduous in circulating recent articles by other authors and pointing to their fresh perspective on existing doctrine.

We have personally enjoyed those benefits of Matthew's work and style. He is generous in inviting our participation in ventures he is sponsoring and relying upon and sharing our work with others. Emails regularly arrive from Matthew – at odd hours, and from distant locations – drawing attention to a recent case, report or development. His helpful response to any query is almost instantaneous.

A particular delight is that Matthew was one of four appointees (and, essentially, the academic representative) to the Administrative Review Council when it was re-established in late 2024. Matthew had earlier been a member of the Council for a term from 2011–14. We saw, as members of the Council at the time, the value and diligence in Matthew's contribution to the Council's discussions, projects and publications. Other members of the Council from government, legal practice and civil society, drew great value from his mastery of public law theory and doctrine and his keen practical perspective.

Matthew – like many others – lamented on many occasions that the Council was left to languish after 2012. Once again, the Council is poised to make a solid contribution to the development of Australian administrative law: its ability to do so is undoubtedly strengthened by Matthew's appointment. In the Council's role of fashioning administrative law in a contemporary setting, Matthew is ideally placed to nurture the essential link between the academy, government, legal practice and the community.

Honorary publications usually appear towards the end of a person's career. The customary aim is to honour a person's contribution and achievements while they are still fresh in people's minds. A distinguishing feature in Matthew's case is that his career is still remarkably active and, undoubtedly, there is a great deal more to come. Matthew has achieved so much already, and his impact is so weighty, that his accomplishments are appropriately being recognised at the mid-point. We are honoured to join in this venture and pay tribute to one of the great scholars of Australian law.

Emeritus Professor Robin Creyke AO    Emeritus Professor John McMillan AO

# CONTENTS

# ABOUT THE CONTRIBUTORS

**Mark Aronson** is an Emeritus Professor of Law at the University of New South Wales, Australia. His published books and articles have spanned several areas of the law, including civil and criminal procedure, evidence law, government liability in tort and judicial review of administrative action.

**Greg Weeks** is a General Member of the Administrative Review Tribunal and a Professor in the ANU College of Law at the Australian National University. He has published widely on judicial review, state liability and remedies against public authorities. He has written extensively with Matthew Groves, most notably alongside Mark Aronson on the two most recent editions of *Judicial Review of Administrative Action and Government Liability*, 6th edn (London, Thomson Reuters, 2017 and 7th edn, 2022), Australia's leading administrative law text. He and Matthew edited two collections of essays: *Legitimate Expectations in the Common Law World* (Oxford, Hart Publishing, 2017) and *Administrative Redress Inside and Outside the Courts: Essays in Honour of Robyn Creyke and John McMillan* (Alexandria, Federation Press, 2019). Matthew and Greg are also the General Editors of the *Australian Journal of Administrative Law*.

**Chantal Bostock** is an Associate Professor in the School of Global and Public Law at the Faculty of Law and Justice at the University of New South Wales, Australia. She has worked as a migration/refugee lawyer in Sydney and as a senior lawyer at the Asylum and Immigration Tribunal and the Law Commission in London and for five years at the Migration Review Tribunal and the Administrative Appeals Tribunal in Australia. Chantal teaches administrative and immigration law and is a member of the NSW Medical Council. She holds an LLM (Syd) and a PhD (UNSW) and has published and delivered papers on a range of topics, including administrative law.

**Robin Creyke AO FAAL** is an Emeritus Professor at the Australian National University. Robin has been an academic, tribunal member for a number of tribunals and worked with organisations related to government law including as Integrity Adviser to the Australian Taxation Office and as a member of the Administrative Review Council. She has co-authored an administrative law text Control of Government Action, two military law texts, and authored material on tribunals and government. She has undertaken several independent inquiries for government, including for the establishment of the Administrative Review Tribunal and is currently working on an inquiry into the national workers' compensation scheme.

**Paul Daly** holds the University Research Chair in Administrative Law and Governance at the University of Ottawa. He previously held academic appointments at the Université de Montréal and the University of Cambridge and has visited at Harvard Law School, Université Paris II Panthéon-Assas, and Louvain Global College of Law. He is an award-winning scholar whose bilingual research has appeared in many leading journals and edited collections and is frequently cited by courts across the common law world. Notable books include *A Theory of Deference in Administrative Law: Basis, Application and Scope* (Cambridge, CUP, 2012) and *Understanding Administrative Law in the Common Law World* (Oxford, OUP, 2021).

**Alison Duxbury** is a Professor of Melbourne Law School, University of Melbourne, and the President of the Australian and New Zealand Society of International Law. Alison's major teaching and research interests are in the fields of international law, in particular international institutional law, human rights law and international humanitarian law. In 2023–24 she was a Visting Fellow at All Souls College and a Visiting Scholar at the Bonavero Institute of Human Rights at the University of Oxford. Alison's publications include *The Participation of States in International Organisations: The Role of Human Rights and Democracy* (Cambridge, CUP, 2011), a co-edited collection (with Matthew Groves), *Military Justice in the Modern Age* (Cambridge, CUP, 2016) and a co-authored book (with Tan Hsien-Li), *Can ASEAN Take Human Rights Seriously?* (Cambridge, CUP, 2019).

**Andrew Edgar** is a Professor of Administrative Law at Sydney Law School. He specialises on administrative law-making. His recent publications focus on regulation-making processes and review of regulations by parliaments and courts. Andrew also has research interests in statutory interpretation and the implementation of international law in domestic law.

**Liam Edwards** is a PhD researcher at Ulster University School of Law and has an LLB from Bangor University. His thesis project, 'Judicial Review and the Devolved Nations', is a mixed-method comparative study on the divergence in the number of judicial review hearings across Scotland, Wales, and Northern Ireland. Prior to this, Liam worked as a researcher at Bangor University School of Law, resulting in a report on judicial review in Wales. Liam's research interests are comparative constitutional and administrative law, devolution, access to justice, and implementation of language rights.

**Emily Hammond** is a Senior Lecturer at the University of Sydney Law School. She teaches and researches Australian public law. Her current research explores how Australian judicial review doctrine reflects a specific constitutional conception of the boundary between judicial and executive power to specify subjects' rights or obligations. Her sole-authored research has been published in leading Australian public law journals, the *CERIDAP Journal*; and appears in Carter and Tomlinson (eds), *Facts in Public Law Adjudication* (Oxford, Hart Publishing, 2023). She is also a co-author of McDonald, Rundle and Hammond, *Principles of Administrative Law*, 4th edn (Oxford, OUP, 2023).

**Cora Hoexter** BA LLB (Natal) MA (Oxon) PhD (Witwatersrand) is a public-law scholar and part-time Professor of Law at the University of the Witwatersrand, Johannesburg. She has written extensively on administrative law, and her publications on this theme are frequently cited by the superior courts of South Africa, including the Constitutional Court. Her books include a leading text, *Administrative Law in South Africa*, first published by Juta in 2007. A third edition, co-authored with Dr Glenn Penfold, appeared in 2021 and a fourth edition is in preparation. Cora has served for many years as South Africa's 'foreign correspondent' to *De Smith's Judicial Review* and has contributed essays to several collections published by Hart Publishing.

**Rain Liivoja** is a Professor and Deputy Dean (Research) at the University of Queensland Law School, where he leads the Law and the Future of War research group. He is also a Visiting Legal Fellow to the Department of Foreign Affairs and Trade, and a Senior Fellow with the Lieber Institute for Law and Land Warfare at the United States Military Academy at West Point. Rain has published on a range of international law issues relating to military operations, as well as on military discipline law from a comparative perspective. His current research focuses on the legal challenges associated with military applications of science and technology. Before joining the University of Queensland, Rain held academic appointments at the Universities of Melbourne, Helsinki and Tartu. He has served on governmental delegations to multilateral meetings on international humanitarian law and arms control.

**John McMillan AO** is an Emeritus Professor at the Australian National University, where he taught administrative and constitutional law from 1983–2003. He is a co-author of *Control of Government Action: Text, Cases and Commentary*, 7th edn (Sydney, LexisNexis, 2025). John has held the statutory positions of Commonwealth and NSW Ombudsman, Australian Information Commissioner, Integrity Commissioner, member of the Administrative Review Council, and member of the Australian Copyright Tribunal. He has conducted independent statutory reviews of the medicinal cannabis scheme, My Health Records Act, Modern Slavery Act and Australian Sports Commission Act.

**Dan Meagher** is Professor and Chair in Law at the Deakin Law School in Australia, teaching and researching in constitutional law and statutory interpretation. Dan has published his scholarship widely in Australian and international law journals, co-edited *The Principle of Legality in Australia and New Zealand* (Alexandria, Federation Press, 2017) with Professor Matthew Groves, *The Legal Protection of Rights in Australia* (Oxford, Hart Publishing, 2019) with Professor Groves and Dr Janina Boughey and is co-author of a leading casebook – *Hanks Australian Constitutional Law: Materials and Commentary*, 11th edn (Chatsworth, LexisNexis,

2021). Dan is Director of Research in the Deakin Law School, comments editor for the *Public Law Review* and an elected Fellow of the Australian Academy of Law.

**Sarah Nason** is a Senior Lecturer at Bangor University. Sarah's research interests include judicial review, comparative administrative law, human rights, and administrative justice. Sarah's monograph *Reconstructing Judicial Review* was published by Hart Publishing in 2016 (Paperback edition 2019). She has also edited a University of Wales Press collection on *Administrative Justice in Wales and Comparative Perspectives* (Cardiff, University of Wales Press 2017), and contributed various articles to the *Modern Law Review*, *Public Law*, *Law and Society*, and the *Journal of Social Welfare and Family Law*; and made contributions to various Oxford University Press, Routledge, Edward Elgar and Hart Publishing collections on public law, administrative justice, and constitutional theory. She is an academic panel member of the UK Administrative Justice Council, and a member of the Editorial Committee of the journal *Public Law* and co-authors the journal's current survey section.

**Ellen Rock** is an Associate Professor in the Faculty of Law & Justice at the University of New South Wales. She is a member of the School of Global and Public Law and the Gilbert + Tobin Centre of Public Law, and is co-director of the Centre's Administrative Law and Justice Project. Ellen's primary research interest is government accountability, focussing on legal and non-legal mechanisms that contribute to the control of public power and the design of accountability systems. She has written widely on these topics, including her monograph *Measuring Accountability in Public Governance Regimes* (Cambridge, Cambridge University Press, 2020). Ellen teaches administrative law at UNSW and holds an appointment as independent legal adviser to the NSW Legislative Council's Delegated Legislation Committee.

**Anita Stuhmcke** is Dean of the Faculty of Law at the University of Technology Sydney, Australia. Anita is widely acknowledged as one of Australia's leading scholars on Ombudsman issues and as a leading international legal scholar in the field. She has a particular research interest in the ways in which law operates as a continuum of effectiveness for social justice, this leads her to interrogate the operation of the Ombudsman institution as an instrument of democratic accountability in terms of the citizen, industry, consumer, government agencies and the wider legal system. Anita is widely cited, nationally and internationally, having published many journal articles, book chapters, written policy submissions which have impacted the development of law and policy in her research field.

**Stephen Thomson** is an Associate Professor at the ANU College of Law at the Australian National University. He has published widely on domestic and comparative public law in several jurisdictions, particularly on administrative law and constitutional law. Stephen is the author of *Administrative Law in Hong Kong* (Cambridge, Cambridge University Press, 2018), *The Nobile Officium*

(Edinburgh, Avizandum/Edinburgh University Press, 2015) and *Administrative Law: A Very Short Introduction* (Oxford, Oxford University Press, forthcoming). He is the co-editor of *Administrative Law (Reissue)* in *The Laws of Scotland: The Stair Memorial Encyclopaedia* (Edinburgh, LexisNexis, 2023) and *Administrative Tribunals in the Common Law World* (Oxford, Hart Publishing, forthcoming). Stephen is the General Editor of the *Federal Law Review*.

**Hanna Wilberg** is an Associate Professor at the University of Auckland Faculty of Law. She specialises in Administrative Law, Social Security, and the Tort Liability of Public Authorities. Her interests also extend to public law more generally, particularly statutory interpretation, Bill of Rights, discrimination and Treaty of Waitangi issues. She is the author of *Administrative Law in Aotearoa New Zealand* (Oxford, Hart Publishing, 2025) and of many articles and book chapters, and co-editor with Mark Elliott of *The Scope and Intensity of Substantive Review: Traversing Taggart's Rainbow* (Oxford, Hart Publishing, 2015). She is a graduate of Otago (NZ) and Oxford, and before joining academia she worked at the NZ Crown Law Office and as a Court of Appeal Judges' Clerk. She has been a visiting scholar at the Australian National University and at the Universities of Cambridge, Toronto and Oxford.

# Introduction: Matthew Groves, His Research and its Impact

GREG WEEKS

> Compliments always embarrass a man. You do not know anything to say. It does not inspire you with words. There is nothing you can say in answer to a compliment. I have been complimented myself a great many times and they always embarrass me – I always feel that they have not said enough.[1]

Upon first meeting Matthew Groves, one might easily conclude that he is an expert. He is, after all, a man of rare intelligence and a sharp wit who does not feel the need to disguise those attributes. The subject of his expertise might be harder to identify – after all, there are experts and experts[2] – although one might understandably speculate that it has to do with cats.[3] It tends to creep up on one that Matthew knows a very great deal about a wide range of topics. For our purposes, that observation has two consequences. The first is that Matthew has been an incredibly prolific[4] writer of universally excellent research. The second is that, while there are evident themes in his research which are revisited from time to time, the complete body of his work covers an extraordinary range of subjects. The chapters in this collection reflect many, but inevitably not all, of Matthew's research interests. Writing

[1] M Twain, 'Robert Fulton Day', (Speech delivered at the Jamestown Exposition, Norfolk, Virginia, 23 September 1907).

[2] The observation of Jordan CJ that 'there are mistakes and mistakes', made in *Ex parte Hebburn Ltd; Re Kearsley Shire Council* (1947) 47 SR(NSW) 416, 420, has almost become an administrative law cliché. It has been repeated frequently (see, eg, *Stanley v Director of Public Prosecutions (NSW)* (2023) 278 CLR 1, 9 [17] per Gageler J) but has also been adapted to apply to topics as diverse as fiduciaries (*Harris v Digital Pulse Pty Ltd* (2003) 56 NSWLR 298, 323 [122] per Mason P), rights (*Kassam v Hazzard* (2021) 106 NSWLR 520, 555 [166] per Leeming JA) and appeals (MJ Leeming, *Authority to Decide: The Law of Jurisdiction in Australia*, 2nd edn (Annandale, Federation Press, 2020) 279).

[3] Matthew has often written and spoken about 'CATs', in the sense of Civil and Administrative Tribunals; see, eg, M Groves, 'Bias by the Numbers' (2020) 100 *AIAL Forum* 60; M Groves and G Weeks, 'The Unique Jurisdiction of Australian Merits Review Tribunals' in S Thomson, M Groves and G Weeks (eds), *Administrative Tribunals in the Common Law World* (Oxford, Hart Publishing, 2024) 129, 143–145; M Groves, 'The Administrative Review Tribunal: A Big Step in Tribunal Justice, 50 Years in the Making' (2024) 98 *Australian Law Journal* 902, 908. Nobody who knows Matthew thinks that these are the cats which interest him most.

[4] Matthew's Deakin University profile listed 162 publications in February 2025: experts.deakin.edu.au/48799-matthew-groves/publications. That number will almost certainly have increased by the time this book is published.

recently, Matthew observed that public law's review and accountability mechanisms 'are patchwork in nature, but a patchwork quilt is still a quilt. It covers what needs to be covered'.[5] Taken cumulatively, Matthew's publications amount to a quilt of impressive coverage.

Even a cursory review of Matthew's published work reveals that he has done an immense amount of work with co-authors. Matthew has a talent for collaborative work and has edited many collections of essays,[6] mostly with a co-editor.[7] Early in his career, he worked extensively with Enid Campbell,[8] who had supervised his doctoral thesis and later recommended him to Mark Aronson and Bruce Dyer as a co-author.[9] As his career has progressed, Matthew has more frequently written with junior colleagues and has done much to further their careers as academics.[10] Matthew's role as an administrative law godfather to junior colleagues has not prevented him from writing with co-authors whose expertise in other subjects complements his own for the purpose of a project.[11] Additionally, Matthew's

[5] M Groves, 'Systemic Failure and Systemic Unfairness' (2023) 30 *Australian Journal of Administrative Law* 209, 210 (footnote omitted). Those wondering about the quilt on the cover of this book have their answer.

[6] Two of these he edited alone: M Groves (ed), *Law and Government in Australia: Essays in Honour of Enid Campbell* (Annandale, Federation Press, 2005); M Groves (ed), *Modern Administrative Law in Australia: Concepts and Context* (Port Melbourne, Cambridge University Press, 2014).

[7] M Groves and H Lee (eds), *Australian Administrative Law: Fundamentals, Principles, and Doctrines* (Port Melbourne, Cambridge University Press, 2007); A Duxbury and M Groves (eds), *Military Justice in the Modern Age* (Port Melbourne, Cambridge University Press, 2016); M Groves and C Campbell (eds), *Australian Charters of Rights A Decade On* (Annandale, Federation Press, 2017); M Groves and G Weeks (eds), *Legitimate Expectations in the Common Law World* (Oxford, Hart Publishing, 2017); D Meagher and M Groves (eds), *The Principle of Legality in Australia and New Zealand* (Annandale, Federation Press, 2017); M Groves, J Boughey and D Meagher (eds), *The Legal Protection of Rights in Australia* (Oxford, Hart Publishing, 2019); G Weeks and M Groves (eds), *Administrative Redress In and Out of the Courts: Essays in Honour of Robin Creyke and John McMillan* (Annandale, Federation Press, 2019); M Groves and A Stuhmcke (eds), *The Ombudsman in the Modern State* (Oxford, Hart Publishing, 2022); S Thomson, M Groves and G Weeks (eds), *Administrative Tribunals in the Common Law World* (Oxford, Hart Publishing, 2024).

[8] See, eg, E Campbell and M Groves, 'Time Limitations on Applications for Judicial Review' (2004) 32 *Federal Law Review* 29; E Campbell and M Groves, 'Award of Costs in Administrative Proceedings' (2004) 11 *Australian Journal of Administrative Law* 121; E Campbell and M Groves, 'Privative Clauses and the Australian Constitution' (2004) 4 *Oxford University Commonwealth Law Journal* 51; E Campbell and M Groves, 'Parliamentary Papers and their Protection' (2004) 9 *Media and Arts Law Review* 113; E Campbell and M Groves, 'Enforcement of Administrative Determinations' (2006) 13 *Australian Journal of Administrative Law* 121.

[9] Starting with M Aronson, B Dyer and M Groves, *Judicial Review of Administrative Action*, 3rd edn (Toronto, Thomson Legal and Regulatory Ltd, 2004).

[10] This has included setting aside the usual convention and putting the names of junior but alphabetically subsequent authors before his own; see, eg, D Meagher and M Groves (eds), *The Principle of Legality in Australia and New Zealand* (Annandale, Federation Press, 2017); G Weeks and M Groves (eds), *Administrative Redress In and Out of the Courts: Essays in Honour of Robin Creyke and John McMillan* (Annandale, Federation Press, 2019); S Thomson, M Groves and G Weeks (eds), *Administrative Tribunals in the Common Law World* (Oxford, Hart Publishing, 2024).

[11] See, eg, M Groves and R Smyth, 'A Century of Judicial Style: Changing Patterns in Judgment Writing on the High Court 1903-2001' (2004) 32 *Federal Law Review* 255; A Duxbury and M Groves (eds), *Military Justice in the Modern Age* (Cambridge, Cambridge University Press, 2016); M Groves and J Murray, 'The Constitutional Price of Justice' (2018) 29 *Public Law Review* 97; M Groves, I Nielsen

fondness for working with junior colleagues has never stood in the way of him convincing a wide range of eminent and successful people to contribute to his books, starting with the Foreword from former Prime Minister Gough Whitlam to his Festschrift for Enid Campbell.[12]

Many of Matthew's co-authors and those to whom he has given an opportunity to contribute chapters to books he has edited have benefitted enormously from his expertise and experience. He is a consummate editor and those with whom he has worked in an editorial capacity have learned a great deal from the experience.[13] It is no surprise that so many of Matthew's co-authors have contributed to this collection.[14]

Matthew's foremost area of expertise is Australian judicial review of administrative action and he has written extensively on many doctrines which fall within that broad label. His research extends beyond the federal arena and embraces the High Court's insistence on there being a single common law of Australia.[15] Emily Hammond's chapter in this collection also explores those themes.[16] She examines the place of state constitutions in understanding jurisdictional error, the centrepiece of judicial review under the Commonwealth Constitution.

Under the broad heading of judicial review, Matthew's particular expertise in issues of procedural fairness is well-known.[17] He has written extensively on aspects of the hearing rule,[18] but his research on the bias rule[19] has been especially

and R Smyth, 'Public Support for the Rule of Law' (2022) 51 *Australian Bar Review* 80; M Groves and A Stuhmcke (eds), *The Ombudsman in the Modern State* (Oxford, Hart Publishing, 2022).

[12] M Groves (ed), *Law and Government in Australia: Essays in Honour of Enid Campbell* (Annandale, Federation Press, 2005).

[13] The most difficult aspect of editing this book has been the fact that Matthew has played no part in it.

[14] See, eg, Matthew's co-authors in: R Creyke and M Groves, 'Administrative Law Evolution: an Academic Perspective' (2010) 59 *Admin Review* 20; A Duxbury and M Groves, 'The Reform of Military Justice' in A Duxbury and M Groves (eds), *Military Justice in the Modern Age* (Cambridge, Cambridge University Press, 2016) xxviii; D Meagher and M Groves, 'The Common Law Principle of Legality and Secondary Legislation' (2016) 39 *University of New South Wales Law Journal* 450; M Groves and A Stuhmcke, 'The Evolution and Future of the Ombuds' in M Groves and A Stuhmcke (eds), *The Ombudsman in the Modern State* (Oxford, Hart Publishing, 2022) 1; S Thomson, M Groves and G Weeks, 'The Distinctive Nature of Tribunals' in S Thomson, M Groves and G Weeks (eds), *Administrative Tribunals in the Common Law World* (Oxford, Hart Publishing, 2024) 1.

[15] See, eg, M Groves, 'Federal Constitutional Influences on State Judicial Review' (2011) 39 *Federal Law Review* 399.

[16] See ch 9 of this volume.

[17] Matthew wrote one of the natural justice chapters in the 3rd edition of *Judicial Review of Administrative Action* and became the sole author of all three of those chapters by the time of the 5th edition. Those chapters are cited frequently in judgments.

[18] See, eg, M Groves, 'Exclusion of the Rules of Natural Justice' (2014) 39 *Monash University Law Review* 285; M Groves, 'The Evolution and Entrenchment of Natural Justice' in M Groves (ed), *Modern Administrative Law in Australia: Concepts and Context* (Port Melbourne, Cambridge University Press, 2014) 205; M Groves, 'Waiver of Natural Justice' (2019) 40 *Adelaide Law Review* 641.

[19] See, eg, M Groves, 'The Rule Against Bias' in M Groves and H Lee (eds), *Australian Administrative Law: Fundamentals, Principles and Doctrines* (Cambridge, Cambridge University Press, 2007) 316; M Groves, 'Waiver of the Rule against Bias' (2009) 35 *Monash University Law Review* 315; M Groves, 'The Imaginary Observer of the Bias Rule' (2012) 19 *Australian Journal of Administrative Law* 188;

influential. It has frequently examined complex issues which go beyond the statements contained in the standard tests.[20] The book chapter on 'The Rule Against Bias' over which Matthew has had primary responsibility for 20 years now runs to over 100 pages and covers that rule's variable application to judicial and administrative decision-makers with encyclopaedic thoroughness.[21] A search of the Jade database shows the frequent judicial citations of Matthew's bias research since 2008 in most Australian jurisdictions. Given that Matthew's work on the bias rule is both so extensive and so celebrated, Paul Daly may have thought that he was on the ultimate hiding to nothing in undertaking to write a chapter on that subject.[22] His analysis of issues of temporal and spatial proximity in the rule against bias is fascinating, although that is not the reason that it will be the first chapter that Matthew reads.

The Australian conception of fairness in administrative law has traditionally been narrow and procedurally focused. The substantive fairness of the outcome of administrative action is seldom directly within the remit of judicial review[23] and is only addressed by merits review proceedings within the scope of reaching the correct or preferable decision on the application of a specific statutory scheme. Matthew's research on conceptions of fairness more broadly has looked beyond the confines of Australian judicial review doctrine while continuing to acknowledge their influence.[24] Matthew's research on fairness has, understandably, shared

M Groves, 'Empathy, Experience and the Rule Against Bias in Criminal Trials' (2012) 36 *Criminal Law Journal* 84; M Groves, 'Public Statements by Judges and the Bias Rule' (2014) 40 *Monash University Law Review* 115; M Groves, 'A Man For All Seasons? The Fair Minded Observer and Royal Commissioners' (2016) 23 *Australian Journal of Administrative Law* 201; M Groves, 'Does One Rotten Apple Spoil the Whole Barrel? Bias in Multi-Member Decision-Making' in G Weeks and M Groves (eds), *Administrative Redress In and Out of the Courts: Essays in Honour of Robin Creyke and John McMillan* (Annandale, Federation Press, 2019) 235; M Groves, 'A Reasonably Reasonable Apprehension of Bias: *CNY17 v Minister for Immigration and Border Protection*' (2019) 41 *Sydney Law Review* 383; M Groves, 'Bias by the Numbers' (2020) 100 *AIAL Forum* 60; M Groves, 'Clarity and Complexity in the Bias Rule' (2020) 44 *Melbourne University Law Review* 565; M Groves, 'Is There a 'Small Town' Exception to the Bias Rule?' (2021) 28 *Australian Journal of Administrative Law* 114.

[20] See *Ebner v Official Trustee in Bankruptcy* (2000) 205 CLR 337, 344 [6] per Gleeson CJ, McHugh, Gummow and Hayne JJ; and *Minister for Immigration and Multicultural Affairs v Jia Legeng* (2001) 205 CLR 507.

[21] M Aronson, M Groves and G Weeks, *Judicial Review of Administrative Action and Government Liability*, 7th edn (London, Thomson Reuters, 2022) 607–709. Matthew has also contributed a more concise treatment of the bias rule to Australia's leading student text: R Creyke et al, *Control of Government Action: Text, Cases and Commentary*, 7th edn (London, LexisNexis, 2025) 545–578.

[22] See ch 7 of this volume.

[23] It has from time to time informed the judicial application of unreasonableness when that ground of review has been more liberally interpreted. That has increasingly been the case since the High Court's decision in *Minister for Immigration and Citizenship v Li* (2013) 249 CLR 332.

[24] See, eg, M Groves, 'Judicial Review and the Concept of Unfairness in English Public Law' (2007) 18 *Public Law Review* 244; M Groves, 'The Insecurity of Fairness in Security Cases' (2013) 24 *Public Law Review* 155; M Groves and G Weeks, 'The Legitimacy of Expectations About Fairness: Can Process and Substance be Untangled?' in J Bell et al (eds), *Public Law Adjudication in Common Law Systems: Process and Substance* (Oxford, Hart Publishing, 2016) 165; M Groves, 'Interpreters and Fairness in Administrative Hearings' (2017) 40 *Melbourne University Law Review* 506; M Groves, 'The Unfolding Purpose of Fairness' (2017) 45 *Federal Law Review* 653; M Groves and G Weeks, 'Fairness, Chance

much ground with his extensive work on tribunals.[25] Recently, Matthew has had much to say about the replacement of the Administrative Appeals Tribunal (AAT) by the Administrative Review Tribunal (ART).[26] That issue is addressed by Chantal Bostock's chapter on the demise of the AAT.[27] Her focus on what can be learned from the abolition of a once highly respected institution aligns closely with Matthew's reformist tendencies.

Matthew has also written frequently about the judiciary. Much of his research in that field has been associated with his expertise on the bias rule[28] but some has looked into issues such as judgment writing.[29] Matthew has also written about judicial behaviour more broadly,[30] including a political and entirely homophobic attack on a sitting judge of the High Court.[31]

Matthew has a deep and abiding interest in legal systems beyond Australian shores and he has contributed regularly to publications from other jurisdictions, including as an Australian 'correspondent' to *De Smith's Judicial Review* over several editions.[32] His comparativist interests will be aroused by two particular

and Discretion in Judicial Review' (2018) 25 *Australian Journal of Administrative Law* 147; M Groves, 'Fairness in Automated Decision-Making' in J Boughey and K Miller (eds), *The Automated State: Implications, Challenges and Opportunities for Public Law* (Annandale, Federation Press, 2021) 14; M Groves, 'Reasons, Fairness and Hearings' (2022) 33 *Public Law Review* 105; M Groves, 'What's in a Name? Fairness and a Reasonable Opportunity: *AB v Independent Broad-Based Anti-Corruption Commission*' (2023) 45 *Sydney Law Review* 525; M Groves, 'Equality of Arms in Administrative Review' (2023) 46 *Melbourne University Law Review* 726.

[25] Most notably in co-editing S Thomson, M Groves and G Weeks (eds), *Administrative Tribunals in the Common Law World* (Oxford, Hart Publishing, 2024), but see also M Groves, 'The Duty to Inquire in Tribunal Proceedings' (2011) 33 *Sydney Law Review* 177; M Groves, 'Do Tribunals Have a Duty to Establish the Competence of Parties Appearing Before Them?' (2013) 20 *Psychiatry, Psychology and Law* 131; M Groves, 'The Power of an Administrative Tribunal to Inform Itself' (2015) 22 *Australian Journal of Administrative Law* 236; M Groves, 'Administrative Justice Without Lawyers? Unrepresented Parties in Australian Tribunals' in S Nason (ed), *Administrative Justice in Wales and Comparative Perspectives* (Cardiff, University of Wales Press, 2017) 346.

[26] See, eg, M Groves and G Weeks, 'Tribunal Justice and Politics in Australia: The Rise and Fall of the Administrative Appeals Tribunal' (2023) 97 *Australian Law Journal* 278; M Groves, 'The Administrative Review Tribunal: A Big Step in Tribunal Justice, 50 Years in the Making' (2024) 98 *Australian Law Journal* 902.

[27] See ch 3 of this volume.

[28] M Groves, 'Emailing Judges and their Staff' (2013) 37 *Australian Bar Review* 69; M Groves, 'Public Statements by Judges and the Bias Rule' (2014) 40 *Monash University Law Review* 115; M Groves, 'Judges and the Media' in G Appleby and A Lynch (eds), *The Judge, the Judiciary and the Court Individual, Collegial and Institutional Judicial Dynamics in Australia* (Cambridge, Cambridge University Press, 2021) 259; M Groves, 'Should Judges Bite Back? Judicial Responses to Public Criticisms of Courts and Cases' (2023) 53 *Australian Bar Review* 231.

[29] M Groves and R Smyth, 'A Century of Judicial Style: Changing Patterns in Judgment Writing on the High Court 1903-2001' (2004) 32 *Federal Law Review* 255.

[30] M Groves, 'Public Comments by Judges of Their Colleagues: An Unhappy Australian Episode' (2016) 8 *Journal of Media Law* 98; M Groves, 'A Man For All Seasons? The Fair Minded Observer and Royal Commissioners' (2016) 23 *Australian Journal of Administrative Law* 201.

[31] E Campbell and M Groves, 'Attacks on Judges Under Parliamentary Privilege: A Sorry Australian Episode' [2002] *Public Law* 626.

[32] Most recently in I Hare, C Donnelly and J Bell, *De Smith's Judicial Review*, 9th edn (London, Sweet and Maxwell, 2023).

contributions to this book.[33] The first of those, by Stephen Thomson, looks at judicial review doctrine in the diverse jurisdictions of Scotland, Hong Kong and Australia.[34] More than that, it is a chapter written in praise of the benefits of comparativism – a point of view shared by its author and this collection's honorand. The second, by Liam Edwards and Sarah Nason, addresses judicial review and administrative justice in the UK's devolved nations of Scotland, Wales and Northern Ireland.[35] It is noteworthy that the authors of both chapters draw attention to the influence of Matthew's work half a world away from Victoria.

Notwithstanding his contribution over many years to a book about judicial review, Matthew's administrative law research has never been so confined and he has written about a wide range of topics. He was a member of the Administrative Review Council (ARC), both before its demise and after its revival,[36] and he has contributed greatly to a wider understanding of an institution whose oversight of Australian administrative law was otherwise not generally appreciated until it was gone.[37] He has co-edited two books on rights protection[38] and has written on rights in various contexts.[39] The metaphorical 'sacred cow' status of the legal world's luminaries has failed to protect them from Matthew's critical gaze.[40] However, perhaps most eye-catching of all is an article he co-authored about the legal management of colonial India's sectarian conflicts concerning sacred cows.[41] The constants in

[33] See also ch 8 of this volume in which Hanna Wilberg looks extensively at the New Zealand and UK ombudsmen and ch 12 of this volume in which Cora Hoexter addresses South African judicial review.

[34] See ch 6 of this volume.

[35] See ch 1 of this volume.

[36] See M Groves and G Weeks, 'Reanimating a Statutory Zombie: the Return of the Administrative Review Council' (2024) 31 *Australian Journal of Administrative Law* 38.

[37] See, eg, M Groves, 'Administrative Justice in Australian Administrative Law' (2011) 66 *AIAL Forum* 18; M Groves, 'Systemic Failure and Systemic Unfairness' (2023) 30 *Australian Journal of Administrative Law* 209; M Groves and G Weeks, 'Institutions and Their Memories' (2023) 30 *Australian Journal of Administrative Law* 83; M Groves and G Weeks, 'The Unique Jurisdiction of Australian Merits Review Tribunals' in S Thomson, M Groves and G Weeks (eds), *Administrative Tribunals in the Common Law World* (Oxford, Hart Publishing, 2024) 129, 145; M Groves, 'The Administrative Review Tribunal: A Big Step in Tribunal Justice, 50 Years in the Making' (2024) 98 *Australian Law Journal* 902.

[38] M Groves and C Campbell (eds), *Australian Charters of Rights A Decade On* (Annandale, Federation Press, 2017); M Groves, J Boughey and D Meagher (eds), *The Legal Protection of Rights in Australia* (Oxford, Hart Publishing, 2019).

[39] See, eg, M Groves, 'Restricting Core Procedural Rights in the Courts' (2013) 37 *Criminal Law Journal* 279; M Groves, 'Judicial Review and Human Rights' (2018) 25 *Australian Journal of Administrative Law* 64; M Groves, 'International Law, Administrative Powers and Human Rights: The Legacy of *Teoh*' in M Groves, J Boughey and D Meagher (eds), *The Legal Protection of Human Rights in Australia* (Oxford, Hart Publishing, 2019) 103.

[40] See, eg, M Groves, 'A Man For All Seasons? The Fair Minded Observer and Royal Commissioners' (2016) 23 *Australian Journal of Administrative Law* 201, 202. Unsurprisingly, for those who know him, Matthew's rare forays into media commentary tend to be particularly withering; see, eg, ABC Radio National, 'The Law Report: apprehended bias' (18 August 2015), www.abc.net.au/listen/programs/radionational-breakfast/the-law-report-apprehended-bias/6705008; ABC Radio National, 'Why was the AAT abolished? The dangers of witnessing wills remotely' (24 January 2023), www.abc.net.au/listen/programs/lawreport/aat-abolished-dangers-of-witnessing-wills-remotely/14134940.

[41] M Groves, 'Law, Religion and Public Order in Colonial India: Contextualising the 1887 Allahabad High Court Case on 'Sacred' Cows' (2010) 33 *South Asia Journal of South Asian Studies* 87.

what might seem an eclectic set of academic interests have been the expertise and erudition which Matthew has brought to every one of his publications.

Matthew's expertise is a symptom of his intellectual curiosity; he is genuinely interested in a wide range of things and writes about many of them.[42] Some of those interests are in highly specialised fields, such as the writ of *habeas corpus*.[43] Some go beyond the usual scope of administrative lawyers; he taught the law of succession to law school students for many years. He has also written extensively on criminal justice.[44] Matthew's interest in military justice[45] is shared by Alison Duxbury and Rain Liivoja. Their contribution to this collection examines the vexed and topical question of how we should deal with criminal offences alleged to have been committed by defence force personnel.[46] Matthew has also written extensively on standing (particularly in the context of environmental concerns).[47] Andrew Edgar shares Matthew's interest in public interest standing and his chapter both reviews the history and posits solutions to persistent problems in that field.[48]

Statutes figure largely in administrative law and Matthew has an interest in some of the more thorny debates concerning statutory interpretation.[49] That interest is addressed by Dan Meagher in his contribution to this collection,

[42] Matthew once included in an email a reference to 'a WWE smackdown', a term with which his correspondents had hitherto been unfamiliar, as they were with the fact that Matthew had a working knowledge of televised wrestling. Matthew has not yet written an article about wrestling; a fleeting reference to wrestling judges was (disappointingly) not meant literally: M Aronson, M Groves and G Weeks, *Judicial Review of Administrative Action and Government Liability*, 6th edn (London, Thomson Reuters, 2017) 747. He may yet do so.

[43] M Groves, 'Habeas Corpus, Justiciability and Foreign Affairs' (2013) 11 *New Zealand Journal of Public and International Law* 587. Matthew has also written the *habeas corpus* chapter for successive editions of M Aronson, M Groves and G Weeks, *Judicial Review of Administrative Action and Government Liability*, 7th edn (London, Thomson Reuters, 2022).

[44] M Groves, 'Empathy, Experience and the Rule Against Bias in Criminal Trials' (2012) 36 *Criminal Law Journal* 84; M Groves, 'Restricting Core Procedural Rights in the Courts' (2013) 37 *Criminal Law Journal* 279; M Groves, 'Prosecutorial Discretion and Constitutional Validity' (2014) 38 *Criminal Law Journal* 193; M Groves, 'The Incomplete Right to Counsel in Criminal Trials' (2018) 42 *Criminal Law Journal* 143; M Groves, 'A Life without Hope – The Victorian Charter and Parole' (2018) 42 *Criminal Law Journal* 353; M Groves, 'Bail in Extradition Proceedings' (2020) 44 *Criminal Law Journal* 298.

[45] M Groves, 'Military Justice, its Punishments and the Constitution' (2011) 35 *Criminal Law Journal* 265; A Duxbury and M Groves, 'The Reform of Military Justice' in A Duxbury and M Groves (eds), *Military Justice in the Modern Age* (Cambridge, Cambridge University Press, 2016) xxviii.

[46] See ch 13 of this volume.

[47] M Groves, 'The Evolution and Reform of Standing in Australian Administrative Law' (2016) 44 *Federal Law Review* 167; M Groves, 'Justice Murphy's Dissent in *Australian Conservation Foundation v Commonwealth* (1980): The Birth of Public Interest Standing in Australia?' in A Lynch (ed), *Great Australian Dissents* (Cambridge, Cambridge University Press, 2016) 189; M Groves, 'Lawfare and the Enemy Within Our Public Law' (2017) 90 *AIAL Forum* 32; M Groves, 'Standing Outside: An Environment of Challenge and Withheld Cures' (2021) 38 *Environment and Planning Law Journal* 111; M Groves, 'Business Competitors, Standing and Judicial Review' (2023) 50 *Australian Business Law Review* 315.

[48] See ch 4 of this volume.

[49] M Groves, 'Administrative Law and Statutory Interpretation: Sidesteps and Missteps in the Struggle for Coherence' in J Barnes (ed), *The Coherence of Statutory Interpretation* (Annandale, Federation Press, 2019) 202; M Groves, 'The Return of the (Almost) Absolute Statutory Discretion' in J Boughey and LB Crawford (eds), *Interpreting Executive Power* (Annandale, Federation Press, 2020) 129.

which seeks to explain just what it is that courts do when interpreting statutes.[50] Statutory context can also be important in determining the boundaries of an electricity distributor's duty to take care to minimise bushfire risks but Mark Aronson's chapter argues that the High Court's turn to statute in a recent case was a massive distraction and a lost opportunity to carve out a new exception to tort law's 'pure omissions' rule.[51]

Matthew has had a longstanding interest in the ombudsman institution.[52] That interest is picked up as the central theme of two chapters in this collection. Hanna Wilberg's chapter argues that full judicial review of ombuds institutions would usually come at the expense of their contributions to administrative justice and it should therefore be limited or even excluded.[53] Anita Stuhmcke's chapter looks at the expansion of bodies called 'ombudsmen' and at the expansion of the number of quite distinct types of portfolios within existing ombuds institutions. She argues for more principled guidance regarding the creation of new bodies and portfolios and laments the increasing marginalisation of individuals as complainants.[54]

At least one of Matthew's research interests has been with him since childhood. In a contribution to an edited collection on ombudsmen, Matthew explained the basis for his extensive research into prisons:

> I spent most of the first four years of my life in prison and only left to start primary school shortly after my fourth birthday. I thought prison was the best place in the world and was very sorry to leave it. Everyone was friendly and seemed very happy. I also had a choice of food at lunchtime. School, by contrast, was a terrible place. It was regimented. I had no freedom of movement. Awful people, I later knew to be called teachers, kept barking orders at me, telling me what I could and could not do. It was many years before I realised my experience of prison was somewhat unusual. I spent my days in a prison because my father worked there and my mother, who suffered from poor health and struggled to manage my younger sister, needed respite. The solution seemed obvious. Send the boy to prison. …
>
> This snapshot of history reveals more than just a bizarre childhood. It also illustrates how some prisons used to operate – relatively lawless places that a thoughtless, though caring, parent could use as a day-care facility.[55]

The story related in Matthew's chapter was in fact more than just a snapshot of history in as much as it led, some years later, to a doctoral thesis on the role of

[50] See ch 5 of this volume. The question in that chapter's title sounds very much like a thing Matthew would ask, in the way he would ask it.

[51] See ch 10 of this volume.

[52] Most notably in M Groves and A Stuhmcke (eds), *The Ombudsman in the Modern State* (Oxford, Hart Publishing, 2022).

[53] See ch 8 of this volume.

[54] See ch 2 of this volume.

[55] M Groves, 'Ombudsmen and Prisons' in M Hertogh and R Kirkham (eds), *Research Handbook on the Ombudsman* (Cheltenham, Edward Elgar, 2018) 319.

administrative law in prison management.[56] Matthew has returned to that issue in subsequent publications.[57]

Matthew's interest in prisons forms part of his broader interest in law reform. That interest shares little ground with, for example, the goal of most Australian law schools to demonstrate a commitment to 'social justice'; Matthew's only published use of that term appeared in a quotation.[58] That is probably no accident, since Matthew has little patience with linguistic imprecision.[59] He has proposed reforms, amongst other things, to tribunals,[60] immigration litigation,[61] standing rules[62] and many other aspects of judicial review.[63] Matthew was also part of the ARC when it proposed modest but timely reforms to judicial review in Australia's federal jurisdiction.[64] The most notable result of the ARC's recommendations was that it was 'defunded into a practical state of abolition a few years later' without any of its proposals for reform having been put into effect.[65] It is immensely pleasing that the ARC has been revived under the Administrative Review Tribunal Act 2024 (Cth) and that Matthew is once again part of its oversight of Australian administrative law.

Matthew's focus in writing about administrative law and the potential for its reform is usually on those who suffer at the hands of the state.[66] His extensive commentary on the Robodebt debacle is a prominent example of that point.[67] Cora

[56] M Groves, *Administrative Law and the Management of Prisons and Prisoners* (PhD thesis, Melbourne, Monash University, 2003).

[57] M Groves, 'Ombudsmen's Jurisdiction in Prisons' (2002) 28 *Monash University Law Review* 181; M Groves, 'The Second Charters of Prisoners' Rights' in M Groves and C Campbell (eds), *Australian Charters of Rights A Decade On* (Annandale, Federation Press, 2017) 187.

[58] M Groves, 'The Changing Role of the Attorney-General' (2024) 52 *Federal Law Review* 131, 149.

[59] See M Groves, 'The Surrogacy Principle and Motherhood Statements in Administrative Law' in L Pearson, C Harlow and M Taggart (eds), *Administrative Law in a Changing State: Essays in Honour of Mark Aronson* (2008) 71, 88–96.

[60] See, eg, M Groves and G Weeks, 'Tribunals – Their Continued Evolution and Reform' (2020) 26 *Australian Journal of Administrative Law* 189.

[61] M Groves and G Weeks, 'Immigration Litigation – Impact, Study and Reform' (2020) 27 *Australian Journal of Administrative Law* 63.

[62] M Groves, 'The Evolution and Reform of Standing in Australian Administrative Law' (2016) 44 *Federal Law Review* 167.

[63] M Groves, 'Reforming Judicial Review at the State Level' (2010) 64 *AIAL Forum* 30; M Groves, 'Reforming Judicial Review (Again)' (2018) 25 *Australian Journal of Administrative Law* 197; M Groves, 'Reforming Judicial Review in Tasmania' (2019) 38 *University of Tasmania Law Review* 1.

[64] Administrative Review Council, *Federal Judicial Review in Australia*, (Report No 50, 2012).

[65] M Aronson, M Groves and G Weeks, *Judicial Review of Administrative Action and Government Liability*, 7th edn (London, Thomson Reuters, 2022), [2.170] 61.

[66] See, eg, M Groves, 'Equality of Arms in Administrative Review' (2023) 46 *Melbourne University Law Review* 726.

[67] See The Hon C Holmes AC SC, *Report*, Royal Commission into the Robodebt Scheme, (2023). In addition to addressing Robodebt in several articles, Matthew also addressed that affair in two separate submissions in response to proposed law reforms: M Groves, 'Submission to the Inquiry into the *Administrative Review Tribunal Bill 2023* and the *Administrative Review Tribunal (Consequential and Transitional Provisions No.1) Bill 2023*' (2023); M Groves and G Weeks, 'Submission in response to the *Administrative Review Reform: Issues Paper*' (2023).

Hoexter's chapter on the rise of 'lawfare' in South African judicial review resonates with several of Matthew's research interests, including the principle of legality and accountability as a central concern of administrative law.[68] She undertakes that task against the history of judicial review in South Africa both before and since constitutional democracy in that country. Ellen Rock's chapter looks at accountability through a different lens, that of the need for government decision-making to be legitimate and impartial and – crucially – to maintain the public's trust in the integrity of those processes. She suggests that a super-abundance of checks and balances could distance both accountability and public trust.[69]

This book collects essays on a wide range of legal issues but their themes are all drawn from the extraordinary research of Matthew Groves throughout his academic career. They stand as a testament to the richness that academic research can achieve when its authors, like Matthew, go beyond the narrowly constructed silos of topical expertise encouraged by law schools and look at law's terrain as something to be explored as broadly as one can. The influence of Matthew's approach to scholarship has been immense and can be seen to some degree in the research of those with whom he has worked closely.

[68] See ch 12 of this volume.
[69] See ch 11 of this volume.

# 1

# Judicial Review and Administrative Justice within and Across the UK Nations: A Tale of Divergence and Convergence

LIAM EDWARDS AND SARAH NASON

As scholars of administrative law and administrative justice, we have been influenced by Matthew's work. Particularly, his kindness to early- and mid-career researchers and his interest in comparative analysis of tribunals and judicial review across systems of multilevel governance. Nason was lucky to welcome Matthew to North Wales in 2015 for a conference on *Administrative Justice in Wales and Comparative Perspectives.* Matthew contributed reflections on the relationship between courts and tribunals in Australian administrative justice. He also discussed how the constitutional division of power in Australia means that rules governing unrepresented parties in Australian tribunals have largely been developed through the supervisory jurisdiction of the courts. Matthew's work has examined the differences between courts and tribunals in the context of both constitutional principle and practical operation. This has included examining the place of institutions, their procedures, and remedies within different conceptions of the nature of administrative justice and its underlying values at both federal and state levels. Matthew's collaborative and curious spirit is one adopted in Nason's work, particularly joining with early-career scholars developing their own experience in comparative administrative law,[1] now seen in our combined contribution to this volume.

The collection, *Administrative Justice in Wales and Comparative Perspectives* ('AJ Wales')[2] which followed our 2015 conference, has since been described as 'a landmark title on the challenges and opportunities of administrative justice in

[1] See, eg, H Pritchard, 'Building a Welsh Jurisdiction Through Administrative Justice', in S Nason (ed), *Administrative Justice in Wales and Comparative Perspectives* (Cardiff, University of Wales Press, 2017) 218.

[2] S Nason (ed) *Administrative Justice in Wales and Comparative Perspectives* ('AJ Wales') (Cardiff, University of Wales Press, 2017).

conditions of small country governance' and as placing Wales 'firmly in the mainstream of contemporary legal discussion'.[3] Administrative justice in Wales is now an established topic of legal research in its own right, with thanks to contributors to the conference and book, as well as Matthew's further support of comparative administrative law research showcasing Wales over subsequent years.[4]

In his chapter in AJ Wales, Matthew noted that scholars should be cautious not to romanticise the developments in Australian tribunals. This is particularly with respect to the unique 'merits review' capability that other jurisdictions sometimes see as an attractive addition to access to justice.[5] Matthew considered that we should also learn from Australia's missteps and mistakes in administrative justice. In particular, we can learn from complexity within a small jurisdiction: 'Australian public law principles are always unusual because most observers, whether looking from within or outside Australia, are surprised that such a relatively small jurisdiction contains such diversity and complexity'.[6] Matthew also noted how in Australia, innovations in administrative justice at the federal level spark reform at the state level, which in turn sparks refinement at the federal level.[7] Our chapter is then loosely based around these three themes. How relatively small nations can contain notable diversity and complexity, especially across multiple layers of governance; how there is interaction between, in our case, central, regional, and devolved administrative justice; and how levels of governance might learn from each other's missteps or mistakes.

In our chapter we take the opportunity to reflect on the development of administrative justice in the UK's four nations, with particular focus on comparing judicial review across the UK's administrative courts and the evolution of tribunals. We explore how several developments have led to increased diversity and complexity, which also manifests in some fragmentation and decentralisation of administrative law and of judicial review. We discuss the implications for understanding administrative justice and multilevel governance.

Our focus is primarily on the UK's devolved nations: Scotland, Wales, and Northern Ireland. Each of these nations now has its own executive and legislature with primary law-making powers, operating under reserved powers devolution settlements. The administration of justice is devolved to Scotland and Northern Ireland, but not to Wales (except for a small collective of 'Welsh tribunals') with Wales also continuing to share a single legal jurisdiction with England.

[3] R Rawlings, reviewing AJ Wales (n 2) www.amazon.co.uk/Administrative-Justice-Comparative-Perspectives-Public/dp/1786831392.

[4] S Nason and L Edwards, 'Making Justice and Rights Work in Wales: The Case for Ground up Constitutional Change' (2022) 4 *Public Law* 224; S Nason and H Pritchard, 'Administrative Justice and the Legacy of Executive Devolution: Establishing a Tribunals System for Wales' (2020) 26(4) *Australian Journal of Administrative Law* 3; S Nason, 'Administrative justice in Wales: A New Egalitarianism?' (2017) 39(1) *Journal of Social Welfare and Family Law* 115.

[5] M Groves, 'Administrative Justice Without Lawyers? Unrepresented Parties in Australian Tribunals' in AJ Wales (n 2).

[6] AJ Wales (n 2) 371.

[7] AJ Wales (n 2) 354.

Whilst the overarching constitutional principle of Westminster parliamentary sovereignty and the asymmetry of the governing devolution agreements mean that the UK cannot be considered a fully federal nation, distinguished commentators such as Cheryl Saunders conclude, 'the UK has enough federal features to be characterised as a federal political system'.[8] The devolved nations have been allowed to operate with a degree of 'permissive authority', such that they have developed a unique constitutional existence. Devolved nation actors have developed their own understandings of the UK's territorial constitution, sometimes diverging from that of UK central government.[9] The characteristics of these 'sub state constitutions', we argue, emerge to a degree in the devolved nations' differing approaches to administrative justice. However, the fundamental value of judicial review gains expression through a lack of divergence across the devolved nations. We begin by considering trends of complexity and diversity, and particularly fragmentation, in UK administrative justice before examining developments across the devolved nations.

## I. Fragmentation of Judicial Review and Administrative Justice

In England and Wales, channelling cases into the High Court 'exclusively' via the judicial review procedure supported the consolidation of general principles of administrative law. Lord Diplock once described the judge-led development of a 'comprehensive system of administrative law' through the judicial review procedure and its predecessors, from the 1950s to the 1980s, as 'the greatest achievement of the English courts' in his judicial lifetime.[10] We note here the implication of 'for Wales, see England'.[11]

Our first argument about the fragmentation of administrative law is that this can be seen in the so-called 'tribunalisation' of judicial review. This is specifically in the development of a new tribunal structure for most of England and Wales, Great Britain, and UK tribunals under the Tribunals, Courts and Enforcement Act 2007 (TCEA). At the apex of this system is an Upper Tribunal, designated as a 'superior court of record'.[12] Certain types of judicial review applications can be determined by the Upper Tribunal, particularly its Immigration and Asylum

[8] C Saunders, *Devolution. Federation. Constitution. From here to where?* The Sir David Williams Lecture, 27 February 2015: www.cpl.law.cam.ac.uk/sites/www.law.cam.ac.uk/files/images/www.cpl.law.cam.ac.uk/legacy/File/cheryl_saunders_david_williams_lecture_2015.pdf.

[9] M Sandford and C Gormley-Heenan, 'Taking Back Control', the UK's Constitutional Narrative and Schrodinger's Devolution' (2020) 73(1) *Parliamentary Affairs* 108.

[10] *R v Inland Revenue Commissioners, ex p National Federation of Self-Employed and Small Business Ltd* [1982] AC 617 (HL) 641.

[11] The *Encyclopaedia Britannica* (1888) entry for Wales famously said, 'Wales: see England'.

[12] TCEA, s 3(5).

Chamber (UTIAC) and its Administrative Appeals Chamber (UTAAC).[13] The nature of this judicial review jurisdiction and its amenability to supervision by the High Court in England and Wales and the Court of Session in Scotland have been analysed by commentators,[14] addressed by the courts in litigation,[15] and subject to legislation that overturned a decision of the UK Supreme Court. Section 2 of the Judicial Review and Courts Act 2022 now excludes higher court judicial review of the Upper Tribunal itself on all but the most extreme grounds of procedural injustice.

The establishment of the Upper Tribunal was based on amalgamating a disparate set of tribunals to foster rationalisation and systematisation. Fragmentation was certainly not an aim. The new tribunal structure was to provide an 'unprecedented opportunity to work towards a more coherent and distinctive system of tribunal justice, drawing together strands of the principles developed from various jurisdictions'.[16] In effect, a separate body of tribunal doctrine that, for various reasons including the specialism of the tribunal judiciary and its closeness to relevant administrative policy, would be subject to less intervention via judicial review in the courts. It had been said that the Upper Tribunal would 'lead on developing the law underlaying administrative justice'[17] and that it would 'come to play a central, innovative and defining role in the new system, enjoying a position in the judicial hierarchy at least equivalent to that of the Administrative Court'.[18] The fragmentation is in the argument that the new tribunals system would develop its own body of administrative law, like the body of law which Lord Diplock considered to be a great achievement of judicial review. However, this time, tribunal administrative law is described as in contrast to 'ordinary lawyers' law',[19] and there is little oversight from the common law supervisory jurisdiction. Two seams of general administrative law running in parallel, with little clarity on their relationship to each other. It was also argued that the Upper Tribunal could begin to perform something like the 'merits review' function of the Australian Federal Administrative Appeals Tribunal. As Matthew's work shows, the origins of this form of review are uniquely situated in Australia's constitutional separation of powers, as well as the steer given by tribunal leaders over time. It would be an uneasy transplant to the UK's administrative justice systems. Although most tribunals across

[13] TCEA, s 15 relating to England and Wales and Northern Ireland, s 21 relating to Scotland.

[14] See. eg, J Bell, 'Rethinking the Story of *Cart v Upper Tribunal* and Its Implications for Administrative Law' (2019) 39 *Oxford Journal of Legal Studies* 74; C Forsyth, 'Blasphemy Against Basics: Doctrine, Conceptual Reasoning and Certain Decisions of the UK Supreme Court' in J Bell, M Elliott, JE Varuhas and P Murray (eds), *Public Law Adjudication in Common Law Systems: Process and Substance* (Oxford, Hart Publishing, 2016) 161.

[15] *R (Cart) v Upper Tribunal* [2010] EWCA Civ 859; *R (Cart) v The Upper Tribunal* [2011] UKSC 28; *Eba v Advocate General for Scotland* [2011] UKSC 29.

[16] R Carnwath, 'Tribunal Justice: A New Start' [2009] *Public Law* 48, 56.

[17] Tribunals Service, *Transforming Tribunals: Implementing Part 1 of the Tribunals, Courts and Enforcement Act 2007* (CP 30/07, 2007) [131].

[18] ibid [178].

[19] *R (Cart) v Upper Tribunal* [2010] EWCA Civ 859 [42] (Sedley LJ).

the UK's various jurisdictions can re-take substantive administrative decisions 'on the merits' standing in the shoes of the initial executive decision-maker, tribunals are a species of court, part of the legislature, not the executive.

Despite the 'new administrative law' aims associated with the Upper Tribunal, analysis so far suggests that the objective of developing a separate but coherent body of tribunal law, or tribunal administrative law, has not yet come to pass. For example, Robert Thomas argues that the work of the Upper Tribunal largely replicates that of its predecessor tribunals and that it is yet to issue any rulings on wider principles of administrative justice to guide tribunals or administrative decision-makers.[20] He argues, for example, that the UTAAC acts primarily as a specialist public law court in the field of social security law, with responsibility for a miscellany of other smaller jurisdictions that, even taken together, generate few claims.

Somewhat paradoxically, both 'tribunalisation' and so-called 'de-tribunalisation' can be associated with the fragmentation of administrative law, and the latter also with a 'decline of administrative justice'.[21] De-tribunalisation is an umbrella term for various reforms, including the abolition of tribunal appeal rights, replacing tribunal appeals with other forms of more bureaucratic redress (such as administrative review), and/or making tribunal appeal rights more difficult to exercise due to legal aid restrictions and fees.

Another aspect of the decline of administrative justice is the lack of holistic oversight following the abolition of the Administrative Justice and Tribunals Council (AJTC). This experience is shared with Australia through the emasculation of the Administrative Review Council,[22] a subject on which Matthew has made significant interventions.[23] However, recently, and more positively for Australia, Matthew argues along with Greg Weeks that a newly proposed ARC under the Administrative Review Tribunal Act 2023 could be stronger than its previous incarnation.[24]

For England and Wales, fragmentation is not only a consequence of tribunalisation and lack of holistic oversight; it can also be seen in the High Court Administrative Court itself. This is through the development of specialist sub-courts

[20] R Thomas, 'UK Tribunals: Structure, History, Constitutional Status and Practice' in S Thomson, M Groves and G Weeks, *Administrative Tribunals in the Common Law World* (London, Bloomsbury Publishing, 2024).

[21] See, eg, R Thomas, 'Current Developments in UK Tribunals: Challenges for Administrative Justice' in AJ Wales; R Thomas and J Tomlinson (eds), 'Mapping Current Issues in Administrative Justice: Austerity and the 'More Bureaucratic Rationality' Approach' (2017) 39(3) *Journal of Social Welfare and Family Law* 380; and M Adler, 'The Future of Administrative Justice' in M Hertogh, R Kirkham, R Thomas and J Tomlinson (eds), *The Oxford Handbook of Administrative Justice* (Oxford, Oxford University Press, 2022) 623.

[22] See, eg, S Nason, 'Oversight of Administrative Justice Systems' in J Tomlinson, R Thomas, M Hertogh and R Kirkham (eds), *The Oxford Handbook of Administrative Justice* (Oxford, Oxford University Press, 2022).

[23] M Groves and G Weeks, 'Tribunal Justice and Politics in Australia: The Rise and Fall of the Administrative Appeals Tribunal' (2023) 97(4) *Australian Law Journal* 278.

[24] M Groves and G Weeks, 'Reanimating a Statutory Zombie: The Return of the Administrative Review Council' (2024) 31(1) *Australian Journal of Administrative Law* 38.

and lists (such as in planning law) and the extent to which its work has become increasingly weighted towards statutory appeals. Increased academic interest in statutory appeals is notable and likely consonant with an increased volume of activity.[25] Nason and Sunkin have noted that the increased use of statutory procedures gives government power to enumerate more specific and limited grounds on which public power may be challenged. The codification process can also be used to add procedural hurdles and circumscribe remedies, avoiding the breadth, flexibility and wider consequences of the inherent supervisory jurisdiction.[26] As Harlow and Rawlings have noted, statutory reform can be used to 'clamp down' on and 'strike back' against judicial review.[27] We argue that, while routes to statutory appeals or reviews can be seen as a positive contribution to access to justice, such intervention also has the potential to further fragment administrative law and increase complexity.

Fragmentation can also be associated with a lack of access.[28] Whilst the grounds of judicial review are said to have expanded dramatically, doctrinal diversity, using the themes of this chapter, is contrasted against the exclusion of people.[29] In England and Wales a range of statutory costs and procedural provisions designed to restrict or exclude access to the Administrative Court's judicial review jurisdiction have impacted caseloads through a combination of practical hurdles and so-called 'chilling effects'. Whilst acknowledging the limitations of an analysis drawn largely from caseload data, Nason constructs a narrative, which she describes as 'perhaps unexpected', of a decline in judicial review activity in England and Wales. This is alongside a lack of clarity about the roles which the procedure should perform in modern administrative law.[30] Outside the immigration context, the overall trend is one of decline in the total number of judicial review applications lodged per year. Applications for civil (non-immigration) judicial review per-annum from around the mid-2010s onwards (up to and including 2023) are approximately one quarter below where they had been at the start of the decade. An average of approximately 1,500 non-immigration claims per-annum has likely now supplanted what was a consistent average of 2,000 claims per-annum going

[25] J Bell and L Fisher, 'Exploring a Year of Administrative Law Adjudication in the Administrative Court' [2021] *Public Law* 505.

[26] S Nason and M Sunkin, 'The Regionalisation of Judicial Review: Constitutional Authority, Access to Justice and Specialisation of Legal Services in Public Law' (2013) 76 *Modern Law Review* 223.

[27] C Harlow and R Rawlings, '"Striking Back" and "Clamping Down": An Alternative Perspective on Judicial Review' in J Bell, M Elliott, JNE Varuhas and P Murray (eds), *Public Law Adjudication in Common Law Systems: Process and Substance* (Oxford, Hart Publishing, 2016).

[28] T Hickman, 'Public Law's Disgrace', UK Const. L. Blog (9 Feb 2017) (available at ukconstitutionallaw.org/)).

[29] C Harlow and R Rawlings, *Law and Administration*, 3rd edn (Cambridge, Cambridge University Press, 2009) 669.

[30] S Nason, 'Plus ça Change? An Empirical Analysis of Judicial Review in Modern Administrative Law' in TT Arvind, L Stirton, R Kirkham, D Mac Síthigh (eds), *Executive Decision-Making and the Courts: Revisiting the Origins of Modern Judicial Review* (Oxford, Bloomsbury, Hart Publishing, 2021).

back to the year 2000.[31] It may well be that fewer individuals are being granted remedies on average per year through the judicial review procedure than perhaps at any point in its history.[32]

Overall, reading judicial review statistics can be a complex task. As exposed, for example, by the Public Law Project's complaint to the Office for Statistics Regulation that a figure relied on by government (that only 0.22 per cent of so-called *Cart* judicial reviews of the Upper Tribunal are successful) was 'entirely incorrect and misleading'. This was because government had relied only on reported cases and artificially deflated the judicial review success rate by assuming the several thousand cases not making it to a final hearing were necessarily failures for the claimant.[33] The fact that fewer people are being granted remedies through judicial review in England and Wales does not, of course, mean that instigating the procedure is of little use to them. Research shows that the *Value & Effects* of judicial review are broad and that those who have not been awarded a remedy often report other benefits from the process.[34]

The Covid-19 pandemic shone a spotlight on what Tom Hickman and Joe Tomlinson call the 'second look' function of judicial review.[35] They consider it initially striking how few judicial review applications reached a final substantive determination during the pandemic. This is given the scope of public law issues that could be raised and that the move to a remote service was swift and relatively uncomplicated compared to other areas of law. The 'second look' function, however, was prominent. This is where the ability to threaten or commence judicial review 'provided an important and empowering lever for affected persons and companies to seek to alter government policies'.[36] Meaningful changes were made to policies to better reflect the balance between public health and individual freedoms without the need for litigation. Notably, in the context of multilevel governance, a high-profile 'second look' threat against the policies or decisions of one UK nation government sometimes resulted in another UK nation government learning from the other's mistakes. This aligns with Matthew's comments about how changes at a central level can be adopted in the states, or in our case, the devolved tiers of governance.

[31] Ministry of Justice, 'Civil justice statistics quarterly' (22 December 2014): www.gov.uk/government/collections/civil-justice-statistics-quarterly.

[32] As explained in Nason (n 30).

[33] See Dr Joe Tomlinson's letter to Ed Humpherson at the Office for Statistics Regulation (20 April 2021): osr.statisticsauthority.gov.uk/wp-content/uploads/2021/06/Dr-Joe-Tomlinson-to-Ed-Humpherson-Use-of-statistics-in-judicial-review-reform.pdf.

[34] V Bondy, L Platt and M Sunkin, *The Value and Effects of Judicial Review: The Nature of Claims, their Outcomes and Consequences* (PLP, London School of Economics, University of Essex, 2016) 'Value & Effects'.

[35] T Hickman and J Tomlinson, 'What Role did Judicial Review Play During the Pandemic?', UK Const. L. Blog (13 May 2024) (available at ukconstitutionallaw.org/).

[36] ibid.

# II. Decentralisation of Judicial Review and Administrative Justice

Decentralisation is another apparent characteristic of complex, diverse, and fragmented judicial review and of administrative justice across UK multilevel governance. For present purposes we see this as taking two specific forms, 'regionalisation' and devolution, and we discuss each in turn.

## A. Regionalisation

In 2007 a Judicial Working Group of a Civil Sub-Committee of the then England and Wales Judges' Council proposed reforms to 'regionalise' judicial review and other Administrative Court claims.[37] The Working Group considered that the clustering of public law legal services around the Royal Courts of Justice in London was 'prejudicial to those who do not live and work in London and the South East'.[38] The Group drew on evidence that London's virtual monopoly over judicial review activity was likely to have had significant adverse effects on access to justice. In 2009, what were then known as 'Regional Administrative Court Centres' opened in Birmingham, Cardiff, Leeds, and Manchester. We focus in this section on the English regions.

Regionalisation was contested. Some lawyers and judges took the view that regionalisation would reduce the quality of representation and adjudication in judicial review. Several argued that this then risked disempowering individuals in local communities as against the state and potentially hampering the development of the law.[39] Through research over several years, we have found there to be no 'instant bonanza' of regional judicial review. To a notable extent, the Regional Administrative Court Centres have been more characterised by the specialisations of local lawyers. For example, cases involving police, prisons and parole in Leeds; medical professions in Manchester (where the General Medical Council is based); and immigration in Birmingham. These specialisations are vulnerable to shocks in the legal services market, which may in part explain declining caseloads in the northern Administrative Court Centres, where legal services were heavily impacted by restrictions on legal aid for prisoners, alongside reduced appeal rights and additional procedural hurdles.[40]

Although data on regional judicial review is complex to interpret, and much relevant detail is not publicly available, our research has suggested a general trend

[37] Civil Sub-Committee of the Judges' Council, Judicial Working Group, *Justice Outside London* (2007) www.judiciary.gov.uk/publications/justice-outside-london/.

[38] ibid 48.

[39] Discussed in Nason and Sunkin (n 26).

[40] ibid.

of increase in claims per head of relevant population outside London and the southeast of England until around 2013. There is a subsequent trend of decline coinciding with legal aid reforms brought in under the Legal Aid, Sentencing and Punishment of Offenders Act 2012 (LASPO). More recently, Marsons and Tan have found that since regionalisation, some 85 per cent of England's judicial review claims have been lodged in London and that regional English judicial review has been broadly in decline in recent years.[41] In their article, they note the work of the Administrative Court Liaison Judge for the Northern and North Eastern Circuit (Leeds and Manchester), Mr Justice Fordham,[42] in improving transparency and guidance on venue decisions. They also mention the recent reinvigoration of the Northern Administrative Law Association (NALA). These matters appear to have had an impact, as we found an increase in claims either issued in or transferred to a northern Court Centre, particularly Manchester, in the most recent Civil Justice Statistics. About 30 per cent of civil non-immigration judicial reviews are now issued outside London in most years, which is a significant change that is unlikely to be reversed. What we haven't seen evidence of, however, is any form of regionally developing jurisprudence, by which we mean 'tailoring'[43] the grounds of judicial review (a phrase often used interchangeably with general principles of administrative law). This might include tailoring to, or being influenced by, local social, economic, political or demographic features, or by particular judges, administrative actors, or policy areas being more prominent in judicial review activity in each region. In this regard, neither 'tribunalisation' nor 'regionalisation' has yet had much discernible impact on the grounds of judicial review or so-called general principles of administrative law.

## B. Devolution

### *i. Judicial Review in Wales*

An Administrative Court Centre was also established in Cardiff in 2009 as part of the 'regionalisation' reforms. The Administrative Court in Wales sits in a somewhat different position from the English Regional Centres. Wales is a nation, not a region, with a primary legislature, the Senedd Cymru/Welsh Parliament. However, England and Wales continue to share a single legal jurisdiction, and much of the administration of justice (including courts, judges, legal aid and the legal professions) remains reserved.

[41] L Marsons and G Tan, 'Levelling Up Judicial Review: Regionalising the Administrative Court in England' (2022) 27(4) *Judicial Review* 281.

[42] Administrative Court Liaison Judge for the Northern and Northeastern Circuit (Leeds and Manchester).

[43] J Bell, A Davies and E Fisher, 'Tailored Judicial Review Doctrine, Tailoring Judicial Review Doctrine' [2024] *Public Law* (forthcoming).

In 2019, looking back over ten years of the Administrative Court in Wales, Gardner and Nason concluded that the Administrative Court in Wales has been a constitutional success and a jurisdictional improvement.[44] On the other hand, they found that the access to justice aims of decentralising the Administrative Court in Wales, as well as in England, have been significantly undercut. This is due to the impacts of legal aid reforms, echoing the points made above about the relative decline of English judicial review.

Gardner and Nason nevertheless found decentralisation in this sense to be a constitutional success because claims of constitutional importance to Wales, such as those relating to the powers of Welsh ministers[45] and to the Welsh language,[46] are now near universally heard in Wales. Their conclusion of jurisdictional improvement is on similar lines, finding that more cases 'wrongly' issued outside Wales[47] have been transferred to Wales over the years, with transfer processes becoming more efficient. Not long after Gardner and Nason's article, the presumption that claims against Welsh public bodies be issued and heard in Wales was strengthened into a Civil Procedure Rule that such claims *must* be issued and heard in Wales.[48] However, concerns have since arisen. Cases from the Western Circuit (southwest England) are now also issued in Cardiff, and official statistics largely fail to distinguish between 'Welsh' and 'English' claims issued in Wales. The practice of holding regular Administrative Court in Wales User Group meetings seems to have lapsed, where such meetings had provided valuable insight into specifically 'Welsh' data.[49]

Public Law Wales,[50] much like NALA in northern England, has raised the profile of public administrative law and human rights in Wales. This has increased practitioner awareness and academic commentary but not yet translated into a culture of public law litigation and developing jurisprudence through judicial review judgments. In part this seems to be due to the extent of settlement activity and a seeming judicial reluctance to entertain more detailed substantive arguments about uniquely Welsh administrative law originating from the Senedd Cymru/Welsh Parliament and Welsh ministers.

[44] S Nason and D. Gardner, 'Ten Years of the Administrative Court in Wales: Success or Failure?' *Essex CAJI* 2019: essexcaji.org/2019/10/15/ten-years-of-the-administrative-court-in-wales-success-or-failure/.

[45] Eg, *R (Brynmawr Foundation School) v Welsh Ministers* [2011] EWHC 519 (Admin) and *R (Sargeant) v First Minister of Wales* [2019] EWHC 739 (Admin).

[46] Eg, *R (The Welsh Language Commissioner) v National Savings and Investments* [2014] EWHC 488 (Admin) and *Driver v Rhondda Cynon Taf County Borough Council* [2020] EWCA Civ 1759 (where both the High Court hearing, and later the Court of Appeal hearing were held in Cardiff).

[47] Under the Civil Procedure Rules Practice Direction 54C – Administrative Court (Venue), with some exceptions, judicial review proceedings should be commenced at the Administrative Court Office for the region with which the claimant is most closely connected.

[48] Civil Procedure Rules, Rule 7.1A Claims against Welsh public bodies to be issued and heard in Wales; and Rule 7.1b Claims against Welsh public bodies to be forwarded for issue in Wales.

[49] As discussed in S Nason and L Edwards, *Reviewing Judicial Review in Wales* (Bangor University/British Academy, 2021).

[50] www.public-law.wales/.

## *ii. Judicial Review in the Devolved Nations*

More generally, providing for policy and legal divergence is an expressed purpose of devolution. By popular democratic support in referenda establishing the devolved governments and legislatures and subsequent elections, voters in the devolved nations at least implicitly accept such divergence. Across the UK nations, judicial review remains a central mechanism through which to hold public power to account. The UK Supreme Court has suggested that the devolved legislatures themselves may be amenable to judicial review on limited common law constitutional grounds as well as statutory grounds. Hypothetical attempts by a devolved legislature to abolish judicial review, or the ordinary role of the courts, are given as prime examples of actions offending constitutional principles.[51]

For his doctoral research, Edwards conducted an analysis of judicial review across the UK's three devolved nations. He examined the number of judicial review judgments per year, revealing that rates of judicial review are different across Scotland, Wales, and Northern Ireland. Edwards studied judicial review judgments reported from 2012–21 inclusive, accounting for cases issued against devolved public authorities – that is, authorities operating under a devolved policy area. As such, the research excluded, for example, immigration claims (a reserved matter under all the devolution settlements).

A total of 823 cases were examined: 317 from Scotland, 78 from Wales, and 435 from Northern Ireland.[52] Adjusting for the respective populations of each devolved nation, for each judicial review judgment reported in Wales, there were four judgments in Scotland and nine in Northern Ireland. Edwards found the rate of judicial review in Scotland per head of population – one judicial review judgment per 173,000 people – close to that found in *The Value & Effects of Judicial Review* research for England and Wales (one per 192,000 people).[53] In contrast, the rate in Wales was one per 406,000 people, and for Northern Ireland, it was one per 43,000 people.

Whilst Edwards's research considers only judicial review applications making it to a final hearing, analysis of civil justice statistics relating to all claims issued reveals a similar picture. For example, Scottish civil justice statistics record that each year, one application (called a petition) is issued for judicial review for each 23,000 people.[54] The Northern Ireland Department of Justice records one application for judicial review per 15,600 people annually.[55] The combined

[51] As discussed in *AXA General Insurance Limited and others v The Lord Advocate and others* [2011] UKSC 46.

[52] L Edwards, 'A Comparative Analysis of Devolved Judicial Review: A Summary' (2024) 29(2) *Judicial Review* 84.

[53] *The Value & Effects of Judicial Review* (n 34).

[54] Scottish Government, 'Civil justice statistics in Scotland 2020-21' (Scottish Government, 28 April 2022) www.gov.scot/publications/civil-justice-statistics-scotland-2020-21/pages/4/.

[55] Northern Ireland Department of Justice, 'NI Courts and Tribunal Service Judicial Statistics for 2021, published today' (Northern Ireland Department of Justice, 24 June 2022) www.justice-ni.gov.uk/news/ni-courts-and-tribunal-service-judicial-statistics-2021-published-today.

statistics for England and Wales record that each year there is one application for judicial review per 26,000 people.

These statistics are reinforced by other research, including that by the Northern Ireland Department of Justice, which noted in 2015 that judicial review cases 'are much more common in Northern Ireland'.[56] Our research in Wales found evidence of a significantly lower incidence of judicial review in Wales compared to parts of England, and in particular when compared to London boroughs.[57] Rates of judicial review in Wales per head of population appear more similar to those of northern English regions. In northern England, especially outside the main cities, rates of judicial review claims are generally very low, especially when claims relating to prisons and the police (significant areas of legal specialism locally) are excluded from analysis.

Some of the difference in the rate of judicial review is likely attributable to the asymmetric scheme of devolution. Wales has a longer list of reserved matters compared to Scotland and Northern Ireland.[58] Many administrative law claims issued by people in Wales will be against England and Wales or UK public authorities. However, even accounting for the differences in the devolution settlements, Edwards still found the incidence of judicial review to be substantially higher in Scotland and Northern Ireland. Of the 317 judicial review judgments in Scotland over the period studied, more than 80 per cent of cases related to policy areas which are also devolved to Wales. For Northern Ireland, which had a significant number of cases relating to police, parole, and prisons (matters not devolved to Wales), still three-quarters of the cases analysed were in policy areas also devolved to Wales.

Edwards's research also disclosed some variation in the type of claimants. For example, in Northern Ireland, over 80 per cent of claimants were individuals, whereas in Wales it was 74 per cent, and in Scotland only 67 per cent. This data relates only to claims reaching a substantive hearing and so could potentially be due to a higher proportion of claims originating from individuals in Northern Ireland (which may well fit with the more developed 'rights culture' and awareness) and/or that individuals in Wales and Scotland are comparatively less successful at the permission stage compared to businesses or organisations. This might also be linked to the different legal aid contexts, discussed further below.

In terms of representation, it can be difficult to identify unrepresented litigants from available data. At least for substantive judgments where the claimant's identity as a litigant in person was specifically recorded, Edwards found only five such cases in Northern Ireland, four in Wales, and three in Scotland during his research period. Nason's earlier research across England and Wales, with data gained under

[56] Northern Ireland Department of Justice, *A Strategy for Access to Justice* (Northern Ireland Department of Justice 2015) 21.7.

[57] Nason and Edwards (n 49).

[58] Scotland Act 1998, Sch 5; Government of Wales Act 2006, Sch 7A; Northern Ireland Act 1998, Sch 3.

privileged access, suggested significant growth in the proportion of judicial review claims issued by unrepresented litigants from 2008 to the mid-2010s. This coincided with cuts to legal aid funding; however, more recent data is not publicly available.

Edwards's research also found that 'success' rates for claimants varied across the devolved nations. Claimants in Northern Ireland and Wales were awarded a remedy at a substantive hearing in approximately 45 per cent of Edwards's sample of claims. This may imply that the permission stage is working adequately to filter out unmeritorious cases through the requirement of 'a reasonable chance of success'.[59] On the other hand, claimants in the Scottish sample were successful in only 28 per cent of final hearings. Practitioner participants in Edwards's research suggested that it is relatively easy to obtain permission to proceed with a judicial review petition in Scotland and that permission criteria may be being applied less stringently, leading to some weaker cases proceeding to a final hearing. This may be due to distinct public law permission requirements having only been introduced more recently in Scotland. However, it may well be that in Northern Ireland and/or Wales, judicial interpretation of the permission stage requirements could be too strict, with some meritorious cases filtered out. We have both heard practitioner anecdotes to that effect, especially in Wales.

That said, and particularly in both Wales and England, the proportion of apparently unmeritorious judicial review claims has been criticised, and reforms have been introduced to stem this apparent tide of weak claims.[60] A significant proportion of claims issued in England and Wales each year are judicially classified as 'totally without merit'.[61] Most claims found to be totally without merit are immigration judicial reviews. Where a claim is classified as such on paper permission, there will be no further opportunity to reargue the point orally, and the claimant will likely be liable for the respondent's costs. That said, despite concerns,[62] there is little evidence of so-called vexatious litigation in the devolved nations.[63]

In Scotland, a 2009 report of the Scottish Civil Courts Review (known as the 'Gill Review') found a steady increase in the number of judicial review petitions that were taking up a disproportionate amount of court time. Subsequently, the Courts Reform (Scotland) Act 2014 amended the Court of Session Act 1988 and introduced a general three-month time limit for bringing applications. This can be increased where the court considers a longer period equitable in the circumstances.

[59] Edwards (n 52).

[60] Ministry of Justice, 'Judicial Review: proposals for further reform' (Ministry of Justice, 4 June 2019) available at consult.justice.gov.uk/digital-communications/judicial-review.

[61] Civil Procedure Rules, Rule 54.12, para 7 and Upper Tribunal Rules, Rule 30; and *Wasif and another v Secretary of State for the Home Department* [2016] EWCA Civ 82. Applications totally without merit are those which are 'bound to fail'.

[62] Northern Ireland Department of Justice, *A Strategy for Access to Justice* (Northern Ireland Department of Justice 2015) 21.10.

[63] A McHarg, 'Access to Judicial Review in Scotland', UK Const. L. Blog (30 July 2013) available a ukconstitutionallaw.org/2013/07/30/aileen-mcharg-access-to-judicial-review-in-scotland/.

The 2014 Act also introduced requirements of sufficient interest and real prospect of success, bringing Scotland largely into line with the rest of the UK.

The proportion of seemingly weak cases being issued has also been seen as problematic in Northern Ireland. For example, Colin Stutt's Review of Access to Justice stated, with respect to claims issued in 2013–14 that:

> 71 are recorded as won or settled, 95 as unsuccessful and 64 as 'other'... I am suspicious of this 'other' category, which probably relates to certificates discharged at an early stage; I do not believe this outcome is likely to be recorded if a substantive benefit were achieved for the client so I regard these cases as unsuccessful ... This means that only 31% of judicial review certificates issued were successful in that year, the lowest success rate of any civil category.[64]

More cautiously, however, the Northern Ireland Audit Office has noted that many judicial review statistics, including on the outcome of cases, have been miscategorised. This is seen as resulting in 'an inaccurate account of the success, or otherwise, that applicants had in challenging the actions and decisions of public bodies'.[65]

'Success' can also come pre-issue or between issue and a final hearing. As we have seen above with respect to Covid-19 policies, even the 'threat' of judicial review can have an impact. In our research, we found that public bodies in Wales have become increasingly alert to judicial review over the years. Our Wales-based research participants considered that authorities were increasingly proactive in ensuring the lawfulness of their procedures and decisions from the outset.[66] In Scotland and Northern Ireland, Edwards found recognition of the 'right first time' agenda and an understanding that judicial review can be an inevitable consequence of poor decision-making.[67]

That said, research generally suggests the incidence of justiciable problems across the nations of the UK does not differ significantly.[68] We should not be artificially reassured that those lower levels of challenge, especially in Scotland and Wales, necessarily imply fewer problems or better decision-making. However, in both Wales and Scotland, research participants suggested that the devolved governments and legislatures might be more conscientious in their pre-enactment assessment of draft policy and legislation than their UK-level counterparts, thus reducing the scope for challenges. In Wales, the need to draft legislation bilingually may provide further opportunities to improve quality. It has also been said that Westminster draftsmen could learn from the clarity, transparency, and approach to updating legislative drafting that occurred in Wales during the

[64] C Stutt, *A Strategy for Access to Justice* (Northern Ireland Department of Justice, 2015) 185.

[65] Northern Ireland Audit Office, *The Judicial Review Process in Northern Ireland* (Northern Ireland Audit Office, 2023) 12.

[66] Nason and Edwards (n 49).

[67] Scottish Government, *Right First Time: A practical guide for public authorities in Scotland to decision-making and the law* (Scottish Government, 2023) 54.

[68] H Genn and A Paterson, *Paths to Justice Scotland: What people in Scotland think and do about going to Law* (Oxford, Hart Publishing, 2001).

Covid-19 pandemic. In evidence to the Welsh Parliament Legislation, Justice and Constitution Committee, former Lord Chief Justice of England and Wales, Lord Thomas, stated that '… nothing could show more the difference between the law of England and the law of Wales than the way legislation was handled during the pandemic …'.[69]

In terms of the 'dynamics of judicial review',[70] our research suggests that Welsh public bodies are more likely to settle than their English counterparts. On the positive side, this avoids costly and lengthy litigation, and claimant solicitors reported generally being happy with the settlements received. On the negative side, this means that opportunities for legal clarification, especially of developing Welsh law, are missed. Our research showed that many claims or potential claims against Welsh ministers also settled early.

A more recent case, not in our original study, was, however, conspicuous in being settled later in the day, by consent after permission and before a substantive hearing. This related to the Welsh ministers' decision to discontinue a particular scheme providing free meals to some schoolchildren during the summer vacation. The High Court declared, by consent, that the ministers were in breach of duties under the Rights of Children and Young Persons (Wales) Measure Act 2011 and the public sector equality duty under section 149 of the Equality Act 2010.[71] As this matter was settled by consent, there is no publicly available judgment on the legal issues that could contribute to the interpretation and development of the law.

Similarly, cases claiming a potential breach of the unique Wellbeing of Future Generations (Wales) Act 2015 (WFGA) have so far failed to pass the permission stage. Court documents obtained under the Civil Procedure Rules have revealed that some duties under the WFGA are considered 'too vague and aspirational' to be judicially enforced.[72] On the contrary, Edwards's research found the courts in Northern Ireland and Scotland more regularly and vigorously dealing with challenges to flagship policies, key legislation, and broader constitutional issues. Such challenges directly question the validity of a devolved legislative provision rather than a public authority decision made under it.[73] As discussed above, there have been cases of constitutional significance issued and heard in Wales. However, the extent of judicial willingness to engage with uniquely Welsh law matters, such as bilingual drafting, as opposed to general administrative law grounds brought

[69] Legislation, Justice and Constitution Committee (22/11/2021) [5]: record.assembly.wales/Committee/12484.

[70] A phrase used by V Bondy and M Sunkin in, *The Dynamics of Judicial Review Litigation: The Resolution of Public Law Challenges Before Final Hearing* (Public Law Project, 2009).

[71] publiclawproject.org.uk/latest/school-meals-welsh-government-admits-failing-to-follow-law/#:~:text=The%20High%20Court%20has%20declared,represented%20by%20Public%20Law%20Project.

[72] See, eg, *R(B) v Neath Port Talbot* (2019) (refusal of permission, unreported) www.bbc.co.uk/news/uk-wales-48272470.

[73] In particular, the courts of Scotland and Northern Ireland are also common initial venues for constitutional challenges that end up before the UK Supreme Court, eg, *Cherry v Advocate General for Scotland* [2019] UKSC 41 or *Allister v Secretary of State for Northern Ireland* [2023] UKSC 5.

against constitutionally important actors (such as Welsh ministers), has been questioned.[74]

Other pre-action differences include that our Welsh research suggested people in certain areas of Wales are less likely than people in most areas of England to seek to use legal methods to resolve concerns/disputes with public bodies. Whilst it was difficult to pinpoint precise reasons for this, there was a perception that it could be linked to a culture of greater deference to authority. This reluctance was also linked to the proportion of the population receiving some form of state social security or welfare benefit and/or receiving care services and the related concern that legal challenge specifically would cause problems for future interaction with public bodies.

Edwards's research, and that of others, finds some evidence of a Scottish reluctance to challenge that comes more from a perspective of 'fatalism or powerlessness',[75] that legal action requires more effort than it's worth. However, as discussed further below, Wales and Scotland both have well-developed administrative justice sectors, with more powerful and accessible commissioners and ombudsmen as compared to England and at the UK level. The other avenues to challenge, as well as relative measures of institutional trust in public authorities, might also be part of this picture.

Considering the approaches of public bodies, participants in Edwards's research from Scotland perceived a hardening of public authority attitudes towards settlement in judicial review, a reduced willingness to engage with potential petitioners until litigation had commenced, and more forceful defences mounted at the permission stage. This may be symptomatic of different responses to strained financial circumstances. Welsh authorities were more likely to settle individual matters to avoid litigation that might later set a costly precedent. Scottish authorities focused their scarce resources on seeing off judicial review petitions at the permission stage. Edwards's research also suggests there is some hardening of public body attitudes towards judicial review in Northern Ireland, again as a side effect of financial challenges coming from a need to prioritise services.

In Wales, the comparative closeness of governance to the public was also seen as a preventative to higher rates of judicial review. Research participants associated the comparative ease of communication between public bodies with greater knowledge sharing and a more consistent approach to judicial review. However, the closeness between central and local government and between government and the kind of third-sector bodies that might normally issue or be otherwise involved in judicial review was seen as problematic to ensuring access to justice for individuals and local communities.[76]

The picture for Northern Ireland and Scotland was perceived to be different. Here, research participants suggested that despite comparatively sized governance,

[74] ACL Davies, 'The interpretation of bilingual legislation/dehongli deddfwriaeth ddwyieithog' (2021) 137 *LQR* 547, 552.

[75] Genn and Paterson (n 68) 182.

[76] Nason and Edwards (n 49).

public bodies were increasingly difficult to communicate with prior to commencing litigation. There was no indication that the third sector, in either Northern Ireland or Scotland, had a particular closeness to government, as was suggested by our research participants in Wales. Rather, the sector in both nations was seen as proactive in seeking out potential claimants and as being a significant source of support for judicial review.

### *iii. The Grounds and Topics of Judicial Review, and Remedies, in the Devolved Nations*

In Edwards's study, illegality (also referred to in the cases as unlawfulness) was the most widely argued ground of review, present in some form in three-quarters of the judgments. The prominence of illegality was also evident in Nason's past systematic analysis[77] and a more recent study by Elizabeth Fisher and Joanna Bell.[78] However, illegality was not the ground of review where courts most often found in favour of claimants. That epithet goes to procedural propriety, principles of which were found to have been breached in around half of all cases in Edwards's study where they were argued.[79] This may well be due to the courts having confidence in their own expertise on matters of fair procedure.

In our past research, we found that whilst there have been some fluctuations, planning, education, and community care have been the most prominent subjects of judicial review claims issued in Wales. Planning is by far the most common topic of substantive judgments relating to Welsh public bodies. Edwards's research shows that planning cases were prevalent across all devolved nations. He also found that such cases were often more successful, across all three nations, where a wider local public interest matter was evident. These matters included public interest in the failure to account for additional traffic,[80] undue impacts on a local listed building,[81] and where a plan to demolish a local leisure centre had adverse effects on the public good as well as being based on insufficient consultation.[82]

Edwards found greater variation in the subject matter of final judgments in Scotland and Northern Ireland. In Scotland, for example, he found a greater proportion of cases relating to civil procedure or more general administrative law issues. In Northern Ireland, a higher proportion of claims involved a human rights argument. Whilst some such cases related to historic issues arising from a legacy of conflict, many did not, indicating that the unique history of Northern Ireland and the nature of the devolution-linked peace process may well have heightened awareness of human rights amongst the legal community and wider population. The insecure

[77] S Nason, *Reconstructing Judicial Review* (Oxford, Hart Publishing, 2016).
[78] Fisher and Bell (n 25).
[79] Nason found similar in her England and Wales systematic analysis of judgments. Nason, (n 77).
[80] *Corbo Properties Ltd's Application for Judicial Review, Re* [2012] NIQB 107.
[81] *R (Martin) v Powys CC* [2018] EWHC 2892 (Admin).
[82] *Guild v Angus Council* [2020] CSIH 50; 2021 SC 83.

nature of government and lack of an effective executive for much of Edwards's research period also appear to have impacted the prevalence of particular remedies. Declarations were more common in Northern Ireland, often in cases where ministers had failed to perform their duties, but where it would involve the courts too closely in politics to issue a mandatory order that would in any event be ignored.

Several cases across Edwards's survey involved legal clarification, even where the claimant was not themselves granted a remedy. Taking an example from Northern Ireland, in *McVeigh's Application for Judicial Review (No. 2)*,[83] while the claimant unsuccessfully attempted to challenge a search warrant of their own property, the court reached broader conclusions about the lawfulness of the search warrant policy.[84] In a case from Wales, *McDonagh v Newport City Council*,[85] the claimant was not awarded a remedy, but the court clarified the meaning of the word 'aversion' in local housing policy, a legal interpretation that improved certainty and predictability for the future.

In our Wales research, participants were clear that judicial review had catalysed forensic examination of law and administrative practice, instigating improvements in the quality of policy and strategic decision-making. These benefits were noted by respondents largely working with claimants and those largely working with defendants. Benefits were evident even where the same decision was ultimately made by the relevant public authority 'on the merits'. Edwards's research in Scotland revealed that public authorities welcomed the benefits of judicial review in improving legal clarity, thereby improving public administration. In Northern Ireland, the comparatively higher rates of success at a substantive hearing for claimants evidences the ability to acquire a tangible remedy across a range of policy issues. Participants in Edwards's Northern Ireland study found that judicial review provides various substantial benefits to claimants, including opening lines of communication between individuals and public bodies and clarifying public authority duties to provide services.

### *iv. Judicial Review in the Devolved Nations: Divergence and Convergence*

Based on the evidence presented, we suggest that the diversity of judicial review caseloads, topics, and the 'dynamics' of judicial review (including pre-litigation activity) across the UK's devolved nations is a product of several factors. These include the historical, political, and social context of each nation, factors which are also related to practitioner and public awareness of the judicial review procedure itself and willingness to use it. The nature of the market for legal services and legal aid also has an impact. This is particularly challenging in Wales, where

[83] *McVeigh's Application for Judicial Review (No. 2), Re* [2017] NIQB 61.
[84] ibid at [59]–[60].
[85] *McDonagh v Newport City Council* [2019] EWHC 3886 (Admin).

responsibility for these matters is not devolved to the Welsh Government or the Senedd Cymru/Welsh Parliament. Northern Ireland has around 60 per cent of the population of Wales but has better access to funding and legal representation due to devolved policies.

Litigation activity is also likely attributable to the development and implementation of new legislation and administrative policies and the life cycle where such may be initially subject to several challenges, followed by legal clarification, stemming the tide of claims. Edwards's study found evidence of judgments providing legal clarification relating to topics of administration in one nation being drawn on with approval in other nations. Indeed, where consistency and further convergence have been most evident is in the development of grounds of judicial review (general administrative law principles) and in matters such as procedure, standing, and time limits.

We have written variously elsewhere about how the developing 'new administrative law' of Wales imposes additional duties on public bodies with respect to sustainable development, health, wellbeing, and the impacts of social and economic disadvantage.[86] It has been suggested that these statutory duties could be codified, alongside existing common law grounds of judicial review, into an Administrative Law Code for Wales.[87] Simon Hoffman has argued further that the Administrative Court in Wales could also make a 'significant contribution to social justice' fostered by '[a]djudication which departs from the traditional approach to judicial review in social welfare fields, to allow (encourage) more judicial activism on substantive human rights issues'.[88] Yet we see no evidence of such developments. Rather, in the alternative, there is reason to believe that claims raising matters of this 'new administrative law' of Wales, some of which require judicial attention and interpretation regardless of whether this is 'activist' or otherwise, are less likely to be granted permission than other topics.

The context of different policy and legislative approaches to socio-economic rights, equality and sustainability is also relevant in Scotland, which can be seen in Scottish responses to a UK Government commissioned Independent Review of Administrative Law (IRAL). The IRAL Panel was established to consider the case for reforming judicial review (procedures, grounds, and remedies) within the UK Government's reserved remit. The Panel received evidence from the Scottish Human Rights Committee that Scotland is on a different 'human rights trajectory' from the rest of the UK. Further, having a dual- or twin-track approach to judicial review could mean remedies for human rights breaches might be different depending on whether the breach related to a devolved or reserved matter.[89]

[86] Nason and Edwards (n 49) and S Nason, 'The 'New Administrative Law' of Wales' [2019] *Public Law* 703.

[87] D Gardner, 'An Administrative Law Code for Wales: Benefits to reap and obstacles to overcome' (2019) 40(3) *Statute Law Review* 273.

[88] S Hoffman, Swansea University, *Submission to the Commission on Justice in Wales* (2018) [3]–[6].

[89] *The Independent Review of Administrative Law* ('IRAL') (CP407, March 2021) 127–128.

Although the substance of the UK's Human Rights Act 1998 is a reserved matter, the devolved nations can implement other human rights and equality conventions into domestic law, including through primary legislation, within their spheres of legislative competence.

Wales has meandered with Scotland along this enhanced human rights trajectory, but reform in both nations has recently stalled. For example, a proposed Human Rights (Scotland) Bill was withdrawn from the Scottish Government's legislative programme.[90] Similar attempts to propose legislative options to strengthen human rights in Wales have been hampered by lack of capacity.[91] A recent judgment of the UK Supreme Court in relation to Scottish legislation seeking to incorporate the UN Convention on the Rights of the Child also appears to support an interpretation of devolution legislation that significantly reduces devolved legislative competence.[92]

It is in Northern Ireland, with a comparatively human rights-aware legal sector and greater public understanding of human rights challenges, where human rights judicial reviews are most common. Other actors in the administrative justice system also have an impact here. Notably, the Northern Ireland Human Rights Commission has a power to bring judicial review claims relating to human rights issues on its own initiative without the need for a 'victim'. The Northern Ireland Public Services Ombudsman has also been proactive in examining human rights breaches in the context of maladministration.

The IRAL Panel noted that its remit did not extend to judicial review in Northern Ireland or Scotland. Nor did it extend to 'Wales only' activity, by which it meant review of powers that may be exercised only in Wales, including powers exercised by either Welsh ministers, UK Government ministers, or both concurrently. However, in this context, IRAL nevertheless recognised that jurisdictionally its recommendations would apply equally to 'Wales only' judicial review. The IRAL report further stated, referring to Northern Ireland and Scotland, that a two-tier system of devolved and reserved judicial review would be undesirable.[93] In the UK Government's response to IRAL, the then Lord Chancellor stated that additional reforms proposed by the UK Government were intended to apply to the jurisdiction of England and Wales only, whilst also voicing concern about risks of fragmentation across the UK.[94]

Scotland and Northern Ireland, where responsibility for the administration of justice is devolved, at least have the potential to reform judicial review should they wish; however, they have largely chosen not to do so, and where they have, this has

[90] See, eg, R McCurdy, 'Human Rights Bill: What is it and why has it stalled?' *The Scottish Herald* 17 October 2024 and K Boyle, *Human rights incorporation in Scotland* (13 September 2024): www.strath.ac.uk/humanities/lawschool/blog/humanrightsincorporation-keynotespeechfromthe2024scottishinternationallawconference/.

[91] See, eg, C Haines, 'Welsh Labour's human rights pledge will miss 2026 deadline', *Nation Cymru* 16 September 2024.

[92] *Reference by the Attorney General and the Advocate General for Scotland – United Nations Convention on the Rights of the Child (Incorporation) (Scotland) Bill* [2021] UKSC 42.

[93] IRAL (n 89) [5.48].

[94] Ministry of Justice, *Judicial Review Reform: The Government Response to the Independent Review of Administrative Law* (March 2021) para 6.

been towards further alignment with England and Wales. This suggests significant support for the value of the judicial review procedure among institutions that are themselves exercising 'delegated' powers and that are themselves subject to judicial review on at least some grounds. This can be taken as a show of support for the procedure, especially alongside other evidence. For example, both the Scottish and Welsh Governments wrote to the IRAL Panel expressing support for existing judicial review procedures and cautioning against any further reforms.[95]

## III. Devolved Tribunals and Administrative Justice

In this section we consider the broader development of administrative justice across the devolved nations. The so-called 'de-tribunalisation' discussed above is not as prominent in the devolved nations. High caseload matters such as immigration are not devolved, and as such, the devolved nations have largely avoided the volume challenges that UK governments have sought to address through adopting administrative review and reducing tribunal access. There has not been the same drive to expand the number of tribunal claims attracting fees or to increase fees where applicable.[96]

Scotland and Northern Ireland have not experienced the extreme cuts to legal aid as have been the case in England and Wales, meaning that tribunal claims and judicial review generally remain more accessible to ordinary people. Northern Ireland has a substantial legal aid budget, far higher per capita than any other nation in Europe.[97] Eligibility for legal aid in Northern Ireland is also broad, permitting a large portion of the population to seek financial assistance with legal advice and representation. Eligibility for legal aid in Scotland is also relatively broad, with most topics of judicial review in scope and advice services being perceived as relatively more accessible. However, financial sums per capita are the lowest across the UK's jurisdictions, with payment rates having stalled and some firms leaving the sector as a result.

Matthew's contribution to AJ Wales, published in 2017, focused on legal representation in Australian tribunals. Until comparatively recently, it had been common to distinguish tribunals and courts across the UK partially based on the less formal and less adversarial nature of tribunals, rendering legal representation less likely to be required. However, the demarcation between courts and tribunals has become much more blurred.[98] Spectrums of practice have been proposed, from the more adversarial to the more inquisitorial, alongside varying levels of

[95] Submissions to IRAL, Welsh Government GOV028 and Scottish Government GOV026.

[96] B Thompson, 'Opportunities and Constraints: Reflections on Reforming Administrative Justice Within and Across the United Kingdom' in AJ Wales (n 2) 171.

[97] European Commission for the Efficiency of Justice (CEPEJ), *European judicial systems CEPEJ Evaluation Report* (Council of Europe, 2022) 142.

[98] See. eg, S Nason and H Pritchard, 'Tribunal Reform and Administrative Justice' in S Thomson, M Groves and G Weeks, *Administrative Tribunals in the Common Law World* (Oxford, Bloomsbury Publishing, 2024).

legal participation, with or without legal representation. The growth of online dispute resolution in its broadest sense and the need to develop online procedural rules have further blurred any existing lines between court and tribunal practices. Perhaps what is notable, and potentially different from Australia, is that the courts, including those of the devolved nations, tend to show considerable respect for specialist tribunal jurisdictions in the development of their own procedures, and with this, their approaches to unrepresented litigants.

Where devolved nations have also followed the lead of the centre is in the amalgamation of tribunals. The Leggatt Review of tribunals, which led to the new TCEA structure, did not extend to devolved tribunals. The Review was nevertheless concerned as to whether the rationalisation envisaged for the new system would be achievable across the range of tribunals operating cross-border in the UK, whilst at the same time maintaining coherence with the devolved systems with which the rationalised tribunals would interact. Subsequently, the devolved nations have pursued their own approaches to tribunal amalgamation. The Tribunals (Scotland) Act 2014 created a statutory framework bringing together existing jurisdictions and providing a structure for the flexible development of new jurisdictions. This structure includes a First-tier Tribunal for Scotland and an Upper Tribunal for Scotland. The Lord President, who is head of the Scottish Judiciary, is also head of the Scottish Tribunals but delegates various roles to the President of Scottish Tribunals. Alongside this, a Review of Civil Justice led to changes in the civil courts, reform of the judicial review procedure, and the creation of a Scottish Courts and Tribunals Service effected by the Court Reform (Scotland) Act 2015.

In Wales, as part of the most recent phase of devolution moving Wales to a reserved powers model, the Wales Act 2017 defined a collection of 'Welsh tribunals' that had developed ad hoc over time. The 2017 Act also created the office of the President of Welsh Tribunals (PWT) to oversee them. The Law Commission has subsequently examined the Devolved Welsh Tribunals,[99] and the Welsh Government issued a White Paper[100] on proposals for amalgamation and systemic reform. The proposals aim to enhance professionalism and judicial independence and to create a new Appeal Tribunal for Wales of equivalent standing to the Upper Tribunal. This would be the first Wales-only 'superior court of record'. Although the systemic reform proposals echo those implemented through the TCEA, so in part following the centre, the Welsh Government's stated aim is also to distance Wales further from England in the administration of justice. The new tribunal's structure is seen as laying the foundations 'for a future where justice is devolved, and Wales administers its own wider system of courts and tribunals'.[101]

When previous UK Conservative governments were considering restricting access to judicial review, there was discussion of whether Welsh ministers and/or

[99] Law Commission, *Devolved Tribunals in Wales Report* (Law Com N. 403; 2021).
[100] Welsh Government, *A New Tribunal System for Wales: White Paper* (2023).
[101] ibid.

the Welsh Parliament could bolster access to justice by creating statutory routes to judicial review (like Upper Tribunal judicial review under the TCEA) to the Welsh tribunals. A key question is whether this might be outside legislative competence, given that 'judicial review' is a reserved matter. In this context it is also significant that the Appeal Tribunal for Wales, if established, would be a devolved 'superior court of record' in contrast to the Administrative Court in Wales, which is a reserved body under the control of the UK Government and Westminster Parliament.

Tribunal judiciary support for an Appeal Tribunal for Wales was relatively lukewarm. The general sentiment was that consistency with tribunal doctrine in developing principles in particular subject areas of administrative law on an England and Wales basis, even in devolved policy areas such as health, property, and standards of local government administration, was valued more than any perceived need to develop a body of 'Welsh' jurisprudence based on the interpretation of Welsh law.[102] This seems consistent with our evidence indicating a lack of support for developing Welsh jurisprudence generally in the Administrative Court.

Turning to Northern Ireland. In 2005, the Northern Ireland Law Centre jointly organised a conference on tribunal reform with the largest tribunal jurisdiction (social security) and the Department for Constitutional Affairs, which was then responsible for the Northern Ireland Courts Service. Proposals for tribunal amalgamation have been developed,[103] including through research that concluded around the time policing and justice powers were devolved to the Northern Ireland Assembly. However, these reforms have not yet been considered a sufficient political priority for enactment. On the other hand, Northern Ireland has led the way in the development of so-called 'ombudsprudence'. The Northern Ireland Public Services Ombudsman was the first UK ombudsman to gain own initiative powers to launch systemic investigations. Wales was next in line, giving its own initiative powers to the Public Services Ombudsman for Wales. The Scottish Public Services Ombudsman does not yet have such powers but has been pursuing them for several years. In contrast, complaints about UK Government departments or other UK public bodies attract a so-called 'MP filter'. Complaints must first be referred to the Parliamentary and Health Services Ombudsman by a Member of the UK Parliament. The Local Government and Social Care Ombudsman in England does not have own-initiative powers.

There are several other factors which contribute to an enhanced administrative justice landscape in the UK's devolved nations. Generally, these nations have a higher number of diverse commissioners acting, for example, as National Human Rights Institutions, as well as determining strategic complaints about administration from younger and older people and, uniquely in Wales, acting as a guardian of

[102] Discussed in S Nason and H Pritchard (n 98).

[103] G McKeever and B Thompson, *Redressing Users' Disadvantage: Proposals for Tribunal Reform in Northern Ireland* (2010) available at: papers.ssrn.com/sol3/papers.cfm?abstract_id=3523975.

the well-being of future generations. It has also been suggested that the extra layer of political representation in the devolved legislatures provides people with additional routes to redress in administrative justice and bolsters public confidence in administration.

The devolved nations have also generally articulated and fostered more holistic conceptions of administrative justice and been able to maintain more searching strategic oversight than has been the case across England and Wales, Great Britain, or the UK.[104] That said, interest in administrative justice and its oversight as a government policy priority has waxed and waned. For example, the Welsh Government's White Paper on the Welsh Tribunals makes no reference to administrative justice. Recent work on administrative justice principles for Scotland, including proposals to legislate for a principles-based approach (similar to that developed, but not progressed, in Wales[105]) has been conducted by the Scottish Law Society[106] without the imprimatur of the Scottish Government.

## IV. Concluding Reflections

Throughout his scholarship, Matthew has stressed the importance of research and evidence, including empirical evidence, to our understanding of the roles, functions, contributions, and impacts of various institutions and procedures of administrative justice. He states, for example: 'Arguments about the precise relationship between judicial and merits review in Australia are largely speculative in the absence of clear empirical research',[107] arguing also that the same evidence 'lacuna' applies to the impact of the AAT on government agencies. Lacunae in evidence bases are something we have sought to focus on in our research, including in this chapter where we present our empirical research into judicial review (whilst noting its limitations). This kind of research, including more systematic research into caseloads and historical archival research, can also demystify areas of public administrative law. For example, it can challenge 'myths', sometimes long-held assumptions about a subject that can be often repeated but divorced from historical context or critical reflection. We note here Matthew's work in busting myths about the historical development of the Australian AAT, its objectives, and the nature of merits review. Matthew has also signalled that a lot can be learnt from small jurisdictions and from the mistakes of various jurisdictions as much

[104] As discussed in Nason (n 22).

[105] Committee for Administrative Justice and Tribunals in Wales, *Administrative justice: a cornerstone of social justice in Wales* (9 December 2016): www.gov.wales/administrative-justice-cornerstone-social-justice-wales.

[106] Law Society of Scotland, Administrative Justice Sub-committee, *A Principles based approach to Administrative Justice: A Proposal for good governance by the Administrative Justice Sub-committee* (April 2024): www.lawscot.org.uk/media/gmohtwyz/a-principles-based-approach-to-administrative-justice-a-proposal-for-good-governance-april-2024-005.pdf.

[107] Groves, AJ Wales (n 2) 350.

as from their successes. Our chapter shows that multilevel governance has allowed for experimentation in administrative justice across the UK's nations. But we also show that, as yet, neither devolution, regionalisation, nor tribunalisation has had much impact on the development of the grounds of judicial review or the so-called general principles of administrative law. This suggests that however much complexity, diversity, or fragmentation there is in procedures, institutions, and oversight of administrative justice and in the subject matter of claims, their prevalence and outcomes for individuals, the core general principles of lawful administration and the basic foundations governing citizen-state interactions remain shared.

# 2

# The Need for a 'New' Template for the Creation of Federal Ombudsman Institutions

ANITA STUHMCKE*

## I. Introduction

This chapter builds upon a 2021 blog post[1] in which I argue that the Australian office of the Commonwealth Ombudsman is no longer fit for purpose. Importantly, I do not believe that the Commonwealth Ombudsman is redundant, requires radical overhaul, or should be abolished. Indeed, I endorse the need for the Ombudsman to continue to address the imbalance of power between the Commonwealth Government as the powerful decision-maker and the powerless and often vulnerable[2] citizen. My concern, however, is that the Commonwealth Ombudsman has lost its way. This is evidenced by the Ombudsman now prioritising the systemic improvement of government administration[3] over individual

* This chapter is funded by a grant from the ARC -Derek Wilding, Karen Lee, David Lindsay and Anita Stuhmcke, ARC Discovery Project – (DP230101322), *Optimising Industry-led Regulation for the Digital Platform Era* Australian Research Council, 1 Mar 2023–28 Feb 2028.

[1] A Stuhmcke 'The Commonwealth Ombudsman: Still Fit for Purpose?' (squarespace.com), 17 September 2021.

[2] Vulnerability can take many forms, for a categorisation of groups of vulnerable people see www.acnc.gov.au/tools/topic-guides/vulnerable-peopleACNC: children and senior; people with impaired psychological functioning; people from a low socio-economic background; people who are Aboriginal or Torres Strait Islanders; people who are not native speakers of the local language; people with low levels of literacy or education; people subject to modern slavery, which involves human exploitation and control, such as forced labour, debt bondage, human trafficking, and child labour. I would add to this list people who have lost their liberty such as prisoners and detainees. This chapter does not conceptualise vulnerability in the way of theorists such as M Fineman, 'The Vulnerable Subject: Anchoring Equality in the Human Condition' (2008) 20 *Yale Journal of Law and Feminism* 2.

[3] A good example of this growing focus on government improvement (which is beyond the scope of this chapter) is the addition of 'audit' roles within the portfolio of the Commonwealth Ombudsman. Some of these include the oversight role of whistleblowing; monitoring of detention facilities and law enforcement oversight re records inspection (thanks to Professor Aronson for this point). An important role/focus of the institution which has become increasingly important since the Commonwealth

citizens' complaints about the government. This shift diminishes the institution's focus on the individual as a stakeholder and negatively impacts both the actual and perceived independence of the institution. In my view, to preserve and promote the institution's hallmark of independence from the government, the ombudsman institution must (re)orient its focus towards the individual complainant.

In this chapter I examine this gap in the coverage of the individual complainant by the Commonwealth Ombudsman. Specifically, I explore how the model has come to prioritise the middle class and advantaged complainants over the vulnerable and disadvantaged. I then suggest that this must be remedied through the proactive and thoughtful construction of new ombudsman offices.[4]

The chapter is divided into four parts. Part II investigates the historical reasons for the creation of the Australian public law ombudsman, identifying the central reason as addressing individual complaints. Part III then provides two case studies that examine the latest developments in new Federal Ombudsman roles. One case study focuses on a 'new ombudsman' aimed at providing consumers with redress against digital platforms like Facebook. The second case study is the new National Student Ombudsman for higher education students, which is a new statutory function of the Commonwealth Ombudsman and will begin taking complaints from 1 February 2025. Part III confirms that there is no standard template for creating ombudsman institutions[5] and that the government approach is to retrofit new ombudsman roles into existing models. This means that the Commonwealth Ombudsman now includes the National Student Ombudsman, and the Telecommunications Industry Ombudsman is the most likely institution to host the Digital Platform Ombudsman.

Part IV notes that integrating new ombudsman roles into existing institutions will embed the problems of the 'old' or existing ombudsman institutions into the new. Specifically, this section demonstrates that both nationally and internationally, the most vulnerable complainants are not typically served by ombudsman institutions. Instead, the individual complainants who do access these institutions tend to be middle-class and advantaged.

This problem must be remedied. To address this, Part IV advocates for a template for the creation of new ombudsman roles. It suggests that using a template will allow for a revival of the 1970s reasons for introducing the Commonwealth

Ombudsman was first introduced in the 1970s is own motion investigations, a virtually non-existent function in the first 2 decades of the office.

[4] Re the use of the term 'ombudsman' or 'ombudsmen' and the gendered nature of the title see the discussion by V Bondy and M Doyle in 'What's in a Name? A Discussion Paper on Ombud Terminology' in M Hertogh and R Kirkham (eds), *Research Handbook on the Ombudsman* (Cheltenham, Edward Elgar Publishing, 2018) ch 26. This chapter uses the term 'ombudsman' throughout in a gender-neutral way.

[5] On this point see also N O'Brien, 'What Future for the Ombudsman?' 86(1) *The Political Quarterly* 72, 74–75.

Ombudsman, thereby addressing the embedded problems of gaps in complainant coverage. This will increase the focus on individual complainants and help promote the real and perceived institutional independence of the ombudsman.

Without a proactive and planned approach to creating new ombudsman roles, the most disadvantaged stakeholders will continue to be overlooked and underserved. Part IV suggests one practical step to address this issue and provide access to vulnerable complainants is through the adoption of the Venice Principles.[6] These Principles are the first independent, international set of standards for the ombudsman institution, equivalent to the Paris Principles, which set out the standards against which national human rights institutions are judged. They thus provide a useful template for ombudsman creation.

The conclusion drawn is that Australian governments should consider utilising the Venice Principles to frame the creation of any new ombudsman. The ombudsman institution exists to address power imbalances within the system of government. It is neither an advocate for the citizen nor is it a reinforcer of the powerful. It is independent from both. Using the Venice Principles ensures a planned and proactive approach to establishing new ombudsman roles, with a focus on the vulnerable complainant.

My intention in this chapter is to use the two case studies of the latest developments in new ombudsman roles to reignite[7] practical protections and scholarly attention regarding the institution's independence. This is critical, as both case studies of new ombudsman roles demonstrate that expediency and efficiency, rather than equity and equality, currently drive ombudsman creation. Without conscious correction, the inevitable result will be limited access to the institution for vulnerable citizens.

## II. The 1970s: The Commonwealth Ombudsman's Historical Focus on the Individual

The socio-political origins of the ombudsman institution were based on addressing the power imbalance between citizens and the government. Globally, it is acknowledged that the central premise of the ombudsman's operation is to promote the rule of law by providing access to justice and effectively resolving individual citizen

[6] *Principles on the Protection and Promotion of the Ombudsman Institution* (the 'Venice Principles') Opinion No. 897/ 2017 Venice Commission 118th Plenary session, Venice 15–16 March 2019, www.venice.coe.int/files/Publications/Venice_Principles_eng.pdf.

[7] The institution can also be a focus of negative attention. For example, see recent events in Western Australia as to the allocation of funds by the Western Australian Ombudsman – D Weber, 'Corruption and Crime Commissioner John McKechnie asks WA Ombudsman Chris Field to consider resigning' 13 April 2024, *ABC News*, www.abc.net.au/news/2024-04-13/wa-ombudsman-chris-field-asked-consider-resigning/103689144.

complaints – functions essential to a healthy democracy.[8] This was also the case in Australia,[9] where in the 1970s, the Commonwealth Ombudsman was established to offer individuals who experienced delays in service, rudeness, or poor decision-making a means to obtain redress quickly, for free, and without losing formal legal rights.[10] The Explanatory Memorandum introducing the Commonwealth Ombudsman legislation in 1976 clearly emphasised the individual complainant, stating that '[T]he essential function of an Ombudsman is to investigate complaints made to {him} about administrative functions of officials ...'.[11]

The primary reason for creating the Commonwealth Ombudsman was to resolve individual complaints from citizens about defective administration by public agencies. This reasoning is confirmed in archival parliamentary material records, which contain confidential files on the concept of the Ombudsman from the 1960s and continue throughout the 1970s.[12] For example, in his policy speech on 13 November 1972, then opposition leader Mr Gough Whitlam stated, '[A]n Ombudsman will be appointed to act as the guardian of the people. He will investigate complaints of unjust treatment by Government departments and agencies, and report directly to Parliament.'[13] The individual complainant was thus central to the creation of the Commonwealth Ombudsman. Consequently, the original proposals envisioned '... an Ombudsman located outside the administrative review system, oriented towards the resolution of individual complaints and generally better at swatting flies than hunting lions'.[14]

The role of the Commonwealth Ombudsman, as originally envisaged, is independent of both the government and the individual and open to all complainants. This function of mediating between the complainant and the government administration, conducting independent investigations, and resolving individual grievances with the power to make recommendations to departments and

[8] For this background see the website of the International Ombudsman Institute, an organisation of more than 200 independent Ombudsman institutions, www.theioi.org/the-i-o-i.

[9] In Australia see the Access to Justice Taskforce, *A Strategic Framework for Access to Justice in the Federal Civil Justice System: A guide for future action, Attorney-General's department, September 2009*, www.ag.gov.au/LegalSystem/Pages/Accesstojustice.aspx.

[10] Australia was the first country to introduce a federal Ombudsman and is the only federation apart from Belgium to have such an office. Many other federal countries, such as the United States, Canada and Germany, have ombudsman operating at state level. There have been proposals for other federal Ombudsman, such as in the United States when in 1969 the American Bar Association proposed a federal Ombudsman: V Hartke, 'Ombudsman: Mediator Between the Citizen and His Government' (1973–74) 10 *California Western Law Review* 325, 351.

[11] Commonwealth Ombudsman, *Annual Report* (1977–78), 3. See also Commonwealth, House of Representatives, Second Reading Speech Ombudsman Bill 1976, *Hansard*, 4 June 1976, 3068 (Mr Ellicott).

[12] Archive file: ECOSOC – Proposal for an 'Ombudsman' in Australia File No 929/1/4.

[13] Archive file, A463 1968/2643 Part 2. Mr Whitlam became Prime Minister on 5 December 1972, five years before the introduction of the Office in 1977.

[14] Senate Standing Committee on Finance and Public Administration, *Review of the Office of the Commonwealth Ombudsman* (December 1991) 14.

agencies sets the Commonwealth Ombudsman apart. It is different from other administrative agencies, such as the Auditors-General or the recently reconstituted Administrative Review Council. These agencies are being established to monitor the whole system of audit and administrative review and to suggest systematic reform to public administration.[15]

The primary reason for creating the Commonwealth Ombudsman was to address individual complaints. This focus on the individual is not surprising, given that in the 1960s and 1970s in Australia, there were limited avenues for the individual to complain about government bureaucracy. Scholars of that time, such as Rowat, suggest that the origins of the Public Law Ombudsman lie in the development of the welfare state, where modern government increasingly intruded into areas of citizens' lives that were previously considered private.[16] As the democratic state developed, it became necessary to impose an ombudsman upon the administrative structure of government, given the government's growing involvement in citizens' daily lives through service provision. As the role of government and bureaucracy expanded dramatically, so did the need for a cost-effective, impartial and efficient forum to investigate and resolve complaints. Importantly, this forum was intended to serve all citizens, not just the wealthy or privileged.

## III. The 2020s: The Ombudsman Institution and the Diminishing Focus on the Individual

Fast forward to the 2020s, and we see the development of two new Australian ombudsman roles: the Digital Platform Ombudsman and the National Student Ombudsman. This section presents each of these new ombudsman roles as brief case studies, focusing on the reasons for their creation. It demonstrates that the motivation behind their introduction is strikingly similar to those of the 1970s creation of the Commonwealth Ombudsman. The individual complainant remains the focus. For the Digital Platform Ombudsman, the goal is to rectify the power imbalance between digital platforms and users by providing a complaint pathway for individual users of platforms like Facebook. Similarly, the National Student Ombudsman aims to give students a voice within large educational providers, in particular universities.

[15] The role of the Ombudsman has been summed up as one 'of investigating, conciliating and cajoling' see Commonwealth, House of Representatives, *Hansard*, 4 June 1975, 3366 (Mr Howard, Bennelong).

[16] Rowat DC (ed), *The Ombudsman: Citizen's Defender* (London, George Allen & Unwin Ltd, 1965). This was also the case in arguments made in the second reading speech by the Honourable Ralph Hanan when the New Zealand Ombudsman Bill was introduced: see Dr B Perry, 'Twenty Five Years of Serving Parliament and the Community' *Victorian Ombudsman Twenty-fifth Report*, (1998) II.

## A. Case Study 1: The Digital Platform Ombudsman

In 2022, the Australian Competition and Consumer Commission (ACCC) recommended the creation of a new independent external ombudsman scheme to address the market power imbalance between consumers and digital platforms.[17] The interim report highlighted that in 2021, '… Australians spent an average of 6 hours and 13 minutes online per day (almost 40% of our waking hours)'.[18] This extensive online presence underscored the need for a digital platform ombudsman to provide a complaint pathway for consumers as:[19]

> The ACCC has growing concerns about the entrenched and durable nature of some large digital platforms' market power and their gatekeeper role, and the impact this has on consumers and business users, especially given the growing reliance of businesses and consumers on a range of digital platform services.

In Interim Report No 5, the ACCC concluded that 'an industry-specific ombuds would be preferable given that an existing body may not have the capability and capacity to undertake this role'.[20] While further consideration should be given to the types of disputes the ombudsman should handle, the ACCC indicated the scheme would primarily resolve user complaints concerning the conduct of the digital platforms, such as unmet contractual expectations (eg, decisions to suspend services or terminate accounts) and/or infringement of an amended Australian Consumer Law (ACL).[21] This call for an ombudsman to resolve digital platform complaints is a recommendation in the Final Report of the ACCC inquiry into Digital Platforms (DPI).[22] The ACCC suggested the Telecommunications Industry Ombudsman (TIO) be considered, or, if that were not feasible, then a standalone ombudsman be established.

I, along with a team of researchers, have endorsed this proposal for the TIO to be a Digital Platform Ombudsman.[23] Our endorsement is based on the fundamental role of the institution in maintaining the 1970s concept of the ombudsman as an independent entity – the 'voice of the voiceless'[24] – where

[17] ACCC, *Digital Platform Services Inquiry: Interim Report No 5 – Regulatory Reform* (September 2022) 16.

[18] ibid 4.

[19] ibid 5.

[20] ibid 103.

[21] For information about the ACCC's proposal to amend the ACL, see ibid 64–71.

[22] *Digital Platforms Inquiry – Final Report* Recommendation 23, 27.

[23] For an analysis of the pros and cons of this proposal see H Raiche, D Wilding, K Lee and A Stuhmcke, *Digital Platform Complaint Handling: Options for an External Dispute Resolution Scheme* (UTS Centre for Media Transition, 2022). See also UTS Centre for Media Transition, *Submission to ACCC Discussion Paper for Interim Report No. 5: Updating competition and consumer law for digital platform services*, April 2022 and Submission to The Treasury, *Digital Platforms: Government Consultation on ACCC's Regulatory Reform Recommendations*, 22 February 2023. The round table was held at UTS on 7 December 2022.

[24] Dr B Perry, 'Twenty Five Years of Serving Parliament and the Community' *Victorian Ombudsman Twenty-fifth Report*, (1998) II, iv.

individuals can seek redress in both the private[25] and the public sectors if they suffer maladministration.[26] Endorsing the TIO as the Digital Platform Ombudsman acknowledges the institution's role in addressing the power imbalance between social media platforms and their users. This imbalance is significant, with users facing stark information asymmetry, limited avenues for complaints, and opaque business practices as digital platforms like Facebook move towards market monopolisation. Our support for the TIO's application to digital platforms is an efficient and practical outcome,[27] especially given that the TIO has advocated to '… lead the world-first Ombudsman service for digital platform complaints'.[28]

It is of interest that our endorsement assumes that the TIO, or any newly created ombudsman, will be independent and assist individual complainants. This assumption aligns with the 1970s model of the ombudsman institution, which aims to address the power imbalance between digital platforms and consumers. This premise promotes the efficacy and role of the ombudsman institution, assuming it will meet the needs of individual users of digital media platforms. The recommendation of the TIO as the ombudsman model is based on evaluating which institution is most equipped, efficient, experienced, and has relevant existing jurisdiction to oversee digital platform complaints. In short, the focus is on selecting the best model for complaint resolution from existing institutions rather than upon evidence of the institution's ability to resolve individual needs.

However, as discussed in more depth in Part IV, the ombudsman model has been found to not serve all groups of individuals equally. This is troubling given that an ombudsman should be independent, impartial and not take sides. Vulnerable groups of potential complainants are particularly under-represented. Access to an ombudsman is weighted towards the privileged and middle class, a current and pressing problem across Australian ombudsman institutions. The TIO is no exception. On 24 August 2022, the Five-Year Independent Review of the

[25] www.fos.org.au/the-circular-5-home/responsible-lending-conduct-obligations-maladministration/.

[26] Maladministration is less serious than corruption and means failing to meet reasonable standards of performance in the discharge of duties: see The ICAC Act – Key Issues for Local Government – Information Paper 11. *Understanding Maladministration* (Local Government Association of South Australia – October 2013), www.lga.sa.gov.au/webdata/resources/files/ICAC_Info_Paper_11_-Understanding_Maladministration.pdf.

[27] This acknowledges that there are other institutions which impact digital media platforms: the Office of the eSafety Commissioner ('eSafety'); the Australian Communications and Media Authority (ACMA); the Digital Industry Group Inc (DIGI); the Australian Competition and Consumer Commission (ACCC); the Office of the Australian Information Commissioner (OAIC); the Australian Small Business and Family Enterprise Ombudsman (ASBFEO); Ad Standards and the Australian Press Council (APC).

[28] *TIO makes the case to lead world-first Ombudsman service for digital platform complaints*, The Telecommunications Industry Ombudsman, 29 March 2023, www.tio.com.au/news/tio-makes-case-lead-world-first-ombudsman-service-digital-platform-complaints; Australia has also led the way with other important world-firsts, like the establishment of an e-Safety commissioner and the Online Safety Act: see M Atkin and L Florance, 29 March 2023, 'Who do you turn to when you're scammed on socials?' *ABC News*, www.abc.net.au/news/2023-03-29/tio-puts-hand-up-new-digital-platforms-social-media-ombudsman/102153394.

TIO[29] focused its accessibility review upon the TIO's approach to working with vulnerable and disadvantaged complainants. The review recommended the TIO develop and implement a 'vulnerability strategy which ensures it can identify, and meet, the needs of vulnerable and disadvantaged complainants'.[30] This strategy is critical in the creation of any new ombudsman or new ombudsman jurisdiction, such as if the TIO takes on the role of Digital Platform Ombudsman.

## B. Case Study 2: The National Student Ombudsman

In a move hailed as 'breathtaking' by student safety advocates,[31] the Federal Government announced on 23 February 2024[32] that a National Student Ombudsman would be established to investigate student complaints and resolve disputes with universities. The call was made to curb '... the sexual violence crisis facing Australia's universities'.[33] The National Student Ombudsman is a new statutory function of the Commonwealth Ombudsman[34] and is part of a national plan to address gender-based violence in higher education, including complaints about sexual harassment, assault and violence. It has been estimated that, on average, 275 students are sexually assaulted per week in Australian universities.[35]

The call for the National Student Ombudsman originates from the 2017 *Change the Course* report[36] by the Australian Human Rights Commission (AHRC). This report highlighted alarming rates of sexual assault and sexual harassment

[29] G McBurnie and J Williams, *Five-year independent review of the Telecommunications Industry Ombudsman*, (Consumer Dispute Resolution Centre, Queen Margaret University), i–ii.

[30] ibid v.

[31] "Breathtaking': education ministers approve national ombudsman to tackle sexual assault at Australian universities', *The Guardian*, www.theguardian.com/australia-news/2024/feb/23/national-ombudsman-sexual-assault-universities-australia.

[32] The Honourable Jason Clare, 'Independent National Student Ombudsman to improve student safety' Ministers' Media Centre (ministers.education.gov.au/clare/independent-national-student-ombudsman-improve-student-safety) stating that 'The functions of the Ombudsman will include:

- considering whether decisions and actions taken by providers are unreasonable, unjust, oppressive, discriminatory or otherwise wrong
- responding to a complaint while a provider is still considering the issue if there are unreasonable delays, or the provider is acting unreasonably
- recommending a provider takes specific steps to resolve the complaint
- sharing information with relevant regulators for further compliance action if needed, and
- offering a restorative engagement process between the student and the provider.'

[33] C Long 'Student ombudsman on the table as governments look to crack down on university sexual assaults' *ABC News*, 6 October 2023, www.abc.net.au/news/2023-10-06/student-ombudsman-considered-university-sexual-assault/102941044.

[34] www.ombudsman.gov.au/__data/assets/pdf_file/0024/304935/Corporate-Plan-2024-25.pdf 4. See Universities Accord (National Student Ombudsman) Act 2024.

[35] C Long, 'Australian universities falling short on key measures to tackle sexual violence, according to new report'. *ABC News* 22 February 2024.

[36] *Change The Course: National Report on Sexual Assault and Sexual Harassment at Australian Universities* (Australian Human Rights Commission, 2017), humanrights.gov.au/our-work/sex-discrimination/publications/change-course-national-report-sexual-assault-and-sexual.

among university students, with 21 per cent experiencing sexual harassment and 1.6 per cent experiencing sexual assault in 2016. The report also revealed an absence of adequate university policies and practices, as a majority of these incidents went unreported to universities. A second student survey in 2021 confirmed these results.[37] The call for a new National Student Ombudsman occurred in November 2023 through a draft proposal by the Commonwealth Department of Education.[38]

The National Student Ombudsman will be '... centred on student voices and needs'[39] and commenced in February 2025. The framing of this new university ombudsman as a response to sexual harassment and assault aligns with the historical function of the institution being to resolve individual complaints.[40] The Ombudsman has investigative and dispute resolution powers '... to ensure domestic and international higher education students have an effective, trauma-informed complaints mechanism to use when they are not satisfied by their provider's response'.[41] The Ombudsman will also have the power to recommend systemic change.[42] This is in keeping with the modern functions of the Commonwealth Ombudsman. The Ombudsman has the power to recommend that universities take specific administrative steps to resolve complaints, which could include changes to provider policies, practices and processes.

This systemic focus aligns with the international development[43] of the ombudsman institution. It is also consistent with the modern development of Australian ombudsman. For example, the most recent Annual Report of the Commonwealth Ombudsman contains a statement by the Ombudsman, Iain Davidson, that the focus of the Commonwealth Ombudsman Office is not only individual complaints:[44]

> The purpose of the Office has never been more important. That is, to provide assurance that government and private sector entities we oversee act with integrity and treat people fairly while influencing enduring systemic improvement in public administration.

[37] R Cox, 'How we got here: sexual assault on campus' *Campus Review* 14 February 2024, www.campusreview.com.au/2024/02/how-we-got-here-sexual-assault-on-campus/; Social Research Centre, National Student Safety Survey, srcentre.com.au/project/national-student-safety-survey/.

[38] Australian Government Department of Education, *Draft Proposal: Addressing gender-based violence in higher education* DRAFT Action Plan, 22 November 2023.

[39] ibid 6.

[40] There is a long history of internal university ombudsmen. In the United States, the first campus ombudsman was established in 1965. See R Smith, 'A Brief History of the Student Ombudsman: The Early Evolution of the Role in US Higher Education' [2020] *Journal of the International Ombudsman Association* 1–10.

[41] ibid.

[42] *Draft Action Plan addressing gender-based violence in higher education publication* (Department of Education, Australian Government), www.education.gov.au/australian-universities-accord/resources/draft-action-plan-addressing-genderbased-violence-higher-education.

[43] *Proceedings of the Second International Ombudsman Conference*, Jerusalem, October 1980, 21, cited in W Haller, 'The Place of the Ombudsman in the world community', Fourth International Ombudsman Conference, 23–27 Canberra 1988, Papers, Commonwealth Ombudsman, Canberra, Australia, 34.

[44] ibid 13.

This statement recognises a holistic approach to system administrative improvement. Australian ombudsman, including the Commonwealth Ombudsman, now dedicate much energy and resources to investigating and reporting recommended changes in policy.[45]

The issue raised is, what does this mean for the independence of the National Student Ombudsman and the institution more generally? Gill and others argue that emphasis by an ombudsman upon improving an entire system can be characterised as a 'managerial ombudsman'.[46] This form of ombudsman emphasises its role in supporting public managers to improve services.[47] While it is not possible to yet categorise the new National Student Ombudsman as a managerial ombudsman, the point squarely raised by Gill et al is the challenge of balancing systemic improvement with individual complaint handling, with the question being, is the ombudsman role '… primarily to settle individual complaints brought by citizens or is it instead to improve the quality of public administration at large?'[48] They note this distinction in functions has variously been labelled 'fire-fighting' and 'fire-watching', 'redress' and 'control' and 'fly swatting' and 'lion taming'.[49] Notably, the 1970s view of a public ombudsman was as a fly swatter or fire fighter and as redress and not control. The next section discusses what this may mean for the individual complainant.

## IV. The Venice Principles: New Ombudsman Need a New Template

Both case studies confirm that there is neither a framework nor a predetermined model for the creation of new Australian ombudsman offices. Across all Australian jurisdictions, there is no single ombudsman model or blueprint for

[45] A Rose, 'The Role of Administrative Review Bodies' (1999) 58(1) *Australian Journal of Public Administration* 65–75, 66.

[46] C Gill, T Mullan and N Vivian, 'The Managerial Ombudsman' (2020) 83(4) *The Modern Law Review* 797–830; see also R Kirkham and C Gill, 'Five Principles for a New Public Services Ombudsman' in R Kirkham and C Gill (eds), *A Manifesto for Ombudsman Reform* (Basingstoke, Palgrave Macmillan, 2020) 13–40 (specifically referring to the creation of a new Public Services Ombudsman). Principle 1 is that the new PSO must have a bolder role in the administrative justice system. Principle 2 is that there should be a presumption for the PSO having an integrated jurisdiction over all English public services, while respecting the UK's devolution settlement. Principle 3 is that the PSO must have a broad range of powers, reflective of those granted to PSOs in other jurisdictions. Principle 4 is that the new PSO must report on how it engages with citizens and on the delivery of administrative justice. Finally, Principle 5 is that the PSO must be subject to multiple accountability routes to ensure that a bolder role and new powers are used appropriately. These principles address the principal controversies which face legislators in creating a new PSO and are designed to provide a guide to legislative reform.

[47] ibid 198.

[48] ibid 15.

[49] ibid.

their creation, establishment, or composition of powers. Each public law ombudsman, as well as many industry ombudsmen, operates under separate legislative frameworks, resulting in varied and nuanced operations. However, basic principles such as independence, jurisdiction, powers, accessibility, procedural fairness and accountability are universally accepted. These principles, often conceptualised as 'soft law', originate from self-appointed regulatory bodies[50] and operational norms.[51]

While nuanced operational models and the application of soft law are not inherently problematic, both case studies reveal an inherent weakness in this approach. The absence of a prescriptive model and hard law results in a lack of rigour and form in creating new institutions. Both the Digital Platform Ombudsman and the National Student Ombudsman illustrate that the reactive creation of Australian ombudsman offices means that the ombudsman 'solution' is retrofitted to fit the problem. This retrofitting often leads to the integration of new ombudsman offices into an existing ombudsman institution. For example, the Digital Platforms Ombudsman is likely to become part of the TIO, and the National Student Ombudsman is integrated within the Commonwealth Ombudsman as a new statutory function.

The outcome of retrofitting is that the new offices are not proactive and are not tailored to the desired outcomes. Consequently, each new office will absorb the problems of the existing ombudsman offices they are folded into. In other words, the Digital Platform Ombudsman will inherit the (good and bad) issues of the TIO, and the National Student Ombudsman will similarly inherit the successes and problems of the Commonwealth Ombudsman.

From inception, both the Digital Platform Ombudsman and the National Student Ombudsman will face challenges in providing access to their services by individual complainants. This may seem surprising, given that the individual complainant was identified in Part 1 as the central reason for the creation of the Commonwealth Ombudsman institution in the 1970s. The institution was created to redress the power imbalance between the governed and the governors. Unfortunately, history has shown that complainants to ombudsman institutions, including the Commonwealth Ombudsman and the Telecommunications Industry Ombudsman, are far from diverse and often exclude vulnerable populations.

[50] In this case this list is from the Australian and New Zealand Ombudsman Association (ANZOA) which has published 'Essential Criteria for Describing a Body as an Ombudsman see www.ombudsman.gov.au/__data/assets/pdf_file/0015/31434/ANZOA-Essential_criteria_for_describing_a_body_as_an_Ombudsman.pdf and the Australian Government's guidance relating solely to private sector Alternative Dispute Resolution *Benchmarks and Key Practices for Industry Based Customer Alternative Dispute Resolution (the Benchmarks and Key Practices)*, treasury.gov.au/sites/default/files/2019-03/key_pract_ind_cust_dispute_resol.pdf.

[51] R Kirkham and A Stuhmcke, 'The Common Law Theory and Practice of the Ombudsman/Judiciary Relationship' (2020) 49 *Common Law World Review* 56–74.

## A. The Individual Complainant – White and Male and Middle Class …

The exclusion of marginalised complainants from ombudsman services is well documented internationally. While there is little empirical research available on ombudsman in Australia, international research identifies the demographic that most frequently complains to an ombudsman institution as '… narrow and middle class'.[52] The general profile of the user of ombudsman services is a man or a woman in middle age with a higher education, a reasonable income and enough bureaucratic competencies.[53]

A 2018 international study by Beqiraj et al found that ombudsman institutions primarily service the white middle class,[54] with not all social groups accessing the institution in the same proportion. More powerful members of society are able to take better advantage of the ombudsman institution, which is designed to support all members of society regardless of race, class, gender or age. This study reflects earlier work such as that by Roosbrocek and Waller who noted that '[i]f wealthier and/or more educated people are the main consumers of the ombudsman's services, then the institution would have failed to achieve its objective to serve people at all socioeconomic levels'.[55]

Roosbrocek and Waller's study found that complaints made to government and industry ombudsman are rarely from socially disadvantaged individuals. These complaints do not come from lower-class, young, or minority groups,[56] as the socially disadvantaged are '… less likely to use the institution.'[57] This research conclusion was drawn from studies conducted in a number of countries, including the Netherlands, the United Kingdom and Belgium. It was noted that non-middle-aged and middle-class individuals with higher education may file complaints with the ombudsman, but they are under-represented.[58] This phenomenon has been labelled as an example of the 'Matthew Effect.'[59]

[52] N Creutzfeldt, 'Managing Complaints: Focusing on Users and Non-users of the System' in R Kirkham and C Gill (eds), *A Manifesto for Ombudsman Reform* (Basingstoke, Palgrave Macmillan, 2020) 112. See also M Hertogh, 'Why the Ombudsman does not Promote Public Trust in Government: Lessons from the Low Countries' (2013) 35(2) *Journal of Social Welfare & Family Law* 245–258.

[53] T Buck, R Kirkham and B Thompson, *The Ombudsman Enterprise and Administrative Justice* (Farnham, Ashgate, 2011).

[54] J Beqiraj, S Garahan and K Shuttleworth, *Ombudsman schemes and effective access to justice: A study of international practices and trends*, International Bar Association, October 2018.

[55] S Van Roosbrocek and S Van de Walle, 'The Relationship between Ombudsman, Government and Citizens: A Survey Analysis' [2000] *Negotiation Journal* 287, 292.

[56] ibid (this finding was based upon a survey of 626 complainants in Belgium).

[57] ibid 287.

[58] ibid 293. This study found that men complained to ombudsmen twice as much as woman, that young and old people were 'severely underrepresented' and a 'near-majority of complainants had a bachelor's or master's degree with blue collar workers also being underrepresented.'

[59] This refers to situations where those who possess certain qualities or possessions will receive more, while the less gifted individuals will receive less. See RK Merton, 'The Matthew Effect in Science' (1968) 159 *Science* 56–63.

In Australia, while not empirically proven, these observations hold true. This is relevant for both the Commonwealth Ombudsman and the TIO – the offices where the National Student Ombudsman and the Digital Platform Ombudsman will be located. For example, the 2010 *Winangali Report*[60] found barriers to making a complaint to the Commonwealth Ombudsman by Indigenous Australians. These barriers included favouritism, inter-family rivalries, fear of reprisals, and the belief that this is their lot in life. Other examples of inequality exist across private industry ombudsman in Australia. For instance, access to the TIO has been proven to be extremely limited, with one survey indicating that only 2 per cent of telecommunications problems were finalised via an 'ombudsman or complaint handling body'.[61]

Australian ombudsman are aware of this issue and aim to improve access by identifying vulnerable populations. The TIO defines vulnerable and at-risk issues for residential consumers as:[62]

- having a serious medical condition, or a registered priority assistance service,
- not having an ongoing mobile or internet issue poses a specific safety risk, or
- needing urgent financial hardship support from their provider.

Identifying and servicing vulnerable populations is a growing theme amongst Australian ombudsmen. The 2022–2023 NSW Ombudsman Annual Report details vulnerable complainants as including:[63]

- Aboriginal people and communities.
- people from culturally and linguistically diverse communities (including newly arrived migrants and refugees).
- people in (or recently released from) custody.
- children and young people.
- people with disability.

In both the international[64] and the Australian context, ombudsman have addressed inequity of access reactively by developing outreach activities and enquiries seeking participation and input from vulnerable communities. For example, the TIO focuses resources upon outreach events, particularly with remote Indigenous

[60] Winangali, *Improving the services of the Commonwealth Ombudsman to Australia's Indigenous Peoples*, November 2010, 29 July 2015, www.ombudsman.gov.au/publications-and-news-pages/publication-pages/speeches/commonwealth-ombudsman/29-july-2015-the-commonwealth-ombudsmans-indigenous-complaint-handling-forum.

[61] Productivity Commission, above n 11; see also Telecommunications Industry Independent Review Report, August 2017 http://www.tio.com.au/__data/assets/pdf_file/0005/253643/2017_0929-TIO-Report-Final.pdf 20.

[62] 'Prioritising complaints from vulnerable and at-risk residential consumers and small businesses', *The Telecommunications Industry Ombudsman*, www.tio.com.au/news/prioritising-complaints-vulnerable-and-risk-residential-consumers-and-small-businesses.

[63] NSW Ombudsman *Annual Report (2022-2023)* 12.

[64] J Beqiraj, S Garahan and K Shuttleworth, *Ombudsman schemes and effective access to justice: A study of international practices and trends*, International Bar Association, October 2018, 5.

communities, to encourage contact and awareness raising.[65] Another example is the Commonwealth Ombudsman commissioning reports on vulnerable communities.[66]

It is inevitable that the insertion of the new ombudsman – the Digital Platforms Ombudsman and the National Student Ombudsman – into existing ombudsman offices will introduce these inequities of access to the newly created ombudsman. It may even be argued that such inequities are structural and that the institution is itself flawed. This phenomenon has been attributed to the nature of the ombudsman institutions themselves. Indeed, the inequity in accessing ombudsman offices is less surprising once the operational aspects of the ombudsman are analysed into their component parts. For example, referring to the United Kingdom, Creutzfeldt observes that every individual that approaches an ombudsman would already have gone through an internal complaints process and have found that to be unsatisfactory.[67] In this sense, the office as a place of last resort militates against its usefulness, as it discourages complainants, especially those who are vulnerable. They are not only less likely to access the institution in the first place, but when they do, they are often unable to navigate the system. Further, Creutzfeldt has observed that user expectations 'to be listened to, to be taken seriously, to speak with someone who has authority to deal with their case appear to run contrary to the budgetary restraints on ombudsman for frontline staff and the need for speed of decision-making'.[68] Indeed in the UK studies have shown that ombudsman offices were increasingly devoting more attention to speedy case disposal.[69]

## B. The Venice Principles should be Adopted in Australia as a Template for New Ombudsman Offices

The reactive, on-demand[70] creation of the two new federal ombudsman is normal for new Australian ombudsman. This pattern, evident in the two case studies, involves first identifying a particular social problem, such as the power of digital

[65] In 2012–2013 the TIO was involved in 72 outreach events see Productivity Commission, *Access to Justice*, 2014, Volume 1, www.pc.gov.au/inquiries/completed/access-justice/report/access-justice-volume1.pdf, p 108 citing the *LAW Survey 2012*, 175.

[66] Winangali, *Improving the services of the Commonwealth Ombudsman to Australia's Indigenous Peoples*, November 2010, www.ombudsman.gov.au/data/assets/pdf_file/0019/34048/improving_the_services_of_the_commonwealth_ombudsman_to_australias_indigenous_peoples.pdf.

[67] N Creutzfeldt, 'Managing Complaints: Focusing on Users and Non-users of the System' in R Kirkham and C Gill (eds), *A Manifesto for Ombudsman Reform* (Basingstoke, Palgrave Macmillan, 2020) 109–126, 113.

[68] ibid 113–114.

[69] C Gill, J Williams, C Brennan and N O'Brien, *The future of Ombudsman Schemes: Drivers for Change and Strategic Responses* (Birmingham: Legal Ombudsman, 2013).

[70] This is also the experience in the United Kingdom see: R Kirkham and A Stuhmcke, 'The Common Law Theory and Practice of the Ombudsman/Judiciary Relationship' (2020) 49(1) *Common Law World Review* 56. See further V Bondy and A Le Sueur, 'Designing Redress: A Study About Grievances Against Public Bodies' (Public Law Project, 2012) accessed 25 October 2019.

platforms and the prevalence of sexual assault at universities; second, proposing an ombudsman scheme or model as the solution to that problem; and third, engaging in stakeholder consultation before drafting legislation to create the ombudsman. At the time of writing, it is the final step – stakeholder engagement – which is being undertaken with respect to the Digital Platform Ombudsman while all steps have been completed with the National Student Ombudsman.

I suggest that this process of ombudsman creation is flawed. The fundamental issue is that the new ombudsman are based on the assumption that the 1970s Commonwealth Ombudsman model still works. In the case of the Digital Platform Ombudsman, the flawed assumption is that the individual complainant will be assisted by the institution to resolve disputes. However, there is no evidence to date that the TIO is equipped to handle complaints from vulnerable digital platform users.

For the National Student Ombudsman, the model embeds the new ombudsman within the existing Commonwealth Ombudsman office without addressing how this will balance with the historical function of handling individual complaints. Additionally, there is no proactive planning on how policy or systemic change will impact the area of sexual assault in universities, which intersects with criminal and tort law rather than focusing solely on administrative law and maladministration, typically the province of the ombudsman institution.

Untested in Australia is whether the ability of individuals to complain may be enhanced if the creation of new ombudsman offices were based on a proactive set of principles. An interesting innovation in this regard has been adopted in Europe with the 2019 Venice Principles.[71] These principles cover all the conditions necessary to ensure properly functioning, independent mediation institutions, from the election or dismissal of an ombudsman to the financial and material safeguards for their activities. The principles apply to both private and public ombudsmen and also protect existing ombudsman offices while providing guidelines for their improvement.[72] Similar to the existing normative framework

[71] *Principles on the Protection and Promotion of the Ombudsman Institution* (the "Venice Principles") Opinion No. 897/ 2017 Venice Commission 118th Plenary session, Venice 15–16 March 2019 see Mini Conference 2018 (www.venice.coe.int/files/Publications/Venice_Principles_eng.pdf). The Venice Principles are issued by the Council of Europe which is an international organisation, based in Strasbourg. It was created to promote democracy, human rights, and the rule of law in 1949 and now includes 46 European countries. Australia is neither a member nor observer of the Council of Europe and therefore not bound by the principles in any way. The Venice Principles, in Principle 13, apply to ombuds with a mandate over 'public administration at all levels and so there would be a question to them applying to a university ombudsman even if the sexual assault university ombudsman is located in the Commonwealth Ombudsman office'.

[72] Principle 25 states: 'These principles shall be read, interpreted and used in order to consolidate and strengthen the Institution of the Ombudsman. Taking into consideration the various types, systems and legal status of Ombudsman Institutions and their staff members, states are encouraged to undertake all necessary actions including constitutional and legislative adjustments so as to provide proper conditions that strengthen and develop the Ombudsman Institutions and their capacity, independence and impartiality in the spirit and in line with the Venice Principles and thus ensure their proper, timely and effective implementation.'

in Australia, the 25 principles are not binding and have been referred to as 'soft law' in Europe.[73]

My suggestion is that the Venice Principles be incorporated into the creation of a new ombudsman to effectively address the issue of complainant access. Specifically the 15th Principle states that: 'Any individual or legal person, including NGOs, shall have the right to free, unhindered and free of charge access to the Ombudsman, and to file a complaint.' Adopting the 15th Principle in the creation of an office would mean that any new Australian ombudsman must demonstrate that it will meet individual needs. This ensures that the creation of a new ombudsman is evaluated based on the institution's ability to serve marginalised or vulnerable complainants. It may also assist ombudsman institutions to demand and receive appropriate levels of funding from government or industry to manage their complaint load.

For instance, the 15th Principle could be applied to the new Digital Platform Ombudsman to proactively assess the institution's ability (or need) to meet the needs of specific categories of marginalised and vulnerable complainants. This is significant given that discussion of vulnerable complainants will raise larger issues of human rights. Indeed the Venice Principles specifically mention the role that an ombudsman plays with respect to human rights in Principle 1.[74]

This relationship between human rights and administrative justice with respect to the operation of the ombudsman institution has been noted in the Australian context. For example, Groves has observed that prisoners, a category of vulnerable complainants, exist within an administrative justice as well as a human rights framework:[75]

> … the role of Ombudsmen in prisons has long been more than its individual parts because their ability to examine both individual complaints and more systemic problems has proven an especially valuable mechanisms to promote useful, practical reform within prisons. For a long time this work was generally considered an instance of administrative justice but the role if Ombudsmen within prisons is generally now conceived within a human rights framework.[76]

In the context of a Digital Platform Ombudsman, Groves's point is one as to whether a human rights framework will apply to its operation.

[73] W Hoffman-Rien, 'The Venice Commission of the Council of Europe – Standards and Impact' (2014) 2 *European Journal of International Law* 597.

[74] Principle 1 – 'Ombudsman Institutions have an important role to play in strengthening democracy, the rule of law, good administration *and the protection and promotion of human rights and fundamental freedoms*. While there is no standardised model across Council of Europe Member States, the State shall support and protect the Ombudsman Institution and refrain from any action undermining its independence.' (Emphasis added).

[75] Groves' point, written 20 years ago, was prophetic as Australia today is being asked (and failing) to deliver on treaty promises made under the Optional Protocol to the Convention against Torture and Other Cruel, Inhuman or Degrading Treatment or Punishment (OPCAT) see L Finlay, 'Australia needs to deliver on our treaty promises' *Australian Human Rights Commission*, humanrights.gov.au/about/news/opinions/australia-needs-deliver-our-treaty-promises, 20 January 2023.

[76] M Groves, 'Ombudsmen's Jurisdiction in Prisons' (2002) 28(2) *Monash University Law Review* 181; M Groves, 'Ombudsmen and Prisons' *Research Handbook on the Ombudsman* 319.

The current call for the new Digital Platform Ombudsman has not identified vulnerable populations such as prisoners in its design. Of course, the issue of prisoner access to communications is vexed. It is also made more complex, as the issue of prisoner use of digital platforms is divergent across many jurisdictions.[77] Prisoners are one of the most vulnerable groups,[78] and state responses to prisoner use of digital platforms and their ability to complain have proven to be extreme. At one extreme, inmates in South Carolina received years in solitary confinement for posting on Facebook while in prison.[79] At the other extreme, an inmate in Australia claims to have had an email address operated on his behalf by intermediaries for over 20 years prior to March 2019 and for over ten years prior to March 2019 had a website in his name on which material was published (again presumably by others, possibly at his request) about him.[80] The added complexity is that prisoners are also within the jurisdiction of state or territory public law ombudsmen and subject to guidelines such as the set of guiding principles for correctional services, known as the Standard Guidelines for Corrections in Australia.[81] In sum, prisoners and digital media show us the pointy end of what 'rights' and vulnerable populations may entail for the setting up of a new Digital Platform Ombudsman.

In sum, the Venice Principles will not solve such complex issues for a vulnerable population such as prisoners, and perhaps that should not be their function. After all, prisoners do not have the same rights as other users of digital platforms. However, the advantage of the Venice Principles is that their application at least

[77] 'Tweeting jailbirds: social media use by prisoners triples', Prisons and probation,| *The Guardian*, www.theguardian.com/society/2018/jul/09/tweeting-jailbirds-social-media-use-by-prisoners-triples.

[78] For instance, in New South Wales, it is increasingly recognised that prisoners require digital literacy upon release. This has been the case in NSW since 2021. See R Lulham, K Bradley and K Wan, *Research and Evaluation Strategy for the Transformation of Prisoner Rehabilitation through Digital Technology*, NSW Government, 2021. In 2022 it was announced that 28 NSW correctional centres would receive custom-configured secure tablets to support their rehabilitation and transition back into the community. See R Chirgwin, 'NSW backs prison tablet project with $40 million' (29 August 2022) *IT News*. This is not only the case in NSW – as in the Australian Capital Territory, prisoners at the Alexander Maconochie Centre have controlled access to internet websites that contain legal resources and educational materials. In Tasmania, a secure network has been developed to assist prisoners in studying by distance education. The University of Southern Queensland is trialling the introduction of portable learning devices in prisons.

[79] 'Now More Than Ever, Prisoners Should Have Some Access to Social Media', Electronic Frontier Foundation (www.eff.org/deeplinks/2020/03/now-more-ever-inmates-should-have-some-access-social-media). Facebook has also stated that it will suspend an inmate's account if staff determined that a profile had been accessed by someone other than the inmate. Facebook said these measures protected the security of the user's account. Facebook also said it treated inmate profiles involved in criminal activity or harassment in the same way it handles accounts belonging to users in the free world. 'Facebook Overhauls Its Inmate Account Takedown Process', Electronic Frontier Foundation (www.eff.org/deeplinks/2015/06/facebook-reforms-inmate-account-takedown-process) 4 June 2015.

[80] *Minogue v Secretary to the Department OF Justice and Community Safety* [2020] VSC 355, [9]. In 2022 it was reported that inmates were using a private Facebook group to find a companion while they served their time – with posts being made by friends and family see 'Facebook: Lonely prisoners look for love', *news.com.au* – Australia's leading news site, www.news.com.au/lifestyle/relationships/dating/lonely-prisoners-look-for-love-on-facebook/news-story/3b259443129a0a21321368e788fb0cde.

[81] D Glass, 'Investigation into the Rehabilitation and Reintegration of Prisoners in Victoria' [2025] *Victorian Ombudsman Report*, [391] Department of Justice, Victoria et al, *Standard Guidelines for Corrections in Australia*, revised 2012.

allows the intersection of vulnerability and ombudsman to be discussed and addressed. This in turn elevates issues of access to ombudsman and human rights and will go some way towards rebalancing the focus of new institutions towards the individual complainant and preventing the tilt towards a focus on government.

## V. Conclusion

In this chapter, I suggest that for the ombudsman institution to remain fit for purpose, a new conceptual foundation for creating ombudsman institutions must be applied.[82] My interpretation of 'fit for purpose' is that Australian ombudsman should prioritise vulnerable and marginalised individuals in society. While recognising that all individuals should be protected by the state, I argue that ombudsman are uniquely positioned and should be proactively supported to promote ethical conduct in addressing the disadvantages faced by these citizens and consumers.

However, this presents a challenge for Australian ombudsman. Reflecting on the discussion of the 1970s Commonwealth Ombudsman in Part II and fast-forwarding to 2024, the most recent Annual Report of the Commonwealth Ombudsman[83] states that the activities of the office are 'Complaint Handling, Investigations, Education, Inspections, Engagement'. Despite this significant expansion of the office's original functions, the 'new' range of activities has not diminished its primary role of complaint handling. In the latest Annual Report, the current Commonwealth Ombudsman, Iain Anderson states:[84]

> Our performance around complaint handling decreased during the year, taking longer to assess and respond to complaints. Complaint management is at the core of what we do and people who raise concerns with us expect clear and simple interactions.

This statement underscores that the original purpose of the office as a 'watchdog' or 'protector'[85] for the ordinary citizen remains core to the mission of the Commonwealth Ombudsman while also acknowledging the need for improvement. Anderson's statement suggests that the office is crucial to the notion that citizens should be able to complain against those that govern them and have their complaints heard and investigated by an independent entity. However, it also highlights that the Commonwealth Ombudsman complaint performance has declined.

Moreover, the quote from the 2024 Annual Report emphasises that complaint management is 'core' to the office's functions. Yet, as discussed in Part IV, the complaints managed are not from the vulnerable and disadvantaged. The two

[82] This leverages off some earlier work I have done on this topic such as 'Australian Ombudsmen and Human Rights' *AIAL Forum* No. 66, 43.

[83] Commonwealth Ombudsman *Annual Report 2022–2023*, 12.

[84] ibid 14.

[85] A Maloney, 'The Ombudsman Idea' (1979) 13 *University of British Columbia Law Review* 380–400, 380.

case studies of the Digital Platform Ombudsman and the National Student Ombudsman illustrate that addressing the needs of individual complainants is the primary reason for the introduction of the new ombudsman.[86] However, there is no prescriptive requirement in Australia that any new ombudsman must take complaints from marginalised groups. The human rights dimension of the operation of an ombudsman is largely absent. There is no soft law principle in Australia that incorporates human rights norms into the complaint-taking function. In this sense, Australia is increasingly out of step with the Venice Principles and jurisdictions which focus the ombudsman institution around vulnerability, such as the Norwegian Ombudsman for Children or the Norwegian Consumer Ombudsman.[87]

The ombudsman institution must be adjusted to align with contemporary principles.[88] The institution's independence cannot be assured if the focus of the ombudsman is diverted away from the citizen/complainant and diluted within the office. This chapter suggests that it is time to review the creation of an ombudsman. The two case studies of the Digital Platforms Ombudsman and the National Student Ombudsman demonstrate that new ombudsmen will always be necessary as long as power inequalities exist. Furthermore, the creation of new institutions is best guided by a set of principles, such as the Venice Principles[89] to prevent and correct recurring systemic flaws.

[86] The last year in Australia has seen calls for ombudsmen to protect individuals across disparate industries. For example, there have been calls for a new ombudsman to resolve the growing number of disputes involving used cars: see *The Sydney Morning Herald* 4 June 2023, 'Used car complaints prompt calls for new ombudsman' (www.smh.com.au/national/used-car-complaints-prompt-calls-for-new-ombudsman-20230604-p5ddui.html).

[87] Some Australian ombudsmen do have such jurisdiction or have institutional practice around vulnerability. With respect to the former see for Summary Offences Act 1998 (NSW) s 9 discussed in Ombudsman Report on NSW Police use of Section 9 Highlights Effects on the Vulnerable, rlc.org.au/article/ombudsman-report-nsw-police-use-section-9-highlights-effects-vulnerable-0; with respect to the latter see Energy & Water Ombudsman NSW, 'Addressing consumer vulnerability' J Young, 24 September 2015 www.ausgrid.com.au/-/media/Files/Industry/Regulation/Planning-for-the-future/Tariffs/Vulnerable-customers-roundtable-Sep-26-2015--EWON-presentation.pdf.

[88] For analysis of the increased usage of the ombudsman model see A Stuhmcke 'The Role of the Telecommunications Industry Ombudsman' (1998) 21 *University of New South Wales Law Journal* 807–834.

[89] Individual State and Federal and Territory ombudsman members of the International Ombudsman Institute (IOI) may claim some operational guidelines by way of the Venice Principle as the General Assembly of the IOI at the World Conference in 2019: 'Venice Commission adopts "Principles on the Protection and Promotion of the Ombudsman Institution"', *IOI News* (www.theioi.org/ioi-news/current-news/venice-commission-adopts-principles-on-the-protection-and-promotion-of-the-ombudsman-institution).

# 3

# The Demise of the Administrative Appeals Tribunal: What Lessons can We Learn for the Future?

CHANTAL BOSTOCK

## I. Introduction

When created in 1975, the establishment of the Administrative Appeals Tribunal (the AAT) was novel and exciting. Its creators gave significant thought to how the administrative law system would work as a whole and what contribution the AAT would make within that system. Despite auspicious beginnings, the AAT has been marred by controversy, particularly evident in the Migration and Refugee Division (MRD), from which I draw many examples.

Following an inquiry in 2022, the Senate Legal and Constitutional Affairs References Committee recommended the abolition of the AAT and the creation of a new federal administrative review tribunal. Relatively soon after, on 16 December 2022, the Attorney-General Mark Dreyfus acted on the Senate's recommendations.[1] What followed was the convening of an expert working group, consultation, and draft legislation following various Committee inquiries.[2] The Administrative Review Tribunal Act 2024 (Cth) (ART Act) received assent on 3 June 2024, and the new Administrative Review Tribunal (ART) came into being on 14 October 2024.[3]

This chapter begins by exploring the role and function of the AAT. It will become evident that in formulating a model of administrative review, the creators of the AAT were concerned with striking the right balance between justice for the individual and administrative efficiency. I then explore the interrelated

[1] J Evans, "Politicised' Administrative Appeals Tribunal Abolished, After Attorney-General Declares Its Reputation Ruined' ABC (online, 16 December 2022), www.abc.net.au/news/2022-12-16/administrative-appeals-tribunal-abolished-by-attorney-general/101781300.

[2] Attorney-General's Department, 'A New System of Federal Administrative Review' (Web Page) www.ag.gov.au/legal-system/new-system-federal-administrative-review.

[3] ibid.

factors leading to the AAT's abolition, including the politicisation of the appointment process and its problematic impact on AAT independence, competence and culture. Next, I explore the related impact on applicants, focusing on vulnerable applicants, particularly within the MRD of the AAT, including the substantial delays in finalising cases on hand. In light of these circumstances, I examine what lessons have been learnt in designing the new tribunal, focusing on key aspects of the new ART. While significant deficiencies under the previous model have been addressed, there remain matters of concern which have not been addressed under the new system. These concerns relate to the revised appointment process, the continued use of strict procedural rules, such as non-negotiable time limits; access to legal representation; and the ART's capacity to undertake proactive decision-making, where appropriate, particularly in the migration and refugee (protection) review context. Without addressing these ongoing issues, the system will not be able to pay sufficient regard to fundamental values, namely accuracy, fairness, cost and timeliness,[4] thereby skewing towards administrative efficiency in the ART, at the expense of justice for the individual.

## II. The Role and Function of the AAT

It is instructive to briefly explore the origins of the AAT. In 1971, the Commonwealth Administrative Review Committee,[5] headed by Justice Kerr (the Kerr Committee), published its report.[6] The findings of the Kerr Committee are important not only because they laid the foundation of our current administrative review system but also because the matters that exercised the minds of the distinguished Committee remain relevant decades later.

The Committee found that it was 'neither correct nor practicable to examine in isolation judicial review in the traditional sense'.[7] In order to assess 'the adequacy of any system of judicial review', a review of the system as a whole was required.[8] Concerned with the expansion of government activities and the increase in powers conferred on decision-makers and the complexity and inadequacy of existing remedies, the Kerr Committee formed the view that citizens[9] should have 'more adequate opportunities' to challenge decision-making.[10] In developing its

[4] R Thomas, *Administrative Justice and Asylum Appeals: A Study of Tribunal Adjudication* (London, Bloomsbury Publishing, 2011) 14.

[5] The Committee consisted of Justice Kerr, Justice Mason, Mr Ellicott, the Commonwealth Solicitor-General and Professor Whitmore, ANU.

[6] Commonwealth Administrative Review Committee, Parliament of Australia, *Commonwealth Administrative Review Committee Report* (1971).

[7] ibid 2.

[8] ibid.

[9] The term 'citizen' was used in the report but in practice, non-citizens, such as visa applicants or those whose visas have been cancelled, may challenge decision-making.

[10] ibid 3, 5, 7–8, 20.

recommendations for reform, the Kerr Committee was mindful of the need to achieve justice for the individual while preserving administrative efficiency.[11] In their view, increased avenues of challenge were not incompatible with administrative efficiency 'provided that the system and procedures selected [were] adapted to the achievement of justice in such a way that administrative efficiency [was] maintained and, further that the system and procedures [were] administered by persons of appropriate capacity and experience'.[12] As will become evident, these matters have been of concern.

The Kerr Committee therefore proposed a sophisticated system of interweaving and complementary mechanisms to challenge decision-making,[13] which included the establishment of the AAT. As the High Court observed, 'the enactment of the AAT Act established a new and substantially unprecedented regime of administrative merits review, distinguished principally by the AAT's jurisdiction to re-exercise the functions of original decision makers'.[14] In contrast to judicial review, the AAT is concerned with the merits of the decision,[15] in other words, 'a consideration of the facts and circumstances relevant to the decision'.[16] The AAT must determine 'whether the decision was the correct or preferable one on the material before [it]'.[17] 'Correct' may be taken to mean the decision 'rightly made',[18] while '"[p]referable" is apt to refer to a decision which involves discretionary considerations'.[19] Bowen CJ and Deane J in *Drake v Minister for Immigration and Ethnic Affairs* observed that its function is 'to determine what decision should be made in the exercise of an administrative discretion in a given case, or where a decision has been lawfully made in pursuance of a permissible policy, to adjudicate upon the merits of the decision or the propriety of the policy'.[20] While not necessarily bound by government policy, the AAT may treat it as 'a relevant factor' in determining the review application.[21] In doing so, however, it cannot 'abdicate its function of determining whether the decision made was, on the material before the AAT, the correct or preferable one'.[22] In deciding the effect of the policy, the AAT must balance 'on the one hand, the desirability of

[11] ibid 3.
[12] ibid.
[13] ibid. See ch 12 (Procedures and Grounds for Review by the Administrative Court), ch 14 (An Administrative Review Tribunal), ch 15 (A General Counsel for Grievances) and ch 17 (An Administrative Procedure Act).
[14] *Frugtniet v ASIC* (2019) 256 CLR 250, 256–257 (Kiefel CJ, Keane and Nettle JJ).
[15] *Shi v MARA* (2008) 235 CLR 286, 297 (Kirby J). As Kirby J noted, judicial review is concerned with 'the legal merits', and 'then often only with any errors of a jurisdictional kind shown to exist at the time of the initial decision': 297.
[16] ibid 327 (Kiefel J).
[17] *Drake v Minister for Immigration and Ethnic Affairs* (1979) 46 FLR 409, 419 (Bowen CJ and Dean J).
[18] *Shi v MARA* (n 15) 327 (Kiefel J).
[19] ibid.
[20] *Drake v Minister for Immigration and Ethnic Affairs* (n 17) 419.
[21] ibid 419 (Bowen CJ and Dean J).
[22] ibid 420 (Bowen CJ and Dean J).

consistency in the treatment of citizens under the law, and on the other hand, the ideal of justice in the individual case'.[23]

Importantly, unless so limited by the statute, the AAT is not limited to a consideration of the facts as at the time of the application and may consider the facts as at the time of its decision.[24] As Cane observes, in contrast to judicial review, merits review 'allows much greater scrutiny of fact-finding and typically involves the making of a substitute decision'.[25] In this context, the AAT's approach to fact-finding assumes particular significance where vulnerable applicants are involved because of the acute power imbalance between the applicant and the state.[26] In the migration and protection context, the focus of this chapter, a vulnerable person may be defined as 'a person whose ability to understand and effectively present their case or fully participate in the review process may be impaired or not developed'.[27] For reasons which will become clear, it has been difficult for vulnerable applicants to participate in the review process.

## III. The Circumstances Leading to the AAT's Abolition

In this section, I explore the circumstances which resulted in the abolition of the AAT beginning with the appointment process.

### A. The Appointment and Re-appointment Process

The appointment and re-appointment process has long been the subject of criticism.[28] The Administrative Appeals Tribunal Act 1975 (Cth) (AAT Act) set out the qualifications for appointment to the AAT.[29] The President, Deputy Presidents, senior members and members were appointed by the Governor-General.[30] The President was required to be a judge of the Federal Court, while Deputy Presidents were either required to be judges of the Federal Court or the Federal Circuit and Family Court, enrolled as a legal practitioner for at least five years or, in the opinion of the Governor General, have special knowledge or skills relevant to the duties

[23] ibid 421 (Bowen CJ and Dean J).
[24] ibid 328 (Kiefel J): 'Where the decision to be made contains no temporal element, evidence of matters occurring after the original decision may be taken into account by the Tribunal in the process of informing itself'.
[25] P Cane, *Administrative Tribunals and Adjudication* (Oxford, Hart Publishing Ltd, 2009) 228.
[26] See M Groves, 'Equality of Arms in Administrative Review' (2023) 46 *MULR* 726.
[27] See AAT, *Guidelines on Vulnerable Persons* (November 2018).
[28] See, eg, ARC, *Better Decisions: Review of Commonwealth Merits Review Tribunals* Report No 39 (Australian Government Publishing Service, 1995) ch 4 'Tribunal Membership'.
[29] AAT Act, s 7.
[30] ibid s 6(1).

of a Deputy President.[31] Similarly, senior and other members were also required to be either enrolled as a legal practitioner for at least five years or have special knowledge or skills relevant to the duties of a senior member or member.[32] The AAT Act further provided that members were appointed for, at most, seven years but could be re-appointed.[33] In order 'to strengthen these weak legal rules', informal appointment processes were utilised.[34] In recent times, for example, following a call for expressions of interest and the establishment of a register, the President of the AAT established a process by which the suitability of applicants would be assessed and appointment recommendations made to the Attorney-General,[35] who was 'not limited to candidates recommended by the President of the AAT' and could 'choose to recommend to Cabinet a candidate for a position that ha[d] not been suggested by the President of the AAT or [was] not on the register'.[36] The Attorney-General would consult with ministerial colleagues in relation to appointments to particular divisions and would make recommendations to Cabinet, which, if approved, would be recommended to the Governor-General.[37] Members seeking reappointment were subject to a reappraisal process by an external reviewer, and if any issues arose, they were invited to an interview before an independent panel.[38] Despite the adoption of such informal appointment processes, 'Ministers routinely retain[ed] the power to appoint candidates who ha[d] neither replied to an advertisement nor ha[d] been recommended by a committee'.[39]

As a consequence, many political appointments were appointed in circumstances which bypassed this informal appointment process.[40] As of April 2022, of the 320 members of the AAT, '70, or 22 per cent, ha[d] a direct political affiliation'.[41] This finding was in keeping with the Australia Institute's research, which similarly found increasing levels of political appointments, which reached '32% of all new appointments', using a broader definition of political appointment.[42] Because of the 'cronyism' within the appointment process,[43] the AAT was described as 'one of

[31] ibid s 7(1), 7(2)(a), (b) or (c).
[32] ibid s 7(3).
[33] ibid s 8.
[34] D Wilkinson and E Morison, *Cronyism in Appointments to the AAT* (The Australia Institute, May 2022) 12.
[35] The Senate Legal and Constitutional Affairs References Committee, *The Performance and Integrity of Australia's Administrative Review System* (Interim Report, March 2022) [4.17]. The interim report outlined the Committee's views and recommendations, which became final.
[36] ibid.
[37] ibid.
[38] ibid [4.26]–[4.27].
[39] Wilkinson and Morison (n 34) 12.
[40] ibid.
[41] D Wood, K Griffiths and A Stobart, *New Politics: A Better Process for Public Appointments* (Grattan Institute, July 2022) 18.
[42] Wilkinson and Morison (n 34) 1.
[43] ibid 6: 'In the Howard and Rudd/Gillard/Rudd administrations, political appointees accounted for 6 and 5 per cent of all appointees respectively. By contrast, during the Abbott/Turnbull/Morrison administration, political appointees accounted for 32 per cent of all new appointments. Within the Abbott/Turnbull/Morrison administration, political appointments were highest during the second

the most notoriously politicised bodies'.[44] While the politicisation of the appointment process has long been documented, its increasing prevalence in more recent times resulted in the Tribunal being described as the 'Liberal Party employment agency'.[45]

In addition, many members were not reappointed. While not an isolated case,[46] the extent of the 'purging of experienced members' was particularly acute in 2017.[47] There was 'a total of 65 of the 77 AAT members with terms expiring', who were not reappointed to the MRD of the AAT.[48] Non reappointment was suspected of being linked to contentious AAT decision-making, something to which I now turn to discuss.

## B. Impact on AAT Independence

O'Connor observes that 'the starting point for tribunal independence is to ask what tribunals require to carry out their functions' as 'independence is not an end in itself'.[49] While the meaning of independence is complex, for current purposes, I focus on its core aspects: institutional and adjudicative independence. Institutional adjudication relates to 'the tribunal's structural and institutional relationship to the executive'.[50] As O'Connor observes, the Executive's power to make decisions relating to 'appointment, reappointment, promotion, term of office, rates of remuneration and allowances, conditions of office, suspension and removal from office … directly affect the financial and career interests of members':[51]

> Institutional independence is about arrangements to ensure that executive powers to appoint and remunerate members do not influence the outcome of tribunal decisions or impair the perception of impartiality.[52]

In contrast, adjudicative independence 'is concerned with the ability of tribunal members and panels to make decisions impartially, free from external interference

Morrison ministry. They climbed from 23 per cent of all appointments during the 2013–2016 Abbott/Turnbull Government to 35 per cent during the 2016–2019 Turnbull/Morrison Government to 40 per cent during the 2019–2022 Morrison Government. In the Abbott/Turnbull/Morrison era, a total of 236 appointments were made': 1.

[44] Evans (n 1).

[45] D Hardaker, The Government's Ransacking of the AAT is Shocking – But the Media Normalises It' *Crikey* (online, 8 April 2022), www.crikey.com.au/2022/04/08/aat-stacking-2022/.

[46] M Seccombe, 'Political Stacking Leaves Appeals Tribunal in Chaos', *The Saturday Paper* (Melbourne, 24 November 2018); C Le Grand, 'Purge of Refugee Review Body' *The Australian* (Sydney, 13 July 2015).

[47] ibid.

[48] J Taylor, 'Brandis Culls AAT Migration Tribunal, with almost 80 to be Shown the Door' *Crikey* (online, 1 June 2017), www.crikey.com.au/2017/06/01/brandis-culls-aat-migration-tribunal/.

[49] P O'Connor, *Tribunal Independence* (The Australian Institute of Judicial Administration Inc, 2013) 7.

[50] ibid 17.

[51] ibid.

[52] ibid.

or improper influence from any source, including the executive, the parties, other external persons, and even from the tribunal head and other members'.[53] While difficult to establish definitively, concerns grew in relation to AAT independence, in particular, but not limited to, its decision-making in the migration and protection context.[54] For example, in the review of visa cancellations, which involved the AAT weighing up different factors contained in legally binding ministerial directions, in coming to the preferable decision, its decision-making as a whole and individual members was the subject of decades-long criticism from, inter alia, the media and the government.[55] Examples of inflammatory headlines include the following: 'Sex Fiend Cabbie to Stay Here';[56] 'Drug Dealer's All Clear'[57] and 'Why Criminals Love Australia'.[58] Its decision-making in relation to protection visas was equally as contentious, with headlines such as 'Tribunal welcomes fake refugees'.[59] As a result, ministers have periodically described AAT decision-making as 'frustrating' and 'infuriating'.[60] Following reports of 39 per cent of cases being overturned by the AAT, one former minister observed as follows:

> [W]hen you've got convictions that run for pages and pages and people who have got dozens and dozens of criminal convictions I don't understand what logic could be applied to allow those people to stay.[61]

Individual AAT members drew significant criticism relating to their decision-making from ministers charged with the appointment process and did not have their appointments renewed.[62] Holmes,[63] for example, was a long-standing and highly experienced member who was not reappointed following her decision to set aside a decision to cancel the visa of a convicted sex offender,[64] but there are

[53] ibid 18.

[54] D Hardaker and J Landis-Hanley, 'You're out! How a Government Tamed the AAT', *Crikey* (online, 25 September 2019), www.crikey.com.au/2019/09/25/how-a-government-tamed-the-aat/.

[55] See C Bostock, 'The Effect of Ministerial Directions on Tribunal Independence' (2011) 18 *AJAL* 161.

[56] K Moor, 'Sex Fiend Cabbie to Stay Here', *The Daily Telegraph* (Sydney, 9 May 2017) 2.

[57] 'Drug Dealer's All Clear', *The Advertiser* (Adelaide, 17 May 2017) 3.

[58] K Moor, 'Why Criminals Love Australia', *The Daily Telegraph* (Sydney, 22 May 2017) 2.

[59] 'Tribunal Welcomes Fake Refugees', *The Australian* (online, 30 May 2017).

[60] C Gribbin, 'Peter Dutton Blames Politics as Bid to Deport Six Refugees Fails' *ABC* (online, 16 May 2017) www.abc.net.au/news/2017-05-16/peter-dutton-blames-politics-over-blocked-bid-to-deport-refugees/8530060; T Minear, 'Axe Falls on AAT' *Herald Sun* (Sydney, 29 June 2017) 2. D Peters, '"Taken for a Ride": Dozens of Foreign Murderers, Rapists and Paedophiles with 'Pages' of Convictions Allowed to Stay in Australia after Tribunal Overruled Orders to Deport Them' *Mail Online* (online, 22 May 2017) www.dailymail.co.uk/news/article-4528290/Peter-Dutton-slams-tribunal-keeping-criminal-asylum-seeker.html.

[61] ibid.

[62] Taylor (n 48).

[63] See, eg, the case of Senior Member Miriam Holmes, who 'was on the receiving end of a media mauling over her decision to grant a bridging visa to an Indian man who'd been convicted of sexual assault': D Hardaker and J Landis-Hanley, 'You're out! How a Government Tamed the AAT', *Crikey* (online, 25 September 2019) www.crikey.com.au/2019/09/25/how-a-government-tamed-the-aat/.

[64] M Koziol, 'George Brandis clears out "infuriating" Administrative Appeals Tribunal', *Sydney Morning Herald* (online, 28 June 2017) www.smh.com.au/politics/federal/george-brandis-clears-out-infuriating-tribunal-20170628-gx071l.html.

other examples as well.[65] In commenting on the perceived high set-aside rate, one former minister suggested that the AAT was 'influenced by politics'[66] but observed that the rejection rate would 'change over time' following appointments and reappointments.[67] In light of this political climate, there was no coincidence that a substantial number of members were not reappointed at that particular time.[68] As a result, there was a view that the chance of success depended on the member hearing the case rather than on the merits of the case.[69] Unsurprisingly, Ghezelbash et al found that protection visa applicants were 'almost twice as likely to be knocked back if they [came] before a tribunal member appointed by the former Coalition government'.[70] As the Senate observed, the politicisation of the appointment process brought into 'serious doubt whether the AAT [could] be fully independent, and its decisions trusted by applicants, the legal profession, or the public more broadly'.[71]

## C. Competence of AAT Members

As noted earlier, under the AAT Act, appointees were required either to be legal practitioners qualified for a certain period of time or to hold special knowledge or skills relevant to the duties of their specific appointment. Leaving aside the longstanding debate relating to whether appointees ought to be enrolled as legal practitioners given the requirements of the role,[72] '[m]embers without legal experience and qualifications require far more training and mentoring'.[73] Yet, as discussed earlier, the Australia Institute found that there was significant variability in the qualifications and experience of political appointees:[74]

[65] See also the case of Emeritus Professor Terry Carney: D Hardaker and J Landis-Hanley, 'You're out! How a Government Tamed the AAT', *Crikey* (online, 25 September 2019) www.crikey.com.au/2019/09/25/how-a-government-tamed-the-aat; Royal Commission into the Robodebt Scheme, Report 2023.

[66] ibid.

[67] ibid.

[68] Koziol (n 64).

[69] Senate (n 35) [5.54].

[70] M Seccombe, 'Odds Stacked against Justice in Politicised Tribunal' *The Saturday Paper* (online, 23–29 July 2022) www.thesaturdaypaper.com.au/news/politics/2022/07/23/odds-stacked-against-justice-politicised-aat; See also D Ghezelbash, K Dorotskar and S Walsh, 'A Data Driven Approach to Evaluating and Improving Judicial Review of Refugee Cases in Australia' (2022) 45(3) *UNSWLJ* 1085.

[71] Senate (n 35) [7.36].

[72] See IDF Callinan AC, *Review: Section 4 of the Tribunals Amalgamation Act 2015 (Cth)* (Report, 23 July 2019). Callinan found that there was 'no necessity to appoint professionals other than lawyers to the AAT': [10.34] and recommended that 'all further appointments, re-appointments or renewals of appointment to the membership of the AAT should be lawyers, admitted or qualified for admission to a Supreme Court of a State or Territory or the High Court': [1.5].

[73] ibid 122.

[74] Wilkinson and Morison (n 34) 29.

> While some political appointees had legal qualifications and significant legal experience, others had low education levels and no professional experience outside of their political employment.[75]

As many as 10 per cent of political appointees had education levels below the level of a bachelor's degree, contrasting with 2 per cent of non-political appointees.[76] Furthermore, 'AAT members with political affiliations perform[ed] worse on average than those without':[77]

> Almost a quarter (24 per cent) of appointees with political connections were well under their performance targets, compared to 17 per cent of non-political appointees.[78]

As will become evident, in light of the ongoing number of cases on hand and the median time in which cases are finalised, the politicisation of the appointment process had an enormous impact, with many 'ill-equipped' members, 'who d[id] not understand the fundamentals' and 'caus[ed] delays', thereby 'affecting the quality of decisions being made'.[79] The reasons for this state of affairs included 'a perceived lack of interest in cases, new Members not having the skills and expertise required for complex cases and the loss of corporate knowledge from Members who were not reappointed'.[80]

There were also reports that with impunity, certain members refused to carry out their decision-making functions[81] while others routinely set aside and remitted decisions to avoid judicial scrutiny.[82] As a result of members struggling to undertake their core decision-making functions, as we shall see, the number of cases on hand grew exponentially.

Furthermore, political appointees were more likely to be appointed as senior members,[83] charged with large caseloads yet 'not experienced enough to guide and influence their members'.[84] These senior members replaced 'very experienced and capable tribunal decision makers', 'creating a big loss in knowledge'.[85] The Senate observed that in short, 'this politicisation [had] a direct impact on the ability of the AAT to perform its legislated functions in a manner that support[ed] proper public administration and effective expenditure of taxpayer funds'.[86]

[75] ibid.
[76] ibid.
[77] Wood et al (n 41) 21.
[78] ibid.
[79] Community and Public Sector Union, 'Statutory Review of the Tribunals Amalgamation' (Submission, 24 August 2018), www.ag.gov.au/legal-system/publications/submissions-received-statutory-review-tribunals-amalgamation-act-2015#:~:text=In%20inviting%20submissions,%20it%20was%20stated%20that%20submissions%20and%20the 5.
[80] ibid.
[81] Seccombe (n 46) 6.
[82] ibid.
[83] Wilkinson and Morison (n 34) 29.
[84] Community and Public Sector Union (n 80) 5.
[85] ibid 6.
[86] Senate (n 35) [7.35].

## D. Culture of the AAT

Matters such as the abovementioned politicisation of the appointment process, the adverse media publicity, its 'suffering' reputation,[87] combined with under-staffing and under-resourcing,[88] had an adverse impact on the culture of the Tribunal. As one former senior member of the AAT observed:

> If you see people just being appointed with no openness, and some of them have been former staff or failed candidates or whatever, it just devastates the morale …[89]

The Community and Public Sector Union (CPSU) also observed that decision-making pressures on members resulted in tension with staff:[90]

> The staff do their best to support members, but they are not their teachers.[91]

Documenting the conflict within the AAT in his report, Callinan went so far as to call for mutual respect and courtesy between members and registry staff.[92]

## E. Backlog and Impact on Review Applicants

While acknowledging that the reasons are multifactorial,[93] including the abovementioned understaffing and under-resourcing, the consequences of a flawed appointment process inevitably also had an impact on the efficiency of AAT decision-making. At the time of drafting his report in 2018, Callinan noted that there were more than 53,282 applications on hand at the AAT.[94] Since 2020, the number of cases on hand has hovered around the 70,000 mark.[95] For example, as of 31 May 2024, there were 69,312 cases on hand at the AAT.[96]

The MRD 'received sustained, high levels of lodgements relating to decisions about protection (refugee) visas'[97] and had 'a growing and ageing on-hand caseload',[98] with 59,543 cases to be determined as of 31 May 2024.[99] In contrast to

[87] Callinan (n 73) [6.261] citing the submission of Emeritus Professor Carney dated 23 August 2018.
[88] ibid [6.116] citing the submission of Community and Public Sector Union dated 24 August 2018.
[89] Crikey (n 54).
[90] Community and Public Sector Union, Statutory Review of the Tribunals Amalgamation (Submission, 24 August 2018) 5.
[91] ibid.
[92] Callinan (n 72) [1.12].
[93] See, eg, Callinan (n 72) who had called for 'the immediate enlargement of the Membership of the MRD': [1.3]. At the time of publication of Callinan's report, there were 53, 282 applications on hand [1.3].
[94] ibid.
[95] From 1 July 2019 to 30 June 2020, there were 72,360 cases on hand; from 1 July 2021 to 30 June 2022, there were 67,720 on hand; and from 1 July 2022 to 30 June 2023, there were 66,131 on hand: see AAT, www.aat.gov.au/about-the-aat/corporate-information/statistics.
[96] AAT Caseload Report for the Period of 1 July 2023 to 31 May 2024, AAT www.aat.gov.au/about-the-aat/corporate-information/statistics.
[97] The Senate Legal and Constitutional Affairs References Committee (n 35) [5.7].
[98] ibid [7.20] citing AAT's submission No 1.
[99] AAT Caseload Report for the Period of 1 July 2023 to 31 May 2024 (n 96).

the median time of 38 weeks to finalise cases in the AAT as a whole, the median time in the MRD as of 31 May 2024 was 234 weeks.[100]

As noted by Callinan, 'there were many instances in which applicants (including many on bridging visas) contrived or deliberately altered their circumstances in Australia for the principal purpose of renewing their visas or establishing a new pathway to a different visa'.[101] Furthermore, '[d]elays also mean[t] that those who are not entitled to stay in the country can stay for extended periods while they are waiting for a decision, creating an incentive to lodge weak claims'.[102] In response, the MRD triaged 'the less complex cases that could be finalised without a hearing or through remote hearings', leaving 'a more complex and aged backlog of cases on hand, which is likely to present significant challenges for the years ahead'[103] and 'contribut[ing] to significant distress and uncertainty for applicants':[104]

> Failure to address these delays leaves people in a very precarious situation. For many their visa status will preclude them from access to Medicare and many will have no work rights ...[105]

For applicants, particularly those affected by torture and trauma and declining mental health, participation in proceedings, including their ability to recall events,[106] becomes more difficult with the passage of time, which may ultimately affect the assessment of their credibility.[107]

Given these circumstances, it was unsurprising that the Senate found that 'the current AAT system [was] not fit for purpose, [was] not working as it should, and it impeded the proper consideration of merits review in this country'[108] and that the Attorney-General decided to proceed with its abolition. In doing so, the Attorney General observed that he wished to end the culture of 'cronyism'[109] found within the AAT as a result of the appointments process:

> ... the former government fatally compromised the AAT. The AAT's dysfunction has had a very real cost to the tens of thousands of people who rely on the AAT each year to independently review government decisions that have major and sometimes life changing impacts on their lives.[110]

[100] ibid.

[101] Callinan (n 72) [1.40]. See also C Nixon, *Rapid review into the Exploitation of Australia's Visa System*, 31 March 2023, 27: 'The faster the merits review process is, the less incentive there is for bad actors to exploit the system'.

[102] Senate (n 35) [5.29], citing Refugee Council of Australia, Submission 16.

[103] UNHCR, Submission to the Performance and Integrity of Australia's Administrative Review System', Submission 17, 6 December 2021, www.aph.gov.au/Parliamentary_Business/Committees/Senate/Legal_and_Constitutional_Affairs/Adminreviewsystem/Submissions 4.

[104] Senate (n 35) [5.29], citing Refugee Council of Australia, Submission 16.

[105] ibid.

[106] J Millbank, '"The Ring of Truth": A Case Study of Credibility Assessment in Particular Social Group Refugee Determinations' (2009) 21(1) *IJRL* 1, 12.

[107] Senate (n 35) [5.25] citing Legal Aid NSW, *Submission 13*.

[108] ibid [7.51].

[109] Evans (n 1).

[110] ibid.

# IV. Key Features of the Administrative Review Tribunal

In this section, I highlight some key, positive features of the ART Act, including its statutory objective, a new appointments process, and its greater emphasis on accessibility, including for the most vulnerable, by way of its procedures, representation, litigation supporters and interpreters, all of which have been designed to address some of the systemic concerns previously discussed.[111]

## A. Revised Statutory Objective

The ART is underpinned by a revised statutory objective, which is as follows:

> The Tribunal must pursue the objective of providing an independent mechanism of review that:
>
> a) is fair and just; and
> b) ensures that applications to the Tribunal are resolved as quickly, and with as little formality and expense, as a proper consideration of the matters before the Tribunal permits; and
> c) is accessible and responsive to the diverse needs of parties to the proceedings; and
> d) improves the transparency and quality of government decision-making; and
> e) promotes public trust and confidence in the Tribunal.[112]

Contrary to the AAT's statutory objective,[113] the ART's statutory objective includes an *independent* mechanism of review. Furthermore, the objective acquires more prominence as it underpins the core functions of the President, judicial and non-judicial deputy presidents,[114] while the parties and their representatives must use their best endeavours to assist the ART to achieve its objective.[115]

## B. Appointments

Following some controversy,[116] Division 3 of Part 8 of the ART Act provides for a new appointment process. The President, judicial and non-judicial deputy presidents, senior and general members are all to be appointed by the Governor-General

[111] It is beyond the scope of this chapter to discuss the full range of innovations, which include the establishment of a Guidance and Appeals Panel.
[112] AAT ct, s 9.
[113] ibid s 2A.
[114] ART Act, ss 193(e), 194(1)(b), 194(2)(b).
[115] ibid s 56(1), (2).
[116] Legal and Constitutional Affairs Committee, Administrative Review Tribunal Bill 2023 [provisions] and related bills, May 2024 [2.27]–[2.45]: As a result of significant pressure, the ART Bill was amended to ensure that the Minister was required to use assessment panels. As the Committee observed, '[t]his means that the Minister would not be able to recommend a candidate for appointment unless they had been assessed as suitable by an assessment panel through a merit-based process': [2.45].

on the recommendation of the minister.[117] With the exception of the judicial deputy presidents,[118] all appointees, including the President, must be assessed by a panel established by the minister[119] as suitable for appointment through an assessment process that is merit-based, publicly-advertised and compliant with the requirements set out in the Regulations.[120] 'Merits-based' is defined in the Act as follows:

> An assessment process for an appointment to an office is merit based only, if:
>
> a) An assessment is made of the comparative suitability of the candidates for the duties of the office, using a competitive selection process;
>
> b) The assessment is based on the relationship between the candidates' skills, expertise, experience and knowledge and the skills, expertise, experience and knowledge required for the duties of the office;
>
> d) The assessment takes into account the need for a diversity of skills, expertise, lived experience and knowledge within the Tribunal.[121]

The inclusion of the definition is 'to ensure that people appointed to the Tribunal are of a high calibre and suited to making decisions and performing the functions of the office that they are appointed to'.[122]

As under the AAT, the President must be a Federal Court judge, while judicial deputy presidents must be either Federal Court or Federal Circuit and Family Court judges.[123] Senior and general members must be enrolled as a legal practitioner for at least seven years or five years respectively or have at least seven or five years' specialised training or experience in a subject matter relevant to the jurisdiction of the Tribunal.[124]

The President and all other appointees are appointed for a period of five years, unless a shorter period is specified in the instrument of appointment and reasons provided.[125] In certain circumstances, the minister may reappoint the President and other appointees for another term, without them having to be reassessed by an assessment panel, after having taken into account the advice of the President in relation to the person's performance against the performance standard.[126]

[117] ART Act, ss 205, 206 and 207.

[118] ibid s 206. Legal and Constitutional Affairs Committee, Administrative Review Tribunal Bill 2023 [provisions] and related bills, May 2024. Revised Explanatory Memorandum, Administrative Review Tribunal Bill 2024 (Cth) [1330]: '[i]t would be unnecessary and inappropriate to apply this [merit-based assessment] process to sitting federal judges, given the common skill set required to sit as a Tribunal member and as a judge'.

[119] ART Act, s 209.

[120] ibid ss 205, 207, 208.

[121] ibid s 4.

[122] Revised Explanatory Memorandum, Administrative Review Tribunal Bill 2024 (Cth) [181].

[123] ART Act, ss 205(3), 206(3).

[124] ibid s 208(3).

[125] ibid ss 205(4), (5), 206(4), 206(5), 207(4), 207(5), 208(5), 208(6).

[126] ibid ss 193, 205(8), s 207(9), 208 (10).

## C. President and Appointees' Functions

Contrary to the AAT Act, the President's functions are set out in considerable detail under the ART Act.[127] With respect to Tribunal membership, the President is tasked with, amongst other things, the following: managing the performance and conduct of members; ensuring that the Tribunal operates efficiently and effectively and continually pursues its statutory objective; provides intellectual leadership, including by promoting best practice in decision-making; and promotes the training, education and professional development of members.[128] The President is assisted in these tasks by deputy and non-judicial deputy presidents, jurisdictional area leaders and the Tribunal Advisory Committee, which must take into account any expressed views of stakeholders.[129]

Designed to strengthen the office bearer's role,[130] the President has been given greater powers to manage appointees, including determining a code of conduct and performance standards for members.[131] The President may investigate breaches of the code of conduct and performance standards and may take various forms of action as a consequence of any breaches.[132]

## D. ART Proceedings

As with the AAT Act, acts and legislative instruments may provide that a decision is reviewable by the ART, and a person whose interests are affected by a reviewable decision may apply for review of the decision.[133] Applicants must lodge applications within the time period set out in either the ART rules or other legislation, although the ART may extend the time period if 'reasonable in all the circumstances to do so'.[134] As was previously the case, there is a carve-out for the time frames relating to the lodgement of migration and protection visa review applications[135] and the decision-maker's obligation to provide the other party a copy of reasons and documents,[136] issues to which I return in due course. The applicant, the decision-maker and other persons affected by the decision are parties to the proceeding, unless the decision-maker elects not to participate in the proceedings.[137]

[127] AAT Act, s 24A.

[128] ibid Part 8. The AAT had a Members' Professional Devlopment Program, which included induction, peer mentoring, periodic evaluation and devlopment and ongoing professional development: see AAT, *Members' Professional Development Handbook* (2nd edn, 2021).

[129] ibid Part 8.

[130] Revised Explanatory Memorandum (n 122) [22].

[131] ART Act Part 8, Subdivision C.

[132] ibid ss 203(1), 203(2).

[133] ibid ss 12, 17.

[134] ibid ss 18, 19(2).

[135] Migration Act 1958 (Cth) (Migration Act) s 347.

[136] ART Act, s 27.

[137] ibid ss 22, 60.

As under the AAT Act, the ART Act gives members significant control over the conduct of proceedings. Subject to the Act and rules, the ART's procedure is within its discretion; it must act with as little formality as a proper consideration of the matters before the ART permits, is not bound by the rules of evidence and 'may inform itself on any matter in such manner as it considers appropriate'.[138] Additionally, and in contrast to the AAT Act, the Tribunal may determine the scope of review by limiting the questions of fact, the evidence and the issues that it considers.[139] It may exercise all the powers and discretions conferred on the primary decision-maker.[140]

In contrast to the AAT Act, however, as far as practicable, the ART must conduct each proceeding in a way that is accessible for the parties, taking into account the needs of the parties.[141] 'Accessible' is defined in the ART Act as 'enables persons to apply to the Tribunal and to participate effectively in proceedings in the Tribunal', including 'adjustments that can reasonably be made to accommodate a person's needs, such as interpreter services for hearings'.[142] Furthermore, the ART must 'ensure that each party to a proceeding in the ART is given a reasonable opportunity to present their case, access any information or documents to which the Tribunal proposes to have regard in making its decision and to make submissions and adduce evidence'.[143] As noted earlier, all parties and their representatives must use their best endeavours to assist the ART to achieve its objective, while decision-makers must also use their best endeavours to assist the ART to make the correct or preferable decision and to achieve the ART's objective.[144]

The ART Act makes provision for a party to a proceeding to be represented,[145] including, contrary to the previous position,[146] in migration and refugee-related proceedings, to have an interpreter and, constituting a significant change, a litigation supporter.[147] In addition, in certain circumstances, parties may apply for legal or financial assistance in relation to ART proceedings.[148]

As under the AAT Act, the ART may summon a person to give evidence or produce documents, to take evidence and to manage proceedings, including the power to give directions, to hold directions hearings and to adjourn.[149]

[138] ibid ss 49(1), 50(1), 52.
[139] ibid s 53.
[140] ibid s 54.
[141] ibid s 51.
[142] ibid s 4.
[143] ibid s 55.
[144] ibid s 56(1), 56(2).
[145] ibid s 66.
[146] Migration Act, s 366A, 427(6).
[147] ibid ss 67, 68.
[148] ibid s 294.
[149] ibid ss 74, 75, 79, 80, 82.

## V. Discussion

Thomas observes that 'the quality of an administrative-legal process is informed by four values', namely the system's 'propensity to produce accurate decisions'; the fairness of the decision-making process, which necessarily includes 'a neutral decision-maker'; and the resources required to fund and the timeliness of the decision-making process.[150] How these values are fulfilled and reconciled allows us to evaluate 'the quality of tribunal adjudication'.[151] In an echo of Thomas' values, the ART's statutory objective, noted earlier, provides that it must provide 'an independent mechanism of review' which balances, amongst other things, fairness and justice with speed, informality and lack of expense yet remains accessible to the parties.[152] While the introduction of the notion of independence provides a new and strong legislative affirmation of the ART's role and function, the objective is 'aspirational or exhortatory in nature'[153] only and provides no explicit guidance on how tensions between the different aspects of the objective ought to be reconciled, given that none 'should be read as having priority above the others'.[154]

The new appointment process is a significant improvement on the previous system, with a publicly-advertised, merits-based process, legislated in the ART Act. Fortunately, as noted earlier, and as a result of significant pressure from, inter alia, the legal community, the draft legislation was amended to require the minister to use assessment panels. However, as also noted above, certain aspects of the appointment process, such as the composition of the panel and its processes, are subject to regulations to enable 'processes to improve over time and to be tailored to particular Tribunal needs where required'.[155] While providing that features of the appointment process be subject to regulations represents an improvement on the previous system, the ease with which they may be amended is of concern. For example, Kate Chaney MP noted that '[g]iven past issues with politicisation of appointments, I am not satisfied that these issues can be appropriately addressed in regulations'.[156] The Law Council of Australia also expressed concern:

> In addition, clause 209 could be strengthened to require that assessment panels must consist of suitably high-level, independent individuals with appropriate expertise. As currently drafted, clause 209 is excessively reliant on the regulations – which are yet to be released – which, in practice, could enable inadequately qualified panels to be

[150] Thomas (n 4) 12–13.
[151] ibid.
[152] ART Act, s 9.
[153] *Fard v Secretary, Department of Immigration and Border Protection* [2016] FCA 417 [80].
[154] Revised Explanatory Memorandum (n 122) [246]: '[an]y tension between them should be resolved in the context of the particular circumstances of each matter'.
[155] ibid [1355].
[156] House of Representatives Standing Committee on Social Policy and Legal Affairs, Inquiry into the Administrative Review Tribunal Bill 2023 and the Administrative Review Tribunal (Consequential and Transitional Provisions No 1) Bill 2023 (Report, February 2024) Additional Comments by Kate Chaney MP, 76.

> established, resulting in poor or inappropriate selections of candidates for the Minister's consideration.[157]

Another change provided for in the ART Act is appointment periods of five years. Five-year appointments do not necessarily represent a 'career pathway'.[158] As noted by Callinan, 'insufficient regard has been had to the fact that a professional person in accepting appointment as a Member can be interrupting a professional career which it will not be easy to re-enter after the conclusion of service as a Member'.[159] As a result, there is still scope, albeit far more limited, for some politicisation of the appointments process. Accordingly, it again brings into question the possible conscious or subconscious effect of Executive criticism on contentious areas of ART decision-making. As Groves observes, 'institutional pressures are often so diffuse and so powerful that they can operate without any form of direct communication', with 'the power of reappointment [being] an obvious form of this power'.[160] No one would disagree with Logan J's comments that

> … any member who allowed himself or herself to be persuaded as to an outcome by partisan or political rhetoric by a Minister, any other administrator or the popular press would be unworthy of the trust and confidence placed in him or her by His Excellency the Governor-General and untrue to the oath or affirmation of office which must be taken before exercising the Tribunal's jurisdiction.[161]

As Logan J further recognises, however, it may be easier said than done:

> For those members who do not enjoy the same security of tenure as judges, that may call at times for singular moral courage and depth of character.[162]

Noting that members should not be 'thin skinned' in the face of scrutiny, Callinan observes that 'the first answer to criticism is the production and publication of good decisions supported by cogent reasons'.[163] This certainly assists, but it is also worthwhile considering the creation of a Tribunal counterpart to the Dutch press judge, whose role is to work with the media.[164] An analysis of the role found that '[p]ress Judges had greatly improved and increased communication between judges and the media and were especially useful in responding to unfair and inaccurate criticisms of cases and personalised criticisms of judges'.[165] A Tribunal counterpart, for example, could point to the difference in the Tribunal decision-making process, in which it holds a hearing where the review applicant may give evidence

[157] Law Council of Australia, Administrative Review Tribunals Bill 2023, Submission to House of Representatives Standing Committee on Social Policy and Legal Affairs dated 2 February 2024, 9.
[158] Callinan (n 72) 123.
[159] ibid [7.14].
[160] M Groves, 'Clarity and Complexity in the Bias Rule' (2020) 44(2) *MULR* 565, 581.
[161] *Singh* (Migration) [2017] AATA 850 (16 June 2017) [18] (Logan J).
[162] ibid.
[163] Callinan (n 72) 174.
[164] M Groves, 'Should Judges Bite Back? Judicial Responses to Public Criticisms of Courts and Cases' (2023) 53 *Australian Bar Review* 231, 258.
[165] ibid.

and be represented.[166] It could also be explained that the Tribunal may also hear from others personally affected by the decision and from relevant experts. Given the lack of tenure, the length of the period of appointment and other aspects of the process, which are not enshrined in legislation, continued vigilance relating to possible politicisation of the process is required. Members must have the freedom to make the correct or preferable decision in the particular circumstances of the case and be certain that their decision-making will not have deleterious consequences in terms of their appointment.[167] Otherwise, the fairness of the decision-making process will be once again compromised.

As noted earlier, the ART's statutory objective pays particular regard to accessibility and responsiveness to the diverse needs of the parties. However, the time limits relating to the lodgement of review applications and applicants' need to specifically request access to Department information with respect to migration and protection visa cases will continue to operate, resulting in an ongoing and significant barrier. Review applicants will have seven days if in immigration detention, nine days for visa cancellations and refusals and, for most other migration and protection reviewable decisions, 28 days from receiving notification of the decision to lodge a review application.[168] The ART cannot extend the period in which to lodge the review application.[169] While time limits are important for administrative efficiency;

> [t]he inflexibility of time limits undermines the ability of the tribunal to deliver effective and efficient justice for applicants. If the tribunal is denied jurisdiction to hear a case, applicants must either apply for judicial review in the Federal Court or they must seek an exercise of the Minister's 'non-reviewable, non-compellable' discretion (see s 351 of the Migration Act). With the backlog in judicial review applications and the overwhelming number of ministerial appeals, it is difficult to see the wisdom in this constraint on the new ART.[170]

The inflexibility of the time limits represents a missed opportunity to enhance the ART's accessibility and responsiveness, which would have provided some of the most vulnerable members of the community an opportunity to substantively challenge the decision.

As was previously the case, the decision maker is not required to give the review applicant a copy of its reasons and documents in its possession or under

[166] See, eg, C Bostock, 'The Value of Adjudicative Independence: Overlapping Conceptions of Administrative Justice in the Administrative Appeals Tribunal's Review of Visa Cancellations' (2020) 27 *AJAL* 154, where I discuss the different approaches to decision-making in primary and merits review.

[167] See, eg, Bostock (n 55).

[168] Migration Act, s 347(3).

[169] Administrative Review Tribunal (Consequential and Transitional Provisions No 1) Act 2024 (Cth) s 347(5).

[170] M Crock, Submission to the Senate Legal and Constitutional Affairs Legislation Committee inquiry into the Administrative Review Tribunal (Miscellaneous Measures) Bill 2024 (23 September 2024).

its control relevant to the review.[171] Instead, 'the applicant is entitled to request the Department provide access to any written material, or a copy of any written material, given or produced to the ART by the Department for the purposes of the review'.[172] The rationale provided is as follows:

> Given the volume of migration and protection matters and the high proportion of people who have copies of their documents, the request-based model provides the appropriate balance between equity, fairness and accessibility and the efficient and effective use of Government resourcing.[173]

Furthermore, there does not appear to be any obligation on the Department to provide information within a prescribed time limit.[174] Nor does the ART's obligation to allow applicants access to any information or documents to which it proposes to have regard in reaching a decision apply in migration and protection visa cases.[175] In these circumstances, where knowledge of the procedural rules is important in order to access and navigate the review process and to increase prospects of success, review applicants are at a serious disadvantage when they are not legally represented.[176] Previously, in migration matters, review applicants were entitled to have an assistant, but not a representative, present at the hearing, who was not permitted to present arguments or address the Tribunal unless there were exceptional circumstances.[177] Protection visa applicants were not entitled to be represented at the hearing.[178] It is a positive development to permit legal representation in ART proceedings, including in relation to migration and protection visa matters. However, it is well established that legal assistance is 'chronically underfunded and unable to meet an ever-increasing demand'.[179] Recognising 'the neglect of Australia's legal assistance sector',[180] the Independent Reviewer of the National Legal Assistance Partnership recently recommended that the Commonwealth undertake a Legal Assistance Impact Assessment 'with a view to adjusting the baseline funding of those services who have substantial

[171] ART Act, s 27; Migration Act, s 336P(2)(g).

[172] Migration Act, s 362A.

[173] House of Representatives Standing Committee of Social Policy and Legal Affairs (n 157) [3.24].

[174] Immigration and Advice Rights Centre, Inquiry into Administrative Review Tribunal Bill 2023 and Administrative Review Tribunal (Consequential and Transitional Provisions No 1) Bill 2023, Submission 23, 2 February 2024, 3.

[175] ART Act, s 55; Migration Act, s 357A(2)(2B).

[176] D Ghezelbash, K Dorotskar and S Walsh, 'A Data Driven Approach to Evaluating and Improving Judicial Review of Refugee Cases in Australia' (2022) 45(3) *UNSWLJ* 1085, 1101: 'The statistics show that applicants with legal representation are on average six times more likely to succeed than self-represented Applicants'.

[177] Migration Act, s 366A.

[178] ibid s 427(6).

[179] Law Council of Australia, 'Access to Justice for All: Open Letter to Ministers' 21 August 2024, lawcouncil.au/access-to-justice-for-all#:~:text=Our%20profession%20is%20calling%20on%20all%20governments%20to%20significantly%20increase.

[180] W Mundy, *Independent Review of the National Legal Assistance Partnership* (Report, March 2024) i.

Commonwealth administrative law caseloads'.[181] Given this broader context, the government's rationale for not extending legal and financial assistance[182] provided for under the ART Act to migration and protection visa matters is not persuasive.[183] It is thus of significant concern that timeliness and government resources are prioritised, despite these longstanding issues which profoundly affect the most vulnerable in our community and could have been easily remedied.

In addition, there are ongoing significant practical, financial and other barriers to obtaining probative material, such as psychological and/or medical reports, which may mean that applicants fall short of the evidentiary threshold required to satisfy decision makers that they meet the relevant criteria.[184] As discussed earlier, the ART is equipped with a number of investigative powers, including the power to inform itself and to summon persons to give evidence or produce documents, many of which mirror those of the AAT. And yet, despite these abovementioned powers, the AAT 'would be placed at the end nearest the courts' on the inquisitorial spectrum[185] for complex reasons, including a limited duty to enquire[186] and, in part, due to:

> … the strength of the legal culture, in part, the unwillingness to move from the known and well established rules of evidence and in part the fact tribunals are sited in an adjudicative system the final tiers of which traditionally operate in an adversarial fashion.[187]

Lack of resources also played a role, an ongoing issue.[188] Although it has gained more resources and members,[189] the ART inherits the AAT's significant backlog of cases, including 40,683 protection visa cases as of 31 May 2024, which take a median time of more than four years to finalise.[190] As Simmons and I have observed elsewhere in relation to determining protection visa review applications, 'there is a disconnect between what may be desirable in terms of maximising an

[181] ibid, Recommendation 4, xiii.

[182] ART Act, s 294; Migration Act, s 336P(2)(l).

[183] House of Representatives Standing Committee of Social Policy and Legal Affairs (n 156) [2.175]: Migration applicants 'are already existing priorities in legal assistance, subject to merit and means, through the National Legal Assistance Partnership'.

[184] See, eg, The Royal Australian and New Zealand College of Psychiatrists, The provision of mental health services for asylum seekers and refugees: Position Statement Last Updated March 2024, www.ranzcp.org/clinical-guidelines-publications/clinical-guidelines-publications-library/the-provision-of-mental-health-services-for-asylum-seekers-and-refugees#:~:text=The%20Royal%20Australian%20and%20New%20Zealand%20College%20of%20Psychiatrists%20(RANZCP)#:~:text=The%20Royal%20Australian%20and%20New%20Zealand%20College%20of%20Psychiatrists%20(RANZCP); D Silove and S Mares, 'The Mental Health of Asylum Seekers in Australia and the Role of Psychiatrists' (2018) 15(3) *BJPsych International* 65–68.

[185] N Bedford and R Creyke, *Inquisitorial Processes in Australian Tribunals* (Australian Institute of Judicial Administration Incorp, 2006) 7.

[186] *Minister for Immigration and Citizenship v SZIAI* (2009) 259 ALR 429; see also M Smyth, 'Inquisitorial Adjudication: The Duty to Inquire in Merits Review Tribunals' (2010) 34 *MULR* 230.

[187] Bedford and Creyke (n 185) 66.

[188] ibid.

[189] Attorney-General's Department, 'Key Features' www.ag.gov.au/legal-system/new-system-federal-administrative-review#key-features-of-the-reform.

[190] AAT Caseload Report For the period of 1 July 2023 to 31 May 2024 (n 96).

applicant's ability to meaningfully participate in the review process and what the Tribunal is required to do to discharge its legal obligations'.[191] For example, in our search of publicly reported AAT cases, we found only one instance where the AAT exercised its power to require the Secretary to arrange for the making of a medical examination considered necessary for the review,[192] a power which is also available to the ART.[193] To promote accurate and fair decision-making, it will therefore be imperative that the ART be acutely mindful of its role and be prepared to invoke its powers in gathering evidence, either by requesting the parties or, where not possible, gathering the evidence itself.[194]

In this high-volume environment, hearings will continue to be crucially important, particularly where vulnerable applicants are involved. While interpreters and litigation supporters will assist in ensuring that applicants meaningfully participate, ultimately, members are expected to 'take control of the hearing' 'with sensitivity'.[195] The ART will be required to ensure that parties are given a reasonable opportunity to present their case,[196] the exact boundaries of which will need to be established on judicial review. Many questions arise, including how active throughout the proceedings will members need to be to ensure that review applicants are given a reasonable opportunity to present their case? Where review applicants are particularly vulnerable, to what extent will the ART be required to exercise its wide powers to gather evidence, in light of its statutory context, including its statutory objective?

As noted earlier, the ART Act stipulates that the merits-based appointment process must take into account the need for a diversity of skills, expertise, lived experience and knowledge within the ART. Qualified and skilled members from different backgrounds are an important starting point. However, as acknowledged in the ART Act, there is renewed emphasis on extensive training and ongoing professional development[197] in matters such as the fundamentals of decision-making and working with a diverse range of applicants, including those with mental and physical disabilities, culturally and linguistically different backgrounds, and victims of torture and trauma.[198] Members should also receive training on important developments such as trauma-informed practice and dealing with victim-survivors of family violence.[199] It will be important to promote a culture of adopting 'an appropriate active investigative approach in hearings',

[191] F Simmons and C Bostock, 'Administrative Review in Refugee Cases: The Vulnerable Persons Guidelines and the Role of Legal Representatives' (2024) 47(2) *UNSWLJ* 448, 472.

[192] Migration Act, s 427(1)(d).

[193] ibid s 353.

[194] Thomas (n 4) 13. See also Cane (n 25) 239.

[195] Bedford and Creyke (n 185) 66.

[196] ART Act, s 55.

[197] ibid s 193.

[198] Revised Explanatory Memorandum (n 122) [1177].

[199] Women's Legal Services Australia, *Inquiry into Administrative Review Tribunal Bill 2023 and Administrative Review Tribunal (Consequential and Transitional Provisions No 1) Bill 2023* Submission 31, 5 February 2024, www.aph.gov.au/Parliamentary_Business/Committees/House/Social_Policy_and_

where appropriate.[200] Members should be encouraged to reflect on their approach to fact-finding in the context of the purpose of the review.[201] As Glass observes, 'it makes a large difference to how the fact-finding is approached depending on whether the point of the review is seen as correctly identifying valid claims, or whether it is seen as correctly identifying invalid claims'.[202] Finally, training relating to member well-being must also be an important focus to avoid the risk of burnout, which affects decision-making. Professional development requiring member self-reflection is crucial so that members recognise the emotional toll of decision-making and take practical steps to achieve 'impartiality'.[203]

## VI. Conclusion

In this chapter, I have set out the circumstances which led to the demise of the AAT. While a brilliant concept, regrettably, its reputation crumbled. The establishment of the ART represents a rare opportunity to begin again. Guided by an expert working group and following consultation, there have been significant changes made, which should lead to an improved administrative review system. Yet we are not out of the woods.[204] While much of the easy work has been done, the more hidden challenges remain. It is therefore crucial that further work is undertaken to ensure that lessons are learnt and acted upon. While the revised appointments process represents a significant improvement on the previous system, for reasons which I have discussed, there remains the possibility of politicisation. In these circumstances, the Tribunal equivalent of a press judge could be created to improve the broader understanding of its role and in the hope that criticism is reduced. Ultimately, it is imperative that ART members are able to come to the correct or preferable decision, 'without fear or favour'. The abolition of the AAT represented a welcome opportunity to consider how practical changes could be made to ensure greater accessibility and responsiveness, particularly to vulnerable review applicants, thereby promoting more accurate and fair decisions. Unfortunately, easily remedied aspects of the system, such as the time limits in order to lodge review applications, access to documents and legal and financial assistance, have not been changed. In addition, one of the most complex and longstanding challenges remains, namely the need to adopt a more investigative

Legal_Affairs/ARTbillsInquiry/Submissions [34]–[35]. See also C Bostock, 'The Impact of Criminal Deportation on Victim-Survivors of Domestic Violence in Australia' [2023] 3 *UNSWLJ The Forum*.

200 The Senate (n 35) [1.31].

201 A Glass, 'Subjectivity and Refugee Fact-Finding' in J McAdam (ed), *Forced Migration, Human Rights and Security* (Oxford, Hart Publishing Ltd, 2008) 223.

202 ibid.

203 K Mack, SR Anleu and J Tutton, 'Judicial Impartiality, Bias and Emotion' (2021) 28 *AJAL* 66, 80–81.

204 For reservations relating to the ART expressed within the context of social security decision-making, see T Brennan, 'The Administrative Review Tribunal as a Response to the Robodebt Scandal' (2024) 31 *AJAL* 17.

approach, particularly where vulnerable review applicants, who do not have access to legal representation or access to evidence, are involved. There will be an ongoing need for highly targeted professional development, including on the ART's full suite of powers and the promotion of a culture which encourages their use. The mandatory review of the ART within six years will ensure that these challenges remain in the spotlight.[205]

[205] ART Act, s 294A.

# 4

# Public Interest Groups in Australian Standing Law: Reconsidering the *North Coast Environment Council* Case

ANDREW EDGAR

## I. Introduction

It is an honour to contribute a chapter to this book dedicated to Matthew Groves' scholarship. I have learned much from Matthew's research, starting from reading his work on polycentric decision-making with Enid Campbell.[1] In this chapter, I revisit the problems and potential solutions for public interest standing in Australian administrative law. Public interest standing applies when the applicant has no personal interest that is affected by the administrative decision, such as their property or financial interests, and they apply to the courts on the basis of representing the public interest, similar to the role traditionally recognised in standing law as being for the Attorney-General.[2] This is not open standing but the ability to represent relevant aspects of the public interest in judicial review proceedings. This aspect of standing law has been an important part of Matthew's scholarship in recent years.[3]

I argue for an approach to public interest standing in Australian law that differs from both Matthew's scholarship and my earlier work on standing.[4] My argument

[1] E Campbell and M Groves, 'Polycentricity in Administrative Decision-Making' in M Groves (ed), *Law and Government in Australia* (Annandale, Federation Press, 2005) 213.

[2] *Batemans Bay Local Aboriginal Land Council v Aboriginal Community Benefit Fund Pty Limited* (1998) 194 CLR 247 [29]–[30].

[3] M Groves, 'Justice Murphy's Dissent in Australian Conservation Foundation v Commonwealth (1980): The Birth of Public Interest Standing in Australia?' in A Lynch (ed), *Great Australian Dissents* (Cambridge, Cambridge University Press, 2016) 189; M Groves, 'The Evolution and Reform of Standing in Australian Administrative Law' (2016) 44 *Federal Law Review* 167; M Groves, 'Standing Outside: An Environment of Challenge and Withheld Cures' (2021) 38 *Environmental Planning Law Journal* 111.

[4] A Edgar, 'Standing for Environmental Groups: Protecting Public and Private Interests' in M Groves (ed), *Modern Administrative Law in Australia: Concepts and Context* (Cambridge, Cambridge University Press, 2014) 140.

is that Australian standing law should be recognised as including a form of public interest standing developed by courts. In contrast to my previous work,[5] I agree with Matthew that there is little need to regard extensions of standing law to be a matter primarily for legislative reform. It is better for courts to recognise public interest standing as a judicially developed principle[6] and for legislation to be left to the adjustment of those principles.

I will also argue that Australian standing law already includes the elements that are required for it and are included in Sackville J's judgment in *North Coast Environment Council Inc v Minister for Resources* ('*North Coast*').[7] While Matthew rightly recognises there are difficulties with *North Coast* relating to its vagueness and uncertainty and its rigid application in some cases,[8] I will argue Sackville J's reasoning includes the elements necessary for a general principle for public interest standing and considerations for applying those principles. The contribution I seek to make in this chapter is to highlight how those elements can be interpreted to provide principles, coherence, and clarity to public interest standing in Australian administrative law.

## II. General Principles and Reforms

### A. *Australian Conservation Foundation v Commonwealth and Onus v Alcoa*

The language and traditional logic for standing in judicial review of administrative action were expressed in *Australian Conservation Foundation v Commonwealth* ('*ACF*').[9] While this case is likely to be very well known, it is necessary to set out its primary elements for background, including the modern special interest test. The application of the special interest test in *ACF* is just as important as the special interest terminology. This case will be explained briefly. It is necessary to highlight its features in order to appreciate the changes that have already occurred and to determine if further changes remain necessary.

The *ACF* case establishes the 'special interest' terminology and the requirement that applicants are to be directly and personally advantaged if they succeed in the proceedings or disadvantaged if not successful.[10] Without this kind of direct impact, the applicant's interest is to be dismissed as a 'mere intellectual or

[5] ibid 159–60.
[6] Groves, 'Standing Outside: An Environment of Challenge and Withheld Cures' (n 3) 129.
[7] *North Coast Environment Council Inc v Minister for Resources* (1994) 55 FCR 492.
[8] Groves, 'The Evolution and Reform of Standing in Australian Administrative Law' (n 3) 176–77; Groves, 'Standing Outside: An Environment of Challenge and Withheld Cures' (n 3) 121–23.
[9] *Australian Conservation Foundation v Commonwealth* (1980) 146 CLR 493.
[10] ibid 527, 530.

emotional concern'.[11] It does not matter that the applicant is an organisation established for purposes relevant to the challenged government action or that it has participated in a public consultation process for the decision being challenged.[12]

These points make things difficult for public interest groups to be granted standing. The Australian Conservation Foundation's interest in bringing proceedings to challenge the Commonwealth's decision under the Environment Protection (Impact of Proposals) Act 1974 (Cth), relating to a resort and tourism facilities in an environmentally sensitive location,[13] was treated as insufficient for standing. The fact that the Australian Conservation Foundation was established for particular purposes, environmental protection, and planned to take actions was treated as something any organisation or person could do, rather than being a special interest.[14] Similarly, the Australian Conservation Foundation's participation in a public consultation process was treated as something any organisation or person can do. Unlike participating in other forms of administrative hearing, this kind of participation does not establish a person's right to ensure the decision-making process and the decision are made according to law.[15] The majority judges' dismissal of these aspects of the Australian Conservation Foundation's interests suggests that it was recognised as having political concerns that many people may have in relation to land uses and environment protection.

The *ACF* case was followed shortly after by another influential standing case determined by the High Court, *Onus v Alcoa of Australia Ltd*.[16] The applicants were two Aboriginal women, rather than a public interest group, who sought injunctions to prevent an aluminium smelter from being constructed on land that held Aboriginal relics. They brought proceedings to protect the relics from being harmed according to the Archaeological and Aboriginal Relics Preservation Act 1972 (Vic). The plaintiffs were of the Gournditch-jmara people who lived in the area on which the smelter was to be constructed and that they, as descendants of Gournditch-jmara people, had responsibilities to protect the relics.[17]

The High Court accepted that the Aboriginal women had standing. The circumstances were distinguished from the facts in *ACF*. The applicants were local people from a small community with cultural and spiritual interests in the relics protected by the relevant Act.[18] The recognition of the Aboriginal women's standing in *Onus v Alcoa* seems uncontroversial now. Is it relevant for public interest groups? Prima facie, it seems not to be. The applicants were two individuals rather

[11] ibid 530.

[12] ibid 531.

[13] T Bonyhady 'Introduction' in T Bonyhady and A Macintosh (eds), *Mills, Mines and Other Controversies: The Environmental Assessment of Major Projects* (Sydney, Federation Press, 2010) 1, 8.

[14] *ACF* (n 9) 531.

[15] ibid 531–32. See also, *Sinclair v Maryborough Mining Warden* (1975) 132 CLR 473; *United States Tobacco Company v Minister for Consumer Affairs* (1988) 20 FCR 520, 530–31.

[16] *Onus v Alcoa of Australia Ltd* (1981) 149 CLR 27.

[17] ibid 31–32.

[18] ibid 37, 42.

than an organisation. While it was relevant that they were descendants and the current generation of the Gournditch-jmara people, they were not representing their Aboriginal group, or Aboriginal people generally in the sense that public interest groups can claim to be representative of particular interests. The applicants' judicial review proceedings challenged actions that engaged their personal responsibilities to protect the relics on the relevant land. They were referred to in the case as 'custodians' of the relics.[19] This could not equate to a form of property, and their interests were not financial, yet their interests in the relics and their potential harm from the aluminium smelter were closely personal.

The language of the judges in *Onus v Alcoa* suggests that plaintiffs who can demonstrate a close interest in the subject matter of the litigation will be granted standing. Justice Gibbs referred to the applicants' interests 'being greater than that of other members of the public'.[20] Stephen J referred to standing law focusing on the 'importance of the concern which a plaintiff has with particular subject matter and of the closeness of that plaintiff's relationship to that subject matter'.[21] These points made by Gibbs J and Stephen J have been highly influential in subsequent cases. They are pitched at a high level of generality, but as we will later see, they are very important for standing for public interest groups.

Brennan J's judgment in *Onus v Alcoa* seems to have been less influential than the judges just referred to; however, it has aspects that are highly relevant for understanding the rationale of public interest standing. Brennan J agreed with the other judges that the applicants' cultural and spiritual connection to the relics provided the basis for their standing to be accepted. However, his reasoning focused much more clearly on the consistency of their cultural and spiritual interests with the heritage characteristics of the Act.[22] This was consistent with a more general analysis he developed in his judgment of the need to broaden the application of the special interest test due to the characteristics of modern legislation. Brennan J stated that,

> A special interest in the subject matter of an action being neither a legal nor equitable right, nor a proprietary or pecuniary interest, will ordinarily be found to arise from modern legislation enacted to protect or enhance non-material interests – interests in the environment, in historical heritage, in culture. … To deny standing would deny to an important category of modern public statutory duties an effective procedure for curial enforcement.[23]

While the judgments in *Onus v Alcoa* by Gibbs CJ and Stephen J have gained attention, Brennan J's judgment provides important guidance for extending standing law. He does this by focusing on the connection between the applicants' interests

[19] ibid 36, 45, 57, 65.
[20] ibid 36.
[21] ibid 42.
[22] ibid 77.
[23] Ibid 73.

and the particular aspect of the public interest reflected in the Act. This is an important element that I will come back to later in the chapter.

The more general point to be made about *Onus v Alcoa* is that the High Court moved beyond the more rigid distinction between direct personal interests and general public interests that underpinned the *ACF* case. Relaxing that distinction enables a more pragmatic, in-between status that can be the basis for standing. It suggests that Australian law may be able to accept standing for applicants where their property or financial interests are not affected by the decision but they have a close connection with the subject matter of the litigation, particularly if their interest is consistent with the public interest concern dealt with by the Act. However, standing will not be accepted if they make a simple claim to the public interest that any person could have.

This is an important development. *ACF* presents what looks like the primary problem for public interest groups. The High Court rejected the applicants' arguments intended to demonstrate the characteristics of its ability to bring proceedings and its relationship to the decision that it sought to challenge. However, the judges' reasoning in *Onus v Alcoa* provides the starting point for an acceptance of public interest standing.

## B. Public Interest Standing – Reforms and Reform Proposals

Justice Sackville's reasoning in *North Coast* engaged closely with *ACF* and *Onus v Alcoa*. I will argue below that his reasoning involves plausible, incremental development of the judges' analyses in those cases. However, *ACF* and *Onus v Alcoa* do not, in themselves, accept public interest standing. *ACF*, of course, denied it to the applicant, and the applicants in *Onus v Alcoa* were not a public interest group. Before examining the reasoning in *North Coast*, it is helpful to refer briefly to other reform proposals.[24]

Recognition of the limitations of standing law as reflected in *ACF* and *Onus v Alcoa* in the 1980s led to two Australian Law Reform Commission inquiries.[25] There have been some legislative reforms to standing that recognise public interest standing. For example, section 487 of the Environment Protection and Biodiversity Conservation Act 1999 (Cth) extends standing to interest groups that are incorporated or established in Australia, have engaged in environment protection or research activities in the previous two years, and whose purposes

[24] For a comprehensive analysis of reforms to standing, see M Aronson, M Groves and G Weeks, *Judicial Review of Administrative Action and Government Liability*, 7th edn (Pyrmont, Thomson Reuters, 2022) 906–12.

[25] Australian Law Reform Commission, *Standing in Public Interest Litigation* (Report No 27, 1985); Australian Law Reform Commission, *Beyond the Door-Keeper: Standing to Sue for Public Remedies* (Report No 78, 1996).

include environment protection or research into environment protection.[26] In the context of Commonwealth merits review, section 15 of the Administrative Review Tribunal Act 2024 (Cth) deems an organisation to be a person whose interests are affected by a decision for the purpose of standing when the 'decision relates to a matter included in the objects or purposes of the organisation or association at the time the decision is made'.[27] These provisions support public interest group standing and do so primarily by accepting the relevance of the purpose of the interest group. Importantly, this had been rejected by the High Court as a relevant factor in *ACF*.

While these legislative reforms are significant developments, they do not apply to judicial review proceedings more generally or to environmental decision-making under other Acts. This has prompted consideration of judicial developments to recognise standing for public interest groups. Matthew Groves has drawn attention to the recognition of public interest standing in the United Kingdom. He has most recently supported the UK Supreme Court's recognition of broad standing in *Walton v Scottish Ministers*[28] and in particular as it applies to environmental groups. He regards this case as taking a small but important step in recognising the public interest basis of environmental concerns being sufficient for standing for environment-protection-minded individuals and groups.[29] This is due to Lord Hope recognising the public interest characteristics of the environment.[30] The environment is a matter of general, rather than individual, concern but will require a public-minded person or organisation to bring proceedings to ensure that decision-makers comply with environmental legislation.

Matthew also supports the development in *Walton v Scottish Ministers* being made by the UK Supreme Court rather than by legislation. He makes an important argument that standing is a technical aspect of judicial review litigation and access to public law remedies. He captures that point as being 'lawyer's law':[31] that is, better understood and managed by judges in judicial review cases, rather than parliaments and legislation. This point can be elaborated by reference to Justice Gibbs' discussion of reform of standing laws in *ACF* and *Onus v Alcoa*. In *ACF*, Gibbs J referred to open standing, as argued by the applicant in that case, being a large step that is more appropriate for reform by parliaments than the courts.[32] In *Onus v Alcoa*, he set out the considerations that underpin standing law that would need to be weighed and balanced in framing changes to standing principles.[33] The

[26] See also A Edgar, 'Extended Standing – Enhanced Accountability? Judicial Review of Commonwealth Environmental Decisions' (2012) 39 *Federal Law Review* 436.

[27] See also Groves, 'The Evolution and Reform of Standing in Australian Administrative Law' (n 3) 190–91.

[28] *Walton v Scottish Ministers* [2012] UKSC 44.

[29] Groves, 'Standing Outside: An Environment of Challenge and Withheld Cures' (n 3) 130.

[30] *Walton v Scottish Ministers* (n 28) [152].

[31] Groves, 'Standing Outside: An Environment of Challenge and Withheld Cures' (n 3) 129.

[32] *ACF* (n 9) 528–29.

[33] *Onus v Alcoa* (n 16) 35.

starting point is that the rule of law suggests broad standing to ensure that laws are complied with. But balanced against this consideration are concerns regarding the need in adversarial litigation for there to be a real legal controversy and the costs to respondents of being sued. While Gibbs CJ stated that standing principles were settled in *ACF*,[34] common law principles develop incrementally, and the factors that he expressed were able, even likely, to be subsequently rebalanced.

I agree with Matthew's argument about incremental steps made by the courts rather than legislation, but not that the step to public interest standing should be limited to environmental cases. However, it is not necessary for Australian courts to adopt the analysis in *Walton v Scottish Ministers* to make this reform. I will argue that *North Coast* is an important incremental step for the recognition of public interest standing in Australia. It engages deeply with *ACF* and *Onus v Alcoa* and provides a plausible analysis for acceptance of the principles in those cases accommodating standing for public interest groups, not only with environment protection interests but also public interest groups generally.

## III. North Coast Environment Council – Primary Features and Potential Difficulties

In this section I examine the primary elements of Sackville J's reasoning in the *North Coast* case and then aspects of the case that are thought to make it not a good basis for reform of standing law.[35] The applicant was an environmental organisation with no personal interest affected by the administrative decision which was being challenged. The applicant sought reasons under the Administrative Decisions (Judicial Review) Act 1977 (Cth) for the minister's decision under the Export Control (Unprocessed Wood) Regulations 1986 (Cth) and its interaction with the Environment Protection (Impact of Proposals) Act 1974 (Cth). Sackville J determined that the environmental organisation had standing.

In the critical part of his analysis in the *North Coast* case, Sackville J structured his analysis by recognising the aspects of the High Court's decision in *ACF* that were insufficient for the applicant to be granted standing and then supplemented that analysis by reference to *Onus v Alcoa* to recognise that the applicant should be granted standing.

Sackville J derived five factors from *ACF*, four being recognised as insufficient for an environmental group to be granted standing. I will focus on the four insufficient factors.[36] The first was the famous point in ACF that an interest in environmental conservation is not sufficient but rather an emotional or intellectual

[34] ibid 35.

[35] For the case law on environmental groups and associations more generally, see Aronson, Groves and Weeks (n 23) 866–68, 876–78.

[36] *North Coast* (n 7) 512.

concern. The second was that an administrator's non-compliance with the law is insufficient for an applicant to be granted standing. The third and fourth were the familiar points from *ACF* that participation in a consultation process for the challenged decision and the environmental objectives of the organisation are not sufficient.

Sackville J recognised that the applicant could not rely only on these issues, but it had provided evidence of additional factors that needed to be considered. He prefaced his analysis of these factors by reference to Stephen J's emphasis in *Onus v Alcoa* on the 'closeness of its relationship' to the subject matter of the decision.[37] The applicant put forward additional factors, and Sackville J boiled them down to the five he found to be most significant:[38]

1. The applicant was the peak environmental organisation for a region of New South Wales with 44 other environmental groups as its members.
2. It had been recognised by the Commonwealth Government due to the grants it had received.
3. It had been recognised by the New South Wales Government as an appropriate representative for environmental matters through membership of advisory committees.
4. It had held conferences and co-ordinated projects on environmental issues and received Commonwealth funding to conduct them.
5. It had contributed to forestry management decision-making, the particular aspect of environmental protection relevant in the case.

After considering the defendant's arguments that these factors were less significant than in earlier cases and analysing the factors in detail, Sackville J determined that the applicant had a special interest that was 'more than an intellectual or emotional concern'.[39] He concluded by emphasising that no concern had been raised to doubt the applicant's capacity to represent the environment in litigation, and it was well-placed to advocate an environmental conservation perspective to counter the economic interest of the forestry business which had applied for a licence to export woodchips.[40]

The final aspect of Sackville J's reasoning to highlight is that he added that it was important to recognise that the connection between the applicant's interests, supported by the evidence provided by the applicant, was consistent with the legislation that was applicable in the case. He stated that the public interest reflected in the Administrative Decisions (Judicial Review) Act 1977 (Cth) and the Environment Protection (Impact of Proposals) Act 1974 (Cth), was 'entirely compatible' with the applicant's interests. Those Acts operated together to enable

[37] ibid 512 referring to *Onus v Alcoa* (n 16) 42.
[38] ibid 512–13.
[39] ibid 513–14.
[40] ibid 514.

access to the reasons for decisions that potentially had adverse environmental impacts.[41]

While we will see that much has been made of Sackville J's five factors that provided the basis for his finding the applicant had standing, there were additional general principles that framed those factors. The two principles were expressed in *Onus v Alcoa*. The first was Stephen J's point about the special interest test being necessarily vague and that it requires courts to assess the closeness of the applicant's concern with the subject matter of the litigation. The information provided by the applicant and distilled in Sackville J's five factors was analysed by Sackville J as evidence supporting the closeness assessment drawn from Stephen J's judgment in *Onus v Alcoa*. Understood in this way, Sackville J's five factors should not be regarded as criteria for public interest group standing. They were a summary of evidence relevant to the closeness assessment drawn from Stephen J's judgment in *Onus v Alcoa*.

The second principle from *Onus v Alcoa* was Brennan J's analysis of standing law being extended to adapt to modern legislation being designed to protect or enhance 'non-material' interests, such as environmental protection.[42] Brennan J emphasised that applicants with interests consistent with the public interest protected by these kinds of Act should be accepted to have standing. While Brennan J's analysis was not expressly drawn on when Sackville J made his primary findings, it was quoted earlier in the judgment[43] and thus added to the conceptual framework applied to the closeness assessment. In particular, this aspect of the conceptual framework was relevant when Sackville J recognised the connection between the applicant's activities and interests and the public interest reflected in the relevant Acts.

There is an additional point that should be highlighted in Sackville J's judgment that was not expressly drawn from *Onus v Alcoa*. It was the significance of his recognition of the applicant's capacity to participate in the litigation. I will argue in Part IV.C that this aspect of Sackville J's reasoning is an important aspect of public interest group standing.

Accordingly, the important features of Sackville J's reasoning can be understood as being his careful avoidance of giving weight to the factors that were insufficient in *ACF*, his heavy emphasis on Stephen J's closeness assessment drawn from *Onus v Alcoa*, and the implied reliance on Brennan J's analysis in *Onus v Alcoa* of the significance of modern legislation for the law of standing. Included in all of this was Sackville J's suggestion that the applicant's capacity to represent the relevant public interest in litigation underpins the closeness assessment when the applicant is a public interest group.

Sackville J's judgment has been subjected to criticism, most of which has focused on the five factors that he examined to determine standing. For example,

[41] ibid 515.
[42] *Onus v Alcoa* (n 16) 73.
[43] *North Coast* (n 7) 506.

Lockhart J in *Right to Life v Secretary, Department of Human Services and Health*[44] doubted the significance of an applicant's recognition by government. Matthew Groves has also criticised the *North Coast* case and its application in subsequent cases. He argues that while the multi-factor analysis enables a holistic assessment, it lacks a general principle, and so it is uncertain how the holistic assessment is to be made and, in particular, how the factors are to be weighed.[45] Importantly, however, Matthew also recognises that this vagueness can be linked back to *Onus v Alcoa* and particularly *ACF*, rather than simply to *North Coast*.[46]

This is an important feature of Matthew's research on standing law. He refers to standing law, in particular in the analysis of UK cases, as involving 'rampant judicial discretion'[47] – which also seems relevant to his analysis of Australian standing law. The problem Matthew identifies with such vagueness is that it raises rule of law concerns.[48] Yet the *North Coast* approach continues to be applied in more recent cases, both accepting and not accepting interest groups' standing and usually without any criticism.[49]

I agree with Matthew that the *North Coast* approach includes vagueness that replicates some of the difficulties in *ACF* and *Onus v Alcoa*. However, I think it is important to recognise the incremental step it makes from those cases in recognising public interest group standing and that, as I argue in the next section, it provides the conceptual framework for developing clearer principles.

## IV. Elaborating the Closeness Assessment

In this part of the chapter, I argue that courts can, and should, move from the vagueness of the closeness assessment to a more structured judicial assessment for determining public interest group standing by clarifying the principles and considerations that are relevant. This is an important step to move beyond the arbitrariness that Matthew highlights in his analysis. I also argue that while *North Coast* involved an environmental group, and they are the most common type of interest group in these cases, the principles and considerations for public interest

[44] *Right to Life v Secretary, Department of Human Services and Health* (1995) 56 FCR 50, 67.

[45] Groves, 'The Evolution and Reform of Standing in Australian Administrative Law' (n 3) 176–77; Groves, 'Standing Outside: An Environment of Challenge and Withheld Cures' (n 3) 121–23.

[46] Groves, 'Standing Outside: An Environment of Challenge and Withheld Cures' (n 3) 123.

[47] Groves, 'The Evolution and Reform of Standing in Australian Administrative Law' (n 3) 198; Groves, 'Standing Outside: An Environment of Challenge and Withheld Cures' (n 3) 125, citing C Harlow and R Rawlings, *Law and Administration*, 3rd edn (Cambridge, Cambridge University Press, 2009) 697.

[48] Groves, 'The Evolution and Reform of Standing in Australian Administrative Law' (n 3) 198.

[49] See, eg, *Boomerang & Blueys Residents Group Inc v New South Wales Minister for the Environment, Heritage and Local Government and MidCoast Council (No 2)* [2019] NSWLEC 202 [78], [85]–[94]; *VicForests v Kinglake Friends of the Forest* [2021] VSCA 195 [69]–[79], [90], [95]; *People of the Small Town of Hawkesdale Inc v Minister for Planning* (2022) 71 VR 550, 566–71 [61]–[85]; *North East Forest Alliance Incorporated (INC1601738) v Forestry Corporation of NSW* [2023] NSWLEC 124 [131].

standing are generally applicable as administrative law principles and, as such, are dependent on the particular statutory scheme.

The most important point to recognise in Sackville J's reasoning in *North Coast* is his reliance on Stephen J's closeness principle from *Onus v Alcoa*. That was the starting point and the concept that influenced his assessment of the evidence provided to the court regarding the public interest group in the case. Interpreting Sackville J's analysis in this way shifts attention from the five factors that supported the interest group's standing in *North Coast*, at least in terms of principle. As we have seen, the five factors were not principles or mandatory considerations but a summary of persuasive evidence of the interest group's closeness to the subject matter of the administrative action being challenged.

## A. Excluding Purely Moral or Political Interests

The first consideration that can elaborate on the closeness principle did not feature expressly in *North Coast* but may be implied from Sackville J's reliance on the closeness principle from *Onus v Alcoa* and his assessment of the applicant's activities. The elaboration is by reference to the function of the closeness principle in the overall law of standing. That is, for the court to be confident that the interest group applicant has interests beyond the kind of political interests and concerns that any person could have, which is the point that raised concerns in *ACF*. The elaborated closeness principle enables courts to examine the track record of the public interest group through evidence of its activities within the particular regulatory area. Interest groups with track records of activities commonly engage with governments in relation to legal developments and administrative decisions. They are likely to have highly developed understandings of the legislative framework and how it has been administered. This not only distinguishes them from the political interests that anyone can have but also makes them well-placed as a judicial review litigant.

When understood in this way, the special interest test for standing in Australian law can be seen to have two aspects. When an applicant's personal interests are affected by the decision, standing is relatively easy to establish. There is little need to assess the applicant's activities in any detail or the consistency of their interests with the public interest protected by the relevant statutory framework. However, it is different when the applicant is a public interest group. The consistency of the applicant's interests with the public interest reflected in the statutory framework becomes very important, and so does the depth of its activities in the particular regulatory context. When these matters are established, standing can be accepted on clear and principled grounds. This extension of standing enables appropriate representatives of the public interest to bring proceedings to protect a matter of public interest reflected in the Act.

The public interest group applicant's interests in *ACF* were characterised as being interests that any person could have, despite the evidence it provided to the High Court of its large membership, recognition by government through receiving grants, and its actions in influencing national environmental policy.[50] This was, importantly, prior to the elaboration of the special interest test provided soon after in Stephen J's closeness analysis in *Onus v Alcoa*.

A better, clearer example of an interest group being excluded for its purely moral and political interests is the Full Court of the Federal Court's decision in *Right to Life v Secretary, Department of Human Services and Health*.[51] The applicant in that case sought to challenge the respondent's decisions to permit health researchers to import and trial the drug mifepristone as an emergency post-coital contraception enabling termination of early pregnancy. The decisions were made under the Therapeutic Goods Act 1989 (Cth) and associated regulations. In separate judgments, Lockhart and Beaumont JJ determined that the applicant did not have standing. Its objects are related to promoting the right to life generally, including against abortion, and by conducting educational programmes directed at legislators making public policy.[52] The Court was provided no evidence of research activities or any other activities that it had carried out, and for Beaumont J, this meant that it could not be granted standing.[53]

Lockhart J focused more in his primary findings on the 'emotional and intellectual' terminology in *ACF*. He characterised the applicant's interest in this manner after referring to its objects. He referred to the importance of free speech in our democratic society, suggesting that there is no restriction for an association with such interests contributing to political discussion. However, standing law requires something more than 'a mere emotional attachment or intellectual pursuit or satisfaction'.[54] He referred to debates about abortion as involving 'deep moral and political questions' that are questions 'any person has as an ordinary member of the public'. He concluded that its interests were 'only an intellectual, philosophical and emotional concern'.[55]

Justice Lockhart included an additional factor in his reasoning. It was that the applicant's interests were unrelated to the public interest characteristics of the Therapeutic Goods regulatory scheme. That scheme related to the 'quality and safety and efficacy' of therapeutic goods.[56] The applicant's interests were simply not addressed in the Act or regulations. Lockhart J referred to this lack of consistency between the applicant's interests and the regulatory scheme as being a 'powerful reason' against the applicant having standing.

The reasoning of the two judges who addressed the standing issue in *Right to Life* goes a long way to elaborate on the 'emotional or intellectual concerns' terminology in *ACF*. Justice Lockhart's reasoning suggests it is primarily aimed at applicants that only have moral or political interests. The applicant's purely moral

[50] *ACF* (n 9) 519.
[51] *Right to Life* (n 44).
[52] ibid 67, 70.
[53] ibid 80–1.
[54] ibid 67–68.
[55] ibid 68.
[56] ibid 68.

and political interest was confirmed by the inconsistency between its interests and the public interest reflected in the Act, as recognised by Lockhart J. Although less clearly stated by Beaumont J in his judgment, he implied that the applicant's lack of research or other activities supported the view that it had purely moral and political concerns.

In the development of the principles underpinning the special interest test and closeness assessment, it is arguable that the emotional and intellectual interest concerns concept remains influential, particularly if relabelled with the more meaningful terminology of 'purely moral and political concerns'. If open standing is not to be accepted and the special interest test is to remain operative, there needs to be a way of distinguishing general from special interests. Purely moral and political concerns, as the *Right to Life* case highlights, are general concerns – concerns that any person in the community is likely to have a view. Accordingly, there are many cases that treat such interests as not sufficient for standing.[57] As Lockhart J suggested, such concerns are suited to advocacy through political institutions rather than the courts.

## B. Public Interest Reflected in the Act

Sackville J in the *North Coast* case referred to the applicant's interests being 'far more than mere intellectual or emotional concerns'[58] and, as we have seen, he did this by drawing on the closeness assessment from Stephen J's judgment in *Onus v Alcoa* to examine the applicant's activities. One of the ways this was assessed by Sackville J was by examining the applicant's interests by reference to the public interest reflected in the Act that grants decision-making or regulation-making powers to the administrator.[59] In *North Coast*, Sackville J conducted this analysis very briefly in the closing stages of his judgment under the heading 'Other cases', suggesting that it was an afterthought. However, this analysis should be regarded as a critical feature of public interest standing.

The analysis of an interest group's activities by reference to the public interest reflected in the Act supports the recognition of the *North Coast* case being the basis for public interest standing generally, rather than limited to environmental groups. Brennan J's analysis in *Onus v Alcoa* makes clear that modern legislation relating to matters such as the environment, heritage and culture (and can be extended to other matters such as animal welfare[60] and consumer protection[61]) are designed to preserve and protect matters beyond property and financial interests that have

[57] Aronson, Groves and Weeks (n 23) 859.
[58] *North Coast* (n 7) 513–4.
[59] ibid 514–5.
[60] Eg, *Animals' Angels eV v Secretary, Department of Agriculture* (2014) 228 FCR 35, 67 [105], 71 [119].
[61] Eg, the consumer protection organisation in *United States Tobacco Company v Minister For Consumer Affairs* (1988) 20 FCR 520 whose standing was accepted but due to its participation in administrative conference.

been the traditional basis for standing. While environmental organisations are the most common form of interest group whose standing is tested in the cases, the *North Coast* analysis is a general test, based on the elaboration of the closeness assessment in *Onus v Alcoa* and an assessment of the consistency of the applicant's interests with the public interest reflected in the Act.

It is also important that in *North Coast* Sackville J referred to the applicant's *interests* being consistent with the public interest protected or enhanced by the relevant Acts rather than its *objects* as an organisation being consistent. This circumvents Gibbs J's point in *ACF* that an organisation's objects being consistent with the relevant Act is insufficient for standing. Sackville J's reasoning can be interpreted as shifting the analysis to a more concrete register in which the applicant's interests are assessed by reference to its activities rather than the more abstract reference to its formal objects as an organisation. Brennan J in *Onus v Alcoa* also used the language of interests being consistent with the public interest characteristics of the Act,[62] but that may simply have been because the applicants in that case were individuals rather than an association.

It may be thought that the High Court's decision in *Argos Pty Ltd v Corbell, Minister for the Environment and Sustainable Development*[63] is not consistent with this reliance on the public interest reflected in an Act. French CJ and Keane J doubted the relevance of any assessment of consistency of the applicant's interests with the scope and purpose of the Act granting the powers for the decision that was challenged, particularly when the case was brought under the Administrative Decisions (Judicial Review) Act 1979 (Cth). However, their Honours' analysis can be distinguished from cases involving public interest groups.

The issue in the High Court in the *Argos* case was whether the lower courts were correct to determine that the applicant, a company with supermarket businesses, had standing under the Australian Capital Territory version of the Administrative Decisions (Judicial Review) Act to challenge a decision made to approve a development including a supermarket on land near the applicant's supermarkets. In standing law practice such cases are referred to as business competitor cases. The lower courts refused standing on the basis that the applicant's business interests were unrelated to the purposes of land use planning legislation. However, the High Court allowed the appeal. French CJ and Keane J decided the case simply on the basis that the applicant's direct business interests were affected.[64] The argument that standing is to be determined by reference to the scope and purpose of the relevant legislation was not accepted.

While the other judges agreed with French CJ and Keane J in regard to the result, their reasoning was different. Nevertheless, it is worthwhile examining French CJ and Keane J's analysis, as it makes an important point for Australian

[62] *Onus v Alcoa* (n 16) 77.

[63] *Argos Pty Ltd v Corbell, Minister for the Environment and Sustainable Development* (2014) 254 CLR 394.

[64] ibid 405 [29], 408–409 [40].

standing law. It is that when an applicant's property or financial interests are affected by the administrative decision they seek to challenge, their standing will likely be accepted without any need for further analysis. It is the kind of material interest that is accepted as being the basis for standing.

French CJ and Keane J's reasoning in *Argos* is not relevant to the different kinds of issues that arise when public interest groups seek standing. The reason standing is controversial for public interest groups is because their property and financial interests are not affected by the administrator's decision. In the context of public interest group standing, the consistency of the applicant's interests with the public interest characteristics of the Act becomes a critical factor.

As we have just seen in relation to *Right to Life*, the *inconsistency* of the applicant's interests with the Therapeutic Goods Act and Regulations was regarded as a 'powerful reason' to refuse standing. It was a strong indication that the applicant's interests were of a purely moral and political character. On the other hand, the *consistency* of the applicant's interests with the public interest reflected in the Act in *North Coast* was an indication that it should be granted standing. While this was not the primary consideration for Sackville J, it was relevant and supported the conclusion that he made.

The consistency of the applicant's interests with the public interest reflected in the relevant Act is accordingly an important way of elaborating the closeness assessment. The public interest characteristics of the Act can be used as one factor that helps to distinguish applicants having moral and political interests that any person could have from applicants whose interests are associated with the public interest reflected in the relevant regulatory scheme. Moreover, the public interest protected by the relevant Act is obviously relevant to the subject matter of decisions being challenged in judicial review proceedings. Judicial review of administrative action nearly always involves decisions made under an Act and administrative law often draws on the scope and purposes of an Act to add substance to the principles for determining whether the administrator made a legal error – such as the matters that the administrator must or cannot consider, the operation of procedural fairness, etc. In the context of elaborating the closeness assessment in standing law, reference to the public interest characteristics of the Act is equally relevant as a matter of statutory context.

It is important to highlight that this approach to public interest standing, primarily drawn from Brennan J in *Onus v Alcoa* and Sackville J in *North Coast*, is designed to apply generally to standing law, rather than to indigenous heritage protection legislation or environment protection legislation, as was relevant in those cases. General application is consistent with the administrative law principles applying to all Acts conferring administrative powers and the principles being adapted to Acts in particular cases. In *Onus v Alcoa* and *North Coast*, the public interest to be protected was clear in the titles of the legislation – the Archaeological and Aboriginal Relics Preservation Act 1972 (Vic) and the Environment Protection (Impact of Proposals) Act 1974 (Cth). The applicant's connection in each case with the public interest characteristics of the Acts was easy to see. But that is not necessarily the case. Other Acts may not be designed to protect or enhance such clear public interests, or they may be designed to balance different, conflicting aspects of the public interest. In such cases, it is likely to be harder to characterise an aspect of the public interest that the Act is designed to protect or enhance, making it difficult for applicants to gain public interest standing. The point is that public interest standing does not need to be limited to decision-making under environmental protection legislation. The principles in *Onus v Alcoa* and *North Coast* enable it to extend to any Act that is designed to protect aspects of the public interest.

## C. Capacity to Litigate

The second consideration that should elaborate the closeness assessment is the organisation's capacity to litigate, a point made by Sackville J in *North Coast*. An organisation with a substantial track record of research and policy engagement activities that are consistent with the public interest reflected in the relevant Act helps to ensure they are not, in Gibbs J's terminology, 'busybodies and cranks and persons actuated by malice' that abuse legal processes.[65] While applicants with personal interests affected by a decision have an obvious motivation to bring a judicial review challenge, for public interest group applicants the strong track record should inform their decision as to whether it is appropriate or necessary to challenge a decision. They are well-placed to assess the lack of, or weak, protection of the relevant aspect of the public interest reflected in an Act. And such a track record should also help to ensure that the applicant is well-placed to provide evidence and make legal arguments relevant to the decision being challenged.

The latter point has been made in the cases. For example, Wilcox J referred to it in *Ogle v Strickland*,[66] a case in which two priests brought proceedings challenging a decision of the Censorship Board under the Customs (Cinematograph Films) Regulations 1956 (Cth) that a film was not blasphemous. The Full Court of the Federal Court accepted that the priests' vocation supported their standing to challenge a censorship decision.[67] In coming to that conclusion, Wilcox J addressed the concern that public interest-focused applicants will inadequately represent the issues to the court.[68] Justice Wilcox dismissed the concern. He cited ten cases brought by public interest-focused applicants. He pointed out that the applicants were successful in half of the ten cases and in 'all of them the issues were fully and competently presented on behalf of the plaintiff'.[69] Wilcox J's point was that public interest groups do not necessarily lack the capacity to litigate effectively.

[65] *Onus v Alcoa* (n 16) 35.
[66] *Ogle v Strickland* (1987) 13 FCR 306.
[67] ibid 320, 324–25.
[68] ibid 323.
[69] ibid 324.

The courts in the United Kingdom have also accepted standing for public interest groups to bring judicial review litigation. One reason that this has been accepted is that their expertise in the particular regulatory context is likely to support litigation processes. The commonly referred to case for this point is *R v Inspectorate of Pollution; Ex Parte Greenpeace.*[70] Greenpeace brought proceedings to challenge the authorisation of radioactive waste discharges from a nuclear reprocessing plant. Justice Otton accepted that Greenpeace had standing.[71] After referring to the number of supporters (presumably financial), its environmental protection objects, and its recognition by United Nations bodies, he referred to its experience in environmental matters and access to scientific and technological experts, enabling it to 'mount a carefully selected, focused, relevant and well-argued challenge'.[72]

Justice Otton made an important point in the *Greenpeace* case. The evidence of a group's membership and support, recognition by government, and activities (as examined by Sackville J in *North Coast*) are important for the court to be confident that the applicant has the capacity to litigate effectively. Evidence of those matters supports the experience and expertise of the public interest group applicant to litigate. While the applicant's capacity to litigate was only briefly mentioned by Sackville J in *North Coast*, it is important to recognise as a matter of principle that it provides a reason for the court's assessment of the scale of the interest group's membership, its involvement in policy development, and research in the particular regulatory area.

The public interest standing cases determined after *North Coast* demonstrate the significance of the capacity to litigate as a guiding concept in standing law and that it is to be determined by reference to the interest group applicant's activities. In *The People of the Small Town of Hawkesdale Inc v Minister For Planning*, ('*Town of Hawkesdale*')[73] the primary issue for the Victorian Court of Appeal was whether the applicant should not have standing due to having conducted no relevant activities.[74] The applicant had been established by eight people from Hawkesdale to oppose a wind farm that had approval in the locality, to correspond with the operators of the wind farm, and to appoint legal representatives and initiate legal proceedings against the operator of the wind farm.[75] The association was established after the administrative decision being challenged had been made.[76]

The trial judge made findings of fact that the association had conducted no activities other than the commencement of the proceedings,[77] and the Victorian

[70] *R v Inspectorate of Pollution; Ex Parte Greenpeace* [1994] 4 All ER 329.
[71] ibid 351.
[72] ibid 350.
[73] *The People of the Small Town of Hawkesdale Inc v Minister For Planning* (2022) 71 VR 550.
[74] ibid 566 [62].
[75] ibid 569 [76].
[76] ibid 566 [65].
[77] ibid 563 [48].

Court of Appeal accepted those findings.[78] The Court of Appeal found the circumstances of the case to be different from two Western Australian cases[79] in which standing was accepted where public interest groups incorporated as associations had strong track records of activities. In one of the Western Australian cases, the association had been recently incorporated but had operated as an unincorporated association for many years.[80] One reason for standing being denied in the *Town of Hawkesdale* case was, therefore, the association's lack of any relevant activities.

While the Court of Appeal in the *Town of Hawkesdale* case did not offer any explanation of why the association's lack of relevant activities is a problem for standing, it seems obvious that it raises doubts over its capacity to litigate. A public interest group without a track record of activities raises doubts over its experience and expertise in contributing to decisions made in the regulatory context. Such doubts will raise concerns about its capacity to litigate. This highlights the importance of this aspect of standing, going beyond the assessment of the consistency of the applicant's interests with the public interest reflected in the relevant statutory scheme. While the applicant in the *Town of Hawkesdale* case may have been able to demonstrate the consistency of its interests in protecting the environment in its town, its lack of activities meant there were doubts over its capacity to litigate. Accordingly, there was good reason for standing to be denied.

## V. Conclusion

Sackville J's analysis in *North Coast* can be interpreted as drawing together what previously looked like disparate threads of the special interest test for standing. It involved plausible incremental developments of the High Court's decisions in *ACF* and *Onus v Alcoa*. It also drew on the earlier Federal Court decision in *ACF v Minister for Resources*,[81] a decision similar to *North Coast* but lacking Sackville J's depth of analysis.[82] Numerous cases have since referred to and applied *North Coast*, and it has taken on the status of an influential trial judge decision of the Federal Court for the law of standing.

Since the *North Coast* case, it is appropriate to recognise that the special interest test applies in two separate contexts for applicants seeking to challenge administrative decisions that affect the applicant, but the decision is not directed expressly to them.

The first context is when the applicant has an individual, personal interest that is affected by the government action. These have been referred to as material

[78] ibid 569 [76].

[79] *Helena Valley/Boya Association (Inc) v State Planning Commission* (1990) 2 WAR 422; *Re MacTiernan; Ex parte Coogee Coastal Action Coalition Inc* (2005) 30 WAR 138.

[80] *Town of Hawkesdale* (n 73) 567–69 [70]–[73].

[81] *ACF v Minister for Resources* (1989) 19 ALD 70.

[82] *North Coast* (n 7) 510–11.

interests in the cases and include when the applicant's property or financial interests are affected, as in the *Argos* case examined in Part IV.B. *Onus v Alcoa* highlights that such interests can be extended to a person's cultural and spiritual interests. Standing is very likely to be accepted and uncontroversial in such cases.

The second context is when the applicant is bringing proceedings to protect public interests. The *North Coast* case indicates that public interest groups can be granted standing and that the closeness assessment becomes critical to determine that the applicant has more than a purely moral and political interest in the decision or regulation being challenged. This is conducted by an assessment of the public interest group's track record of relevant activities. While in many cases the track record assessment seems to be conducted without any guiding principle, I have argued in this chapter that the track record assessment is to ensure that the applicant's interests, demonstrated through its activities, align with the public interest reflected in the relevant Act and demonstrate its expertise and experience in the regulatory area sufficient to accept its capacity to litigate.

In a series of articles in the last ten years, Matthew has grappled with the difficulties of public interest standing and put these important issues for judicial review of administrative action onto the scholarly agenda. The most relevant for this article is his concern that standing law in Australia is too vague and uncertain, risking arbitrariness. I agree with that assessment and the risks involved, and I hope to have shown that revising the key features of the *North Coast* case provides the starting points for a more principled judicial assessment.

# 5

# What is the Legal Status of Statutory Interpretation in Australia and Why does it Matter Anyway?

DAN MEAGHER*

## I. Introduction

This chapter seeks to explore an issue which at first blush may appear of theoretical or academic interest only – what is the legal status of statutory interpretation as undertaken by courts in Australia? As Julian Murphy has observed, the development of common law is informed by – indeed must conform to[1] – the Australian Constitution, so 'it may not matter a great deal whether the law of statutory interpretation is conceived of as pure "common law", workings out of Chapter III judicial power, or something in between'.[2] That is certainly true, so long as the body of interpretive rules, principles and presumptions used by the courts to determine the legal meaning of statutes remain stable and accepted by the judicial and political arms of government. Indeed, the notion that the precise legal status of statutory interpretation may not really matter has an echo of the High Court's pragmatic view in *Plaintiff S10* of the ultra vires debate in administrative law:

> It is in this sense that one may state that 'the common law' will usually imply, as a matter of statutory interpretation, a condition that a power conferred by statute upon the executive branch be exercised with procedural fairness to those whose interests may be adversely affected by the exercise of that power. If the matter is understood in that

* My thanks are due to Lisa Burton Crawford and Rosalind Dixon for organising the Principle of Legality Workshop held on 16 August 2024 at the University of Sydney Law School where an earlier version of this chapter was presented. Thanks also to Mark Aronson, Jacinta Dharmananda, Peter Gerangelos, Emily Hammond, Luciana Morón, Jason Varuhas and Greg Weeks for their very helpful comments and suggestions on that earlier version.

[1] *Lange v Australian Broadcasting Corporation* (1997) 189 CLR 520, 566 (per curium).

[2] JR Murphy, 'Constitutionally Protective Statutory Interpretation' (PhD Thesis, University of Melbourne, 2022) 188.

> way, a debate whether procedural fairness is to be identified as a common law duty or an implication from statute proceeds upon a false dichotomy and is unproductive.[3]

I suspect this common-sense pragmatism – where theory is no substitute for the analytical rigour of case law and doctrine and the accumulated wisdom they represent – is one which Matthew Groves would wholeheartedly support. So much is apparent from the opening salvo in Matthew's chapter in *Interpreting Executive Power*, the excellent recent collection edited by Janina Boughey and Lisa Burton Crawford: 'I am no fan of legal or other philosophy, but even I cannot ignore the greatest American thinker of our time – Homer J Simpson. Among his many piercing thoughts on life was the rhetorical question 'donuts. Is there anything they can't do?'[4]

To address an issue that may attract the sobriquet of 'purely academic interest only' may, then, seem misplaced in a volume to honour Matthew's intellectual legacy! Be that as it may, I hope to demonstrate that the legal status of statutory interpretation is worthy of analysis and may prove of practical use also.

I have always had an interest in the issue due to its prominence in the United States. There, the formal absence of federal common law has attracted scholarly interest as to the legal basis of judicially developed interpretive principles.[5] And, relatedly, the extent to which Congress could provide for legislated interpretive directives compatibly with the strict separation of judicial power established by the United States Constitution.[6] With a unified system of common law in Australia, we do not have the American jurisprudential anxiety regarding the legal status of statutory interpretation. But the Australian Constitution did consciously adopt an American-style separation of powers. And, most relevantly for present purposes, the separation of judicial power from that of the political arms of government is (like in the United States) particularly strict. This constitutional parallel gives the issue a salience in the Australian context which is presently underexplored.[7]

[3] *Plaintiff S10/2011 v Minister for Immigration and Citizenship* (2012) 246 CLR 636, 666 (Gummow, Hayne, Crennan and Bell JJ) (footnote omitted) ('*Plaintiff S10*').

[4] M Groves, 'The Return of the (Almost) Absolute Statutory Discretion' in J Boughey and L Burton Crawford (eds), *Interpreting Executive Power* (Annandale, The Federation Press, 2020) 129 where the reference was made regarding the explanation of discretion by reference to donuts offered by R Dworkin in *Taking Rights Seriously* (Cambridge, MA, Harvard University Press, 1977).

[5] See, eg, A Gluck, 'Intersystemic Statutory Interpretation: Methodology as 'Law' and the *Erie* Doctrine' (2011) 120 *Yale Law Journal* 1898.

[6] See, eg, LD Jellum, "Which is to be Master,' The Judiciary or the Legislature? When Statutory Directives Violate Separation of Powers' (2009) 56 *UCLA Law Review* 837; NQ Rosencrantz, 'Federal Rules of Statutory Interpretation' (2002) 115 *Harvard Law Review* 2085.

[7] But see J Basten, *Constitutional Dimensions of Statutory Interpretation* (Conference Paper, University of Melbourne Law School, 24 July 2015); P Emerton and LB Crawford, 'Statutory Meaning without Parliamentary Intention: Defending the High Court's 'Alternative Approach' to Statutory Interpretation' in LB Crawford, P Emerton and D Smith, *Law Under a Democratic Constitution: Essays in Honour of Jeffrey Goldsworthy* (Oxford, Hart Publishing, 2019); The Hon M Kirby AC, 'The Never-Ending Challenge of Drafting and Interpreting Statutes – A Meditation on the Career of John Finemore QC' (2012) 36 *Melbourne University Law Review* 140, 171–172; Murphy (n 2) 177–189;

In any event, what prompted this chapter was a deceptively simple question asked of me by Professor Larry Alexander at a Faculty seminar at the University of San Diego Law School a few years ago – could Parliament abolish the principle of legality? I reflexively and (probably) unsatisfactorily answered yes. From memory my answer had two parts: As a common law principle, it was, by definition, vulnerable to abolition so long as the statute did so clearly. But even so, the courts would likely resist or work around it by creative interpretive means, just like they do when faced with seemingly watertight privative clauses. But since that seminar I have often returned to Larry's question. Once you scratch its surface, you quickly strike a number of deep-lying principles and values which, in the Australian context, find some reflection and recognition in the Constitution. That being so, the 'answer' to Larry's question is far more difficult and interesting than I first realised when I gave my perfunctory answer. It requires, in my view, giving serious consideration to the legal status of the interpretive principles developed (over centuries) and applied by the courts to determine the legal meaning of statutes to facilitate the resolution of legal disputes. That is the aim of my chapter. To do so, I will consider a series of real and hypothetical legislated interpretive directives, including, of course, one which seeks to abolish the principle of legality. As to the latter, my jurisprudential and political hope is that it remains a hypothetical. But the trajectory and content of legislative activity in two areas of core concern to Matthew's scholarship – migration law and prison discipline – suggest the future possibility of such a provision.

The chapter proceeds as follows. Part II will outline those existing judicial statements on (and academic consideration of) the legal status of statutory interpretation. This will include those on the principle of legality specifically and the significance of the High Court's enigmatic proposition in *Zheng* that 'the preferred construction by the court of the statute in question is reached by the application of rules of interpretation accepted by all arms of government in the system of representative democracy'.[8] Building on the High Court's existing Chapter III jurisprudence, Part III will offer a constitutional proposition regarding judicially-developed interpretive principles and presumptions which are applied to facilitate the exercise of judicial power. The compatibility with that proposition of a spectrum of legislative interpretive directives – some real, others hypothetical – will be the focus of Part IV. The analysis undertaken in this Part will shed important light on the scope and rationale of the constitutional proposition offered and help to clarify the legal status of statutory interpretation in Australia. Part V concludes.

D Smith, 'Is the High Court Mistaken About the Aim of Statutory Interpretation' (2016) 44 *Federal Law Review* 227, 245–249.

[8] *Zheng v Cai* (2009) 239 CLR 446, 455–456 (French CJ, Gummow, Crennan, Kiefel and Bell JJ) ('*Zheng*').

## II. Judicial Statements on the Legal Status of Statutory Interpretation

In *Plaintiff S10*, the following proposition was made in the joint judgment of Gummow, Hayne, Crennan and Bell JJ regarding the legal status of statutory interpretation in Australia:

> The principles and presumptions of statutory construction which are applied by Australian courts, to the extent to which they are not qualified or displaced by an applicable interpretation Act, are part of the common law. In Australia, they are the product of what in *Zheng v Cai* was identified as the interaction between the three branches of government established by the Constitution. These principles and presumptions do not have the rigidity of constitutionally prescribed norms, as is indicated by the operation of interpretation statutes, but they do reflect the operation of the constitutional structure in the sense described above.[9]

In terms of legal status, the proposition is clear – it's common law; and as such, the relevant principles and presumptions (judicially-developed and applied) can be 'qualified or displaced' by statute.[10] But what of the references to the Constitution and 'constitutional structure'? Does this suggest a higher, maybe quasi-constitutional status for these interpretive tools? The applicable statement in *Zheng* to which the High Court refers said 'judicial findings as to legislative intention are an expression of the constitutional relationship between the arms of government with respect to the making, interpretation and application of laws'.[11] That specific proposition, though controversial,[12] may be unremarkable in general terms as to the status of statutory interpretation. It may simply posit that the relevant principles and presumptions perform, necessarily, a small 'c' constitutional function in fixing the legal meaning of statutes. Those statutes are the final product of another arm of government. They are made by a democratically elected Parliament through an often slow, deliberative and constitutionally mandated process of bicameralism. That too is significant for the nature and permissible scope of judicial interpretation. It is, however, the constitutional duty of the executive arm of government to secure the administration of those statutes. This may be the interaction to which the High Court refers and the 'constitutional' role that statutory interpretation performs within it. As French CJ observed in *Momcilovic*, '[t]he common law in its application to the interpretation of statutes helps to define the boundaries between the judicial and legislative functions. That is a reflection

[9] *Plaintiff S10* (n 3) 666 (footnote omitted). It might reasonably be argued that this statement (made in 2012) accepts the validity of the Acts Interpretation Act 1901 (Cth) including, most importantly, ss 15AA and AB. The analysis undertaken in Part IV.B below regarding s 15AA and AB supports this view. My thanks to Mark Aronson for this point.

[10] *SAS Trustee Corporation v Miles* (2018) 265 CLR 137, 162 (Edelman J).

[11] *Zheng* (n 8) 455 (French CJ, Gummow, Crennan, Kiefel and Bell JJ).

[12] See R Ekins and J Goldsworthy, 'The Reality and Indispensability of Legislative Intentions' (2014) 36 *Sydney Law Review* 39.

of its character as 'the ultimate constitutional foundation in Australia'.[13] Patrick Emerton and Lisa Burton Crawford, however, have offered a more sophisticated and substantive account as to the interpretive significance of the 'constitutional structure' reference in *Zheng*.

> [I]f interpretive principles do and must reflect the constitutional structure, then the fact than an interpretive principle has been accepted by the branches of government cannot demand its continued application if the courts subsequently discover that its constitutional foundation was flawed. And conversely, it must be possible for new interpretive constraints to be discovered, as our understanding of the Constitution increases, and as new forms of legislation are enacted and the distribution of powers between the legislative, executive and judiciary plays out in the context of these.[14]

The first part of this account – that interpretive principles must reflect the constitutional structure – may be considered a specific manifestation of the High Court's proposition that '[o]f necessity, the common law must conform with the Constitution'.[15] The second part, however, contemplates the articulation of 'new interpretive constraints' which are derived from the text and structure of the Constitution. This adds, arguably, a big 'c' Constitutional dimension to the small 'c' ones outlined in the first part of their account and above regarding the interaction between the three arms of government producing the relevant interpretive principles. It is this constitutional dimension of statutory interpretation in Australia that will be further explored in Part III.

Before doing so, however, what are we to make of the more enigmatic statement from *Zheng* that 'the preferred construction by the court of the statute in question is reached by the application of rules accepted by all arms of government in a system of representative democracy'?[16] In terms of *parliamentary* acceptance, Emerton and Crawford reject this proposition. They do support the High Court's denial in *Zheng* that authentic notions of legislative intention exist and are indispensable to ascertain the legal meaning of statutes.[17] But then suggest that a contradiction arises with the enigmatic statement above: 'If Parliament is incapable of holding a mental state (such as an intention) then it cannot 'know' or 'accept' a principle of statutory interpretation, either'.[18] And as to the empirical basis of that acceptance, '[i]t is also unclear what evidence could lead the Court to conclude that certain principles were known and accepted'.[19] Similarly, John Basten has observed that it 'sounds like an empirically justifiable statement, but that too may be doubted because the Court has never offered a factual basis for it'.[20]

[13] *Momcilovic v The Queen* (2011) 245 CLR 1, 46 (footnote omitted) ('*Momcilovic*').
[14] Emerton and Crawford (n 7) 61.
[15] *Lange* (n 1) 566.
[16] *Zheng* (n 8) 455–456.
[17] Emerton and Crawford (n 7) 45–52.
[18] ibid 61.
[19] ibid.
[20] Basten (n 7) 7.

If the accuracy of this important proposition may be doubted as a factual matter, what, then, is its possible significance? In Basten's view, 'it seems to be a normative statement: that is, being pronounced by the courts (or rather the High Court) it *should* be accepted by all arms of government'.[21] If so, that is important, for it suggests *ultimate* judicial control, supervision and, if need be, refinement of those principles and presumptions which are applied to determine the legal meaning of statutes.

We can see evidence of this dynamic when the High Court has revisited and refined statutory presumptions which involve the other arms of government. In *Bropho*, for example, the Court held that a strong and inflexible presumption of Crown legislative immunity could no longer be justified in Australia's contemporary (commercial and governmental) context.[22] This recognised that 'the activities of the executive government reach into almost all aspects of commercial, industrial and developmental endeavour'.[23] The Court's reasoning for this important refinement of interpretive principle was sound. But to do so, necessarily, involved a judicial reworking of a principle which had long underpinned the Crown's legal – indeed constitutional – relationship with Parliament.

More recently, the Court has done likewise regarding the presumption that a statute does not impose criminal liability on the Crown.[24] The Attorney-General of the Commonwealth had argued that the presumption should be applied to read down a Northern Territory statute 'to have no penal application in the case of a body corporate created by the legislature of a body politic other than the Northern Territory'.[25] That argument was rejected unanimously. The Court did, however, note that the reasoning for (and rationale of) the presumption 'did not emerge from a vacuum. It was founded on centuries of intellectual and jurisprudential wrangling between the Parliament and the Crown in England, from which Australia inherited its system of constitutional monarchy.'[26] But like in *Bropho*, those circumstances and (historical) considerations no longer pertained. These are significant refinements of interpretive principle (concerning the other arms of government) which, being pronounced by the High Court, *should* now be accepted by all arms of government.

This proposition may also underpin the interpretive account offered above by Emerton and Crawford regarding 'constitutional structure'. That the process and principles of statutory interpretation fall squarely within the constitutional domain of the courts and are, therefore, its primary responsibility. The origins of that proposition can probably be traced to Chief Justice Marshall's iconic statement from *Marbury v Madison*: 'It is emphatically the province and duty of the

[21] ibid (original emphasis).
[22] *Bropho v Western Australia* (1990) 171 CLR 1 ('*Bropho*').
[23] ibid 19 (Mason CJ, Deane, Dawson, Toohey, Gaudron and McHugh JJ).
[24] *Chief Executive Officer, Aboriginal Areas Protection Authority v Director of National Parks* [2024] HCA 16.
[25] ibid [6] (Gageler CJ and Beech-Jones J).
[26] ibid [261] (Jagot J).

judicial department to say what the law is. Those who apply the rule to particular cases, must of necessity expand and interpret that rule.'[27] In Australia, 'the principle of *Marbury v Madison*… is accepted as axiomatic'.[28] That principle, however, connotes the power and duty of the courts to pronounce on the compatibility or otherwise of legislation with the Constitution. Yet the discharge of that core function requires, necessarily, the court to first determine the legal meaning of the impugned statute. A statute must be interpreted before it can be judicially reviewed.

Even so, to accept that it is 'emphatically the province and duty of the judicial department to say what the law is' is not a proposition which entails a judicial monopoly on the articulation and development of the relevant interpretive principles to be applied. The permissibility (and reality) of legislative interpretive directives was, for example, expressly noted by the High Court in *Plaintiff S10*.[29] But in Australia (like the United States), the proposition does have a large 'c' constitutional dimension. Judicial power is a constitutional concept the application of which often requires judges to interpret a statute to determine the relevant legal rights and obligations.[30] That being so and '[i]f statutory interpretation is at the core of the judicial function, the Commonwealth Parliament must be constrained in its ability either to expand or diminish that function.'[31]

## III. The Constitutional Dimension of Statutory Interpretation

The High Court has long recognised that Chapter III of the Constitution established a strict separation of judicial power from the political arms of government.[32] This proposition, it said, was clear from the text and structure of the Constitution and 'could not be considered accidental to the institution of federalism'.[33] As the Privy Council noted on appeal in *Boilermakers*, 'in a federal system the absolute independence of the judiciary is the bulwark of the constitution against encroachment whether by the legislature or by the executive'.[34] The exclusivity of judicial power to Chapter III courts secured that independence. Yet the most striking

[27] *Marbury v Madison* 5 US 137 (1803) 177. In the United States this foundational separation of powers principle mandates also that the judgments of federal courts are final. Consequently, the Supreme Court has held invalid a legislative direction which required federal courts to reopen cases which they had finally stayed in the exercise of inherent jurisdiction: *Plaut v Sprendthrift Farm Inc* (1995) 514 US 211, 218–219 (Scalia J, delivering the opinion of the Court). My thanks to Peter Gerangelos for bringing this case to my attention.

[28] *Australian Communist Party v Commonwealth* (1951) 83 CLR 1, 263 (Fullagar J).

[29] *Plaintiff S10* (n 3) 666.

[30] Australian Constitution, s 71.

[31] Basten (n 7) 1.

[32] *R v Kirby; Ex parte Boilermakers' Society of Australia* (1956) 94 CLR 254 (*Boilermakers*).

[33] ibid 276 (Dixon CJ, McTiernan, Fullagar and Kitto JJ).

[34] *Attorney-General (Cth) v R; Ex parte Australian Boilermakers'* Society (1957) 95 CLR 529, 540–541.

aspect of the High Court's contemporary Chapter III jurisprudence is its willingness to explore the novel doctrinal consequences which may be said to follow from that exclusivity. The constitutional concept of 'judicial power' and what is required, institutionally and procedurally, for its exercise has informed this jurisprudence.[35] Relevantly, the Court has recognised principles of incompatibility,[36] equal justice,[37] due process,[38] and an entrenched minimum provision of judicial review.[39] These doctrinal developments (and Chapter III protections) have been extended to state and territory courts.[40] The justification for which is the integrated Australian court system which Chapter III of the Constitution established.[41]

In any event, it is the following proposition which has underpinned important aspects of the High Court's contemporary Chapter III jurisprudence that is of present relevance to my inquiry:

> [T]he grants of legislative power contained in s 51 of the Constitution, which are expressly 'subject to' the provisions of the Constitution as a whole, do not … extend to the making of a law which requires or authorizes the courts in which the judicial power of the Commonwealth is exclusively vested to exercise judicial power in a manner which is inconsistent with the essential character of a court or with the nature of judicial power.[42]

Much then turns on what *are* the essential attributes of a court, what *is* the nature of judicial power and, most importantly, *when* a law occasions inconsistency with either of these constitutional criteria. The High Court has stated, for example, that

> [a] law that purports to direct the manner in which judicial power should be exercised is constitutionally invalid. However, a law which merely prescribes a court's practice or procedure does not direct the exercise of the judicial power in finding facts, applying law or exercising an available discretion.[43]

This posits an important constitutional distinction between 'permissible regulation' of the judicial process and 'impermissible interference' with an essential court attribute or core judicial function.[44] To identify that distinction – which may be more a spectrum than a bright line – requires an understanding of the Chapter III concept of 'judicial power'. Only then is it possible to determine the

[35] See M Foster, 'The Separation of Judicial Power' in C Saunders and A Stone (eds), *The Oxford Handbook of the Australian Constitution* (Oxford, Oxford University Press, 2018) 672.

[36] *Grollo v Palmer* (1995) 184 CLR 348, 365 (Brennan CJ, Deane, Dawson and Toohey JJ).

[37] *Wong v The Queen* (2001) 207 CLR 584, 608 (Gaudron, Gummow and Hayne JJ).

[38] *Bass v Permanent Trustee Co Ltd* (1999) 198 CLR 334, 359 (Gleeson CJ, Gaudron, McHugh, Gummow, Hayne and Callinan JJ).

[39] *Plaintiff S157/2002 v Commonwealth* (2003) 211 CLR 476, 482–483 (Gleeson CJ), 513–514 (Gaudron, McHugh, Gummow, Kirby and Hayne JJ).

[40] *Kable v Director of Public Prosecutions (NSW)* (1996) 189 CLR 1 ('*Kable*'); *North Australian Aboriginal Legal Aid Service Inc v Bradley* (2004) 218 CLR 146.

[41] *Kable* (n 40) 102–103 (Gaudron J).

[42] *Chu Kheng Lim v Minister for Immigration* (1992) 176 CLR 1, 27 (Brennan, Deane and Dawson JJ) (footnote omitted).

[43] *Nicholas v R* (1998) 193 CLR 173, 188 (Brennan CJ) (footnotes omitted).

[44] See *Graham v Minister for Immigration and Border Protection* (2017) 263 CLR 1, 21–24 (Kiefel CJ, Bell, Gageler, Keane, Nettle and Gordon JJ).

extent to which the nature and process of statutory interpretation undertaken by Australian courts has a constitutional dimension.

The High Court has said that to define 'judicial power' with precision is neither possible nor desirable.[45] Even so, it is well established that to exercise judicial power involves the following: 'The unique and essential function of the judicial power is the quelling of [legal] controversies by the ascertainment of the facts, by the application of the law and by exercise, where appropriate, of judicial discretion.'[46] A core aspect of the judicial function is, then, to apply the relevant (common, constitutional or statute) law. This, necessarily, requires judges to ascertain what the law is. When that law is statute law, the courts must determine the legal meaning of those parts contested or impugned. That requires statutory interpretation. As Mark Leeming has observed extra-judicially, '[i]t is an essential characteristic of judicial power to determine the legal meaning of legislation.'[47] It is in this regard, as noted above, that 'statutory interpretation is at the core of the judicial function.'[48] If so, then statutory interpretation as undertaken by the courts in the exercise of judicial power has a constitutional dimension.

Yet that is to state an important proposition at a high level of abstraction. What is that constitutional dimension, and when is parliamentary involvement in or interference with this core function impermissible? This requires an account of constitutionally impermissible interference in the context of statutory interpretation. To that end, the following proposition may be offered:

> A legislative interpretive directive is invalid if it either directs a court as to the way they must exercise judicial power, or it impermissibly interferes with an essential attribute or core function of a court.

This constitutional proposition is, again, stated in quite general terms. Yet I hope to demonstrate that, if accurate, it provides the necessary touchstone to undertake the analysis in Part IV. As will be seen, much will turn on what constitutes *impermissible* interference, a notion which is context-dependent and often a matter of degree. To exercise judicial power, the courts must have at their disposal the interpretive tools which enable them to determine the legal meaning of the relevant statute. In a common law tradition, like Australia, the relevant body of interpretive principles has been developed and refined by the courts over centuries. That was a constitutional necessity as the final arbiters of statutory meaning in the context of settling legal disputes. That tradition and body of (common) law formed – and still forms – the backdrop against which the Constitution was enacted and is to be applied.[49] The common law of statutory interpretation forms an important part of that inherited legal tradition.

[45] See *Precision Data Holdings Ltd v Wills* (1991) 173 CLR 167, 188–189 (Mason CJ, Brennan, Deane, Dawson, Toohey, Gaudron and McHugh JJ).

[46] *Fencott v Muller* (1983) 152 CLR 570, 608 (Mason, Murphy, Brennan and Deane JJ).

[47] M Leeming, 'Power' in Saunders and Stone (n 35) 780.

[48] Basten (n 7) 1.

[49] See Sir O Dixon, 'The Common Law as an Ultimate Constitutional Foundation' in *Jesting Pilate and Other Papers and Addresses*, 2nd edn (William S Hein & Co. Inc, 1997) 204.

To recognise this inherited and continuing tradition is not to ignore that the Commonwealth Parliament in its first year of operation enacted the Acts Interpretation Act 1901 (Cth)('AIA'). The long title of which said it was '[a]n act for the Interpretation of Acts of Parliament and for Shortening their Language.' So, at federation the Parliament took immediate steps to provide instructions aimed at reducing the length and complexity of *its* statutes. That is significant. For as Dennis Pearce has noted, '[t]he manner in which legislation is constructed and presented can provide assistance as to its meaning.'[50] Yet it may fairly be said that the many definitions and rules laid down by the AIA took as the relevant *interpretive* baseline the existing body of common law principles and presumptions.[51] The common law of statutory interpretation was (and is) supplemented, clarified and sometimes refined but not superseded. That, arguably, is still the case with the AIA and its State and Territory equivalents – at least on the judicial view[52] – even for the general interpretation rules in Part 5 including sections 15AA and AB. These important provisions will be examined in more detail in Part IV.

The relevant point for present purposes is that statutory interpretation is at the core of the judicial function. To quell legal controversies, the courts must have at their disposal the interpretive tools which enable the legal meaning of statutes to be ascertained. In Australia, the relevant body of interpretive rules and presumptions is primarily supplied by the common law, supplemented by statute and informed by the Constitution.[53] The constitutional proposition which emerges is that Parliament cannot deprive the courts of the tools which are necessary to perform their interpretive function in the exercise of judicial power. To do so constitutes an impermissible interference with an essential attribute or function of a court.

# IV. Legislated Interpretive Directives

## A. Statutory Definitions and Default Rules

The constitutional conferral of legislative power on Parliament necessarily entails that Parliament is responsible for the content of statutes. That content is a parliamentary statement about what the law is. If so, then it seems permissible for Parliament to provide specific guidance (whether internal or external to a statute) which may enhance the clarity of that content.[54] This, for example, is an important

[50] D Pearce, *Interpretation Acts in Australia*, 2nd edn (London, LexisNexis Butterworths, 2023) 60.

[51] Dixon (n 49) 203–205. As Pearce notes, it was not until the 1980s that Australian Parliaments first incorporated interpretive directives into their Interpretation Acts – (n 50) 3.

[52] See, eg, *Thiess v Collector of Customs* (2014) 250 CLR 664, 672 (French CJ, Hayne, Kiefel, Gageler and Keane JJ).

[53] See, eg, the account of statutory interpretation in the Australian constitutional context offered by French CJ in *Momcilovic* (n 13) 44–50.

[54] Smith (n 7) 249.

aim of a definition section. It is part of the statute's content which aims to make clearer Parliament's statement of the relevant law. To supply the content of *its* statutes, including the internal definition of key terms and concepts, is quintessentially the constitutional domain of Parliament. And to the extent that these definitions and default rules provide (greater) clarity as to a statute's content, this will assist those interpreting a statute (including the courts) in determining its meaning.

Importantly, however, such definitions and directives do not interfere with the judicial function to interpret the relevant statute – including the definition sections or default rules themselves – should that need arise in the context of litigation. Only then would it engage the constitutional proposition offered above. Take, for example, the recent case of *Harvey*.[55] There, the High Court had to determine the legal meaning of an internal statutory definition which was unclear as to whether it was exhaustive or non-exhaustive. The definition itself provided the relevant content to the phrase 'infrastructure facility' for the purposes of the Native Title Act 1993 (Cth).[56] But as the meaning of that phrase was not clear in the context of the litigation, the exercise of judicial power required statutory interpretation.[57] There can, therefore, be no constitutional objection to *internal* statutory definitions and default rules which provide (greater) clarity as to a statute's content. But if the meaning of a definition (or the scope of a default rule) is not clear in the context of litigation, it is for the courts to finally determine it. Any legislative attempt to direct *that* interpretive process would engage the constitutional proposition.

Is it the same for *external* statutory definitions and default rules, such as those contained in the AIA and its state and territory equivalents? In principle, one would assume so. But there is one important distinction between internal and external legislative directives. The latter, by definition, involve general interpretive directives to be applied to other statutes. They are in this regard facilitative. In the context of litigation, the issue will usually be the legal meaning of the other (more specific) statutes. That is the relevant context in which the external legislative directives must be applied. Again, in principle, there can be no constitutional objection to *external* statutory definitions and default rules which seek to provide (greater) clarity to the content of other statutes enacted by the same Parliament. But these external (general) legislative directives cannot trump the legal meaning of other (specific) statutes. If, for example, the courts determine that the meaning of 'land' within the context of a specific Commonwealth statute is at odds with the definition of 'land' provided in the AIA, then the former controls.[58] This possibility and consequence is acknowledged in the simplified outline of the AIA provided in section 1A: 'A provision of this Act is subject to a contrary intention in

[55] *Harvey v Minister for Primary Industry and Resources* [2024] HCA 1 ('*Harvey*').
[56] Native Title Act 1993 (Cth) s 253.
[57] See J Dharmananda, 'Sliding Doors: *Harvey* and the Dual Legal Gateways to Extrinsic Materials' (2024) 35(2) *Public Law Review* 105.
[58] AIA, s 2.

other Commonwealth legislation.'[59] It would, therefore, offend the constitutional proposition if a general (external) directive of the AIA mandated its application even when contrary to the legal meaning of other Commonwealth statutes. In the context of litigation that would amount to an impermissible usurpation of the court's interpretive function.

## B. Interpretive Methodology Directives

The AIA (and its state and territory equivalents) contain specific directives as to interpretive methodology. These are comparatively recent developments in the law of statutory interpretation. Section 15AA of the AIA, for example, was incorporated by amendment in 1981, with its current version (detailed below) provided in the Acts Interpretation Amendment Act 2011 (Cth).[60]

> In interpreting a provision of an Act, the interpretation that would best achieve the purpose or object of the Act (whether or not that purpose or object is expressly stated in the Act) is to be preferred to each other interpretation.

Before considering its compatibility with the constitutional proposition, it must otherwise be a valid law of the Commonwealth. That requires identification of the relevant head of legislative power in the Constitution which supports its validity. In the second reading speech for the Statute Law Revision Bill 1981 (Cth), the Commonwealth Attorney-General explained the purpose of incorporating section 15AA into the AIA:

> [T]he general approach to be adopted to statutory interpretation is something which this Parliament can-and at this stage should-address. The volume and complexity of legislation are assuming daunting proportions and the task of understanding and applying it grows in proportion. Increasingly the more significant decisions our courts are called upon to make turn on a point of statutory interpretation ... The effect of the provision to be inserted in the Acts Interpretation Act will be to confirm that in interpreting provisions regard is to be had to the object or purpose underlying the Act in question. I am not among those who would say that the general approach of our courts is at present overly legalistic, but I do think that there is scope for expressly stating that the statutes we make are to be interpreted in a purposive manner.[61]

The Commonwealth Attorney-General considered that the Parliament *can* (and should) provide such an interpretive directive to confirm that the legislation *it* makes be given a purposive construction. On this account, it would seem incidental to the execution of legislative power to provide this kind of interpretive methodology directive. If so, then section 15AA would be supported by section 51(xxxix) which authorises Parliament to legislate on matters incidental to the execution of

[59] See Pearce (n 50) 8–15.
[60] Statute Law Revision Act 1981 (Cth) s 115.
[61] Commonwealth, *Parliamentary Debates*, Senate, 27 May 1981, 2167 (Peter Durack, Attorney-General).

any power vested by the Constitution in the Parliament.[62] Interestingly, however, the Attorney-General also recognised that 'under our constitutional arrangements it is the function of an independent judiciary to interpret the law and no proposals which we make can or should undermine the freedom that this function requires'.[63] To do so acknowledged (implicitly) the constitutional proposition. On providing an American perspective of section 15AA, Professor Frickey (one of America's leading statutory interpretation scholars) considered that a purposive interpretation of it led to the following:

> [It] is to understand s 15AA as encouraging courts to consider statutory purpose as an important determinant (along with other traditional tools such as textual analysis and canonical analysis) in constructing the list of permissible interpretations. One says 'encouraging' rather than 'mandating' because the latter understanding might, as suggested to the author by James Emmett, trench upon fundamental principles of the Australian constitutional separation of powers as they apply to the judicial power to interpret law.[64]

This account also suggests the permissible interaction between interpretive methodology directives (such as section 15AA) and the core interpretive function of the courts. It suggests the confirmatory and supplementary nature of section 15AA to the judicially developed and applied principles of statutory interpretation. An important point which, arguably, the Commonwealth Attorney General made as well when he said the effect of section 15AA 'will be to *confirm* that in interpreting provisions regard is to be had to the object or purpose underlying the Act in question'.[65] These accounts as to the proper scope of section 15AA have been confirmed in contemporary statements of interpretive principle offered by the High Court. In *Thiess*, for example, the Court stated that to attribute meaning to a statutory text, it 'must be considered in context. That context includes legislative history and extrinsic materials'.[66] And, as for purpose:

> Objective discernment of statutory purpose is integral to contextual construction. The requirement of s 15AA of the Acts Interpretation Act 1901 (Cth) that 'the interpretation that would best achieve the purpose or object of [an] Act (whether or not that purpose or object is expressly stated …) is to be preferred to each other interpretation' is in that respect a particular statutory reflection of a general systemic principle.[67]

This posits contextual construction as the Court's interpretive methodology. It makes clear also that statutory purpose is an important *part* of this methodology but is not the methodology itself. Moreover, the legislative directive as to purpose made by section 15AA is said to confirm (or reflect) a 'general systemic

[62] See *Gazzo v Comptroller of Stamps (Vic)* (1981) 149 CLR 227, 235–236 (Gibbs CJ).
[63] *Parliamentary Debates* (n 61).
[64] P Frickey, 'Structuring Purposive Statutory Interpretation' (2006) 80 *Australian Law Journal* 849, 856.
[65] *Parliamentary Debates* (n 61) (my emphasis).
[66] *Thiess* (n 52) 671. But see Smith (n 7) 245–247.
[67] ibid 672.

principle' which, presumably, was pre-existing and judicially developed. So, whilst section 15AA may be an 'unqualified statutory instruction'[68] regarding statutory purpose, the Court has integrated it within *its* interpretive methodology. That being so, section 15AA and its state and territory equivalents are compatible with the constitutional proposition. Parliament has provided an instruction regarding one aspect of contextual construction. But the core interpretive function of courts – including the methodology used to perform this function in the exercise of judicial power – remains squarely within the constitutional domain of the judiciary.

The Court, unsurprisingly, has reasoned in a similar manner regarding legislative history and extrinsic materials. Other aspects of contextual construction for which Parliament has provided an instruction. Section 15AB (and its state and territory equivalents) provides that 'consideration may be given' to 'any material not forming part of the Act [if] capable of assisting in the ascertainment of the meaning of the provision'.[69] As Jacinta Dharmananda has observed, '[t]he section makes it discretionary to refer to extrinsic sources and then only in three circumstances.'[70] To confirm that the meaning of a provision is the ordinary meaning.[71] To determine the meaning of a provision when it's 'ambiguous or obscure'.[72] Or to determine the meaning of a provision when its ordinary meaning is 'manifestly absurd or is unreasonable'.[73] But authoritative statements of interpretive principle made by the High Court after section 15AB was enacted make clear that for contextual construction – the Court's methodology – 'there are no thresholds for recourse to extrinsic sources nor is application of the contextual principle discretionary'.[74] So, for example in *SZTAL*, the following statement was made in the joint judgment of Kiefel CJ, Nettle and Gordon JJ:

> The starting point for the ascertainment of the meaning of a statutory provision is the text of the statute whilst, at the same time, regard is had to its context and purpose. Context should be regarded at this first stage and not at some later stage and it should be regarded in its widest sense.[75]

There is, then, a divergence between the judicial and parliamentary approaches to when recourse may be had to extrinsic materials. Even so, as Dharmananda notes, '[a]part from occasional judicial comment about the surprising state of affairs, courts have applied one or the other, or both, without apparent concern.'[76] A point to which Edelman J referred in *Harvey*. The divergent common law and statutory

[68] *SZTAL v Minister for Immigration and Border Protection* (2017) 262 CLR 362, 375 (Gageler J) ('*SZTAL*').

[69] This interpretive directive was incorporated into the AIA by s 6 the Acts Interpretation Amendment Act 1984 (Cth).

[70] Dharmananda (n 57) 105.

[71] AIA, s15AB(1)(a).

[72] ibid s15AB(1)(b)(i).

[73] ibid s15AB(1)(b)(ii).

[74] Dharmananda (n 57) 106.

[75] *SZTAL* (n 68) 368 (footnotes omitted).

[76] Dharmananda (n 57) 105 (footnote omitted).

'gateways'[77] notwithstanding, there will 'very rarely be a difference in practice'[78] as to when and what extrinsic materials are judicially accessed. That's primarily due to the ease with which the 'ambiguity' threshold will be met in litigation where the legal meaning of a statute is at issue.[79] Yet this divergence, especially its judicial explanation, suggests something of importance regarding the legal status of statutory interpretation. In *Harvey*, for example, Edelman J made clear that the common law approach to extrinsic materials holds doctrinal sway:

> An expansive approach to the extrinsic materials to which s 15AB permits recourse is also consistent with the nature of that provision as generally facilitative and as one which is designed to expand resort to information in extrinsic materials and not as one that is intended to constrain the development of the common law rules of statutory interpretation.[80]

This *facilitative* account of section 15AB presumably refers to the provision's role in assisting the core judicial function of fixing the legal meaning of a statute to determine a legal controversy. If so, then section 15AB's interpretive directive (as with section 15AA) supplements the extant body of judicially developed principles and presumptions. Its discretionary and complimentary nature secures its compatibility with the constitutional proposition. And, as the later statement of interpretive principle from *SZTAL* above makes clear, the common law has indeed developed to open an alternative 'gateway'[81] to extrinsic materials which is less restrictive than section 15AB and non-discretionary. Again, the important point for present purposes is the judicial view that the content and application of interpretive methodology is ultimately part of the court's core function.

If, however, the sections 15AA and AB directives were expressed as mandates, would they offend the constitutional proposition? One could argue that the manner in which the High Court has explained and justified both provisions might lead to that conclusion. And, to recall, that was certainly the view of Professor Frickey regarding section 15AA and an apparent parliamentary concern as well when sections 15AA and 15AB were incorporated into the AIA.[82] Yet such an argument is hard to make, in my view. Indeed, section 15AA *is* expressed in mandatory terms. A point which Gageler J (as he then was) noted in *SZTAL*.[83] But on the judicial view, it is a directive as to purpose which is only *one* of the sources of statutory meaning to which a court refers in the interpretive process. Relevantly, if the text in context (considered in its widest sense and in the first instance) yields more than one possible meaning, then its legal meaning *must* be that which best

[77] ibid.
[78] *Harvey* (n 55) at [113] (Edelman J).
[79] ibid.
[80] ibid [114] (footnote omitted).
[81] Dharmananda (n 57) 105.
[82] See Commonwealth, Parliamentary Debates, Senate, 8 March 1984, 582 (Gareth Evans, Attorney-General). My thanks to Jacinta Dharmananda for this point.
[83] *SZTAL* (n 68) 375.

achieves the identified statutory purpose. That is perfectly consistent with the constitutional proposition. So too would be the section 15AB directive if expressed in mandatory terms. For that is precisely the common law position in Australia regarding recourse to extrinsic materials, as Dharmananda noted above.[84] The common law must, of course, conform to the Constitution. To settle legal disputes using an interpretive methodology which fixes the legal meaning of a statutory text by always considering its context and purpose clearly meets this characterisation.

But what if section 15AA mandated an interpretive methodology – such as strict textualism – which is antithetical to the High Court's (current) approach? On the one hand, there is a decent argument that courts *could* still perform its core function of determining the legal meaning of statutes to resolve legal disputes. But that determination would be made using a mandated interpretive methodology at odds with the contextualism which is judicially preferred. Let us assume that strict textualism involves the prohibition of recourse to extrinsic materials in order to fix the legal meaning of a statute. If so, then such a directive requires the repeal or rewording of section 15AB as well to make clear that prohibition. But strict textualism – at least of the kind advocated in the United States by Justice Antonin Scalia and others[85] – does consider statutory context. But that context is limited to the relevant statute, other statutes, textual canons and (controversially) substantive canons.[86] It excludes consideration of legislative history.

So, would it be constitutionally problematic if section 15AA mandated strict textualism and section 15AB, to facilitate it, prohibited judicial recourse to any extrinsic parliamentary materials when interpreting a statutory provision? Clearly enough, there would be judicial resistance to such legislative mandates as to interpretive methodology. And, to the extent textually possible, that would likely manifest in courts reading down those directives to incorporate, or rather assimilate, them into the judicially preferred method of contextualism. That, for example, has been the experience in those American states which have legislated interpretive methodology mandates.[87] As Abbe Gluck has observed, the American 'state cases indicate that courts will find ways around legislated methodological rules they do not like, and that judges may be unwilling to relinquish authority over interpretive methodology'.[88] That judicial disposition seems likely as well in Australia.

Yet let us assume in the Australian context that a prohibition on judicial recourse to extrinsic materials *in all interpretive circumstances* was crystal clear, so that reading it down would amount to judicial legislation, not interpretation. If section 15AB was expressed in those terms, would it offend the constitutional proposition? In this context, one should not underestimate judicial interpretive

[84] Dharmananda (n 57) 105–106.

[85] See, eg, A Scalia and BA. Garner, *Reading Law: The Interpretation of Legal Texts* (St. Paul, Thomson/West, 2012); A Scalia, 'Originalism: The Lesser Evil' (1989) 57 *University of Cincinnati Law Review* 849.

[86] Scalia and Garner (n 85) 16–41.

[87] See A Gluck, 'The States as Laboratories of Statutory Interpretation: Methodological Consensus and the New Modified Textualism' (2010) 119 *Yale Law Journal* 1750, 1771–1811; Jellum (n 6) 842–847.

[88] ibid 1786.

ingenuity. It has long been the case throughout the common law world, for example, that courts have preserved court access and review powers in the teeth of comprehensive privative clauses.[89] In Australia specifically, the High Court stated in *Plaintiff S157* that a particularly strict privative clause must 'be construed conformably with Ch III of the Constitution, specifically, s 75'[90] which provides an entrenched minimum of judicial review through the constitutional writs of mandamus, prohibition and injunction.[91] Such an approach may be instructive for present purposes. Relevantly, the use of Chapter III of the Constitution to underpin an approach which maintains judicial control of interpretive methodology in the teeth of a comprehensive section 15AB is certainly possible. If so, the compatibility of such a provision with the constitutional proposition is never squarely confronted. To use an interpretive technique of constitutional avoidance – or constitutionally conforming interpretation – seems the likely judicial response in Australia.[92] To do so would also avoid direct confrontation with the political arms of government in contested legal terrain. A prudent approach which uses the restrained language of legal principle and reasoning to alert those political actors that a constitutional red line is being approached. Further, to seek alignment of the judicial role with constitutional principle in this way *may* serve to buttress the legitimacy of the court's interpretive approach in this contested terrain.[93]

However, for the purposes of this chapter, I do want to squarely confront the constitutional proposition. The issue is a difficult one. On the one hand, as Justice Edelman recently observed in *Harvey*, '[u]ntil relatively recently in the life of the common law, it was impermissible to have regard to information contained in extrinsic materials as part of the context to determine the meaning that Parliament was taken to have intended.'[94] The courts were, then, required and able to discharge their core interpretive function to finally determine legal disputes without recourse to extrinsic materials. If so, would a mandated statutory return to this old common law position *now* offend the constitutional proposition? If the courts determined the legal meaning of statutes in litigation satisfactorily for centuries, why couldn't they do so again? I think the answer is that they could. But, as detailed above,

[89] See M Aronson, M Groves and G Weeks, *Judicial Review of Administrative Action and Government Liability*, 7th edn (London, Thomson Reuters, 2022) 1127–1130.

[90] *Plaintiff S157* (n 39) 506 (Gaudron, McHugh, Gummow, Kirby and Hayne JJ).

[91] ibid 513.

[92] See LK Weis, 'Australia: Techniques of Developing Legislation and the Common Law to Align with Constitutional Legal Norms' in M Klatt (ed), *Constitutionally Conforming Interpretation: Comparative Perspectives Volume 1: National Reports* (Oxford, Hart Publishing, 2022) 381–406.

[93] My thanks to Mark Aronson for pointing out that courts must always have one eye on their own legitimacy when articulating interpretive principle and undertaking statutory interpretation; and to maintain that legitimacy courts must do so in a manner which recognises the constitutional limits of their own interpretive role and respects those of the political arms of government regarding the content and administration of legislation. To strike this constitutional balance is particularly important in those cases which involve strong and controversial policy positions taken by the political arms of government in statute. On which see Sir G Brennan, 'Courts, Democracy and the Rule of Law' (1991) 65 *Australian Law Journal* 32, 36–40.

[94] *Harvey* (n 55) at [108].

they would no doubt resist (if and where possible) such a statutory mandate. That would likely occur for two related reasons. The courts would consider this legislative intervention to be trespassing on their constitutional domain of determining the interpretive methodology needed to facilitate the exercise of judicial power, and in doing so, such a mandate would roll back decades of common law development of that methodology and return to an approach which, in the judicial view, is far less capable of fixing accurately the legal meaning of statutes. Even so, Parliament might offer the same kind of reasons for the old common law rule to justify its new mandate. That rule was underpinned by rule of law and access to justice considerations as the High Court explained in 1977:

> It is established by many decisions of the highest authority that material of that kind may not be used as an aid to the construction of a statute. This rule is neither irrational nor outmoded. It is based upon sound practical reasons. Conflicting opinions as to the meaning or effect of a Bill may be expressed in the course of debate – perhaps sometimes even disingenuously – and it will often be impossible to say that any particular view is more authoritative than another. The debates in Parliament would often introduce a new source of argument and confusion, rather than provide a guide to the construction of a statute. The need to have regard to the parliamentary debates for the purpose of construing a statute would render the law less certain, and the burden of having this additional material available for consideration and of examining it, in many cases for no worthwhile result, would tend to aggravate the delay and increase the cost of litigation.[95]

On the contemporary judicial view, these considerations do not justify a complete prohibition on recourse to extrinsic materials. Indeed, on the contrary.[96] But the important point for present purposes is whether such a statutory mandate would offend the constitutional proposition. One might argue that it does not if Australian courts could still satisfactorily (though maybe not optimally on the judicial view) determine the legal meaning of statutes in litigation without recourse to extrinsic materials. One further, speculative point is that extrinsic materials are those generated by Parliament itself as part of the legislative process which is, quintessentially, its constitutional domain. If so, then should it not be permissible for Parliament to take the view that, on balance, *its* preparatory materials are not reliable sources of statutory meaning?

On the other hand, it might be argued that to deprive judges of an important source of contextual meaning is problematic. That is especially so for the High Court (indeed all Australian courts), as the raison d'etre of the modern approach to statutory interpretation is text in context.[97] But more importantly, as noted

[95] *Commissioner for Prices and Consumer Affairs (SA) v Charles Moore (Aust) Ltd* (1977) 139 CLR 449, 461 (Gibbs J).

[96] See *Port of Newcastle Operations Pty Ltd v Glencore Coal Assets Australia Pty Ltd* (2021) 274 CLR 565, 594 (Kiefel CJ, Gageler, Gordon, Steward and Gleeson CJ).

[97] See *CIC Insurance Ltd v Bankstown Football Club Ltd* (1997) 187 CLR 384, 408 (Brennan CJ, Dawson, Toohey and Gummow JJ). Alternatively, if this kind of legislative interpretive directive relied

above, the core interpretive function of courts – *including the methodology used to perform this function in the exercise of judicial power* – falls squarely within the constitutional domain of the judiciary. If so, then *any* statutory mandate which directs the courts as to how it must discharge its interpretive function may be constitutionally suspect. On this account, the relevant constitutional point is not the court's institutional capacity to interpret statutes without recourse to extrinsic materials. Rather, it is maintenance of the judicial responsibility to determine *how* they discharge *their* core interpretive function.[98]

There are other statutory interpretive mandates that may also offend the constitutional proposition. In *Momcilovic*, for example, there are suggestions that in Australia's constitutional context, a statutory mandate like section 3 of the Human Rights Act 1998 (UK) may be incompatible with Chapter III of the Constitution.[99] There, courts must give a statute an interpretation which is compatible with (the European Convention on) human rights 'so far as it is possible to do so'.[100] To the extent that this has authorised a jurisprudence which has involved the judicial rewriting of statutes, that is something which is prohibited under Australia's constitutional separation of powers.[101] Moreover, a directive which prohibited the courts from considering anything other than the text of the contested statutory provision(s) in determining its legal meaning may be impermissible statutory interference. This kind of mandate would, again, be constitutionally suspect, for it directs the courts as to *how* it must discharge *its* core interpretive function. It also deprives the courts of important and relevant statutory context to such an extent that it cannot discharge its core interpretive function. A court could, of course, fix *a* meaning to such statutory words. But without this necessary context, it could not determine its *legal* meaning. If a court cannot consider a contested provision in the wider context of that statute or the statute book more generally, *then it no longer has at its disposal the interpretive tools which enable its legal meaning to be ascertained.* The italicised passage in the previous sentence is an important touchstone for the constitutional proposition. It is a Rubicon which legislated interpretive directives cannot cross.

## C. Abolishing the Principle of Legality

On the principle of legality, French CJ in *Momcilovic* relevantly observed that it 'does not constrain legislative power'.[102] 'It is expressed as a presumption that

on the incidental power for support, then a court may query its validity on characterisation grounds for not being necessary or appropriate to the execution of legislative power.

[98] My thanks to Jacinta Dharmananda for drawing this perspective to my attention.

[99] See, eg, *Momcilovic* (n 13) 44–50 (French CJ), 87–93 (Gummow J), 123 (Hayne J), 175–183 (Heydon J), 208–211, 217 (Crennan and Kiefel JJ).

[100] Human Rights Act 1998 (UK) s 3.

[101] *Momcilovic* (n 13) 45 (French CJ).

[102] ibid 46.

Parliament does not intend to interfere with common law rights and freedoms except by clear and unequivocal language for which Parliament may be accountable to the electorate.'[103]

The susceptibility of the common law rights and freedoms which legality protects to statutory diminution or abolition is, then, doctrinally orthodox. It reflects the long-settled constitutional relationship between Parliament and the courts. As Gageler J (as he then was) observed regarding legality …

> … any common law principle or presumption of interpretation must surely have reached the limit of its operation where its application to read down legislation plain on its face would frustrate an object of that legislation or render means by which the legislation sets out to achieve that object inoperative or nonsensical.[104]

If so, then it seems plausible that the principle of legality could be abolished by a sufficiently clear legislative mandate. Yet if one accepts the constitutional proposition, the doctrinal situation may not be so clear-cut. Importantly, the High Court's statements regarding the status of legality do so in the context of individual statutes infringing specific common law rights and freedoms which fall within the protective scope of the principle. So, for example, the joint judgment of French CJ, Kiefel, Bell, Keane, Nettle and Gordon JJ in *IBAC* stated that

> common law rights are to be regarded as abrogated by statute only by the use of language which manifests a clear intention to do so. The principle of legality means that common law rights will not be taken by a court to have been displaced by legislation save where the intention to do so is 'expressed with irresistible clearness'.[105]

These statements do not address or contemplate legislative abolition of the principle itself. The distinction is an important one. Consider, for example, that the principle applies to (and so protects) 'the rules of procedural fairness in the exercise of statutory powers'.[106] Yet there can be no objection to a statute which modifies or excludes with sufficient clarity the common law requirements of procedural fairness for specific kinds of administrative decision-making.[107] This involves one common law right (presumptively protected by legality) being abrogated in a specific legislative context. That, as the High Court has routinely held, is constitutionally permissible.[108] It reflects the doctrinal orthodoxy of Parliament's constitutional relationship with the courts noted above.

The preceding analysis suggests the following possibility as well. Parliament could, in my view, seek to abrogate all relevant common law rights and freedoms which might be engaged in the application of an individual statute. If done with

[103] ibid (footnote omitted).
[104] *R v Independent Broad-Based Anti-Corruption Commissioner* (2016) 256 CLR 459, 481 ('*IBAC*').
[105] ibid 471 (footnote omitted).
[106] *Momcilovic* (n 13) 47 (French CJ) (footnote omitted).
[107] See Aronson, Groves and Weeks (n 89) ch 8.8: Exclusion and Statutory Modification.
[108] *Plaintiff S10* (n 3) 654–655 (French CJ and Kiefel J), 668 (Gummow, Hayne, Crennan and Bell JJ), 672–673 (Heydon J).

sufficient clarity and precision, this seems constitutionally permissible. To do so is an extreme example of the doctrinal orthodoxy outlined above. The statute's very specific and circumscribed content makes clear Parliament's intended meaning. The statute also trumps legality in the doctrinally orthodox manner. Relevantly, the common law rights and freedoms engaged are specifically identified and then abrogated through 'clear and unequivocal language for which Parliament may be accountable to the electorate'.[109] Yet this kind of *individual statute* leaves the principle of legality itself fully intact and does not interfere with the core interpretive function of the courts (or the interpretive tools used to perform it) nor direct them as to the way they must exercise judicial power. If so, this statute is compatible with the constitutional proposition.

However, what if an individual statute stated that in its interpretation the principle of legality cannot be applied? On the one hand, the intent of such a statute seems indistinguishable from the constitutionally permissible one considered in the previous paragraph. On the other, the statute seeks to abrogate the principle itself from the interpretive tools available to judges to determine its legal meaning. But unlike the statute considered above, it does not trump legality in orthodox doctrinal terms. It fails to identify and abrogate the relevant common law rights with textual clarity and precision. Without the performance of this necessary statutory work, the attempt to abrogate legality in this context and manner would likely fail. That failure, however, is primarily due to the statute not fulfilling the orthodox doctrinal conditions required for the abrogation of common law rights and freedoms. But is this kind of statute also constitutionally impermissible? It does not seek to legislatively abolish the principle of legality, only preclude its availability in determining the legal meaning of *this* statute. But it does interfere with the interpretive tools used by courts to perform a core function and, arguably, provides a methodological directive to them as to how (in this specific statutory context) they must exercise judicial power. If so, then this statute may be constitutionally suspect. Yet a judicial reckoning with the compatibility of this statute with the constitutional proposition is unlikely. As the statute fails to abrogate legality for the reasons detailed above, it becomes unnecessary to address its validity.

Finally, we arrive at Larry's question. Let us assume that Parliament seeks to abolish the principle of legality by amending the AIA in the following terms:

> In interpreting a provision of an Act, courts are prohibited from using the principle of legality to facilitate determination of its legal meaning.

This is a general legislative mandate the aim of which is to deprive courts of an interpretive tool used to ascertain the legal meaning of statutes which engage fundamental rights. Even so, the courts still have at their disposal the principal sources of statutory meaning – text, purpose and context – to perform their interpretive role. To be sure, this mandate deprives the courts of an important aspect

[109] *Momcilovic* (n 13) 46 (French CJ).

of the wider (common law) context in which statutes are situated. But one might reasonably observe that with the core tenets of the modern – contextual – approach to statutory interpretation largely intact, courts still have the capacity to determine the legal meaning of statutes to resolve legal disputes.

Yet the problem is that statutes have the capacity to engage fundamental rights in a multitude of different ways and in often unforeseen factual contexts, and increasingly so. That some rights are more fundamental than others and the intensity and scope of their statutory infringement are variable.[110] The principle of legality is the interpretive tool which mediates the range of (sometimes discordant) factors from which a statute's legal meaning must be derived. In these contexts, legality is not the only contextual source of statutory meaning, but it is a critical one and can be decisive. To deprive courts of an interpretive tool which enables the legal meaning of many statutes to be ascertained is, then, constitutionally problematic. Maybe, again, the courts could hold that this general attempt to abolish legality fails for not fulfilling the orthodox doctrinal conditions required to abrogate common law rights and freedoms. But that would deprive the provision of meaning and effect, something which the High Court considers interpretively impermissible.[111] So, if a court accepts that the purpose and meaning of this statutory mandate are clear but cannot make sense of a statute without applying legality, then it is unable to perform its core interpretive function. It is being deprived of an essential attribute which enables the determination of a statute's legal meaning and so facilitates the exercise of judicial power. It is also a statutory mandate which directs the courts as to *how* it must discharge *its* interpretive function. If so, then to amend the AIA in the above terms may offend the constitutional proposition.

This is a striking proposition. If correct, then legality *is* a constitutional (interpretive) principle. But to recognise this does not involve judges unilaterally converting common law rights and freedoms into constitutional ones. That would amount to the judicial creation of a constitutional bill of rights contrary to section 128 of the Constitution. As my above analysis explained, these common law rights and freedoms remain susceptible to statutory abrogation if done with precision and clarity. So, even though legality is a constitutional principle – immune from legislative abolition in the manner detailed above – it does not otherwise constrain legislative power. The principle itself is constitutional. But the rights and freedoms which fall within its protective scope exist at common law. In orthodox doctrinal terms, they remain vulnerable to statutory interference.[112]

[110] See D Meagher, 'Fundamental Rights and Necessary Implication' (2023) 51 *Federal Law Review* 102, 119–127.

[111] *Project Blue Sky Inc v Australian Broadcasting Authority* (1998) 194 CLR 355, 382 (McHugh, Gummow, Kirby and Hayne JJ).

[112] The existence of a constitutional rule with content that is sourced to the common law (and so vulnerable to statutory abrogation) is not unique in the Australian context. It exists with the relationship between common law prerogative powers and the repository of those (and all other Commonwealth executive) powers in s 61 of the Australian Constitution – see *Barton v Commonwealth* (1974) 131 CLR 477.

# V. Conclusion

One hopes the legislative possibilities considered in Part IV.C remain hypothetical. Common law rights, freedoms and principles – including those which underpin the law of statutory interpretation – are fundamental for good reason. They represent the accumulated judicial wisdom of centuries. To legislatively disturb, without compelling justification, those principles and presumptions which enable the courts to fix accurately the legal meaning of statutes is politically imprudent and constitutionally dubious. Yet institutional comity cuts both ways. The application of judicial power involves the interpretation and application of legislation to resolve legal disputes. The discharge of this core function requires judicial maintenance of the constitutional distinction between statutory interpretation and judicial legislation.

This chapter sought to identify the legal status of judicially developed principles and presumptions of statutory interpretation in Australia. They are, as the High Court has explained, creatures of the common law. Yet the core interpretive function of the courts is performed in the exercise of judicial power which, in Australia, is a constitutional concept. Consequently, a constitutional proposition was offered regarding statutory interpretation which built upon the High Court's Chapter III jurisprudence. To exercise judicial power, the courts must have at their disposal the interpretive tools which enable them to determine the legal meaning of the relevant statute. That being so, a legislative interpretive directive is invalid if it either directs a court as to the way they must exercise judicial power or it impermissibly interferes with an essential attribute or core function of a court. This doctrinal framework was used to assess the validity of legislative interpretive directives, some real and others hypothetical, including whether Parliament could abolish the principle of legality. The most striking proposition to emerge was that, in Australia, legality may be a constitutional principle. Should Parliament ever legislate in these terms, the legal status of statutory interpretation will matter.

# 6

# The Doctrine and Scope of Judicial Review: Comparative Reflections on Three Jurisdictions

STEPHEN THOMSON*

One of the most rewarding aspects of a comparative study of law is the increased objectivity that it gives about a law and legal system.[1] It helps one to understand that rules do not have to be the way that they are. That things can be done differently. That some things work better or worse than elsewhere. That what is difficult in one jurisdiction is relatively uncomplicated in another. That rules should not be taken for granted and that there is much to be learned and understood when a law and legal system are stripped back to their doctrinal and institutional roots. Comparative law teaches one as much about their own legal system as it does others. It allows one to see the wood as well as the trees.

I have been fortunate to research and teach public law in three quite different legal systems – Scotland, Hong Kong and Australia. With the common denominator between all three being English law, which features to a more or less prominent extent in all three legal systems, I can also claim familiarity with the public law of a fourth jurisdiction. This transition through legal systems has been a challenging and fascinating learning process. Coming from my PhD, which investigated the constitutional basis for judicial review in Scotland, exploring the nuanced and evolving jurisprudence of a half-a-millennium-old court to, at the other end of the scale, teaching the case law on Australia's comparatively formulaic Administrative Decisions (Judicial Review) Act 1977, has required me to constantly question and challenge my basic assumptions about judicial review and broader issues of public

* I thank Mark Aronson and Greg Weeks for very helpful comments on a draft of this chapter. Any errors and the views expressed within are of course my own.

[1] See generally L Ehrlich, 'Comparative Public Law and the Fundamentals of its Study' (1921) 21(7) *Columbia Law Review* 623; DP Kommers, 'The Value of Comparative Constitutional Law' (1976) 9 *The John Marshall Journal of Practice and Procedure* 685; R Dixon and T Ginsburg, 'Introduction' in T Ginsburg and R Dixon (eds), *Comparative Constitutional Law* (Cheltenham, Edward Elgar, 2011) 1–15; and U Kischel, *Comparative Law* (Oxford, Oxford University Press, 2019) 45–86.

law, the rule of law and constitutionalism. And then there has been administrative law in Hong Kong, where the law was far more similar to English law than that of Scotland and framed by a quasi-constitutional code – the Basic Law of the Hong Kong Special Administrative Region – the likes of which has no analogue in either England or Scotland. These experiences have also led me to be active in the fields of comparative administrative law and comparative constitutional law, and comparative law has made me a better public lawyer not only in general but in each of the jurisdictions where I have been active.

Professor Matthew Groves requires no convincing as to the merits (Australian public law joke) of comparativism in public law research and teaching. He is not only one of the most accomplished go-to experts on Australian administrative law[2] but has also researched legal systems as various as England and Wales,[3] Canada,[4] Hong Kong[5] and India.[6] When I was invited to contribute a chapter to this festschrift marking and celebrating the work and achievements of Professor Groves, I was, in equal measure, honoured and excited to accept. I have not only learned from many enlightening and stimulating discussions with Matthew on all matters public law but have also had the easy pleasure of working with him, most recently as a co-editor (along with my excellent colleague and co-editor of this festschrift, Professor Greg Weeks) of *Administrative Tribunals in the Common Law World*.[7] Matthew not only has extensive and deep expertise as a public lawyer but also has that increasingly rare quality in today's world – humility. I hope he will not mind me stating here in print that he does not hide behind titles or airs and graces but is thoroughly down to earth. This has not only made Matthew a pleasure to get to know and to work with but also imbues his work with authenticity and intellectual sincerity. Matthew's work is solid, no-nonsense scholarship and, in an industry increasingly characterised by metrics and gimmicks, I can pay his work no higher compliment.

This chapter represents not only an opportunity for me to write something that I think may be interesting to Matthew and hopefully to the readership at large, but also to offer a more personal reflection which ties together the physical and

[2] Among his many influential works are the seminal text M Aronson, M Groves and G Weeks, *Judicial Review of Administrative Action and Government Liability*, 7th edn (London, Thomson Reuters, 2022) and articles including M Groves, 'Substantive Legitimate Expectations in Australian Administrative Law' (2008) 32 *Melbourne University Law Review* 470, M Groves, 'Exclusion of the Rules of Natural Justice' (2013) 39(2) *Monash University Law Review* 285, and M Groves, 'Should We Follow the Gospel of the Administrative Decisions (Judicial Review) Act 1977 (Cth)?' (2010) 34 *Melbourne University Law Review* 736.

[3] M Groves, 'Judicial Review and the Concept of Unfairness in English Public Law' (2007) 18 *Public Law Review* 244.

[4] M Groves, 'The Differing and Disappearing Standards of Judicial Review in Canada' (2009) 16 *Australian Journal of Administrative Law* 211.

[5] M Groves, 'The Rule Against Bias' (2009) 39 *Hong Kong Law Journal* 485.

[6] M Groves, 'Law, Religion and Public Order in Colonial India: Contextualising the 1887 Allahabad High Court Case on 'Sacred' Cows' (2010) 33 *Journal of South Asia Studies* 87.

[7] S Thomson, M Groves and G Weeks (eds), *Administrative Tribunals in the Common Law World* (Oxford, Hart Publishing, 2024).

intellectual aspects of my own journey through legal systems. But I will not pretend that a comparative study of law has led me to all the answers; in some ways it has raised more questions than answers. That alone has value, for I am more hesitant than ever to jump to conclusions. In the age of the internet and an increasingly interconnected world, there is more opportunity than ever – and less excuse for failing to seize that opportunity – to examine how things are done elsewhere, even for those that are not or cannot be internationally mobile. Yet comparative public law still seems to be little taught and little researched in most universities in a way that suggests that many scholars' focus and expertise are still drawn along national lines.

## I. Scotland: An Oddity as the Norm

In some ways, Scotland's law of judicial review bears remarkable similarity to its English counterpart. The courts of both jurisdictions apply common legislation like the Human Rights Act 1998 and various immigration, taxation and employment statutes.[8] There has been held to be 'no substantial difference' between the common law grounds of judicial review in England and Scotland.[9] Various procedural idiosyncrasies have in Scotland been erased in the past decade by aligning them with England – these include the introduction of a requirement for permission to be obtained,[10] a move towards England's more public law-oriented 'sufficient interest' test applied to applicants for review,[11] and the introduction of a designated time limit for making a judicial review application.[12] When viewed through these lenses, one might wonder why Scotland would generate any special comment or interest in a judicial review context as distinct from England.

But differences there are, and major ones at that. First is the doctrinal core of judicial review in Scotland, which is one of confinement to jurisdiction; not quite regardless, but with markedly less emphasis on the presence of a sufficient public (law) element for the availability of review.[13] Judicial review developed in Scotland through review of a range of bodies, including temporal courts, ecclesiastical courts, arbiters and various boards and commissions. Without retrospectively imposing a unified jurisprudential narrative on the courts, this was almost never articulated in terms of a public/private divide. It is possible in Scotland to competently seek

[8] Statutes applicable to Great Britain or the UK pronounced in English or Irish appeals will generally – but not always – be followed in the Scottish courts: G Maher and TB Smith (eds), 'Sources of Law (Formal)', Vol 22, *The Laws of Scotland: Stair Memorial Encyclopaedia* (London, LexisNexis, 1987) [282].

[9] *West v Secretary of State for Scotland*, 1992 SC 386, 413.

[10] Court of Session Act 1988, s 27B (as inserted by the Courts Reform (Scotland) Act 2014, s 89).

[11] Court of Session Act 1988, s 27B (as inserted by the Courts Reform (Scotland) Act 2014, s 89). See also *AXA General Insurance Co Ltd v Lord Advocate* [2011] UKSC 46, [171].

[12] Court of Session Act 1988, s 27A (as inserted by the Courts Reform (Scotland) Act 2014, s 89).

[13] See S Thomson, 'The Doctrinal Core of the Supervisory Jurisdiction of the Court of Session' [2016] *Public Law* 670.

judicial review of a private company or organisation performing purely private law functions. The absence of a sufficient public law element, by contrast to England,[14] will not of itself prove fatal to the application.

This blends into, and is related to, the markedly different approach to remedies in the two jurisdictions. During my undergraduate degree at Edinburgh, I would sometimes hear it being said that in England the principle follows the remedy, whereas in Scotland the remedy follows the principle. This was usually left to speak for itself, and it took me some time to understand what, in practical terms, it meant. A significant part of English judicial review's comparative formalism is its being shackled to the historical niceties of the prerogative writs of certiorari, mandamus and prohibition, of course now rebadged and rebranded as quashing orders, mandatory orders and prohibiting orders.[15] The prerogative writs were – and the prerogative orders are – to a great extent determinative of the scope of judicial review in England.[16]

Yet a public law education in Scotland teaches that it is not necessary to have this discrete system of remedies for the purposes of judicial review. The supervisory jurisdiction of the Court of Session – Scotland's supreme civil court of almost 500 years' standing – was to a great extent developed through the remedies of advocation, suspension and reduction. Advocation was largely based on jurisdictional deficiencies and was replaced with notes of appeal in 1868.[17] Suspension and reduction, which remain as civil remedies and are supplemented by declarator, interdict, implement, restitution and payment,[18] broadly covered the same grounds as advocation. However, these remedies are available in both judicial review procedure *and* ordinary procedure. An order of reduction, for example, can be used to invalidate a wide range of acts and instruments, from an ultra vires decision of a local authority exercising statutory discretion, to a fraudulent document issued by a private trustee. An order of specific implement can be used to compel acts as various as a licensing board to provide a statement of reasons for a decision to a recalcitrant executor who refuses to perform a testamentary instruction. An order of interdict can be used to prohibit the deportation of an asylum seeker just as it can be used to prohibit a company director from disposing of shares. But it is the action of reduction that has in many ways been key.

Of the four jurisdictions with whose laws of judicial review I am most familiar, Scotland is the least formalistic by a considerable degree. The relatively formless and general nature of the Scottish remedies was regarded by the late J.D.B. Mitchell, formerly Professor of Constitutional Law at Edinburgh, as contributing to the relative formlessness and generality of judicial review more broadly.[19] The remedies,

[14] *O'Reilly v Mackman* [1983] 2 AC 237; *Cocks v Thanet District Council* [1983] 2 AC 286; *Davy v Spelthorne Borough Council* [1984] AC 262; *Roy v Kensington and Chelsea and Westminster Family Practitioner Committee* [1992] 1 AC 624.

[15] Civil Procedure Rules, CPR 54.2.

[16] JDB Mitchell, *Constitutional Law* (London, W. Green, 1964) 210–211 and 250–251.

[17] Court of Session Act 1868, ss 64–65 and 76.

[18] Rules of the Court of Session, r 58.13.

[19] JDB Mitchell, *Constitutional Law* (London, W. Green, 1964) 210–211 and 250–251.

doctrine and jurisdictional tests in Scots judicial review have, in comparative terms, great flexibility. This brings clear advantages. While *R v Panel on Take-overs and Mergers, ex parte Datafin plc* was a welcome development in the liberalisation of English judicial review,[20] the public/private divide continues to cause real problems for determining the availability of judicial review.[21] Comparatively, these problems have barely featured in Scotland. If a body has exceeded its jurisdiction, the supervisory jurisdiction of the Court of Session – the primary jurisdiction of judicial review – is potentially engaged. This does not lead to the floodgates being opened because it is not a doctrinal free-for-all. If remedies sound in other areas of law, such as contract, the courts have ruled that those other avenues must be pursued instead of judicial review.[22] That can be as much about pragmatism as anything else.

When the seminal case of *West v Secretary of State for Scotland*, which is an authoritative (re)statement of the law of judicial review in the modern period, was decided, there were concerns that all manner of persons and bodies could now be caught by judicial review. This was because Lord President Hope (as he then was) held that:

> [t]he cases in which the exercise of the supervisory jurisdiction is appropriate involve a tri-partite relationship, between the person or body to whom the jurisdiction, power or authority has been delegated or entrusted, the person or body by whom it has been delegated or entrusted and the person or persons in respect of or for whose benefit that jurisdiction, power or authority is to be exercised.[23]

This formulation, it was said, could render company directors subject to judicial review,[24] as well as trustees[25] and sporting referees.[26] (It was also questioned whether such a test would adequately capture exercise of prerogative power.[27]) True enough, private golf clubs were successfully judicially reviewed,[28] which doubtless sounds outlandish to readers from other legal systems. But for the most part this did not materialise, and in any event the tripartite relationship test was an innovation without a clear historical basis.[29] What was true in the *West* judgment was that the 'competency of the application [to the supervisory jurisdiction] does not depend upon any distinction between public law and private law, nor is

[20] *R v Panel on Take-overs and Mergers, ex parte Datafin plc* [1987] QB 815.

[21] See S Thomson, 'Into the Quagmire: Social Media Platforms and the Limits of Judicial Review' [2024] *Public Law* 692.

[22] *West v Secretary of State for Scotland*, 1992 SC 386, 413; and see S Thomson and D Edwards (eds), 'Administrative Law (2nd Reissue)', *The Laws of Scotland: Stair Memorial Encyclopaedia* (London, LexisNexis, 2023) [104]–[108].

[23] *West v Secretary of State for Scotland*, 1992 SC 386, 413.

[24] Where 'A' was the Articles of Association, 'B' was a company director and 'C' was a shareholder.

[25] Where 'A' was the truster, 'B' was a trustee and 'C' was a beneficiary.

[26] Where 'A' was the sporting rules, 'B' was a referee and 'C' was a player or participant.

[27] *Cf Council of Civil Service Unions v Minister for the Civil Service* [1985] 1 AC 374.

[28] See, eg, *Crocket v Tantallon Golf Club*, 2005 SLT 663, *Wiles v Bothwell Castle Golf Club*, 2005 SLT 785, and *Smith v Nairn Golf Club* [2007] CSOH 136.

[29] See S Thomson, 'The Doctrinal Core of the Supervisory Jurisdiction of the Court of Session' [2016] *Public Law* 670.

it confined to those cases which English law has accepted as amenable to judicial review'.[30] The doctrinal basis for this assertion was confirmed by my own close historical analysis in my doctoral research.[31] In fact, Lord President Hope went even further in *West*, stating that, in relation to the competency of an application to the supervisory jurisdiction, it is not correct to describe judicial review as a 'public law remedy'.[32]

What this all means is that many of the conundrums about the side of the putative public/private divide on which a body sits are largely avoidable. The advantages of this approach were sounded by Sir William Wade and Christopher Forsyth who wrote that in Scotland '[j]ustice can … be done in cases which lie beyond the reach of the rigid English system with its misguided public and private law dichotomy, and procedural obstacles and dilemmas are avoided'.[33] In a system in which a public/private divide is recognised, wherever that line is drawn, there will be bodies which straddle it, either by their nature, powers or personnel. Publicly-owned companies, private companies that operate public infrastructure and private companies that perform regulatory functions are all difficult to classify as public *or* private; and that classification is important in England and other jurisdictions because judicial review ('public law') procedure is discrete from ordinary ('private law') procedure. Choosing the wrong procedure can be fatal to an application,[34] so this is hardly a theoretical concern. Yet if judicial review procedure is only going to entertain public law matters, and ordinary procedure is only going to entertain non-public law matters – as embodied in the procedural exclusivity principle – then such cases must be shoehorned into one or the other by reference to the extent to which public law matters are in play.[35] Of course, one must also choose the correct procedure in Scotland, but the availability of judicial review will not depend on the extent to which so-called public law matters are at issue. Additionally, the same common law remedies are available. To this extent, the Scottish system seems less of a hostage to fortune as the public/private divide evolves.

The unusual, perhaps unique, approach to judicial review that is taken in Scotland is not without its disadvantages. 'Floodgates' concerns did not materialise post-*West*, as noted, but there seems to be little at the doctrinal level preventing them from opening. Their remaining closed is largely attributable to procedural protections and the fact that most of what may be considered non-traditional

[30] *West v Secretary of State for Scotland*, 1992 SC 386, 413.

[31] S Thomson, 'The Constitutional Basis of Judicial Review in Scotland' (PhD thesis, University of Edinburgh, 2013).

[32] *West v Secretary of State for Scotland*, 1992 SC 386, 413.

[33] That line has appeared in previous editions, but most recently in C Forsyth and J Ghosh, *Wade and Forsyth's Administrative Law*, 12th edn (Oxford, Oxford University Press, 2023) 518.

[34] *O'Reilly v Mackman* [1983] 2 AC 237; *Cocks v Thanet District Council* [1983] 2 AC 286. But see *Wandsworth London Borough Council v Winder* [1985] AC 461.

[35] *Davy v Spelthorne Borough Council* [1984] AC 262; *Roy v Kensington and Chelsea and Westminster Family Practitioner Committee* [1992] 1 AC 624.

public law matters would be captured by other areas of law like contract, delict (tort), property law and so on. They will therefore not come for judicial review and the courts can prevent them from doing so for that reason alone. But crucially this will not be because they do not concern matters of 'public law'. Yet a flip side of flexibility is lack of certainty or specificity, and while there has been a general 'doctrinal ease' with which to get matters into judicial review, remedies have also been obtained in judicial review-type cases using ordinary procedure.[36] In the past, the consequences of this may have been less significant, but with the relatively recent introduction of a permission requirement, time limit and sufficient interest test comparable to those in England, those consequences may now be greater.

There is also the fact that the vast majority of Scots judicial review cases are what would uncontroversially be regarded as concerning public law matters: immigration, social welfare, licensing and the like. While the doctrinal differences in Scotland are therefore important, indeed key to understanding differences in the scope of review in Scotland, they should not be taken to overstate the extent to which judicial review is substantially different in that jurisdiction. An objection might therefore be made that what are essentially more marginal cases are being taken to characterise judicial review as a whole. But this would be to commit a logical error. The fact that most judicial review cases that are respectively litigated in the English and Scottish courts concern matters that are, substantively, also amenable to review in the other does not mean that there is doctrinal equivalence between those jurisdictions. Indeed, the fact that a whole class of cases are amenable to judicial review in Scotland, but not in England, points to material differences between the two jurisdictions even if the volume of such cases is low. What is perhaps a greater challenge is how the distinctiveness of Scots judicial review, including its unique doctrinal approach, is to be explained and defended if Scots judicial review *procedure* is increasingly aligned with its English counterpart, as it recently has been.[37] Procedural matters are not always, and not necessarily, divorced from substantive or doctrinal considerations. However, if this increasing procedural alignment is indicative of alignment in any other sense, that could be an innovation that contradicts almost half a millennium of relative doctrinal coherence.

## II. Hong Kong: A Common Law System in Transition

Bearing more similarity to English judicial review than does its Scottish counterpart, judicial review in Hong Kong is modelled on that of England. This should not be particularly surprising given that an 1844 Hong Kong statute imported

[36] *Gunstone v Scottish Women's Amateur Athletic Association*, 1987 SLT 611; and *Graham v Ladeside of Kilbirnie Bowling Club*, 1990 SC 365. See also *Tait v Central Radio Taxis (Tollcross) Ltd*, 1989 SC 4.

[37] See above.

almost wholesale the law of England to the Crown colony.[38] This general position remained in place until 1966, when more scope for divergence from English law was established,[39] but with Hong Kong law continuing to be based on English law. Moreover, the Judicial Committee of the Privy Council – a convergent force on the legal system – was the final court of appeal for Hong Kong. This continued to be the case until the handover of sovereignty over Hong Kong from the United Kingdom to the People's Republic of China on 1 July 1997, though English law, and in particular the English common law, continues to be persuasive in the Hong Kong courts.[40] While English decisions also have persuasive effect in the Scottish courts, English law has never been directly imported into Scots law.

One of the main differences under Hong Kong's post-handover designation as a Special Administrative Region of the People's Republic of China, established as such under Article 31 of the PRC Constitution, is that Hong Kong law operates under a central constitutional code in the form of its Basic Law. Although the Basic Law is an enactment of the National People's Congress (and thus capable of ready abolition, by contrast with most constitutional texts), and is itself subject to the PRC Constitution,[41] it clearly serves a basic constitutional function by dispensing and allocating state power among institutions and restraining those institutions in accordance with law and principles of constitutionalism.[42] But this presents for the researcher, teacher and indeed practitioner a dimension not readily encountered in England: constitutional judicial review. In Scotland, such a thing exists in the context of devolution, with the Scotland Act 1998 and supplementing legislation creating and empowering a Scottish Parliament and Scottish Executive (now Scottish Government[43]) with major legislative and executive power, respectively. But, outside that context, judicial review is largely reserved for the administrative law sphere rather than the constitutional law sphere as it exists in other common law systems. In England, where devolution is generally not a direct concern, this constitutional aspect is even less pertinent. It might be said that the Human Rights Act 1998, sometimes referred to as a 'quasi-constitutional' statute, provides a ground for constitutional review. However, the Human Rights Act 1998 neither allocates nor restrains the basic powers of state institutions (including the

[38] Supreme Court Ordinance (No 15 of 1844).

[39] Application of English Law Ordinance 1966.

[40] See also The Hon. Mr Justice Tang PJ, 'The Common Law and the Market Place of Ideas' (speech to the Chancery Bar Association (5 May 2017) (available at www.hkcfa.hk/filemanager/speech/en/upload/186/The%20Common%20Law%20and%20the%20Market%20Place%20of%20Ideas.pdf).

[41] By decision of the National People's Congress, the Basic Law is compliant with the PRC Constitution despite the fact it is textually at odds with it and most of the PRC Constitution is not enforced within Hong Kong – Decision of the National People's Congress on the Basic Law of the Hong Kong Special Administrative Region of the People's Republic of China (adopted at the Third Session of the Seventh National People's Congress on 4 April 1990).

[42] Though the rule of law and constitutionalism – and the Basic Law's constraining power – are receding: see, eg, S Thomson, 'The New Constitutional Disorder: The Unlawful Application of Mainland Chinese Law to Hong Kong' (2018) 54(1) *Texas International Law Journal* 115.

[43] Scotland Act 2012, s 12.

legislature) and is not constitutional review par excellence. Note in this regard that Australia, to which we will soon turn, has a central constitutional code but no federal bill of rights.[44]

Clearly constitutional law does exist in England (and Scotland), and it has been litigated in recent high-profile cases including *R (on the application of Miller) v Secretary of State for Exiting the European Union*[45] and the prorogation cases.[46] But these cases are not litigated by reference to a central constitutional code and in that regard represent a sharp departure from the norm in other western legal systems. Hong Kong has moved in the other direction, from a legal system in which there was no central constitutional code (barring the Letters Patent and Royal Instructions) to one in which there is (the Basic Law). And while the Basic Law contains various continuity provisions, importantly including for present purposes Article 8, which states that the common law and rules of equity shall continue to be in force, this is not enforced by a pre-existing institution because the Court of Final Appeal was established only at the point of Handover.[47] The Court of Final Appeal's powers of judicial review therefore flow from the Basic Law and legislation but not from a predecessor institution. This is a different constitutional dynamic from Scotland, for there the Court of Session survived the transition from Scotland as a sovereign entity to Scotland as a constituent jurisdiction of a newly created sovereign United Kingdom of Great Britain.[48] It is also a different constitutional dynamic from Australia, where the High Court was created soon after the establishment of the new sovereign state of Australia,[49] albeit with a constitutional avenue to appeal to the Judicial Committee of the Privy Council,[50] which has since become defunct.[51] In Hong Kong, the Court of Final Appeal was established as a new institution at the point when the jurisdiction passed from one continuing sovereign state (the United Kingdom) to another (the PRC).

Hong Kong's Basic Law has been differentiated from the Australian Constitution by the Hong Kong courts. In the context of a constitutional challenge to administrative tribunals, it was stated that:

> Given the theme of continuity, it would be very surprising if the effect of the Basic Law, upon its proper interpretation, were to outlaw these administrative tribunals and bodies for ousting the jurisdiction or usurping the judicial functions of the courts of judicature of the HKSAR. Or put another way, the Basic Law should be interpreted in such a way

[44] Some Australian states and territories do have a bill of rights, namely the Australian Capital Territory, Queensland and Victoria.

[45] *R (on the application of Miller) v Secretary of State for Exiting the European Union* [2017] UKSC 5.

[46] *R (on the application of Miller) v The Prime Minister* and *Cherry v Advocate General for Scotland* [2019] UKSC 41.

[47] Basic Law, Arts 81–82; Hong Kong Court of Final Appeal Ordinance (cap. 484).

[48] Treaty of Union 1707, Art XIX.

[49] Judiciary Act 1903 (Cth).

[50] Australian Constitution, s 74.

[51] Privy Council (Limitation of Appeals) Act 1968; Privy Council (Appeals from the High Court) Act 1975; Australia Act 1986 (Cth), Australia Act 1986 (UK).

> as to enable, so far as violence is not done to the principle of the separation of powers as understood in the tradition of the English common law, the continued existence and development of administrative tribunals and bodies. This calls for a flexible and realistic, as opposed to an idealistic, approach to the doctrine of the separation of powers, and a purposive and contextualised interpretation of the scope and meaning of 'judicial power' in the Basic Law, rather than following indiscriminately the strict interpretation adopted by the Australian courts towards their own Constitution, which was written under very different circumstances in order to serve its own unique purposes.[52]

This 'flexible and realistic' approach to the separation of powers has unfortunately been taken to new levels in Hong Kong as the rule of law and constitutionalism have been increasingly weakened in recent years. The 2016 oath-taking controversy saw elected legislators who failed to properly take their oaths in accordance with law barred from retaking them by intervention of the National People's Congress Standing Committee ('NPCSC'). A judicial review application by the Chief Executive which inter alia sought to restrain the President of the Legislative Council from re-administering their oaths failed to obtain interim remedies,[53] but before judgment could be delivered on the perpetual remedies sought,[54] the NPCSC issued a binding interpretation which tied the court's hands by effectively rewriting the law on oath-taking.[55] Article 158 of the Basic Law, which provides that 'judgments previously rendered shall not be affected' by NPCSC interpretations, did not, it turned out, prevent the NPCSC from issuing an interpretation during litigation with the clear intention of dictating its outcome. While strictly none of the institutions concerned transgressed the constitutional limitations on their powers, the ability of a non-judicial body to intervene in active litigation with clear political objectives is a serious challenge to the rule of law.

This incident was closely followed by the West Kowloon Station Co-Location Arrangement controversy, which has been one of the gravest assaults on the Basic Law as a constitutional document. Hong Kong's Legislative Council enacted legislation which sought to disapply the applicability of the Basic Law from part of Hong Kong territory by declaring it to be:

> [A]n area lying outside Hong Kong but lying within the Mainland for the purposes of –
>
> the application of the laws of the Mainland, and of the laws of Hong Kong, in the Mainland Port Area; and
>
> the delineation of jurisdiction (including jurisdiction of the courts) over the Mainland Port Area.[56]

[52] *Luk Ka Cheung v Market Misconduct Tribunal* [2009] 1 HKLRD 114, [36] (A Cheung J).

[53] *Chief Executive of HKSAR v President of Legislative Council* [2016] 6 HKC 144.

[54] ibid 417.

[55] Interpretation of Article 104 of the Basic Law of the Hong Kong Special Administrative Region of the People's Republic of China by the Standing Committee of the National People's Congress (adopted by the Standing Committee of the Twelfth National People's Congress at its Twenty Fourth Session on 7 November 2016).

[56] Guangzhou-Shenzhen-Hong Kong Express Rail Link (Co-location) Ordinance (cap. 632), s 6(1).

This means that the area in question is, except in relation to limited matters, legally regarded as Mainland China rather than Hong Kong and subject to the laws and courts of Mainland China. Yet, leaving aside situations where a decolonising power cedes sovereignty over one or more former colonies,[57] the idea that ordinary legislation can disapply a constitutional code from part of a territory and disclaim jurisdiction over it is repugnant to the very idea of constitutionalism. Not only had the executive which promoted this initiative and the legislature which enacted it acted in violation of the Basic Law in so doing,[58] but the courts also failed to uphold two challenges to its constitutionality,[59] thus achieving the rare accomplishment of all three branches of the state acting unconstitutionally.[60] The Hong Kong Bar Association regarded the Basic Law's integrity as having been 'irreparably breached'.[61]

More recently – and notoriously – the PRC enacted a national security law for Hong Kong on 30 June 2020,[62] later supplemented by local legislation.[63] With their sweeping criminalisation of dissent, claim of extraterritorial jurisdiction and disapplication of existing legal protections, the national security laws have begun to dismantle many of Hong Kong's existing rule of law protections and practices of constitutionalism. A two-tier judiciary has been established, with only judges specially designated by the Chief Executive authorised to hear national security cases:[64] an absurdity, for if a judge is trusted to make decisions which can destroy a person's livelihood, remove access to their children or end their liberty, how could they not be trusted to hear a national security case? A Committee for Safeguarding National Security was established with vaguely defined jurisdiction,[65] and its decisions were deemed 'not amenable to judicial review'.[66] Just when common lawyers would be ready to step in and make the *Anisminic*[67] objection to that ouster clause, the Hong Kong courts have confirmed (in the high-profile Jimmy Lai case) that the Committee is not subject to judicial review.[68]

[57] For example, in relation to the UK Parliament providing for an end to British sovereignty and jurisdiction over Hong Kong (Hong Kong Act 1985) and the UK Parliament enacting the constitution of a sovereign Australia (Commonwealth of Australia Constitution Act 1900) and the termination of British legislative authority over Australia (Australia Act 1986).

[58] Both in general and in relation to multiple specific provisions.

[59] *Leung Chung Hang, Sixtus v President of the Legislative Council* [2018] HKCFI 2657; *Kwok Cheuk Kin v Secretary for Justice* [2021] HKCA 871.

[60] See further S Thomson, 'The New Constitutional Disorder: The Unlawful Application of Mainland Chinese Law to Hong Kong' (2018) 54(1) *Texas International Law Journal* 115–148.

[61] *Statement of the Hong Kong Bar Association on the Decision of the NPCSC of 27 December 2017 on the Co-Operation Agreement between the Mainland and the HKSAR on the Establishment of the Port at the West Kowloon Station of the Guangzhou-Shenzhen-Hong Kong Express Rail Link for Implementing Co-location Arrangement* (Press release, Hong Kong Bar Association, 27 December 2017), 6.

[62] The Law of the People's Republic of China on Safeguarding National Security in the Hong Kong Special Administrative Region (30 June 2020) ('NSL 2020').

[63] Safeguarding National Security Ordinance (Ord No 6 of 2024).

[64] NSL 2020, Art 44.

[65] NSL 2020, Arts 12–15.

[66] NSL 2020, Art 14.

[67] *Anisminic Ltd v Foreign Compensation Commission* [1969] 2 AC 147.

[68] *Lai Chee-ying v The Committee for Safeguarding National Security of the HKSAR* [2024] HKCA 611.

And this really represents what is happening to the rule of law in Hong Kong. With a stream of Overseas Non-Permanent Judges exiting the Court of Final Appeal, including Lord Collins, Lord Reed and Mr Justice Spigelman, some of the world's leading common law judges are no longer prepared to play their part in a system increasingly characterised by lip service to the rule of law. Lord Sumption, who resigned from the Court on 4 June 2024, stingingly wrote of a 'growing malaise in the Hong Kong judiciary', 'honourable people with the liberal instincts of the common law … [who] have to operate in an almost impossible political environment created by China'. He continued:

> An oppressive atmosphere is generated by the constant drumbeat from a compliant press, hardline lawmakers, government officers and China Daily, the mouthpiece of the Chinese government. A chorus of outrage follows rare decisions to grant bail or acquit. There are continual calls for judicial 'patriotism'. It requires unusual courage for local judges to swim against such a strong political tide. Unlike the overseas judges, they have nowhere else to go.
>
> Intimidated or convinced by the darkening political mood, many judges have lost sight of their traditional role as defenders of the liberty of the subject, even when the law allows it. There are guarantees of freedom of speech and assembly in both the Basic Law and the National Security Law, but only lip-service is ever paid to them. The least sign of dissent is treated as a call for revolution. Hefty jail sentences are dished out to people publishing 'disloyal' cartoon books for children, or singing pro-democracy songs, or organising silent vigils for the victims of Tiananmen Square.
>
> Hong Kong, once a vibrant and politically diverse community is slowly becoming a totalitarian state. The rule of law is profoundly compromised in any area about which the government feels strongly.[69]

While this erosion of the rule of law does not have obvious, immediate ramifications for bread-and-butter administrative law decisions about licences or urban planning consents, the 'national security' tentacles will doubtless find their way into immigration, education and policing decisions. Hong Kong's new national security era, in which dissent is increasingly viewed as unpatriotic or some kind of existential threat, will also see meaningful reforms to some institutions, like administrative tribunals, even less likely.[70] It must also be borne in mind that the Legislative Council now has no effective opposition following electoral reforms and a broader clampdown on dissenting voices.[71] The whole legal, constitutional and political ecosystem in which judges work and individuals live has changed.

[69] J Sumption, 'The rule of law in Hong Kong is in grave danger' (10 June 2024, *Financial Times*) (www.ft.com/content/60c825be-b70a-4152-895f-f6127974570a).

[70] S Thomson, 'Administrative Tribunals in a Hybrid Regime: The Case of the Hong Kong Special Administrative Region' in S Thomson, M Groves and G Weeks (eds), *Administrative Tribunals in the Common Law World* (Oxford, Hart Publishing, 2024) 251–270.

[71] Basic Law of the Hong Kong Special Administrative Region, Annexes I and II, as amended in accordance with the Decision of the National People's Congress on Improving the Electoral System of the Hong Kong Special Administrative Region (adopted at the Fourth Session of the Thirteenth National People's Congress on 11 March 2021).

Whereas the limitations of England's formalistic law of judicial review have been explored in the Scottish context, everything is relative. English judicial review upholds comparatively strong rule of law standards, allowing government to be held to account not only within the bounds of constitutional and statutory restrictions but also common law standards. The common law grounds of review allow the individual to demand higher standards of decision-making from government and public bodies. This depends on judges remaining faithful to their central mission of the dispensation of justice without fear or favour and playing their role in a system with a separation of powers.[72] The Court of Final Appeal sits in the Old Supreme Court Building in central Hong Kong, upon which is a blindfolded statue of Lady Justice bearing a sword in one hand and the scales of justice in the other. Is the metaphorical blindfold still firmly in place for the Hong Kong judiciary? Are the scales still evenly tipped? Lord Sumption's indictment would suggest not, at least in national security cases. This 'growing malaise' could easily seep into bread-and-butter administrative law cases where the government is increasingly given the benefit of the doubt. Doctrines like deference could be abused or conveniently deployed to duck sensitive political matters. The direction of travel towards an increasingly authoritarian system, despite the strong rule of law heritage left by English law, is not inspiring of confidence.

## III. Australia: Formalism Writ Large

Jurisdiction to judicially review in Australia is rooted in section 75 of the Australian Constitution, particularly section 75(v) but also section 75(iii). These respectively state that:

> In all matters:…
>
> (iii) in which the Commonwealth, or a person suing or being sued on behalf of the Commonwealth, is a party; …
>
> (v) in which a writ of Mandamus or prohibition or an injunction is sought against an officer of the Commonwealth;
>
> the High Court shall have jurisdiction.

Section 75(v) expressly grants the High Court jurisdiction to award mandamus, prohibition or injunction against an officer of the Commonwealth, but

[72] Hong Kong clearly has a separation of powers and an executive-led system, even though these have been pitted as mutually exclusive in a largely vacuous and emotionally-charged dispute. See, eg, former Secretary for Justice Teresa Cheng's nonsensical tirade which continues to be carried on the Hong Kong Department of Justice website: T Cheng, '*An executive-led system, with the executive, legislature and judiciary performing constitutionally designated roles*' (originally published in the *South China Morning Post*, 9 September 2020) (Department of Justice, www.doj.gov.hk/en/community_engagement/speeches/pdf/sj20200909e1.pdf).

this has been held to encompass jurisdiction to award certiorari as an ancillary remedy.[73] It has also been held that superior courts have an inherent power to grant declaratory relief.[74] The High Court's judicial review jurisdiction has been closely replicated in the Federal Court.[75] Section 75 of the Constitution (and section 39B of the Judiciary Act 1903) are limited in their conferral of judicial review jurisdiction, however, inasmuch as their applicability is determined by the identity of the party being sued: namely the Commonwealth or an officer of the Commonwealth.

This was supplemented by an important piece of legislation called the Administrative Decisions (Judicial Review) Act 1977 ('ADJR Act'). To slightly simplify, the relevant part of the Act for present purposes is section 5(1) which provides that:

> A person who is aggrieved by a decision to which this Act applies … may apply to the Federal Court or the Federal Circuit and Family Court of Australia for an order of review in respect of the decision on any one or more of the following grounds …

Section 5 then proceeds to list the grounds of review, which is not so much a codification of the common law grounds (and the High Court considered it only a restatement of those grounds[76]), not least because it offers almost nothing by way of definition or elaboration. As to a 'decision to which this Act applies', one must turn to section 3, which defines this in the following terms:

> [A] decision of an administrative character made, proposed to be made, or required to be made (whether in the exercise of a discretion or not and whether before or after the commencement of this definition):
>
> under an enactment …; or
>
> by a Commonwealth authority or an officer of the Commonwealth under an enactment …;
>
> other than:
>
> a decision by the Governor-General; or
>
> a decision included in any of the classes of decisions set out in Schedule 1.

This expands the Federal Court's (but not the High Court's) judicial review jurisdiction by inter alia allowing for judicial review where the person being sued is not the Commonwealth or an officer of the Commonwealth. In relation to section 3(1) in particular, it is the source of the act or decision that determines jurisdiction rather than the identity of the person being sued. To that extent it is a welcome and important expansion of judicial review jurisdiction.

However, this triumvirate of jurisdictional bases for judicial review – section 75 of the Constitution, section 39B of the Judiciary Act 1903 and the ADJR Act – has

[73] *Re Refugee Review Tribunal, ex parte Aala* (2000) 204 CLR 82.
[74] *Ainsworth v Criminal Justice Commission* (1992) 175 CLR 564 at 581.
[75] Judiciary Act 1903 (Cth), s 39B.
[76] *Kioa v West* (1985) 159 CLR 550; *Australian Broadcasting Tribunal v Bond* (1990) 170 CLR 321.

facilitated a hyper-technical approach to the determination of jurisdiction and its scope. In relation to section 75, there is case law on what constitutes a 'matter'.[77] Under the ADJR Act, there is a whole jurisprudence on the meaning of 'decision',[78] 'administrative character'[79] and 'under an enactment'.[80] While the ADJR Act is a statute and the terms of statutes will inevitably require interpretation, it seems wholly unnecessary to have three discrete avenues of review. Moreover, they do not even encapsulate the full gamut of review. Not only are some areas of decision-making largely reviewed under other legislation – notably review of migration decisions under the Migration Act 1958 (Cth) – some decisions would fail to be captured by any of these routes.

The quintessential example of this is *NEAT Domestic Trading Pty Ltd v AWB Ltd*.[81] AWB Ltd was a private company with a monopoly over wheat export under the Wheat Marketing Act 1989. AWB (International) Ltd ('AWBI') was 'nominated company B' in terms of section 57(3B) whose consent in writing must be given before the Wheat Export Authority could grant a bulk-export consent. AWBI's refusals to grant consent were challenged under the ADJR Act. The application for review failed, but there has been disagreement on what exactly is the ratio of the case. One interpretation is that AWBI's 'decision' was not made under an enactment because AWBI did not derive its authority to make the 'decision' under an enactment but from its private incorporation; another that AWBI made its 'decision' in pursuit of its private interests and therefore not 'under an enactment' (in pursuit of public law objectives). But the idea that a private company which can wield a singular veto over the award of export permits is operating only in the domain of private law – and the idea that legislation could create a scheme which insulates such a function from judicial review – is to adopt the most formalistic understanding of public law accountability. Had *Datafin*-style reasoning been adopted, AWBI's decision would more likely have been subject to review (bearing in mind there were also issues of statutory interpretation in play). In other words, while the main sources of Australian judicial review provide jurisdiction on the basis of the identity of the party being sued (under section 75 of the Constitution or section 39B of the Judiciary Act 1903) or the source under which the act or decision was made (under the ADJR Act), none of them provides jurisdiction on

[77] *Re Judiciary and Navigation Acts* (1921) 29 CLR 257; *Fencott v Muller* (1983) 152 CLR 570; *CGU Insurance Limited v Blakeley* (2016) 259 CLR 339.

[78] *Australian Broadcasting Tribunal v Bond* (1990) 170 CLR 321; *Pegasus Leasing Ltd v Federal Commissioner of Taxation* (1991) 32 FCR 158; *Telstra Corp v Australian Competition and Consumer Commission [No 2]* (2007) 240 ALR 135; and the cases discussed in Aronson, Groves and Weeks (n 2) 83–107.

[79] *McWilliam v Civil Aviation Safety Authority* (2004) 142 FCR 74; *Roche Products Pty Ltd v National Drugs and Poisons Schedule Committee* (2007) 163 FCR 451; *Applied Medical Australia Pty Ltd v Minister for Health* (2016) 246 FCR 555; and the cases discussed in Aronson, Groves and Weeks (n 2) 107–116.

[80] *NEAT Domestic Trading Pty Ltd v AWB Ltd* (2003) 216 CLR 277; *Griffith University v Tang* (2005) 221 CLR 99; and the cases discussed in Aronson, Groves and Weeks (n 2) 116–133.

[81] *NEAT Domestic Trading Pty Ltd v AWB Ltd* (2003) 216 CLR 277.

the basis of the nature of the power exercised. And the negative consequences of this are plain to see.

Another case which is well known in Australian administrative law circles, and which further demonstrates the accountability deficits in Australian judicial review, is *Griffith University v Tang*.[82] Griffith University excluded a PhD student because of allegations of academic misconduct. Noting that the university enjoyed statutory powers,[83] the student sought judicial review of the exclusion decision under Queensland's Judicial Review Act 1991 (Qld), which the High Court accepted could be construed by reference to 'under an enactment' decisions under the ADJR Act. The High Court stated that a decision 'made … under an enactment' had to be expressly or impliedly required or authorised by the enactment and must itself confer, alter or otherwise affect legal rights or obligations. Applying these tests to the facts, it was held that:

> The decisions of which the respondent complains were authorised, albeit not required, by the University Act … But that does not mean that the decision of which the respondent complains were 'made under' the University Act in the sense required to make them reviewable under the Review Act. The decisions did not affect legal rights and obligations. They had no impact upon matters to which the University Act gave legal force and effect.[84]

This is an even more formalistic system for determining the scope of judicial review when contrasted with that of England. In some ways England's system of judicial review is more remedy-driven than Australia's (inasmuch as the remedy-driven part of Australian judicial review is largely confined to review under section 75 of the Constitution and section 39B of the Judiciary Act 1903), but the Australian approach is rather more characterised by a technical search for the right constitutional or statutory formula to provide the basis for judicial review jurisdiction. It is a very fragmented approach which lacks doctrinal coherence.

This view was not lost on all of the judges in *Tang*, because Kirby J in his dissent opined that the majority had adopted 'an unduly narrow approach to the availability of statutory judicial review directed to the deployment of public power'.[85] That view has a great deal to commend it. This was the *Datafin* problem 20 years later – and with the benefit of the *Datafin* judgment to show how it could be done – but without the judiciary seizing the opportunity to substitute hypertechnicality for doctrinal pragmatism. Just as the Panel on Takeovers and Mergers would have been beyond legal recourse had the scope of judicial review not been reframed in *Datafin*, so too did the PhD student – whom, by the way, was not in a contractual relationship with the university – have no recourse without the High Court taking the same approach in *Tang*. As Mark Aronson helpfully pointed out to me, it was

[82] *Griffith University v Tang* (2005) 221 CLR 99.
[83] Griffith University Act 1998 (Qld).
[84] *Griffith University v Tang* (2005) 221 CLR 99, 132.
[85] *Griffith University v Tang* (2005) 221 CLR 99, 133.

recently held in South Australia that an assessment of a family's circumstances conducted by a government department, which was adverse but had no legally adverse consequences, was not subject to judicial review because that enquiry could have been conducted by a private individual. It was therefore not a decision made in the exercise of statutory power and not amenable to judicial review, even though South Australia has no equivalent to the ADJR Act.[86]

It is decisions like these that have led me to develop quite a critical view of Australian judicial review (though clearly these criticisms pale in comparison to the direction of travel in Hong Kong).[87] Who are these decisions supposed to serve? The statutory (and constitutional) patchwork quilt had already established tests for judicial review jurisdiction that lacked doctrinal coherence. The High Court, through decisions such as those in *NEAT* and *Tang*, has only added to that incoherence. While the courts cannot be blamed for unhelpfully framed legislation or constitutional provisions, they can be criticised for further descending into the quagmire of hypertechnicality or being reluctant to engage squarely with these issues.[88] The judicial response might be that it is for the legislature, not the judiciary, to amend the statutory framework if it so desires; and that is, of course, a correct position. But this does not justify the making of decisions when interpreting those statutes that seem more concerned with some kind of predetermined linguistic meaning than a just interpretation of statutory provisions or a rational common law which smoothes the edges of those provisions. If there is a fair choice to be made between interpreting a provision in a way which maximises or consolidates state power and one which strengthens the position of the individual against the state, why in general would a court choose the former approach?[89] A fundamental rationale of judicial review is to protect the individual in their dealings with the state, rather than to find cracks in the statutory scheme and then prise them open to the detriment of the individual.

The consequences of the fragmented and under-rationalised framework for judicial review in Australia and the courts' restrictive approach to determining the scope of review seriously risk leaving the individual insufficiently protected against the changing nature of public and governmental power in Australia. As Mark Aronson rightly wrote:

> [The Australian] courts should … recognise that public power is increasingly exercised from places within the private sector, by non-government bodies, and according

[86] *CNM v Chief Executive, Department for Child Protection* [2024] SASC 118; extending the reasoning of *L v State of South Australia* (2017) 129 SASR 180.

[87] I am far from the first to subject them to criticism – Mark Aronson noted at least 25 articles most of which were critical of these judgments on doctrinal and policy terms as far back as 2007, and there have been more since: see M Aronson, 'Private Bodies, Public Power and Soft Law in the High Court' (2007) 35(1) *Federal Law Review* 1, fn 6.

[88] See J Boughey and G Weeks, "Officers of the Commonwealth' in the Private Sector: Can the High Court Review Outsourced Exercises of Power?' (2013) 36(1) *UNSW Law Journal* 316.

[89] Consider D Stewart, '*Griffith University v Tang*, 'Under an Enactment' and Limiting Access to Judicial Review' (2005) 33(3) *Federal Law Review* 525.

> to rules found in management manuals rather than statute books. If judicial review is about the restraint of public power, it will need to confront these shifts in who exercises public power, and in the rules by which they exercise it.[90]

Janina Boughey and Greg Weeks have contended that *Datafin* is not suitable for application in the Australian context because this would simply shift the uncertainty to what constitutes a 'public' or 'private' power (ie, adopt the English problems) and that it cannot be reasonably accommodated within the language of section 75(v) of the Australian Constitution.[91] The first objection is a legitimate one, but in my submission it would be a better situation than the current approach adopted by the High Court and the broader legal framework. The second objection presents a more significant obstacle because section 75(v) places emphasis on the identity of the body under challenge, ie, 'an officer of the Commonwealth'. However, neither the challenge in *NEAT* nor *Tang* invoked the High Court's section 75(v) jurisdiction, instead comprising statutory challenges. A more *Datafin*-type approach could have been adopted in those cases, and even in cases invoking section 75 jurisdiction, the court could adopt more of a *Datafin*-type approach under section 75(iii), in particular by reference to a party 'being sued on behalf of the Commonwealth'. Moreover, there are other ways of expanding the scope of judicial review in Australia, for example, its application to bodies subject to one or more rules of natural justice, as Matthew Groves has discussed in the context of Victoria's Administrative Law Act 1978.[92] This is a somewhat inverted test whereby scope is determined by reference to the applicability of a ground of review, rather than the establishment of scope being determined prior to a consideration of grounds, but it still points to the potential for the remit of Australia's judicial review to be significantly expanded.

## IV. Comparative Law: Seeing the Wood as Well as the Trees

This is not the place to relitigate the doctrinal and policy credentials of the likes of *NEAT* and *Tang*, but it does beg the question of how, comparatively, Australia fares in terms of judicial review's ability to appropriately handle the tenacious public/private divide problem. The answer, or at least my answer, is that it does not fare well. These decisions, and their failure to be overturned or substantially modified some 20 years later, suggest that Australian judicial review has lost sight of its core function. The finger cannot be pointed solely at Parliament for creating such a fragmented statutory scheme for review given the courts' tenuous decisions in this area.

[90] Aronson (n 87) 1, 2.
[91] Boughey and Weeks (n 88) 316, 331–337.
[92] M Groves, 'Should the *Administrative Law Act 1978 (Vic)* be Repealed?' (2010) 34(2) *Melbourne University Law Review* 452.

English law has improved its resilience to the conundrums generated by the public/private divide through *Datafin*-type decisions. It has by no means solved the issue, and there remain serious problems with its remedy-driven, cart-before-the-horse approach to the scope of judicial review, but it has – by *judicial* innovation – put itself on a stronger footing. Hong Kong, which also features in this chapter, has followed *Datafin* and on this point is similar in position to England.[93]

The Scottish courts are less constrained overall such that, of these jurisdictions, bodies are least likely in Scotland to avoid the crosshairs of judicial review because of some failure to fit into a predetermined formula of amenability to review, whether along remedy-driven and 'sufficient public (law) element' lines (as in England) or the lines of exacting but under-rationalised statutory criteria (as in Australia). To the extent that this makes the law on judicial review in Scotland 'better' in this regard, it is not because it was better designed as such – apart from anything else, it is largely historical accident that has led Scots law to be less of a hostage to fortune in terms of the public/private divide. The problems posed by publicly-owned companies (whether at the national, devolved or local level) and public services performed by private corporations could hardly have been envisaged when Scots judicial review was undergoing substantial development in the nineteenth century. But the fact that Scots judicial review is less hamstrung by these problems is difficult to dispute.

Critical as one may be of the Australian High Court's decisions, it is not simply a matter of pointing out that the Scottish courts have not tied themselves in knots in a comparable manner and therefore that if only the High Court of Australia would learn some lessons from their Scottish counterparts, the troubles of Australian judicial review would be resolved. For a start, Australia's law of judicial review is, as discussed, heavily framed and conditioned by the two main statutes through which applications are made, namely the Judiciary Act 1903 and the ADJR Act.[94] The Australian Parliament would have to repeal or make significant amendments to parts of these statutes (though I am tempted to argue that they should). But the whole manner in which judicial review has developed in the two jurisdictions is different. The jurisdictional foundation of the Court of Session's supervisory jurisdiction is found in a very old statute, namely the College of Justice Act 1532. And even that imported pre-existing powers from older, predecessor institutions. It barely needs to be said that the law and legal system looked very different then and that matters have since come a long way. In Scotland, the Court of Session has played a key role in shaping its own jurisdiction throughout the centuries.[95] Judicial review in Scotland seems more a product of slow evolution than one of antecedent design.

[93] An authoritative statement of the law in Hong Kong on this matter remains Hon A Cheung J's (as he then was) statement in *Anderson Asphalt Ltd v Secretary for Justice* [2009] 3 HKLRD 214, [57].

[94] And, as discussed, section 75 of the Australian Constitution which provides the basis for the High Court's original jurisdiction.

[95] See S Thomson, 'The Doctrinal Core of the Supervisory Jurisdiction of the Court of Session' [2016] *Public Law* 670; S Thomson, 'The Constitutional Basis of Judicial Review in Scotland' (PhD thesis, University of Edinburgh, 2013).

Does this scenario adequately translate into the Australian context, where the system was necessarily one of design (of course, it has also evolved)? Australia as a country, and its core federal institutions, only came into existence in 1901. Much of modern Australian administrative law can be traced to the Kerr Committee Report of 1971.[96] This was a very different age in which to start thinking about the role of a central court in a newly formed sovereign state. It was also a very different context, where the powers of the High Court of Australia and bodies of legislation and government had to be articulated in a central constitutional code, something that has never had to be done in the same way in relation to Scotland.[97] Even if Scotland were to become an independent sovereign state and enact its own central constitutional code, the situation would still be different from that of Australia. In Australia, the states already had their own supreme courts with their own powers. These were reserved in the Australian Constitution of 1901 but supplemented by the creation of federal jurisdiction supervised by the High Court. There was no Australian federal or high court before this 'constitutional moment'. In Scotland, the situation is different. The main institution of judicial review, namely the Court of Session, predates the current state (the United Kingdom) by some 125 years and itself embodied jurisdictional powers from even older institutions. The Treaty of Union 1707 served as a conduit for many of those powers. Should the Court of Session be retained as the supreme civil court in Scotland after independence, as it probably would be, it would likely continue to enjoy the same perennial jurisdiction that it has done under previous sovereign states. A new Scottish Constitution would therefore probably confirm the Court of Session's existing jurisdiction rather than conferring it afresh. In various ways this is the reverse of the Australian example.

But just how different are these constitutional systems? Australia has been said to have a constitutionally entrenched minimum of judicial review; but this legal rule has come from the High Court.[98] While no comparable textual 'guarantee' is found in the likes of Scotland – save a rather oblique reference in Article XIX of the Treaty of Union – the Court of Session has likewise asserted the constitutional status of its own supervisory jurisdiction. In both legal systems the courts play a key role in asserting an enduring constitutional basis for judicial review. This is not to understate the significance of section 75 of the Australian Constitution, but to caution against the notion that it is self-executing and to suggest that these systems may not be as different at a more fundamental level than is often supposed. A rejoinder may be that no legislation could override the Australian Constitution.

[96] Commonwealth Administrative Review Committee, *Report: August 1971* (October 1971).

[97] Again, this is not wholly true by reference to the Treaty of Union 1707 which expressly reserves pre-existing powers of the College of Justice (including the Court of Session). But the Treaty, for better or worse, has never played the kind of constraining constitutional role that Australia's Constitution – or many western constitutional codes – have. The Treaty of Union rarely forms the subject of litigation, and even more rarely successful litigation.

[98] *Plaintiff S157/2002 v Commonwealth* (2003) 211 CLR 476; and, at the state level, *Kirk v Industrial Relations Commission of New South Wales* (2010) 239 CLR 531.

Yet the fate of ouster clauses in Scotland[99] is broadly the same as in England,[100] and judicial resistance to ouster of common law jurisdiction to review is found in Scottish cases from as early as the eighteenth century.[101] And while the supremacy of Parliament may be cited, there are the perennial problems with this both from a UK and Scottish (as opposed to English) perspective – it has no provision in the Treaty of Union 1707 or the Acts of Union 1800, it does not necessarily find the same historical traction in Scotland,[102] and there is in any event precedent in Scotland for even an act of the monarch being struck down as ultra vires.[103] So is this another constitutionally entrenched minimum of judicial review, but one that is more nuanced than in Australia?

This is the value of comparative law: being able to recognise that the status quo is not the only way of doing things and that other options exist. Those might be concluded to be better, worse, similarly good/bad or altogether inappropriate (for example, due to constitutional differences) depending on the comparison being made. But neither the status quo nor basic doctrinal assumptions are inevitable. Perhaps this chapter raises more questions than answers, but it does provide some answers. Must a legal system have a discrete class of public law remedies? No. Must the scope of judicial review be drawn on public/private (law) lines? No. Must there be a discrete permission stage? No. Must there be a 'fixed' time limit for applying for review? No. The idea that these are inevitable characteristics of a common law system of judicial review is false. Let the pros and cons of procedural exclusivity, or a discrete class of public law remedies, be weighed up, and if they are concluded to be substantially in the negative, then abolish or reform them. This seems to be a far more rational and less dogmatic basis for designing laws and legal systems. Comparativism should be practised in courts, lawmaking, legal research and legal education if doctrinal tunnel vision is to be avoided. Alignment between jurisdictions should not be pursued for its own sake, but an abstention from reform should be based on an informed conclusion that the status quo works well. Are readers, in whichever legal system they are located, satisfied that it does?

[99] See *Eba v Advocate General for Scotland* [2011] UKSC 29; and S Thomson and D Edwards (eds), 'Administrative Law (2nd Reissue)' in *The Laws of Scotland: Stair Memorial Encyclopaedia* (London, LexisNexis, 2023) [47]–[51] and [109]–[110].

[100] *Anisminic Ltd v Foreign Compensation Commission* [1969] 2 AC 147; *R (on the application of Privacy International) v Investigatory Powers Tribunal* [2019] UKSC 22.

[101] For example, in *Lord Prestongrange v Justices of the Peace of Haddington*, 1756 Mor 7350; *Countess of Loudon v Trustees on the High Roads in Ayrshire*, 1793 Mor 7398; and reiterated in 19th century cases such as *Lord Advocate v Police Commissioners of Perth* (1869) 8 M 244, 246; and *Stirling v Commissioners of Police of the Burgh of Turriff* (1874) 1 R 935.

[102] *MacCormick v Lord Advocate*, 1953 SC 396, 411.

[103] *Officers of State for Scotland v Lord Dunglas* (1838) 1 D 300.

# 7

# On Time and Space: Proximity in the Law of Bias

PAUL DALY

## I. Introduction

In my contribution to this volume, I address the law of bias and offer a proposal designed to enhance analytical clarity. Lawyers should incorporate proximity, with temporal and spatial dimensions, into the analysis of alleged bias. Simply put, the closer the source of bias in time and space to the decision at issue, the more plausible any claim that a decision-maker is biased.

My focus will be on administrative law, where the relevant general legal principles are highly contextual and unpredictable in their application to specific cases. As I explain in the first section of this chapter, the law of bias has evolved significantly over time, most importantly in response to the rise of the administrative state in the twentieth century: the hard-edged rules of natural justice became progressively softer and now form a context-sensitive set of principles to be applied with due attention to the nuances of particular areas of regulation, taking account of all the relevant circumstances of individual cases. Context sensitivity comes at the expense of predictability, however, which is the problem I tackle in this chapter.

As I set out in the second section, demonstrating bias requires an applicant to identify a relevant source of bias – such as a prior relationship between an adjudicator and one of the parties, prejudicial comments or predispositions, and prior involvement in a matter – and articulate a logical connection between the source and the decision made. I briefly introduce the test of a 'reasonable apprehension of bias' and discuss by reference to a series of cases involving statistical evidence the importance of articulating a logical connection between a source of bias and a decision.

With the groundwork laid, I then turn in the third section to proposing greater analytical clarity in the form of focus on spatial and temporal proximity. My proposal for greater analytical clarity in this context-sensitive area of law builds on the suggestion of Justice Stephen Gageler (as he then was), enthusiastically endorsed by Professor Matthew Groves, that a third step should be introduced to the assessment of bias cases. Their third step requires consideration of the reasonableness of the claim of bias. In my view, this third step is a valuable addition to the framework for assessing bias, but I would go further and introduce spatial and temporal proximity as key considerations. As I explain, by reference to decided cases, the closeness in space and time of a source of bias to the decision taken helps to sharpen the analysis of bias claims.

My focus in what follows will mostly be on Canadian cases, with a spattering of Irish and Australian authorities. I think that Professor Groves would approve. One of the wonders of the magisterial textbook he co-authors with Professors Aronson and Weeks is its reference to comparative materials: the book is firmly grounded in Australian law but takes a broad perspective encompassing developments elsewhere in the common law world. In any event, though there may be nuances here and there, I think the law of bias can fairly safely be said to be uniform in its application across the jurisdictions I refer to, such that the cases discussed below would have come out the same way wherever they arose.

## II. The Problem

There is a problem with the common law of bias as applied to administrative decision-makers. Comprised of a set of heavily context-sensitive principles, it is difficult to predict the application of the law of bias in advance. The Privy Council noted how '[t]his is a corner of the law in which the context, and the particular circumstances, are of supreme importance', which makes generalisation hazardous.[1] As Professor Groves observes in a magisterial study of the area, the 'potential level of difference in judicial assessment of bias claims is inevitable'.[2]

The historical evolution of the common law explains why. Previously, the no-bias principle was one of the two rules of natural justice. These were *nemo iudex in sua causa* (no one shall be a judge in their own cause) and *audi alteram partem* (hear both sides).[3]

When the prerogative writs were used to control judicial decision-making, the courts originally required strict compliance by decision-makers with these two rules of natural justice. Gradually and incrementally, over a period of many years, the courts extended the scope of the prerogative writs to cover a broad range of administrative decision-making. With the growth of the administrative state in the wake of the Industrial Revolution, the extension of the franchise and crises of war and depression, it became necessary to adapt the strict rules designed to regulate *judicial* decision-making to an *administrative* context.

[1] *Man O'War Station Ltd v Auckland City Council (No 1)* [2002] UKPC 28; [2002] 3 NZLR 577 [11] (PC).

[2] M Groves, 'Clarity and Complexity in the Bias Rule' (2020) 44 *Melbourne University Law Review* 565, 568.

[3] Contemporary understandings of the latter rule are now addressed under the label of the hearing principle, which is not the subject of this chapter.

One consequence was that it became entirely unrealistic to require all decision-makers to respect the rules of natural justice to the letter. This was particularly obvious in respect of the hearing principle. Given that the modern administrative state was making decisions about matters ranging from housing benefits and immigration status to tariffs payable to providers of public services, to require full-on hearings for all manner of administrative decisions would be entirely impractical.

It also became increasingly obvious in respect of the no-bias principle. For example, administrative tribunals were, from their earliest days, peopled by members with expertise in a particular area and significant prior knowledge of issues likely to arise.[4] They were not detached, impassive arbiters wearing 'the inscrutable face of a sphinx'.[5]

When states later created regulatory agencies to manage complex sectors of the economy, like stock markets and utilities, the problem became more acute: such agencies have rule-making, rule-interpreting and rule-enforcing functions that are often exercised by the same people; those doing the interpretation and enforcement will often have been participants in the industry prior to becoming regulators; and regulators are expected to engage in dialogue with the regulated community and broader public. These roles, individually and in combination, are anything but judicial.

Administrative decision-makers are very far removed from the Sphinx-like judge, detached from society and applying law to fact dispassionately, for whom the *nemo iudex* rule was developed. Indeed, it should be said that even today's judges are not expected to imitate their forebears by remaining aloof on the dais; rather, the no-bias principle is relaxed even in its application to members of the judiciary in recognition of the desirability of judges engaging with civil society.[6] Accordingly, the rules developed for previous eras have morphed into context-sensitive standards appropriate for this one, generating, however, a lack of predictability in the application of the standards in any given case.

## III. The Law

Acknowledging the changes wrought by the emergence of the modern administrative state, the courts began to relax the rules of natural justice, taking an avowedly context-sensitive approach to their application, whereby the exigencies of natural justice would vary from case to case.[7] The modern no-bias principle is

[4] C Stebbings, 'Comment: A Victorian Legal Legacy – the Bespoke Tribunal' (Council on Tribunals, *Adjust*, April 2007) 3.

[5] *R. v Nat Bell Liquors*, [1922] 2 AC 128, at 159. I appreciate that Lord Sumner was writing there of judicial review for error on the face of the record, but the 'sphinx' point has been picked up on in the bias context: *Brouillard Also Known As Chatel v The Queen*, [1985] 1 SCR 39, at [17].

[6] *Yukon Francophone School Board, Education Area #23 v Yukon (Attorney General)*, 2015 SCC 25, [2015] 2 SCR 282, at [59].

[7] The definitive treatment remains D Mullan, 'Fairness: The New Natural Justice' (1975) 25 *University of Toronto Law Journal* 281.

an exemplar of this. Courts must ask if the reasonable observer, appraised of the relevant facts, would have a fear that the decision-maker would not determine the matter impartially:

> [T]he apprehension of bias must be a reasonable one, held by reasonable and right minded persons, applying themselves to the question and obtaining thereon the required information. [T]hat test is 'what would an informed person, viewing the matter realistically and practically – and having thought the matter through – conclude. Would he think that it is more likely than not that [the decision-maker], whether consciously or unconsciously, would not decide fairly?'[8]

Often, the test for bias is expressed in terms of the view a 'reasonable observer' would take of the relevant facts. But there is no such corporeal entity that a court can appeal to: the 'reasonable observer' is purely a judicial construct.[9] What is required – from judges – is an 'abstract judicial assessment of the conclusions of a fictional person'.[10] And then the 'device of the informed observer becomes more difficult to apply as the courts attribute relevant knowledge from the case or decision at hand'.[11]

The High Court of Australia has set out a two-step process for determining whether there is bias. As Professor Groves has put it, the test 'requires claimants to first identify the source of the claimed bias and then articulate how that source might have the effect claimed'.[12] Ultimately, '[t]here must be an articulation of the logical connection between the matter and the feared deviation from the course of deciding the case on its merits'.[13]

## A. Sources of Bias

As to the first step, there are a variety of sources of bias. A prior relationship with a party, prejudicial comments before or during a decision-making process, prior involvement in the decision-making process and prejudicial conduct during a hearing can in principle make a decision-maker's position untenable.[14] I will return to these in more detail below.

[8] *Committee for Justice and Liberty v National Energy Board*, [1978] 1 SCR 369, at 394.

[9] AA Olowofoyeku, 'Bias and the Informed Observer: A Call for a Return to *Gough*' (2009) 68 *Cambridge Law Journal* 388, 393–396.

[10] Groves (n 2) 579.

[11] ibid 583.

[12] ibid 567.

[13] *Ebner v Official Trustee in Bankruptcy* [2000] HCA 63; (2000) 176 ALR 643, 345, approved in *Saxmere Co Ltd v Wool Board Disestablishment Co Ltd* [2009] NZSC 72; [2010] 1 NZLR 35. See also *CNY17 v Minister for Immigration and Border Protection* [2019] HCA 50, [21], [69]. For a not dissimilar formulation, see *R (Royal Brompton and Harefield NHS Foundation Trust) v Joint Committee of Primary Care Trusts* [2012] EWCA Civ 472 [125] per Arden LJ.

[14] See P Daly, *Understanding Administrative Law in the Common Law World* (Oxford, Oxford University Press, 2021) ch 2.

## B. Connecting a Source to a Reasonable Apprehension of Bias

As to the second step, the importance of articulating a logical connection can be appreciated by reference to a series of cases from around the common law world in which unsuccessful claims of bias were raised on the basis of statistical evidence purporting to demonstrate pre-judgment about classes of claimant.

In *ALA15 v Minister for Immigration and Border Protection*,[15] the applicant was unsuccessful in seeking the recusal of a judge of the Federal Circuit Court. The applicant adduced evidence that the judge in question only found in favour of an immigration applicant in 0.79 per cent of the matters he heard, finding in favour of the respondent minister 99.21 per cent of the time. In those 0.79 per cent of matters, moreover, the minister admitted that the decision in question was vitiated by a fatal error. By contrast, other judges (considered as a group) found in favour of applicants 10.8 per cent and 12.2 per cent of the time in immigration and refugee matters, respectively.

The court held that this statistical evidence was insufficient to demonstrate bias, especially because the well-informed observer would have to consider not only raw statistics but also the more general context of the underlying cases: 'a close analysis of some, many, or all of the relevant judgments reveal that they had been determined on a reasonable and plausible basis' or as 'a consequence of human frailty'.[16] On its own, the fact that one judge might be more likely than another to find in favour of or against an applicant is not evidence of bias.[17] Ultimately,

> the mere fact that a particular judge has decided a number of cases, the facts and circumstances of which are unknown, one way rather than another, does not go any way to assisting the hypothetical observer making an informed assessment as to whether that judge might not bring an impartial and unprejudiced mind to the resolution of the question in a particular proceeding before that judge.[18]

The Federal Court of Canada reached the same conclusion, on almost identical grounds, in *Turoczi v Canada (Citizenship and Immigration)*.[19] There was evidence that the Member who had rejected T's refugee claim had only made decisions favourable to claimants in 1.9 per cent of cases he heard in the same year. The court rejected the application for judicial review because, without more, the statistics did not satisfy the test for bias:[20] the

> informed reasonable person, thinking the matter through, would demand a statistical analysis of this data by an expert based upon and having taken into consideration all of the various factors and circumstances that are unique to and impact on determinations

[15] *ALA15 v Minister for Immigration and Border Protection* [2016] FCAFC 30.
[16] ibid at [38].
[17] ibid at [39].
[18] ibid at [41].
[19] *Turoczi v Canada (Citizenship and Immigration)* 2012 FC 1423.
[20] ibid at [13]–[15].

> of refugee claims before he or she would think it more likely than not that the decision-maker would not render a fair decision.[21]

An interesting Irish case is to the same effect: *C.S.B v The Minister for Social Protection*.[22] Here, the mother of a young boy who had been diagnosed with autism was refused a domiciliary care allowance by the minister. Her argument was 'that the Department of Social Protection in effect operates a policy whereby the opinions of its medical assessors are dutifully followed by departmental deciding officers, irrespective of the medical evidence actually submitted by claimants'.[23] Affidavit evidence from the Department suggested that it would indeed be 'unusual' for deciding officers not to defer to medical experts.[24] Remarkably, the particular decision-maker here had followed the medical assessors in 3,806 out of 3,806 cases, 100 per cent of the time, with no particular bias in favour of or against claimants. The first-instance judge found that the decision-making process had been tainted by undue deference to the medical assessor and sent the decision back for fresh consideration, but this conclusion was reversed on appeal. It was not enough to observe that 'the deciding officer invariably follows the views of the medical assessor'.[25] Without more, the statistics were insufficient to demonstrate that the deciding offer had a fixed and irrevocable view that the medical assessor's views were binding: 'statistics alone do not, however, prove the existence of a fixed policy position'.[26] If statistical evidence is insufficient to win a case like this one, it will always be insufficient.[27]

In these cases, the statistical evidence could not, on its own, furnish a logical connection between the alleged predisposition and the impugned decisions.[28]

The conclusions do, on their face, seem surprising: even a 100 per cent rejection rate is not enough, on its own, to indicate a case of prejudgment. One appreciates that drawing the line can be difficult – 90, 95, 99 per cent – but when the data are overwhelming, perhaps courts could draw the fairly obvious conclusion that the decision-maker is not likely to look favourably on a particular class of applicant.

[21] ibid at [15].

[22] *C.S.B v The Minister for Social Protection* [2016] IECA 116.

[23] ibid at [9].

[24] ibid at [10]–[11].

[25] ibid at [30].

[26] ibid at [33].

[27] See the comments of the first-instance judge:

> [T]he policy whereby deciding officers generally defer to the opinions of department medical assessors in the manner and circumstances described has yielded a situation in the instant case in which there has been an abdication of statutory duty by the deciding officer who decided B.'s initial application. Indeed the manner of implementation of such policy in the case of the deciding officer who decided B.'s initial application is such that the court finds it has vitiated the decision-making process employed in relation to that application; this is because the deference manifested by this particular deciding officer to the opinion of medical assessors has been proven to be so great that the court concludes that the medical assessor's opinion volunteered in the course of the consideration of B.'s initial application was in fact determinative of that application … ([2014] IEHC 186, at [26]).

[28] See also the principle that de minimis financial interests do not justify recusal: *Pearlman v Manitoba Law Society Judicial Committee* [1991] 2 SCR 869.

Nonetheless, the point for present purposes is only the analytical one, that the applicant must identify a logical connection. These extreme cases help to make that crucial point.

## IV. Proximity and Intensity: Time and Space

In an interesting intervention, Justice Stephen Gageler suggested that there is a third step to the analysis of any bias claim. Having identified the source of bias and articulated a logical connection between the source of bias and the decision in question, the court must then turn its mind to a 'consideration of the reasonableness of the apprehension of that deviation being caused by that factor in that way'.[29]

Professor Groves agreed that Gageler J's suggested new step could 'introduce a greater level of transparency into the bias rule' by enabling judges 'to provide their own assessment of bias claims'.[30]

I also agree. In this section, I will attempt to demonstrate how this third step can provide a greater degree of analytical clarity in response to the well-known problem of uncertainty described above. What matters in terms of reasonableness, I suggest, is the temporal and spatial closeness of the ground of bias to the decision taken.

I will demonstrate the strength of this proposition by reference to three sources of bias: prior relationship with a party, prejudicial comments and prior involvement in a decision-making process. I will also consider a fourth, conduct during a hearing. Drawing mostly on Canadian case law, I will observe that considerations of temporal and spatial proximity help to explain how bias cases are decided.

### A. Prior Relationship

I will consider three Canadian decisions in this section. They each relate to the prior relationship between a decision-maker and a party to a matter.

The issue in *Committee for Justice and Liberty v National Energy Board*[31] was the perceived lack of impartiality of the Chair of the National Energy Board in a quasi-judicial proceeding. In the proceeding, the Board had to consider which, if any, of the competing applications for a Mackenzie Valley pipeline should be granted a certificate of public convenience under section 44 of the National Energy Board Act.[32]

[29] *Isbester v Knox City Council* 2012 FC 1141, at [59]. For a philosophical approach to the issue, see L Jacobs, 'From Rawls to Habermas: Towards A Theory of Grounded Impartiality in Canadian Administrative Law' (2014) 51 *Osgoode Hall Law Journal* 543.

[30] Groves (n 2) 587.

[31] *Committee for Justice and Liberty v National Energy Board* [1978] 1 SCR 369.

[32] RSC 1970, c N-6.

Prior to his appointment to the Board, the Chair had been the president of a Crown Corporation involved in studies of the physical and economic feasibility of a Mackenzie Valley pipeline. The Chair attended meetings of a study group and, indeed, participated in the group's unanimous decision on the ownership and routing of the pipeline, just a few months before his appointment to the Board. The application arising from the study group's work was filed about five months after the Chair's appointment to the Board. The Crown Corporation remained an active member of the study group through the application process up to the point where concerns about impartiality were raised.

A majority of the Supreme Court held that the Chair should have recused himself. One of the applicants before the Board 'was born' out of the 'deliberations and decisions' of the study group.[33] As a member of this group, the Chair 'was not a mere cipher'[34] but had to apply his 'own judgment' and his 'own talents to the joint project',[35] including assessing its '[e]conomic and financial feasibility',[36] with significant 'latitude' in pursuing the interests of the Crown Corporation.[37] Ultimately, the Chair 'had a hand in developing and approving important underpinnings of the very application which eventually was brought before the panel'[38] and supported the decision to make the application[39] in circumstances where the question the Board had to answer was 'not only … whether a particular application for a pipeline will succeed but also … whether any pipeline will be approved'.[40] Accordingly, a well-informed observer would have formed a reasonable apprehension that the Chair would be predisposed to decide in a way favourable to the application arising from the study group's work.

For three dissenting judges (as well as three judges at the Federal Court of Appeal who found there was no reasonable apprehension of bias), it was important that the pipeline plan had long been in the offing: 'the problem was that of routing and of ownership and it is to these two points and to these two points only that Mr. Crowe gave his attention',[41] whereas many other points also fell to be considered by the Board, that there had been modifications to the proposal since the Chair's involvement and the fact that the Chair had signed a Board report raising 'many question marks' about the application process.[42] This was, in other words, a fairly close case, with many judges taking a different view of the facts from the perspective of a well-informed observer.

[33] [1978] 1 SCR 369, at 375.
[34] ibid at 386.
[35] ibid at 387.
[36] ibid at 390.
[37] ibid at 387.
[38] ibid at 389.
[39] ibid at 390.
[40] ibid at 391.
[41] ibid at 403.
[42] ibid at 405.

The issue in *Wewaykum Indian Band v Canada*[43] arose after the Supreme Court dismissed the appeals of two bands which had claimed exclusive possession of a reserve. The reasons for the decision were written by Justice Binnie. It came to light after the decision had been released that Justice Binnie had acquired some knowledge of the underlying dispute in 1985–86 when he was Associate Deputy Minister for Justice, in which capacity he oversaw all litigation involving the federal government (save for tax matters and cases from Quebec).

The Supreme Court held that there was no reasonable apprehension of bias. First, Justice Binnie's prior involvement in the matter was of 'a limited supervisory and administrative nature':[44] 'he was never counsel of record, and played no active role in the dispute after the claim was filed'.[45] In his role as Associate Deputy Minister, Justice Binnie was involved in setting the 'strategic orientations' of 'thousands of files', and the issue he had discussed in relation to this one was of a high-level nature as it related to reserves in British Columbia generally.[46] Second, a 'lengthy period' of 15 years had elapsed between his earlier involvement and the Supreme Court decision.[47] In addition, Justice Binnie stated that he had no recollection of the matter. These considerations led the Supreme Court to conclude that Justice Binnie need not have recused himself.

My third case is *Canadian Union of Postal Workers v Canada Post Corporation*.[48] This case arose from special federal legislation passed in 2011 to compel striking Canada Post workers to return to work. One component of the back-to-work legislation was that a 'final offer' arbitrator would be appointed. Both Canada Post and the Union would make their 'final offer', and the arbitrator would choose between them. Once the arbitrator had chosen, the 'final offer' would become the binding collective agreement between the parties.

The Federal Court held that the arbitrator nominated by the federal government should have recused himself. The arbitrator had previously represented Canada Post in litigation against a different Union about pay equity. Although his active involvement in the litigation ended almost a decade prior to his nomination as arbitrator, he remained a partner at the firm handling the litigation until 2009. The case only ended in 2011 and continued to have repercussions on Canada Post's operations.

Here, a reasonable apprehension of bias existed because of the short passage of time between the arbitrator's prior involvement (especially given the continuing importance of the underlying dispute for Canada Post), the fact that the arbitrator 'had formed ties with various managers at Canada Post during this mandate',[49] and

[43] *Wewaykum Indian Band v Canada* 2003 SCC 45, [2003] 2 SCR 259.
[44] ibid at [82].
[45] ibid at [83].
[46] ibid at [84].
[47] ibid at [88].
[48] *Canadian Union of Postal Workers v Canada Post Corporation* 2012 FC 975.
[49] ibid at [89].

the similarity of the issues in the arbitration and the prior litigation, both of which dealt 'with the relationship between employees and management at Canada Post'.[50]

Two factors explain why these cases were decided the way they were: time and space.

In terms of *time*, the length of time from the prior involvement was a key consideration. In *National Energy Board*, the Chair's involvement preceded the hearing by only a few years, and the application was made to the Board just five months after the Chair's appointment to the Board. In *Canada Post*, the arbitrator had been directly involved in a similar matter for many years and indirectly involved until a couple of years before his appointment. By contrast, 15 years had elapsed in *Wewaykum* between Justice Binnie's prior involvement and his deliberation on the matter in the Supreme Court.

In terms of *space*, the nature of the prior involvement was also significant. In *National Energy Board*, the Chair was a key player in the development of recommendations relating to a Mackenzie Valley pipeline, and the application which was before the Board was born out of the work done by the study group of which the Chair was a member. In *Canada Post*, the arbitrator was lead counsel for the company for many years (albeit that the intensity of his involvement had diminished in the years leading up to his appointment) on a matter also relating to pay and conditions in Canada Post. By contrast, in *Wewaykum*, Justice Binnie did not have a hands-on role in the litigation, as his involvement related to high-level matters of policy in relation to Indigenous land matters in British Columbia generally and not to the specifics of the particular file: Justice Binnie's perspective as Associate Deputy Minister was significantly more high-level than his perspective as a Supreme Court judge.

I would suggest, therefore, that in *National Energy Board* and *Canada Post*, there was both temporal and spatial proximity: the prior involvement was close in time to the decision in question and related to substantially similar issues as those to be considered in the hearing. By contrast, in *Wewaykum*, the prior involvement was ancient history and had not required Justice Binnie to take a substantive position on the issues that eventually came before the Supreme Court, meaning that temporal and spatial proximity were lacking.

## B. Prejudicial Comments

Comments made by a decision-maker may give rise to a reasonable apprehension of bias. It is useful to contrast the statements at issue in two Canadian cases.

On the one hand, in *Newfoundland Telephone Co. v Newfoundland (Board of Commissioners of Public Utilities)*,[51] a lay member of a regulatory board made comments to the media before and during a rate-setting hearing.

[50] ibid at [90].

[51] *Newfoundland Telephone Co. v Newfoundland (Board of Commissioners of Public Utilities)* [1992] 1 SCR 623.

One of the issues related to the recovery of salary costs by a utility company from ratepayers. The member was reported, before the hearing, as describing executive pay packages as 'ludicrous' and 'unconscionable' and stating that the costs should be borne by shareholders in the utility, not ratepayers: 'I'm not having anything to do with the salary increases and big fat pensions.' After the hearing began, the member continued to speak to the media. He reiterated his view that 'it is unfair to expect ratepayers, the consumers, you and I to pay for this kind of extravagance', suggesting that the packages were 'excessive' and could not be justified 'at all': 'very clearly there is a significant level of executive over compensation'. The Supreme Court of Canada held that, 'viewed cumulatively', these statements generated a reasonable apprehension of bias.[52]

On the other hand, in *R. v Pickersgill, ex parte Smith*,[53] a speech on transportation policy by a member of the Canadian Transport Commission did not give rise to a reasonable apprehension of bias. The speech in question was given about six weeks before the opening of a rate-setting hearing under a new statutory scheme. The fate of the so-called 'The Canadian' passenger trains run by Canadian Pacific Railway was at issue in the hearing. The applicants argued that the member's speech revealed a bias in favour of granting the railway company's application to discontinue the train service, as it allegedly indicated a predisposition to favour the economic interests of railway companies, to the neglect of the public interest (which, in turn, was a factor to be considered under the statutory scheme). Wilson J considered that several factors militated against a finding of bias. The member had not specifically mentioned 'The Canadian' or the Canadian Pacific Railway.[54] While he had expressed an understanding of the economic challenges facing railways, he did not indicate that his eyes were closed to consideration of the public interest.[55] To the extent that passages of the speech suggested favouritism to the interests of the railways, they had to be read in light of his closing remarks, which described the statutory scheme as having 'twin objectives': 'securing the most adequate and efficient methods of total transport and of distributing the benefits of increased efficiency and lower cost fairly among the transport industries, their customers, and the Canadian public'.[56] Considering the speech as an 'integrated whole', there was no basis for a finding of bias.[57]

These contrasting decisions can be understood in terms of time and space. In *Newfoundland Telephone*, the problematic comments were made immediately prior to and during the hearing process: they were temporally proximate to the decision; the comments also touched directly on a set of the precise issues that were to be considered in the decision; there was also spatial proximity. But in *Pickersgill*, there was a lapse of time between the comments and the decision (six weeks), and the

[52] ibid at 643.
[53] *R. v Pickersgill, ex parte Smith* (1970), 14 D.L.R. (3d) 717.
[54] ibid at 724.
[55] ibid at 726.
[56] ibid at 728.
[57] ibid at 729. See also *Teksavvy Solutions Inc. v Bell Canada*, 2024 FCA 121, at [52], emphasising that engagement on policy issues by regulators can be constructive and in the public interest.

comments were couched in generalities, not in specifics: here, temporal and spatial proximity were absent. Hence, I suggest the different outcomes and the analytical utility of thinking about bias issues in terms of time and space.

I would add to these two another pair of cases addressing prior conduct that might have been indicative of bias. On the one hand, in *Beaverford v Thorhild (County No. 7)*,[58] a municipal councillor was precluded by reason of bias from adjudicating on whether or not to grant a quarrying permit because he had recently introduced a legislative proposal that would have imposed an outright ban on quarrying and required a subsequent supermajority to reverse the ban: the legislative proposal was close in time to the decision at issue and took a very strong view on precisely the same subject matter, so considerations of proximity weighed heavily in favour of a conclusion of bias.[59] On the other hand, in *Francis v Canada (Citizenship and Immigration)*,[60] a refugee adjudicator was not tainted by bias on the basis of articles he had written previously about anomalies in the refugee determination process and the threat of immigration to Canada's social cohesion: the comments in the articles were broad, general and concerned 'a societal question that is unrelated to the case at bar',[61] thus lacking spatial proximity, and predated the adjudicator's appointment, meaning temporal proximity was also lacking.

## C. Prior Involvement in a Matter

In this section, I will draw a contrast between an Australian decision and one from Canada, again to support my proposition that the law relating to bias is best understood in terms of temporal and spatial proximity.

At the centre of the tale of *Isbester v Knox City Council*[62] was a dog, Izzy, who had attacked and injured a person. Legislation in the Australian province of Victoria gave the Council the power to order that a dog be destroyed in such circumstances. The problem here arose from the involvement of a Mrs Hughes in the decision-making process. As the Council's Co-ordinator of Local Laws, she had been an active participant in the investigation that led to the initiation of legal proceedings in the Magistrates' Court relating to Izzy. Subsequently, she sat on the panel that ordered Izzy's destruction.

For the majority (Kiefel, Bell, Keane and Nettle JJ.), the key question was the interest Mrs Hughes would have in seeing charges brought to their successful conclusion: 'The interest of a prosecutor may be in the vindication of their opinion that an offence has occurred or that a particular penalty should be imposed,

[58] *Beaverford v Thorhild (County No. 7)* 2013 ABCA 6.
[59] ibid at [30]–[31].
[60] *Francis v Canada (Citizenship and Immigration)* 2012 FC 1141.
[61] ibid at [35]–[36].
[62] (n 29).

or in obtaining an outcome consonant with the prosecutor's view of guilt or punishment.'[63] As Gageler J put it, writing separately,

> a person who has been the adversary of another person in the same or related proceedings can ordinarily be expected to have developed in that role a frame of mind which is incompatible with the exercise of that degree of neutrality required dispassionately to weigh legal, factual and policy considerations relevant to the making of a decision which has the potential adversely to affect interests of that other person.[64]

Here, Mrs Hughes' prior investigative involvement tainted her later participation with a reasonable apprehension of bias, as 'her involvement in the prosecution of the charges created an interest in the final outcome of the matter':

> Having participated in obtaining the conviction for the offence …, she organised the Panel hearing and drafted the letter advising the appellant of it [and] supplied the Panel with evidence, including further evidence she had obtained as relevant to the future housing of the dog. If Ms Hughes could not actually be described as a prosecutor with respect to the [final] decision …, she was certainly the moving force.[65]

As she had a 'material part' in the decision, it had to be quashed.[66]

Most instances of prior involvement in a decision-making process will 'typically' invalidate a decision, certainly where the same person wears the hats of investigator, prosecutor and adjudicator.[67] However, there are cases in which prior involvement has not risen to the level required to generate a reasonable apprehension of bias. Again, this can be understood in terms of temporal and spatial proximity. Consider the decision of the Court of Appeal for Saskatchewan in *DeMaria v Law Society of Saskatchewan*.[68] The issue here related to the role of in-house counsel at the Law Society, a person who 'among other capacities, acts as legal advisor to the Executive Director of the Law Society and to the Law Society itself, prosecutes all instances of lawyer misconduct, handles general litigation involving the Law Society, and prosecutes instances of unauthorised practice of law'.[69]

The facts giving rise to an allegation of bias were unusual. They involved contact between the Benchers of the Law Society (that is, the senior members who chair committees and, ultimately, make decisions in the name of the Society) and the in-house counsel:

(a) … the Bencher who served as chair of the A&E Panel [ie, the discipline committee] contacted the Law Society's in-house counsel on an ex parte basis

[63] ibid at [46].
[64] ibid at [63].
[65] ibid at [43]–[44].
[66] ibid at [48].
[67] D Brown and J Evans, *Judicial Review of Administrative Action in Canada* (Thomson Reuters, looseleaf) s 11.20.
[68] *DeMaria v Law Society of Saskatchewan* 2015 SKCA 106.
[69] ibid at [31].

about the A&E Panel's final decision before it was released to the parties and also invited the Law Society's in-house counsel to play golf with him;

(b) ... the Benchers who sat in review of the A&E Panel's decision breakfasted with the Law Society's in-house counsel on the day of the hearing and met with him on an ex parte basis after the Bencher review hearing; and

(c) ... one Bencher is 'friends' on Facebook with the Law Society's in-house counsel.[70]

As to the email of the decision and accompanying golf invitation, the Court of Appeal characterised the communication as an 'imprudent and out-of-place addition to a surprisingly *ex parte* email',[71] but only 'a single flippant display of familiarity between a Bencher and the in-house counsel for the Law Society'.[72] This was not enough to ground a finding of bias, given the 'institutional limitations and administrative arrangements at the Law Society'[73] and the ability of the Benchers to 'expertly divorc[e] themselves from friendship and affinity to dispassionately assess a matter on the basis of advocacy and reasoned argument on the facts and law'.[74] In a spatial sense, the communication was not sufficiently 'on point', as it had no relation to the substance of the matter being decided. It was also significant that the email communication was of a final decision: temporally speaking, the decision had already been made and could not be affected by the 'careless slip of familiarity' that had occurred.[75]

As for the breakfast, this was 'ill-considered'[76] (no doubt because of its temporal proximity to the hearing) but nonetheless understandable given the multiple roles played by in-house counsel for the Law Society.[77] Spatial proximity was lacking because the in-house counsel had perfectly legitimate reasons for attending a breakfast meeting. As for the social media relationship, without more, 'that unadorned fact is indicative of nothing more than the two individuals know each other, which would be presumed in any event from their respective offices within the corporate structure of the Law Society'.[78]

## D. Conduct at a Hearing

Lastly, I will consider two contrasting cases on a decision-maker's conduct at a hearing. These cases do not involve consideration of temporal proximity, as the conduct occurred at the hearing itself. Temporal proximity is, nonetheless, a

[70] ibid at [36].
[71] ibid at [44].
[72] ibid at [45].
[73] ibid at [44].
[74] ibid at [45].
[75] ibid at [44].
[76] ibid at [47].
[77] ibid at [48].
[78] ibid at [49].

relevant consideration to the extent that a hearing has (as is commonly the case these days) multiple steps: it will often be the case that the parties to an adjudication convene at a pre-hearing conference at which the adjudicator may express tentative views about relevant issues, with a view to ensuring that the parties' evidence and submissions are appropriately focused. In this section, I will focus on spatial proximity.

Begin with *R. v Gooliah*,[79] where an immigration adjudicator was held to have demonstrated bias during a hearing as his conduct demonstrated that his mind was 'made up' even before the hearing commenced.[80] There were two issues, one relating to whether the relevant authorities had authorised a pre-apprenticeship trial and one relating to an alleged change from one immigration class to another.

On the pre-apprenticeship issue, the adjudicator's conduct of the hearing indicated that he was not engaged in an objective search for truth but rather sought 'to find justification or support for a point of view to which, in advance of the relevant testimony, he was already firmly committed':[81]

> Noting that there was no written record evidencing the Branch's permission to Gooliah as claimed, he called as a witness one Farr, an officer of the Immigration Branch, for the purpose of establishing that there had in fact been no such permission. To this witness he first of all made a preliminary statement that Gooliah had no evidence of permission. Against that background he then put a series of questions clearly inviting, as indeed they received, the concurrence of the witness in the conclusion that Gooliah had not been given the consent of an Immigration Officer to work in pre-apprenticeship trial.[82]

On the second question, the hearing was 'equally unsatisfactory',[83] as the adjudicator prevented counsel for G from obtaining relevant information due to a 'hostile attitude'[84] and 'excessive zeal',[85] with the result that G did not know the case against him. In a nutshell, the adjudicator had pre-formed views on precisely the subject matter of the hearing: the spatial proximity could not be closer (and, of course, temporal proximity was also present).

Contrast *College of Physicians & Surgeons (Ontario) v Casullo*.[86] Here, C had been found guilty of professional misconduct because he had a financial interest in a laboratory to which he directed an excessive number of testing requests. Members of the disciplinary committee became impatient and were demonstrably annoyed with C during his testimony. There was 'obvious annoyance'.[87] However, spatial proximity was lacking. The annoyance related only to the question of C's financial interest in the laboratory, not to the question of the excessiveness of the

[79] *R. v Gooliah* (1967), 63 DLR (2d) 224.
[80] ibid at 233.
[81] ibid at 234.
[82] ibid at 233.
[83] ibid at 234.
[84] ibid at 235.
[85] ibid at 236.
[86] *College of Physicians & Surgeons (Ontario) v Casullo* [1977] 2 SCR 2.
[87] ibid at 11.

tests: C was questioned separately on these distinct issues, which in turn were dealt with separately in the committee's reasons. Thus, unlike in *Gooliah*, where the problematic conduct pertained directly to the subject matter in issue, here the problematic conduct related to a separate issue. It did not occupy the same space as the final decision, and thus there was no finding of bias.

## V. Conclusion

Professor Groves has produced the leading Australian work on the law of bias. As he has explained, with characteristic detail and care, this is an area of the law which gives rise to a significant degree of unpredictability in practice. Along with Justice Gageler (as he then was), Professor Groves suggested that the introduction of a third analytical step into the analysis of bias issues could help to bring some clarity to the law in this difficult area. I agree and, by reference to the concept of proximity – with temporal and spatial dimensions – have suggested that greater analytical clarity can be achieved. Proximity will hardly solve all the problems in this area, but it may provide a useful tool with which to address them.

# 8

# Judicial Review of the Ombuds Office: Good for Administrative Justice?

HANNA WILBERG*

Public sector Ombuds offices[1] are an important part of the administrative justice system across common law jurisdictions today. They provide accessible and often effective recourse to persons who are aggrieved at public administrative decisions, and also broader systemic oversight of the conduct of public administration.

But what happens when things go wrong? We can think of many examples. The Australian Ombudsman missed serious illegality in the infamous Robodebt scheme.[2] A complainant may be aggrieved at their complaint being rejected at the initial triaging stage. An official may consider that they were wrongly criticised in an Ombuds office report. Should judicial review be available to address such issues? In some jurisdictions, the Ombuds office's work is protected by a privative clause. Should courts give any effect to such clauses?

My frame of reference for addressing these questions is administrative justice. The question is what approach will promote good administrative decision-making, accessible and effective recourse for aggrieved individuals and effective implementation of the social objectives of administrative regimes.[3] I propose a proportionality enquiry based on case law in other similar contexts. Applying that enquiry, I argue that, in terms of administrative justice, the disadvantages of

* I would like to thank audiences at the Public Law Conference, Ottawa, 2–5 July 2024; the ICON-S Australia-NZ Chapter Conference, Sydney, 29–30 August 2024; and at seminars at the Auckland High Court, the University of British Columbia and the University of Auckland. Special thanks to Alexandra Allen-Franks, Lisa Burton-Crawford, Jodi Gardner, Dean Knight, Janet McLean, Mary Liston, Vernon Rive, Arie Rosen, Nicole Roughan, Robert Thomas, Rayner Thwaites, and Joshua Yuvaraj. Thanks also to several students in my Administrative Law class of 2021 who wrote excellent essays on this topic. For excellent research assistance on Ombudsman legislation, thanks to Jack Mckenzie.

[1] I am using the term 'Ombuds office' to avoid the gender specific 'Ombudsman' and also to make the point that these are institutions staffed by teams of investigators, not just individual officers.

[2] *Report of the Royal Commission into the Robodebt Scheme* (Commonwealth of Australia, 2022).

[3] For an introduction to administrative justice, see S Halliday and C Scott, 'Administrative Justice' in P Cane and HM Kritzer (eds), *The Oxford Handbook of Empirical Legal Research* (Oxford, Oxford University Press, 2010) 469; T Mullen, 'Access to Justice in Administrative Law and Administrative Justice' in E Palmer, T Cornford, A Guinchard and others (eds), *Access to Justice: Beyond the Policies and Politics of Austerity* (Oxford and Portland, Oregon, Hart Publishing, 2015) 69, 70–75.

judicial review of Ombuds office determinations outweigh the benefits in many contexts. Judicial review should be restricted or excluded in those contexts.

An exploration of these issues seems appropriate for celebrating the work of Professor Matthew Groves. He has written much on administrative justice and has just recently co-edited an excellent collection of essays on the Ombuds office.[4] More particularly, I hope to emulate some of our honorand's work that I most admire in offering a doctrinal administrative law analysis drawing on administrative justice policy arguments.[5] In addition to being an outstanding scholar, Matthew stands out for his generosity as a colleague and mentor. As one who has greatly benefited from that generosity, I am delighted to contribute to this Festschrift.

Part I lays the foundation for my argument. This part outlines A. the administrative justice advantages of the Ombuds office, B. the statute and case law on judicial review of Ombuds office determinations, and C. two lines of cases in which courts in other contexts have accepted limits on judicial review: first, NZ cases that have given effect to partial privative clauses and second, UK cases that have adopted a proportionality enquiry to determine how much judicial review is required by the rule of law.

In Parts II to IV, I develop my argument. In Part II, I propose an administrative justice proportionality enquiry that combines the approaches in the two lines of cases outlined earlier. In Parts III and IV, I apply that enquiry to argue that in many contexts, administrative justice would be best served by restricting or excluding judicial review of Ombuds office's determinations.

The analysis in this chapter is confined to public sector Ombuds offices handling complaints about public administration. There is a wide range of other Ombuds schemes, dealing with complaints about banking, financial services, legal services, and others. Different considerations may, to some extent, apply to such schemes.

The jurisdictions covered are Aotearoa New Zealand and the United Kingdom. In other common law jurisdictions such as Australia and Canada, the law on access to judicial review is so different that analysis of this chapter's questions for those jurisdictions must wait for a separate paper. We will detour to Australia, however, to draw on some notable experiences with the Ombuds office's work there.

# I. Foundations for the Argument

## A. The Ombuds Office and Administrative Justice

As noted, my frame of reference is administrative justice. Ombuds offices are considered very effective at serving administrative justice.[6] The three commonly

[4] M Groves and A Stuhmcke (eds), *The Ombudsman in the Modern State* (Oxford, Hart Publishing, 2022).

[5] See, eg, M Groves, 'Equality of Arms in Administrative Review' (2023) 46 *Melbourne University Law Review* 726.

[6] See, eg, T Mullen, 'A Holistic Approach to Administrative Justice?' in M Adler (ed), *Administrative Justice in Context* (Oxford, Hart Publishing, 2010) 383, 401–02.

listed objectives of administrative justice are getting administrative decisions right the first time around, putting errors right with the minimum of difficulty for the affected person, and learning from errors.[7] In addition to serving the interests of individual justice, where these objectives are achieved, that also promotes the proper implementation of public administrative regimes and their social objectives.[8]

Ombuds offices receive and investigate complaints from members of the public about exercises of power by public administrative authorities.[9] Some Ombuds offices also have the power to investigate on their own motion.[10] Any form of maladministration is within their remit,[11] and in Australia and New Zealand they may also consider the merits.[12] The outcome of an investigation is a report on the problems identified and a recommendation as to the appropriate remedy, rather than a binding order.[13] There is a broad discretion as to what remedies to recommend. Recommendations command much respect and have a very high rate of acceptance and implementation.[14] Ombuds offices have powers to 'name and shame' non-compliant authorities by reporting them to Parliament,[15] but those rarely need to be exercised.

One of the main strengths of Ombuds offices is their accessibility. This helps them achieve the second of the three objectives of administrative justice – putting errors right with minimum difficulty for the affected person. Complainants bear no costs and need no representation; there is no onus on them to establish the complaint. Rather, the Ombuds office takes the initiative in the investigation once a complaint has been received. A qualification must be noted, however. The reality of resource constraints means that Ombuds offices employ triaging protocols to screen complaints and determine which of them merit further investigation. This entails a risk that unrepresented complainants with valid complaints may fail to persuade the Ombuds office to investigate.

[7] White Paper, *Transforming Public Services: Complaints Redress and Tribunals* (Cm 6243, 2004) at [1.5], [1.7].

[8] See Mullen (n 3) 71.

[9] Ombudsmen Act 1975 (NZ), s 13 and sch 1; Parliamentary Commissioner Act 1967 (UK), ss 4 and 5 and sch 2; Local Government Act 1974 (UK), s 24A(1) and (2) and s 25; Ombudsman Act 1976 (Cth), s 3 and s 5(1)(a) and s 3.

[10] Ombudsmen Act 1975 (NZ), s 13(3); Public Services Ombudsman (Wales) Act 2019, s 4; Local Government Act 1974 (UK), s 24A; Ombudsman Act 1976 (Cth), s 5(1)(b); The Parliamentary Commissioner in the UK lacks this power.

[11] Parliamentary Commissioner Act 1967 (UK), s 5(1)(a); Local Government Act 1974 (UK), s 26(1)(a).

[12] Ombudsmen Act 1975 (NZ), s 22(1) and (2); Ombudsman Act 1976 (Cth), ss 15(1); GDS Taylor, 'May Judicial Review Become a Backwater?' in M Taggart (ed), *Judicial Review of Administrative Action in the 1980s: Problems and Prospects* (Auckland, Oxford University Press, 1986) 152, 173.

[13] Ombudsmen Act 1975 (NZ), s 22(3); Local Government Act 1974 (UK), ss 31(1)–(3B); Ombudsman Act 1976 (Cth), ss 15(2)–(3).

[14] See, for instance, Office of the Ombudsmen, *Report of the Ombudsmen for the year ended 30 June 2008* [2008] AJHR A.3 (NZ) at 24; Taylor (n 12) 173; Commonwealth Ombudsman, *2005–2006 Annual* Report (Aus).

[15] Ombudsmen Act 1975 (NZ), s 22(4); Parliamentary Commissioner Act 1967 (UK), ss 10(3) and 10(3A); Ombudsman Act 1976 (Cth), ss 16(1) and 17.

Ombuds offices are also considered effective at promoting the third objective, for authorities to learn from their errors. This in turn feeds into the first objective: it makes it more likely that the authority will in future get it right the first time.

Ombuds offices have two strengths in this regard. First, Ombuds offices usually adopt collaborative processes for their investigations. They work closely with the authorities concerned to work out what happened, what went wrong and how it can be put right. This approach serves the second objective in that it allows the Ombuds office to put errors right, often without a full investigation and formal recommendation. In addition, the process can, at least potentially, be a learning and reflective process for the officials involved.[16] Second, the Ombuds office's recommendations can go beyond remedies addressing the particular grievance. They can include explicit recommendations for improvements to systems.[17]

## B. The Current Law on Judicial Review of the Ombuds Office

The current law on judicial review of Ombuds office determinations is very different in the two jurisdictions to be discussed. In Aotearoa New Zealand, surprisingly, there is no recorded attempt to bring judicial review proceedings against the Ombuds office concerning the discharge of its complaints jurisdiction under the Ombudsmen Act. The only reported judicial review cases concern other powers held by the office.[18] The reasons for this absence have not, to my knowledge, been studied.

There is a privative clause in section 25 of the Ombudsmen Act 1975 (NZ),[19] purporting to exclude judicial review of Ombuds office determinations. As is well known, the courts' usual approach to privative clauses since *Anisminic* is effectively to disregard them, applying a strong presumption that Parliament could not have intended to exclude judicial review.[20] Whether that applies to section 25 has never been tested.[21]

[16] M Hertogh, 'Coercion, Co-operation, and Control: Understanding the Policy Impact of Administrative Courts and the Ombudsman in the Netherlands' (2001) 23 *Law and Policy* 47.

[17] Ombudsmen Act 1975 (NZ), s 22(3); Ombudsman Act 1976 (Cth), s 15(2).

[18] Most cases (eg, *Wyatt Co (NZ) Ltd v Queenstown-Lakes District Council* [1991] 2 NZLR 180 (HC)) concern the jurisdiction under the Official Information Act 1982 (NZ), where the Ombuds office's recommendations can become binding: s 32 of that Act. Extended litigation ending with *Financial Services Complaints Ltd v Chief Ombudsman* [2022] NZCA 248 concerned refusal of permission for a private complaints scheme to use the 'Ombudsman' name.

[19] Previously Parliamentary Commissioner (Ombudsman) Act 1962, s 21.

[20] *Anisminic v Foreign Compensation Commission* [1969] 2 AC 147 (HL); *R (Privacy International) v Investigatory Powers Tribunal* [2019] UKSC 22, [2020] AC 491; *Bulk Gas Users Group v Attorney-General* [1983] NZLR 129 (CA).

[21] The litigation concerning the office's other powers did not engage the privative clause: its effect is expressly excluded by the Official Information Act 1982, s 29; and it was held not to apply to the power to decide who may use the 'Ombudsman' name: *Financial Services Complaints Ltd v Chief Ombudsman* [2016] NZHC 634.

In contrast, judicial review proceedings challenging an Ombuds office's determinations are relatively common in the United Kingdom.[22] A number of such challenges have been successful. Courts have noted the need for judicial restraint in this context.[23] Yet successful grounds of review have included that findings simply were not justified,[24] inadequate reasoning in support of findings,[25] misunderstanding the scope and nature of the Ombuds office's powers[26] and breach of natural justice.[27] Successful challenges have been brought both by dissatisfied complainants[28] and by authorities under investigation.[29] We might expect also to see challenges by individual officials who have been criticised in reports – certainly that has happened in Australia.[30] Turning to privative clauses, the two English public sector Ombuds office regimes both lack such a clause.

The questions explored in this chapter are whether courts *should* allow judicial review of Ombuds office determinations and whether they should give effect to privative clauses in this context, departing from the usual *Anisminic* approach.

## C. Reasons for Limiting Access to Judicial Review in Other Contexts

In order to help answer the questions identified in the previous paragraph, it is useful to look at other contexts where courts have limited access to judicial review or given effect to privative clauses. I will outline the reasoning in two such lines of cases: New Zealand cases that have given effect to partial privative clauses and English cases that have accepted limits to how much judicial review is required by the rule of law. That reasoning will provide the basis for my proposed test for access to judicial review of Ombuds offices.

[22] For surveys, see K Keith, 'Judicial Control of the Ombudsmen?' (1982) 12 *Victoria University of Wellington Law Review* 299; *A Database of Case Law on the Ombudsmen Sector* caselaw.ombudsmanassociation.org/ (accessed 20 December 2024) (this covers both public and private sector Ombudsman schemes).

[23] *R v Parliamentary Commissioner for Administration, ex parte Dyer* [1994] 1 WLR 621 at 626–27.

[24] *R v Commissioner for Local Administration, ex parte Croydon London Borough Council* [1989] 1 All ER 1033 at 1045–46.

[25] *R v Parliamentary Commission for Administration, ex parte Balchin (No 1)* [1996] EWHC Admin 152; *R v Parliamentary Commissioner for Administration, ex parte Balchin (No 2)* (2000) 79 P&CR 157; *R v Parliamentary Commissioner for Administration, ex parte Balchin (No 3)* [2002] EWHC 1876 (Admin); *R (Turpin) v Commissioner for Local Administration* [2001] EWHC Admin 503.

[26] *R v Local Commissioner for Administration, ex parte Eastleigh Borough Council* [1988] 1 QB 855 (CA).

[27] *Turpin* (n 25).

[28] See, eg, ibid, and the other cases cited in n 25.

[29] See *Croydon* (n 24); *Eastleigh* (n 26).

[30] See, eg, *Kaldas v Barbour* [2017] NSWCA 275, (2017) 350 ALR 292.

### *i. Reasons for Giving Effect to Partial Privative Clauses (New Zealand)*

The courts in Aotearoa New Zealand give effect to certain types of privative clauses. They follow the *Anisminic* orthodoxy of ignoring such clauses when the clause in question simply purports to exclude access to the courts. However, they give effect to what we may call 'partial' privative clauses: provisions that channel challenges into alternative statutory avenues before allowing access to the courts by way of judicial review or appeal. Our interest is in the reasoning used to decide when to give effect to these clauses.

The reasoning generally involves two elements, as we will see. First, the courts give effect to these clauses to the extent that this does not deprive those aggrieved by decisions of an effective avenue of recourse. If there are any gaps in the available legal scrutiny, courts insist on exceptions to the effect of the privative clause to ensure that scrutiny is available. Second, courts recognise that there are good policy reasons to require recourse to statutory avenues. Those policy reasons include, in particular, the valuable role of statutory avenues in securing administrative justice.

Some cases have considered partial privative clauses in terms of the right to judicial review in section 27(2) of the New Zealand Bill of Rights Act 1990. The arguments for giving effect to partial ouster of that right can be put in terms of section 5, which allows demonstrably justified limits on rights.[31]

The channelling kind of partial privative clause is generally not needed in the UK, since the English courts in any event require applicants for judicial review to have exhausted their statutory remedies.[32] However, where statutes provide appeal or review rights as the exclusive remedy and subject to a time limit, English courts have given effect to such provisions for reasons similar to those in the NZ cases.[33]

The most well-established effective partial privative clause in NZ protects decisions of the Employment Court. This clause, unusually, restricts the available grounds of review.[34] The courts have consistently given full effect to this provision.[35] The longstanding legislative policy of restricting access to the ordinary courts in employment matters[36] originally reflected a concern that the general courts might

[31] See, eg, *Affco New Zealand Ltd v Employment Court* [2017] NZCA 123, (2017) 14 NZELR 349 at [30]–[37].

[32] See I Hare, CM Donnelly and J Bell, *De Smith's Judicial Review*, 9th edn (London, Sweet & Maxwell, 2023) [16-014]–[16-023].

[33] *R v Secretary of State for the Environment, ex parte Ostler* [1977] QB 122 (CA), affirming the pre-*Anisminic* authority of *Smith v East Elloe Rural District Council* [1956] AC 736 (HL). See also M Elliott, 'Through the Looking-Glass? Ouster Clauses, Statutory Interpretation and the British Constitution' in C Hunt, L Neudorf and M Rankin (eds), *Legislating Statutory Interpretation: Perspectives from the Common Law World* (Toronto, Carswell, 2018) 131, 135.

[34] Currently s 193 of the Employment Relations Act 2000.

[35] *New Zealand Rail Ltd v Employment Court* [1995] 3 NZLR 179 (CA) at 607; *Parker v Silver Fern Farms Ltd* [2011] NZCA 564, [2012] 1 NZLR 256; *Affco* (n 31).

[36] See also *Bulk Gas* (n 20) at 133.

not be sympathetic to the legislative attempt to address the power imbalances in this field.[37]

The explanation offered more recently was that speedy and informal dispute resolution was important in the context of employment disputes, which involve dynamic relationships requiring good faith.[38] Further, it was relevant that both the Employment Relations Authority and the Employment Court are 'specialist bodies'; and that most parties, by the time they apply for judicial review, have already had hearings in both of these fora.[39] This represents administrative justice reasoning: speed, informality and specialisation are among the reasons commonly given in the administrative justice literature for preferring statutory avenues of recourse to judicial review.[40]

Other partial privative clauses involve channelling grievances into alternative statutory avenues, as described earlier. The leading authority for giving effect to these is *Tannadyce*,[41] concerning such a provision in the Tax Administration Act 1994. The Act provides for merits review of tax assessments, and taxpayers can elect between the High Court or the Taxation Review Authority as the forum for this review. Any other proceedings are excluded by section 109.

The Court saw no need for the usual presumption against ouster of judicial review in this context.[42] The statutory avenue was more effective than judicial review since it included access to the High Court and could deal with all grounds of review as well as the merits. The Court contemplated some very limited exceptions to the effect of the privative clause to cover cases where the statutory avenue cannot assist.[43] Aside from that, it recognised the advantages of the statutory 'one-stop shop' process: it is more efficient and prompt, and it prevents taxpayers gaming the system.[44] Once again, these are administrative justice advantages. There is a long line of cases in which partial privative clauses have been given effect for similar reasons.[45]

The few cases in which partial private clauses have not been given effect can be explained on the basis of the same reasoning. The statutory avenues were not considered adequate, particularly in light of what was at stake. Two notable instances are *Zaoui (No 2)* and *H (SC 52/2018) v Refugee and Protection Officer*.

[37] See *Samuels v Employment Relations Authority* [2018] NZ Emp C 138 at [21]; HW Arthurs, 'Rethinking Administrative Law: A Slightly Dicey Business' (1979) 17 *Osgoode Hall Law Journal* 1.

[38] *Affco* (n 31) at [38].

[39] ibid at [39].

[40] See, eg, Mullen (n 6) 396; SH Legomsky, *Specialized Justice* (Oxford, Clarendon Press, 1990) 8–13.

[41] *Tannadyce Investments Ltd v Commissioner of Inland Revenue* [2011] NZSC 158, [2012] 2 NZLR 153.

[42] ibid at [70], [72].

[43] ibid at [58]–[59]. A strong dissent only argued for more generous exceptions: at [7], [11]–[17], [24], [35]–[38].

[44] ibid at [54]–[55], [57], [71].

[45] See also, esp, *Love v Porirua City Council* [1984] 2 NZLR 308 (CA); *Ramsay v Wellington District Court* [2006] NZAR 136 (CA) at [30]–[33].

In *Zaoui (No 2)*,[46] a security risk certificate had been issued against Mr Zaoui which, if confirmed, required him to be deported despite having refugee status. The certificate was subject to review by the Inspector-General, and then to an appeal to the Court of Appeal on a question of law with a tight time limit of only three days. On an application for judicial review of a determination by the Inspector, the Court applied the usual presumption against giving effect to a privative clause.[47] The reasons included that judicial review was especially necessary in this context, given the determination's impact on liberty and security of the person.[48] Further, the scope of the appeal right was too restricted for it to be the exclusive remedy.[49]

*H (SC 52/2018) v Refugee and Protection Officer*[50] concerned a clause in the Immigration Act 2009 which requires unsuccessful refugee claimants to exercise a statutory appeal to the Immigration and Protection Tribunal before they may seek leave to apply for judicial review. The Court acknowledged the legislative policy to 'prevent duplicative proceedings' but insisted that it must 'prevent injustice occurring when a statutory process fails'.[51]

The particular situation in this case called for an exception from the clause for two connected reasons. First, there was a fundamental breach of natural justice in the Officer's first-instance decision, and as a result the merits of the refugee claim were not considered at that stage at all.[52] Second, the statutory scheme was intended to afford refugee claimants two hearings on the merits: one by the Officer at first instance and then on appeal by the Tribunal.[53] This reading of the statutory scheme seems likely to have been influenced by the importance of what was at stake, although the Court did not mention this. The Act provided for significant safeguards in the first instance process that were not replicated in the appeal process. A fair hearing in the Tribunal would therefore not 'cure' the breach at first instance.[54] Nor did the Tribunal's powers under the Act allow it to remedy this by remitting the matter for reconsideration by the Officer.[55] *Tannadyce* was distinguished on the basis that the appeal process in that case included access to the High Court and was sufficiently comprehensive to render judicial review unnecessary.[56]

In summary, New Zealand courts give effect to partial privative clauses if they do not deprive challengers of recourse that is adequate, judged in light of what is at stake. Courts acknowledge the administrative justice arguments in favour of requiring alternative statutory avenues to be used.

[46] *Zaoui v Attorney-General (No 2)* [2005] 1 NZLR 690 (CA).
[47] ibid at [16], [101], [105], [179]–[181].
[48] ibid at [16].
[49] ibid at [92], [102]–[104].
[50] *H (SC 52/2018) v Refugee and Protection Officer* [2019] NZSC 13, [2019] 1 NZLR 433.
[51] ibid at [63].
[52] ibid at [14], [64] and [77].
[53] ibid [43], [70]–[74].
[54] ibid [41], [43], [65]–[69], [82].
[55] ibid [71], [74]. The Act also appeared to preclude the Officer reconsidering his own decision: ibid [17], [29]–[30].
[56] *H* (n 50) at [87].

### *ii. Proportionality Enquiry Governing Review of Tribunals (UK)*

In the United Kingdom, two leading cases establish that there can be limits to judicial review of administrative tribunals that are of a sufficiently judicial nature. Such limits may be found with or without a privative clause – the question turns at least as much on the court's assessment of whether judicial review is needed. The two main principles applied by the courts to answer that question are the rule of law and proportionality.

First, in *Cart*, the Supreme Court considered the scope for judicial review of decisions of the Upper Tribunal.[57] This Tribunal is designated a 'superior court of record', and appeals from it go directly to the Court of Appeal.[58] It hears appeals from the First-tier Tribunal that require leave. The limited rights of appeal from the Tribunal do not include an appeal from its refusal to grant permission for an appeal to it. The issue in *Cart* was whether and when judicial review is available to challenge this type of non-appealable decision of the Upper Tribunal. There was no privative clause.

The Supreme Court imposed restrictions on access to judicial review, albeit lesser restrictions than the Court of Appeal would have adopted.[59] That Court would have restricted judicial review to cases of excess of jurisdiction in the narrow sense that there was no power to enter the enquiry[60] or there was a breach of fundamental justice. The Supreme Court instead adopted the criteria for second appeals in the courts system: the case must either raise an 'important point of principle affecting large numbers of similar claims', or there must be a 'compelling reason', such as 'the extremity of the consequences for the individual'.[61]

The Court here can be seen as adopting the civil justice concept of proportionate dispute resolution[62] while insisting on the rule of law. The question, as the Court saw it, was what level of independent external scrutiny of tribunal decisions is required by the rule of law. A 'principled but proportionate approach' was needed.[63] One reason for restricting judicial review was the special status of the Upper Tribunal and the evident legislative intention to make the tribunal structure more self-contained.[64] The other main reason was that more liberal availability of review would involve a disproportionate use of limited judicial resources.[65] Lord Brown saw such disproportionality as compromising the rule of law itself: 'The rule of law is weakened, not strengthened, if a disproportionate part of the courts'

[57] *R (Cart) v Upper Tribunal (Public Law Project Intervening)* [2011] UKSC 28, [2012] 1 AC 663.

[58] Tribunals, Courts and Enforcement Act 2007 (UK), ss 3(5) and 13.

[59] *Cart* (n 57) at [44], [110], [130].

[60] This was the sense of jurisdiction prior to *Anisminic* (n 20).

[61] *Cart* (n 57) at [57]; see also at [130]–[131].

[62] White Paper, *Transforming Public Services: Complaints, Redress and Tribunals* (Cm 6243, 2004) part 2. See also the Civil Procedure Rules: their 'overriding objective' is 'enabling the court to deal with cases justly and at proportionate cost' (rule 1.1).

[63] *Cart* (n 57) at [51].

[64] ibid at [57], [120], [123], [127].

[65] ibid at [47], [89], [104], [124]–[127].

resources is devoted to finding a very occasional grain of wheat on a threshing floor full of chaff.'[66]

The rule of law did always require that another, more senior, judge could look at a case and check for error. However, it did not always require further checks after that, as that may not be proportionate.[67] In the case of the tribunal system, there was a 'real risk' that the Upper Tribunal might become, in reality, the final arbiter of law, developing a special 'local law' applied by the tribunal system. That was not what Parliament intended. It represented a risk of serious errors affecting large numbers of people.[68] Judicial review therefore had to be available for that kind of case, but not more generally. Unrestricted access to judicial review would not be proportionate.

The second case is the Supreme Court's decision in *Privacy International*.[69] The majority declined to give effect to the privative clause at issue in that case, reiterating the usual approach.[70] However, the decision is also notable for a clear acceptance that there are limits to how much judicial review is required by the rule of law and that a privative clause may be given effect if the court considers that consistent with the rule of law.[71]

The plurality judgment given by Lord Carnwath favoured an extension of the approach established in *Cart* for determining the scope of review of the Upper Tribunal. On this approach, it is a question for the court in each case what degree and type of scrutiny amounts to sufficient and proportionate protection of the rule of law.[72] Part of the answer is that the rule of law always requires access to the general courts. This is to ensure that statutory bodies do not develop a 'local law' different from the general law of the land.[73]

However, restrictions on judicial review can in some contexts be consistent with the rule of law. In relation to the tribunal at issue in this case, Lord Carnwath suggested that permission for judicial review of its decisions should be granted only in cases raising points of general significance.[74] His other example of appropriate limits is found in the provisions, mentioned earlier, that substitute statutory avenues equivalent to judicial review and make those subject to time limits. In the planning cases, such provisions strike a 'proportionate balance between effective judicial review, and the need for certainty to enable such decisions to be acted on with confidence'.[75]

[66] *Cart* (n 57) at [100].
[67] ibid at [56].
[68] ibid at [42]–[44].
[69] R *(Privacy International) v Investigatory Powers Tribunal* [2019] UKSC 22, [2020] AC 491.
[70] ibid at [99]–[111], [161]–[167].
[71] ibid at [144]. See further H Wilberg, 'The Limits of the Rule of Law's Demands: Where *Privacy International* Abandons *Anisminic*', *UK Constitutional Law Blog* (11 September 2019) (available at ukconstitutionallaw.org/).
[72] *Privacy International* (n 69) at [132], and generally at [127]–[134], [144].
[73] ibid at [112], [138]–[139].
[74] ibid at [112].
[75] ibid at [130]; see further at [79]–[80], [133]–[134].

The approaches in *Cart* and the *Privacy International* plurality were applied by the Court of Appeal to give effect to a privative clause in *LA (Albania)*.[76]

# II. Proposing a Test Based on these Two Lines of Cases

## A. Summary of the Approaches in the Two Lines of Cases

In summary, the English cases recognise that how much and what kind of judicial scrutiny is necessary turns on a proportionality assessment in light of limited judicial resources and other public interest considerations such as the need for certainty in planning law. Relevant factors include the importance of what is at stake, whether there is an important point of principle that is likely to arise in a large number of cases, and whether the concern about developing 'local law' applies. This reasoning can justify limiting access to judicial review in the absence of a privative clause, and it can also be used to justify giving effect to a privative clause. It is therefore relevant to my questions in this chapter.

The New Zealand approach to partial privative clauses involves departing from the usual *Anisminic* approach and giving effect to such a clause if that does not deprive claimants of effective avenues of recourse. This has been held to turn on the nature and scope of the alternative statutory avenues and on whether the avenues include access to the High Court. It may also depend on the gravity of the alleged error and the importance of what is at stake.

The courts also acknowledge the good administrative justice reasons for such clauses. These have included the advantages of the alternative avenues compared to judicial review in terms of their scope (usually merits review), speed, informality and specialist nature. The reasons also include the public interest in finality – avoiding too many opportunities for challenge and their use to 'game the system'.

The point has not been put in terms of proportionality, except in the few cases where the provision for justified limits in section 5 of the Bill of Rights Act is used. Indeed, the New Zealand cases generally only give effect to partial privative clauses if and to the extent that available avenues are fully adequate. On that basis, the administrative justice reasons do little independent work: the clause is given effect simply because there is no downside to it. Even where section 5 of the Bill of Rights is invoked, there is no real proportionality enquiry: no weighing of the administrative justice reasons against any need for more adequate recourse.

This last feature of the New Zealand cases contrasts with the United Kingdom cases, where the competing considerations have been weighed to arrive at a proportionate compromise position: access to judicial review may be limited if the need for it is not especially strong and is outweighed by reasons for limits. On the other hand, the New Zealand cases have acknowledged a much fuller set of

[76] *R (LA (Albania)) v Upper Tribunal* [2023] EWCA Civ 1337, [2024] 1 WLR 1673.

good reasons for restricting judicial review, including in particular administrative justice reasons. My proposal is that the two approaches should be combined to achieve a more complete proportionality enquiry into the justification for limiting access to judicial review.

## B. Combining the Approaches in the above Two Lines of Authority

Combining the two approaches yields a proportionality test for deciding on access to judicial review, which can be used to decide when judicial review should be available against the Ombuds office. The three questions to ask are: (1) are there good policy reasons for limiting access to judicial review (in particular administrative justice considerations such as speed and informality, but also conserving limited judicial resources and promoting certainty or finality); (2) are there alternative avenues of recourse, and how adequate are those; and (3) are the good policy reasons for limits strong enough to outweigh any need for more adequate avenues of recourse?

Answers to the third question depend on two variables. First, there are two interests that might call for more adequate redress. Each can vary in strength, thus affecting the proportionality balance. One is the strength of the affected individual person or entity's right to legal recourse. This turns on the importance of what is at stake and also on the gravity of the error. The other is the strength of the public interest in the maintenance of the rule of law. This turns on the gravity of the error and on its significance beyond the case at hand (is there a risk of developing 'local law'; does the issue concern a general point of law that is likely to recur repeatedly?).

When focusing on the individual right to recourse, the answer also depends on a second variable: who is the individual person or entity seeking to challenge the Ombuds office? Is it the original complainant, the authority under review, or an individual official in that authority?

In Parts III and IV, I address these two variables, in the following order. Part III focuses on protecting the individual right to recourse. It examines the different arguments for each of the three types of challengers. Part IV examines arguments about ensuring maintenance of the rule of law. First, however, let me briefly comment on the nature of my proposed test.

## C. A Question of Degree Rather than a Categorical Enquiry

A proportionality test such as the one I propose is a question of degree: the answers should not take the form of binary categories. Complete exclusion of review is best understood as merely one end of a spectrum of answers. Where there are good reasons for excluding review, but they do not entirely outweigh the need for more adequate avenues of recourse, an appropriate answer may be review that is limited in terms of the available grounds, the intensity of review or the remedies awarded.[77]

This approach is to be distinguished from an approach that would allow or exclude judicial review based on categories. For instance, it is tempting to say that judicial review must be available where the Ombudsman office has exceeded its jurisdiction in the narrow sense. However, that category was rightly dismissed as unhelpful and unduly technical in *Cart*.[78] Considerations such as the nature and gravity of the alleged error are relevant to the approach proposed here, but they are questions of degree, and function as factors to be weighed in the balance.

## III. Proportionate Protection for the Individual Right to Recourse

As noted, when we focus on the individual right to recourse, the answers to my proportionality test vary according to who is the individual person or entity seeking to challenge the Ombuds office: the original complainant, the authority under review, or an individual official in that authority. Let me take these in turn.

### A. Challenges by the Original Complainant

In challenges by the original complainant, there are several good reasons for limiting access to judicial review. These usually outweigh any need for judicial review as a more adequate avenue of recourse for this type of challenger, as I will show in this section. Only exceptionally will these good reasons be outweighed by the need for more adequate individual recourse. They may also occasionally be outweighed by the need to maintain the rule of law, where that concern is especially strong, as discussed in Part IV.

#### *i. Administrative Justice Reasons and Other Policy Reasons for Limiting Judicial Review*

At least three good reasons can be identified for limiting access to judicial review challenges by the original complainant. The first is the strongest, as it directly concerns administrative justice. As we saw earlier, the Ombuds office jurisdiction has significant strengths from this perspective. The main problem with judicial review of Ombuds office determinations is that it may undermine one of the major strengths.

[77] For the varying forms of judicial restraint, see DR Knight, *Vigilance and Restraint in the Common Law of Judicial Review* (Cambridge, Cambridge University Press, 2018).

[78] *Cart* (n 57) at [39]–[40], [111].

Recall that the Ombuds office jurisdiction is considered effective for the objective of putting errors right with minimum difficulty for the person affected, due in significant part to its accessibility. This accessibility in turn is largely due to its informality. The problem is that the availability of judicial review may have an impact on an Ombuds office's approach to its tasks and may detract from this informality.

In particular, it has been argued that regular instances of close judicial scrutiny of an Ombuds office's reasoning, such as were seen in the *Balchin* litigation in the UK, may impair informality and hence accessibility.[79] It might be thought that encouraging fully reasoned reports must be a good thing. However, this is in fact in tension with the need to process a high volume of complaints within the inevitable resource constraints; it is liable to lead to unacceptable delays.

The second and third reasons for limiting judicial review may not count for very much by themselves, but they are worth mentioning alongside the main reason. The second reason is that the Ombuds office's limited resources are generally better used for dealing with complaints than for defending judicial review applications, unless there are strong reasons for considering judicial review necessary.

The third reason is the privative clause, where there is one. On the one hand, it is well established that courts will disregard these if they are full privative clauses, primarily because giving effect to them would compromise the rule of law. On the other hand, there is no getting past the fact that this approach is in tension with parliamentary sovereignty.[80] Arguably, therefore, Parliament's decision to include a private clause should register at least as a factor in determining when and to what extent judicial review is available.[81]

### *ii. Weighing the Need for Judicial Review against Good Policy Reasons for Excluding it*

Let us turn then to the second and third parts of my proposed proportionality test. What alternative avenues of recourse are available to the original complainant, how adequate are those for individual recourse, and is any need for judicial review as a more adequate avenue outweighed by the disadvantages of allowing judicial review?

Elliott and Varuhas have suggested that judicial review may be less necessary for Ombuds office determinations because the Ombuds office is itself an avenue of recourse.[82] Why should that matter? I suggest this alludes to several points. First,

[79] P Giddings, 'Ex p Balchin: Findings of Maladministration and Injustice' [2000] *Public Law* 201. But *cf* R Kirkham and E O'Loughlin, 'Judicial Review and Ombuds: A Systematic Analysis' [2020] *Public Law* 680, arguing that review plays a positive role of structuring the law and providing detail of good administration standards for Ombuds offices.

[80] Elliott (n 33).

[81] That used to be the approach in Canada: *Dunsmuir v New Brunswick* [2008] SCC 9, [2008] 1 SCR 190 at [52].

[82] M Elliott and JNE Varuhas, *Administrative Law: Text and Materials*, 5th edn (Oxford, Oxford University Press, 2017) 779; see also Keith (n 22) 322.

there is another decision in play – the original decision by a public authority that was the subject of the complaint to the Ombuds office. Second, the main grievance is against that decision. Finally, the Ombuds office is not an exclusive avenue for addressing that main grievance: other avenues of recourse directly against that original decision remain available. However, we should acknowledge that there is also a second fresh grievance against the Ombuds office relating to its handling of the complaint. I will address the extent to which judicial review of Ombuds office determinations may be needed and justified for each of these two grievances in turn.

In relation to the original and main grievance, arguably an appropriate and often better remedy when the complainant is not satisfied with the Ombuds office's response is to start afresh. A fresh challenge may be brought directly to the original decision, using other available avenues, rather than challenging the Ombuds office's determination.[83]

What other avenues are available for such a further fresh challenge to the original administrative decision? A statutory review or appeal route is usually not available in the cases we are concerned with: if it had been available, the Ombuds office would ordinarily not have accepted the complaint for investigation in the first place.[84] Another informal avenue is to seek the assistance of the complainant's local Member of Parliament. If broader systemic issues are involved, complaints by multiple affected persons may also lead to some form of public inquiry. For instance, in relation to the Australian Robodebt scandal, the main problems were missed by the Ombuds office – a very unfortunate failure. They were subsequently identified by a Royal Commission of Inquiry.[85]

Finally, the complainant may also challenge the original decision by judicial review. This is not an informal and accessible avenue and hence would not normally count as an adequate alternative in terms of administrative justice. However, that objection does not apply where the choice is between seeking judicial review of the Ombuds office or judicial review of the original decision: if the complainants can afford the former, then presumably they can afford the latter.

Judicial review, of course, does not offer a broad jurisdiction to deal with maladministration: the grounds are limited to legality and procedural propriety, and remedies are limited to quashing the decision and remitting it for reconsideration. For complaints such as delay or rudeness, therefore, the only available alternative will be one of the informal alternatives.

In many cases, however, the complaint about the original decision was on grounds that would also be available in a judicial review of the original decision. In *Turpin*, for instance, that complaint was that the claimants had not had an adequate opportunity to comment before a planning decision affecting them was taken. In such cases, judicial review of the original decision is a more direct and effective

[83] For a similar objection to judicial review of a settlement offer, see *XY v Attorney-General* [2016] NZHC 1196, [2016] NZAR 875 at [36]–[37].

[84] Ombudsmen Act 1975 (NZ), s 13(7)(a); Parliamentary Commissioner Act 1967 (UK), s 5(2)(a).

[85] *Report of the Royal Commission into the Robodebt Scheme* (Commonwealth of Australia, 2022).

route for addressing the original grievance. In comparison, a successful judicial review of the Ombuds office results merely in requiring that office to reconsider. The original grievance then still has to be addressed by the Ombuds office recommending a remedy to the original decision-maker, and the original decision-maker accepting that recommendation. Why choose such a roundabout route?

We should note that in some cases, judicial review of the original decision faces a timing problem. By the time the Ombudsman has disposed of a complaint, the time available for judicial review may have expired, or the delay may count as a reason to deny a remedy in the exercise of the remedial discretion. However, there may still be better solutions than allowing judicial review of the Ombuds office determination in such a case.

Where there is a discretion to still allow review of the original decision, as in New Zealand,[86] the fact that the delay was due to pursuing a complaint via the Ombuds office ought to be a factor in favour of allowing judicial review and granting remedies despite the delay. If quashing the original decision would be unduly disruptive – for instance, in a planning case where construction has already taken place – then a declaration could still be granted to record any administrative flaw in the decision. Where no such discretion exists, perhaps that could be a reason to allow judicial review of the Ombuds office determination. However, in terms of access to redress against the original decision, it might make more sense to create exceptions to judicial review time limits than invite the roundabout route via judicial review of the Ombudsman.

Turning, then, to the complainant's second grievance: the fresh grievance against the Ombuds office. When, if ever, should judicial review be available to address this? It helps to further distinguish between three possible aspects. One is the grievance that the Ombuds office did not do its job: it should have resolved the original complaint but failed to do that because they got it wrong. That is indirectly addressed if the original complaint is upheld on another avenue of recourse. Where that is available, it is arguably adequate.

A second possible aspect of the fresh grievance concerns being treated badly, such as rudeness or being treated dismissively by Ombuds office staff. A complainant's avenues of redress in that regard are limited. The complainant's constituency MP may once again be in a position to assist informally. The Ombuds office's formal accountability is commonly to Parliament, but Parliament's role is usually limited to receiving periodic reports from the Ombuds office.[87] Some Ombuds offices are subject to other forms of regular auditing,[88] but those do not offer individual recourse. However, judicial review would not address this second aspect of

[86] There is no general time limit on judicial review, and delay is merely a factor going to the remedial discretion.

[87] See, eg, Ombudsman Act 1975 (NZ), ss 22(4), 29; Standing Orders of the New Zealand House of Representatives, SO 404. See R Kirkham, 'Decentred Regulation of the Ombudsman Sector: UK Style' in M Groves and A Stuhmcke (eds), *The Ombudsman in the Modern State* (Oxford, Hart Publishing, 2022) 187, 192–93.

[88] Kirkham (n 87) 195.

the fresh grievance either, as the grounds of review do not extend to this type of complaint.

The final possible aspect of the fresh grievance is a standard administrative law complaint about the Ombuds office's reasoning and process. As we saw, such complaints have been entertained in the UK. Surely there must be recourse for a breach of natural justice or for a clear reasoning error,[89] such as where the Ombuds office failed to notice that new evidence had contradicted one of its earlier findings?[90] I would argue not.

In terms of proportionate use of judicial resources, there must be doubts whether the most expensive avenue of recourse should be available for general error correction in relation to the least expensive avenue. Additionally and more importantly, nothing of substance is at stake in such challenges since the substantive grievance is against the original decision. Nor are occasional challenges of this kind likely to improve the quality of Ombuds determinations in the bulk of cases that do not make it to the courts. Some form of regular audit would be much more likely to promote quality across the board.[91]

As for natural justice, such challenges would in any case succeed very rarely against the Ombuds office, for two reasons.[92] First, the requirements of natural justice vary with context, and a complainant's natural justice rights in the context of an Ombuds investigation are likely to be limited. Second, courts ought to adopt a deferential stance on this issue, because as an informal administrative justice institution, the Ombuds office regulates its own procedure.

In summary, then, in challenges by the original complainant, any need for more effective redress against the Ombuds office is usually outweighed by the disadvantages of judicial review of Ombuds office determinations. The cure is worse than the disease. The balance favours judicial review at most in a few relatively exceptional cases. The additional concern about maintaining the rule of law that may also feature in some challenges by the original complainant is discussed in Part IV below.

## B. Challenges by the Authority under Investigation

In challenges by the authority under investigation, additional considerations apply. This is the context in which the disadvantages of judicial review of Ombuds office findings and recommendations most clearly and consistently outweigh the need for it as part of adequate avenues of recourse.

[89] For such a view, see A Stuhmcke, 'Ombudsman Litigation: The Relationship between the Australian Ombudsman and the Courts' in G Weeks and M Groves (eds), *Administrative Redress In and Out of the Courts* (Sydney, Federation Press, 2019) 155, 175.

[90] As, eg, in *Balchin (No 3)* (n 25) at [48].

[91] Kirkham (n 87) 195.

[92] See, eg, *Dyer* (n 23); but *cf Turpin* (n 25).

### *i. Administrative Justice Reasons to Limit Judicial Review*

Turning first to the reasons for limiting judicial review challenges by the authority under investigation, the reason is that two key administrative justice strengths of the Ombuds office could be compromised by allowing such challenges. First, its accessibility: there are no fees, and there is no burden on a complainant to make good their complaint. Allowing judicial review of Ombuds office findings and recommendations by the authority under investigation severely undermines that accessibility. Such a challenge threatens to deprive the complainant of the favourable outcome gained by the Ombuds office's accessible proceedings. It requires them at least to await the further outcome of the judicial review proceedings, and beyond that it makes it desirable for them to obtain legal representation to participate in those formal proceedings. Once that occurs, clearly the benefit of accessibility has been lost. If judicial review is available to the authority under investigation every time the Ombuds office upholds a complaint, then complainants can no longer count on recourse via the Ombuds office being accessible.

Second, we saw that the Ombuds office's effectiveness for all three administrative justice objectives is due in significant part to the collaborative style of investigation. The concern in this regard is that the collaborative approach may be undermined if it became common practice for authorities to litigate Ombuds office findings and recommendations.

In addition to these two reasons, all three reasons for limiting review by the original complainant (discussed in section A. above) also apply in challenges by the authority under investigation.

### *ii. Weighing Good Reason for Limits against Need for More Adequate Recourse*

The above good reasons have to be weighed against the countervailing considerations at the second and third step of the proportionality test. What avenues of recourse are available to the authority other than judicial review, and how adequate are those? If judicial review would be a more adequate avenue, is the need for it outweighed by the disadvantages of allowing judicial review?

Other than judicial review, no formal legal avenues are available to the authority under investigation if it has concerns about the Ombuds office's findings and recommendations. The available alternative avenues flow from the informal, collaborative and recommendatory nature of the Ombuds office's jurisdiction. The authority can seek to persuade the Ombuds office to reconsider. Failing that, the law generally allows the authority to refuse to comply and explain its disagreement. Alternatively, an authority could comply while registering its protest.

Where a central government authority refuses to comply, the Ombuds office may report the matter to Parliament.[93] The relevant minister can then be held to

[93] Ombudsmen Act 1975 (NZ), s 22(4); Parliamentary Commissioner Act 1967 (UK), ss 10(3) and 10(3A); Scottish Public Services Ombudsman Act 2002, s 16.

account for the refusal, having to explain and justify the reasons for it.[94] In the UK, authorities who refuse to comply have also been held to account in the courts. However, a refusal to comply will be upheld so long as the authority has considered the Ombuds office's finding and recommendation and has cogent reasons for declining to accept or follow it.[95] Subject to such close scrutiny, an authority is within its lawful powers in declining to follow a recommendation.

The position appears to be different for local government entities in the UK.[96] However, that is a questionable position, and it is doubtful that it would be followed elsewhere.

The options available to an authority under investigation clearly do not represent full and perfect recourse. However, authorities are not powerless in their dealings with the Ombuds office. The office is reliant on their cooperation both for carrying out its investigations and to give effect to its recommendations.[97] It thus has reason to engage with an authority that contests a finding.

Is it proportionate to confine authorities to such informal and imperfect recourse? I would argue that the adverse effect of judicial review on accessibility for complainants easily outweighs any need for more effective recourse for the authority. While the available recourse is not perfect, that must also be seen in light of the limited nature of what is at stake. Public authorities have no legitimate self-interest.[98] They can claim access to recourse only for the sake of the public interest served by their activities. In that regard, there are two points to note.

First, the cost of compliance with an individual recommendation is generally small (both the financial cost and the extent to which it may compromise public interest objectives). Second, an Ombuds office finding and recommendation does not set a precedent, and neither does an authority's compliance with it. Broader repercussions, therefore, are limited.

The only cases where judicial review should perhaps be available to authorities under investigation are those where there is a sufficiently strong rule of law argument. That is addressed in Part IV below. Some successful challenges have quite clearly gone beyond this and should not have been entertained in the view taken here.[99]

The argument above does not apply where the entity under investigation is not a public authority, such as in *JR55*, which involved a medical practitioner in private practice.[100] The jurisdiction of some public Ombuds offices does extend in this way beyond public authorities. It is strongly arguable that the Supreme Court was

[94] *R (Bradley) v Secretary of State for Work and Pensions* [2008] EWCA Civ 36, [2009] QB 114 at [60], [63], [136]–[137]. The authority may also have the opportunity to have its comments included in the report to Parliament: Ombudsmen Act 1975 (NZ), s 22(5).

[95] *Bradley* (n 94) at [71]–[72], [91], [95]; *R (Equitable Members Action Group) v HM Treasury* [2009] EWHC 2495 (Admin).

[96] *Eastleigh* (n 26) at 867; distinguished but explained and approved in *Bradley* (n 94) at [54]–[58], [139].

[97] Keith (n 22) 323.

[98] M Elliott, 'Judicial Review's Scope, Foundations and Purposes: Joining the Dots' [2012] *New Zealand Law Review* 75, 79.

[99] See, eg, *Croydon* (n 24).

[100] *Re JR55's Application for Judicial Review (Northern Ireland)* [2016] UKSC 22, [2016] 4 All ER 779.

right in allowing the medical practitioner to challenge a recommendation to pay compensation to a patient.[101] The Ombuds office here acted as a public authority imposing a significant burden on a private individual, who did have a legitimate self-interest. We ordinarily expect access to some right of appeal or review in such a situation. This in turn raises questions about the wisdom of extending the Ombuds office's jurisdiction to private persons on the same terms as its jurisdiction over public authorities. The breadth and discretionary nature of the Ombuds office's jurisdiction are arguably appropriate only for public authorities that lack a legitimate self-interest.

## C. Challenges by Individual Officials Criticised in Reports

Another area where Ombuds office findings impact private individuals is where the investigation concerns a public authority, but identified individual officials are criticised in a published report. That is damaging to the official's personal reputation and career.[102] Should judicial review be available to such officials to protect their legitimate private interest? Of the three types of challengers, this is the one that raises by far the most difficult issues in striking the balance between considerations for and against allowing judicial review.

In this context, the mere fact that the Ombuds office's report is only recommendatory is no answer to an official's claim to access judicial review. Commissions of inquiry and coroners, for instance, also have only recommendatory powers. Yet they are amenable to judicial review where their findings have a real impact on a claimant's reputation.[103] Some Ombuds office legislation expressly provides for a right to be heard for any individual who is to be the subject of adverse comment[104] – arguably that should be enforceable by judicial review.

No adequate alternative avenues are available. Employment law proceedings are available to the official if the official is disciplined or otherwise disadvantaged in their employment as a result of the Ombuds office's comments. But such proceedings do not deal with the reputational damage caused by a published report containing criticism of individuals. Defamation proceedings are the usual means for individuals to vindicate their reputation. But unless bad faith can be shown, such proceedings are excluded in this context.[105]

[101] The difference between the practitioner and a public authority is discussed ibid at [11], [20] and [24].

[102] K Del Villar, 'Who Guards the Guardians? Recent Developments Concerning the Jurisdiction and Accountability of Ombudsmen' (2003) 36 *AIAL Forum* 25, 26.

[103] See *Re Erebus Royal Commission; Air New Zealand Ltd v Mahon* [1983] NZLR 662 (PC); also, eg, *Carroll v Auckland Coroner's Court* [2013] NZHC 906, [2013] NZAR 650.

[104] Ombudsman Act 1975 (NZ), s 22(7); Ombudsman Act 1976 (Cwth), s 8(5)(b). The Local Government Act 1974 (UK), s 30(3) instead provides that individuals should not be named unless necessary.

[105] Ombudsman Act 1975 (NZ), s 26(1)(a) and (4); Defamation Act 1992 (NZ), ss 16, 18 and sch 1, pt 2, cl 3; Parliamentary Commissioner Act 1967 (UK), s 10(5); Local Government Act 1974 (UK), s 32(1).

The informal recourse that is adequate for the authority under investigation does not avail the individual official. Unlike the authority, the official cannot refuse to comply with a recommendation, and in any event such refusal would not deal with the harm from adverse publicity. The official may perhaps register their protest about the finding, but such a move will have much less impact than an authority registering its protest.

It is, of course, true that even individual officials are not powerless vis-à-vis the Ombuds office. The public authorities on whose cooperation the Ombuds office depends are, after all, made up of individual officials. If the Ombuds office acquires a reputation for not treating officials fairly in their investigations and then ignoring their protests, then this cooperation may dry up. Nonetheless, individual officials have no real recourse in relation to a particular criticism made of them.

On the other hand, however, the countervailing considerations are equally strong. All of the reasons for denying access to judicial review against the Ombuds office apply. In particular, allowing review on the application of an individual official would undermine the accessibility of the Ombuds office no less than judicial review on the application of authorities under investigation.

The best answer may be that courts faced with such claims should balance the competing considerations for and against judicial review on a case-by-case basis. The case for judicial intervention is strongest where a published report has found serious wrongdoing by named individual officials. For Ombuds offices, the lesson is that they should avoid assigning blame to named individuals in public reports as much as possible.

Indeed, where findings of serious wrongdoing against individuals are likely to be needed, arguably the Ombuds office is not an appropriate agency to investigate – such matters should be allocated to less informal agencies. A major Australian Ombudsman inquiry into the New South Wales Crime Commission and Police Integrity Commission, which did result in attempted legal action against the Ombudsman by an individual official,[106] may be a good illustration of this problem.[107]

## IV. Proportionate Protection for the Rule of Law

So far the discussion has focused on litigants' rights of recourse and what limits on such rights are proportionate for the sake of protecting the administrative justice advantages of the Ombuds office. The remaining question, to be addressed in this Part, concerns the public interest in the maintenance of the rule of law: when does this interest outweigh the disadvantages of judicial review against the Ombuds

[106] *Kaldas v Barbour* [2017] NSWCA 275, (2017) 350 ALR 292.

[107] For discussion, see M Aronson, 'Ombudsmen and Crime Busters: Ships Passing in the Night' in G Weeks and M Groves (eds), *Administrative Redress In and Out of the Courts* (Sydney, Federation Press, 2019) 178, esp 193.

office? The disadvantages have already been outlined. Recall that the strength of those disadvantages depends on who is bringing the challenge: the strongest disadvantage applies in challenges brought by the authority under investigation or an official within it.

The available alternatives do not involve legal accountability. Is that necessary? There is a general concern that the Ombuds office would be above the law unless it is subject to judicial review. Responding to that, Ken Keith argued that significant accountability is achieved by virtue of the fact that the Ombuds office has to maintain the respect and goodwill of the public authorities it supervises, as already discussed.[108]

The need for legal accountability may also be somewhat diminished because the Ombuds office has no policy agenda of its own. In this regard, it differs both from primary decision-makers and from the administrative tribunals that are usually subject to judicial review. Primary decision-makers are charged with implementing the policy of a particular regime. That, rather than compliance with the law, is their focus. For administrative tribunals with a merits review jurisdiction, policy implementation is at least an aspect of their role too.[109] In contrast, an Ombuds office, much like courts, has no inherent reason not to resolve complaints in accordance with the law.

Most importantly, in challenges by the original complainant, nothing of substance is directly at stake (the substantive grievance is against the original decision), as argued earlier. Much the same goes for challenges by the authority under investigation, as the authority has no legitimate self-interest to protect. In light of that, legal accountability may not be a proportionate use of limited judicial resources in these types of cases.

If we accept that the rule of law does not require judicial review of Ombuds office determinations in all cases, then attention can shift to identifying and weighing particular factors that may make for a stronger rule of law concern. According to *Cart* and *Privacy International*, these include the gravity of the error, whether it concerns a general point of law that is likely to recur in other cases, and whether there is a risk of 'local law' developing. The last of these does not apply to the Ombuds office. There is no concern about creating 'local law',[110] because Ombuds office findings and recommendations do not generate binding precedent.

The other two factors, however, are relevant. Judicial intervention may be warranted on rule of law grounds if the alleged error is a serious error and if that error is likely to be repeated many times unless it is addressed by a judicial ruling.

Any error in the interpretation of the Ombuds office legislation is likely to have such general significance. That includes, for instance, errors concerning

[108] Keith (n 22) 323.

[109] R Thomas, *Administrative Law in Action: Immigration Administration* (Oxford, Hart Publishing, 2022) 4–11.

[110] This concern is also open to question in any event: see, eg, Arthurs (n 37). However, it is not necessary to pursue that point here.

which authorities may be investigated. Authorities that are subject to the Ombuds office's jurisdiction may also wish to have clarification on whether purely commercial contracting decisions are a proper lawful subject of Ombuds office attention. Indeed, Ombuds office legislation expressly provides for jurisdictional issues to be resolved by the courts;[111] often on the application of the Ombuds office itself.[112]

However, in some cases, challenges to the reasoning in particular cases have been dressed up as raising issues about the interpretation of statutory tests, such as the concept of maladministration.[113] That is not the kind of case in which judicial intervention is especially warranted.

Legislative design solutions can minimise the chances of these kinds of issues arising. For instance, disputes about which agencies may be investigated are much less likely to arise when the Ombuds office legislation defines the jurisdiction by means of a list of entities subject to the jurisdiction,[114] as is often the case.[115] Providing such a list may seem a blunt and inflexible approach, but it has obvious advantages in terms of avoiding litigation.

## V. Conclusion

I have argued for applying a proportionality test to decide when judicial review of Ombuds office determinations should be available: balancing administrative justice reasons for avoiding judicial review against any need for more adequate avenues of recourse against the Ombuds office. The application of the proportionality test depends on whether our focus is on protecting the individual right to recourse or on maintaining the rule of law. When focusing on the individual right to recourse, it depends on whether the challenge is brought by the original complainant, the authority under investigation or an individual official in that authority. When focusing on the public interest in the rule of law, it depends on whether there is a serious legal error that is likely to be repeated many times.

We have also seen that in several contexts, the likelihood of disputes requiring judicial intervention can be reduced by good legislative design. This includes avoiding inappropriate extensions of the Ombuds office jurisdiction. The office is an informal avenue for dealing with maladministration by public authorities. It is arguably not suitable for regulating private businesses or for investigating serious individual wrongdoing.

[111] See, eg, Ombudsman Act 1974 (NSW), s 35B.
[112] Ombudsmen Act 1975 (NZ), s 13(9).
[113] *Eastleigh* (n 26) seems open to doubt on this basis.
[114] Keith (n 22) 320.
[115] See, eg, Ombudsmen Act 1975 (NZ), s 13 and sch 1; Parliamentary Commissioner Act 1967 (UK), s 4 and sch 2; Public Services Ombudsman (Wales) Act 2019, s 31 and sch 3. But *cf*, eg, Ombudsman Act 1976 (Cwth), s 5(1)(a) and ss 3–3A.

Based on this analysis, the starting point should be to avoid judicial review of Ombuds office determinations. In most contexts, the administrative justice reasons for avoiding judicial review are stronger than any need for more adequate recourse: the cure would be worse than the disease. Judicial review should be allowed only in occasional cases and only on limited grounds. Types of cases where the balance may favour judicial review are where the original complainant truly has no alternative recourse for a significant grievance, where an individual official has been subjected to serious public criticism in an Ombuds office report, or where the need to maintain the rule of law is especially strong.

Some greater accountability for the Ombuds office may well be desirable in some jurisdictions that currently lack this.[116] But to achieve this, we should search for options other than judicial review: options that are less likely to undermine the distinctive administrative justice benefits of recourse to the Ombuds office.

[116] For discussion, see Kirkham (n 87).

# 9

# The Constitution, Separated Judicial Power and Judicial Review in the Australian States

EMILY HAMMOND

## I. Introduction

This chapter explores how Australian judicial review doctrine accommodates separation of powers principles and the flexibility of Australian state constitutions. Specifically, it explores this dynamic in the application of a central judicial review doctrine – 'jurisdictional error'. The chapter contends that the doctrine expresses a fundamental commitment to the conditionality of state power over subjects through denying inherent executive authority over rights. It then explores how this idea fares in relation to two constitutional reference points: the scheme for the exercise of separated judicial power located in Chapter III of the Constitution and the flexibility afforded for Australian states to vest judicial power outside courts on executive branch actors. It argues that a separation of powers perspective on jurisdictional error usefully draws attention to a fundamental constitutional principle of government under law at both Commonwealth and state levels. Conversely, there are two aspects of jurisdictional error which seem anomalous when viewed from a separation of powers perspective. These may be attributable to the influence of concerns to ensure the flexibility of state constitutions. While judicial review doctrine must respect the flexibility of state constitutions, there is a need for a more nuanced approach that better accommodates both elements in tension, flexibility and separation of powers principles.

My analysis in this chapter seeks to reflect a signature theme of Matthew Groves' scholarship: despite the prominence of the Constitution in judicial accounts of judicial review since the late 1990s, the separation of powers principles located in Chapter III of the Constitution do not exhaust the constitutional influences on judicial review of executive action. Groves' scholarship steadily reflects the insight that the dominant Australian conception of judicial review has its roots in state cases. As such, it accommodates the flexibility of state constitutional arrangements, which lack the rigid institutional separation of judicial from non-judicial power that applies at the Commonwealth level. This perspective mitigates against reductionist thinking that overstates Chapter III's determining force on judicial review doctrine.[1] For example, the constitutional understanding of executive power that finds expression in entrenched review of executive action for jurisdictional error (discussed in Part II below) does not originate in the Constitution but is rather drawn from an anterior common law constitutional understanding which, in Australia, began life at the state level. Or, as Groves would put it more pithily, the idea may gain prominence in the context of Chapter III but it is 'arguably also a [s]tate based chicken coming home to roost'.[2]

## A. Jurisdictional Error in Australian Judicial Review of Executive Action

Jurisdictional error has become the central organising concept of Australian judicial review of administrative action. The Constitution entrenches minimum provisions for judicial review for the Commonwealth and each state, ie, specified supervisory jurisdictions that cannot be removed or impaired by ordinary legislation.[3] These entrenched supervisory jurisdictions are identified in terms of review for correction of jurisdictional error. The doctrine of jurisdictional error thereby contributes to a key institutional expression of the rule of law in Australia, defining the entrenched measure of legal accountability for the exercise of public powers under law.

Groves has been sceptical of jurisdictional error and its entrenchment at the state level.[4] Recognising the uncertain and open-ended nature of the doctrine, Groves has described jurisdictional error as 'soft-centred' – 'an evolving and expanding concept' akin to a 'doctrinal black hole, seeming to consume all around it, while shedding no light to outside observers who might wonder how it all works'.[5] Relatedly, he has questioned what it adds to constitutional doctrine and whether the constitutional

[1] Compare M Groves, 'The Return of the (Almost) Absolute Discretion' in J Boughey and LB Crawford (eds), *Interpreting Executive Power* (Annandale, Federation Press, 2020) 129, 133–5. See also M Groves, 'Federal Constitutional Influences on State Judicial Review' (2011) 39 *Federal Law Review* 400.

[2] M Groves, 'Federal Constitutional Influences on State Judicial Review' (2011) 39 *Federal Law Review* 400, 434.

[3] That is, the entrenched minimum provisions for review identified, for Commonwealth powers, in *Plaintiff S157/2002 v Commonwealth* (2003) 211 CLR 476 and, for state powers, in *Kirk v Industrial Court (NSW)* (2010) 239 CLR 531. These review jurisdictions of the High Court and state Supreme Courts respectively deny legislative power to oust the jurisdiction or impose procedural restrictions on their exercise inconsistent with their place in the constitutional structure: *Bodruddaza v Minister for Immigration & Multicultural Affairs* (2007) 228 CLR 651 (inflexible time-limit on applications); *Graham v Minister for Immigration and Border Protection* (2017) 263 CLR 1 (radical restrictions on the court's access to information about the decision under review).

[4] M Groves, 'Federal Constitutional Influences on State Judicial Review' (2011) 39 *Federal Law Review* 400, esp 414–8.

[5] M Groves, 'Judicial Review and Human Rights' (2018) 25(1) *Australian Journal of Administrative Law* 64, 67.

role of courts requires the incorporation of jurisdictional error.[6] Without any expectation of meeting this forceful and well-grounded scepticism about the concept, I suggest a mitigating consideration. Namely, the concept of jurisdictional error focuses attention on an important aspect of the conditionality of state power over subjects in our constitutional context. Before turning to elaborate this point, it is necessary to say something further about the meaning of jurisdictional error.

Though it has a solid common law basis, jurisdictional error has been substantively iterated in Australian caselaw since judicial recognition of the entrenched provision for review. From that caselaw, an analytic account of jurisdictional error emerges which runs something like this: The term 'jurisdictional error' expresses a conclusion about the legal consequences of an error.[7] It signifies that an error has taken the decision-maker beyond their authority to decide. Such an error renders a purported decision 'invalid'. In turn, 'invalidity' means that a purported decision under statutory authority does not determine rights by force of statute. The essence of jurisdictional error is that it results in 'a decision which has been made in fact lacking characteristics necessary for it to be given force and effect by the statute pursuant to which the decision-maker purported to make it'.[8] Within this account, it is treated as axiomatic that a statute empowering decisions determining rights will only operate on rights through the decisions it authorises. In this analytic, jurisdictional error means that a decision made in fact will not be a factum for the statute's operation to affect rights.[9]

There is flexibility built into this conception of jurisdictional error at two points. First, flexibility is built into the method of identifying whether an error is an invalidating (aka jurisdictional) error. In the case of decision-making under an Act, jurisdictional error 'consists of a material breach of an express or implied condition on the valid exercise of a decision-making power conferred by that Act'.[10] Whether an error can be so characterised is a question of statutory interpretation, informed by evolving common law principles of statutory interpretation.[11] This applies to the two key dimensions of jurisdictional error:

[6] M Groves, 'Federal Constitutional Influences on State Judicial Review' (2011) 39 *Federal Law Review* 400, 417.

[7] M Aronson, M Groves and G Weeks, *Judicial Review of Administrative Action and Government Liability*, 7th edn (London, Thomson Reuters, 2021) 789–91.

[8] *Hossain v Minister for Immigration and Border Protection* (2018) 264 CLR 123, 133 [24] (Kiefel CJ, Gageler and Keane JJ).

[9] That is, the decision's status as 'the incidental or ancillary determination of circumstances as a factum for the operation of the legislative will': *British Imperial Oil Co Ltd v Commissioner of Taxation (Cth)* (1926) 38 CLR 153, 176 (Isaacs J). The decision made in exercise of statutory authority is viewed as 'adjunct to legislation', a 'factum on which the operation of [statute] depends'/'the factum by reference to which the Act operates to alter the law in relation to the particular case': *R v Trade Practices Tribunal; Ex parte Tasmanian Breweries Pty Ltd* (1970) 123 CLR 361, 371 (McTiernan J), 378 (Kitto J). See also *Attorney-General (Cth) v Alinta Ltd* (2008) 233 CLR 542, 577–579 [94]–[97] (Hayne J).

[10] *Hossain v Minister for Immigration and Border Protection* (2018) 264 CLR 123, 135 [31] (Kiefel CJ, Gageler and Keane JJ).

[11] *MZAPC v Minister for Immigration and Border Protection* (2021) 273 CLR 506, 521 [30] (Kiefel CJ, Gageler, Keane and Gleeson JJ).

> Just as identification of the preconditions to and conditions of an exercise of decision-making power conferred by statute turns on the construction of the statute, so too does discernment of the extent of non-compliance which will result in an otherwise compliant decision lacking the characteristics necessary to be given force and effect by the statute turn on the construction of the statute.[12]

Second, flexibility is also present in relation to the consequences that may be attributed to an invalid purported decision. As succinctly put by Aronson, Groves and Weeks, invalidity is a 'bundle' of possible legal consequences, and the term 'is still used even where some of those consequences may not apply to a particular context'.[13] Consequences of invalidity that vary include: whether the decision is open to collateral attack;[14] whether the purported decision suffices to enliven a second actor's statutory powers;[15] and whether the decision-maker can re-open the decision irrespective that it has not been set aside in judicial review.[16] These variable consequences of invalidity in purported statutory decisions can be contrasted with the one fixed consequence mentioned earlier – that the invalid statutory decision does not have statutory force:

> A decision made outside jurisdiction is not necessarily to be regarded as a 'nullity', in that it remains a decision in fact which may yet have some status in law. But a decision made outside jurisdiction is a decision in fact which is properly to be regarded for the purposes of the law pursuant to which it was purported to be made as 'no decision at all'.[17]

A purely analytic account of jurisdictional error does not adequately convey the constitutional values it serves or the constitutional influences on its application. Before turning to these matters, it is first necessary to briefly sketch some key features of the constitutional context.

## B. Constitutional Context for Judicial Review

Judicial review of executive action in Australia adapts the British common law supervisory jurisdiction of Westminster superior courts to the distinctive context set by the Constitution.[18] Each of the original British colonies in Australia – now

[12] *Hossain v Minister for Immigration and Border Protection* (2018) 264 CLR 123, 133–4 [27] (Kiefel CJ, Gageler and Keane JJ).

[13] M Aronson, M Groves and G Weeks, *Judicial Review of Administrative Action and Government Liability*, 7th edn (London, Thomson Reuters, 2021) 791.

[14] ibid 813–21.

[15] Eg, efficacy to enliven a statutory avenue of appeal or review is not necessarily affected by jurisdictional error: see, eg, *Collector of Customs (NSW) v Brian Lawlor Automotive Pty Ltd* (1979) 24 ALR 307; *Plaintiff M174/2016 v Minister for Immigration and Border Protection* (2018) 264 CLR 217.

[16] *Minister for Immigration and Multicultural Affairs v Bhardwaj* (2002) 209 CLR 597.

[17] *Hossain v Minister for Immigration and Border Protection* (2018) 264 CLR 123, 133 [24] (Kiefel CJ, Gageler and Keane JJ).

[18] Compare M Groves and G Weeks, 'The Creation of Australian Administrative Law: The Constitution and its Judicial Gate-Keepers' in S Jhaveri and M Ramsden (eds), *Judicial Review of*

the states – has a Supreme Court invested with jurisdiction enabling judicial review on applications for certiorari, mandamus and prohibition. The British model is also seen in the provision made, upon federation, for judicial review within the newly established Commonwealth level of government. Section 75(iii) and (v) of the Constitution ensured that the newly established High Court of Australia would have an equivalent supervisory jurisdiction in respect of Commonwealth powers to that exercised by Supreme Courts in relation to state powers.

Federation necessarily saw some departures from the British model. Enacting the Constitution as the compact for the federation was understood to introduce judicially-enforceable limits on the government powers of all polities within it and a distinctive framework for the development of Australian common law. One of the changes introduced by federation was the structure of an integrated national system of courts under Chapter III of the Constitution. Chapter III declares the High Court ('the Court') to be the apex court for federal and state matters. It also defines the scope of Commonwealth judicial power by reference to nine categories of subject matter, identified in sections 75 and 76, and provides for that Commonwealth judicial power to be exercised by the Court, federal courts, and state courts. This is seen as bringing all courts, federal and state, into an integrated national system for the administration of a national common law and the exercise of federal jurisdiction.

Within the terms of Chapter III, there are two aspects of particular significance for judicial review of executive action. The first, already mentioned, is the provision of entrenched supervisory jurisdictions of the Court and each of the state Supreme Courts. As adverted to, section 75(iii) and (v) of the Constitution deny Commonwealth legislative power to exclude or impair the Court's jurisdiction to issue mandamus, prohibition, injunction and certiorari for jurisdictional error in the exercise of Commonwealth powers. Section 73 of the Constitution denies state legislative power to exclude or impair a state Supreme Court's jurisdiction to enforce the limits of state powers by granting prohibition, mandamus and certiorari on grounds of jurisdictional error.

A second aspect of significance for judicial review is the Chapter III provision that judicial power in identified subject matters be exclusive to courts. This is the primary separation rule established by Chapter III. This primary separation rule generates a mandate for judicial review. This arises because non-courts cannot conclusively determine legal rights with respect to the identified subject matters. To do so would usurp the judicial power (to conclusively determine rights) exclusively vested in courts under Chapter III. Clearly, executive bodies are routinely authorised by statute to make decisions that affect rights by force of statute – administrative decisions to grant, revoke or alter permits, and licences and visas; require payments to be made or specific actions undertaken; or even place a person into detention, etc. Not infrequently, these decisions are made according

*Administrative Action Across the Common Law World: Origins and Adaptation* (Cambridge, Cambridge University Press, 2021).

to enacted criteria that would be suitable for application in judicial decision-making, and not infrequently decision-makers are required to act 'judicially' in the sense of affording procedural fairness and maintaining the reality and appearance of impartiality. Across such instances, usurpation of judicial power is avoided because an executive determination of rights is not conclusive in the same way as a judicial order may be. Judicial review is critical to give practical expression to that distinction. It offers a mechanism for authoritative adjudication on whether rights are as specified in a purported administrative decision.

For the present discussion, it is important to address the impact of Chapter III's primary separation rule on state constitutions. Significant alteration to the doctrine was made relatively recently. In *Burns v Corbett*[19] ('*Burns*'), the Court recast the scope of the primary separation rule. To take a step back: soon after federation, and certainly by 1918, it was recognised that *Commonwealth* judicial power cannot be conferred on any office or institution that is not a 'court' within the meaning of Chapter III.[20] The Constitution's positive provision for Commonwealth judicial power to be vested in courts was exhaustive and impliedly prohibited Commonwealth judicial power from being vested otherwise. This understanding of the primary separation rule as a rule pertaining only to *Commonwealth* judicial power continued for 100 years. However, the '*Burns* restriction' identified by a majority of the Court in 2018 recalibrated Chapter III's primary separation rule, revealing it to also be applicable as a limit on *state* legislative power to confer *state* judicial power on non-courts – albeit only on those subject matters identified in sections 75 and 76 as falling within the potential scope of federal jurisdiction.[21] The *Burns* majority returned to the premise of the primary separation rule, that Chapter III is the only source of Commonwealth power to confer or invest judicial power in the subject matters identified in sections 75 and 76.[22] On the assumption that Commonwealth legislative power in relation to adjudication of these matters is both paramount and limited, their Honours concluded that Chapter III impliedly denies *state* legislative power to outflank the choices given to Commonwealth Parliament in relation to adjudication of those subject matters.[23] In this way, Chapter III was held to necessarily deny

[19] *Burns v Corbett* (2018) 265 CLR 304.

[20] As definitively established in *Waterside Workers' Federation of Australia v J W Alexander Ltd* (1918) 25 CLR 434.

[21] *Burns v Corbett* (2018) 265 CLR 304. Specifically, the view of the majority is that this is a limitation derived from Chapter III's exhaustive scheme for the exercise of judicial power on the field described by ss 75 and 76 (and *not*, as the minority justices considered, an effect of Judiciary Act 1903 (Cth) provisions overriding state laws conferring state jurisdiction on non-court tribunals).

[22] *Burns v Corbett* (2018) 265 CLR 304, 335 [43], 341 [55], 345 [64] (Kiefel CJ, Keane and Bell JJ), 346 [68], 364 [119] (Gageler J).

[23] Chapter III empowers the Commonwealth Parliament to replace a state court's *state* jurisdiction with *federal* jurisdiction, so that appeals lie directly to the High Court; or to make a federal court's jurisdiction exclusive of that which belongs to or is invested in state courts: see *Burns v Corbett* (2018) 265 CLR 304, 356–7 [96]–[99] (Gageler J) and, to similar effect 335–7 [43]–[45] (Kiefel CJ, Keane and Bell JJ).

states the constitutional option of vesting judicial power in federal subject matters in non-courts.

The *Burns* ruling is a significant incursion on the flexibility of state constitutional arrangements. Until *Burns*, the orthodox view was that Chapter III did not impose any strict institutional separation of judicial power on the states. Following *Burns*, that orthodoxy holds true for the exercise of state judicial power on subject matters that fall *outside* the nine classes of subject matter in sections 75 and 76 of the Constitution. But in respect of those subject matters, judicial power is exclusive to courts.

In addition to these two features of Chapter III of direct relevance to judicial review (entrenched review; the primary separation rule), another aspect of Chapter III warrants mention as relevant context for the discussion to follow. This is the scheme in Chapter III to protect core characteristics of separated judicial power. This scheme, as progressively elaborated by the Court, protects the constitutional conception of 'courts' as repositories of separated judicial power and prevents courts from being co-opted to perform functions incompatible with this conception. The scheme emerges from distinct restrictions on Commonwealth and state legislative powers, albeit with some areas of overlap. Principally, the '*Boilermakers* restriction' prevents the Commonwealth from vesting non-judicial power in courts,[24] while the '*Kable* restriction' precludes states from entrusting their courts with functions incompatible with the essential characteristics of courts as repositories of separated judicial power.[25] The complexities attending the application of these restrictions are not important for the present discussion. What is important is that there is an area of overlap which protects the institutional integrity of all courts that are entrusted with the exercise of separated judicial power under Chapter III.

## II. Jurisdictional Error Through a Chapter III Lens

The discussion in this Part concerns the impact of the Chapter III primary separation rule on the doctrine of jurisdictional error in Australia. I argue that the association of jurisdictional error with the primary separation rule usefully focuses attention on the defining characteristics of executive power. This in turn clarifies certain constitutional values embedded in entrenched review of executive action for jurisdictional error. These values include long-standing commitments concerning the conditionality of state power over subjects, including a commitment to the executive's inherent incapacity to determine rights.

[24] *R v Kirby; Ex parte Boilermakers Society of Australia* (1956) 94 CLR 254; affirmed *Attorney-General of the Commonwealth v The Queen* (1957) 95 CLR 529. This restriction applies to 'bare' non-judicial functions, so allows for conferral of non-judicial functions 'auxiliary or incidental' to judicial powers.

[25] So named for the leading authority, *Kable v Director of Public Prosecutions (NSW)* (1996) 189 CLR 51.

## A. The Conditionality of State Power Over Rights

The primary separation rule (making separated judicial power exclusive to courts) assumes a conception of the distinctive characteristics of both executive and judicial powers. One perspective on this distinction, touched on earlier, emphasises the distinctive qualities of judicial power. It is only through an exercise of judicial power that the state conclusively determines rights. Thus, judicial review for jurisdictional error ensures against executive usurpation of separated judicial power by ensuring an avenue to seek a conclusive judicial determination as to whether an executive assertion of statutory or prerogative power determines rights in the way it purports.

Another perspective on the distinction between judicial and executive power focuses on the qualities of executive power, specifically, the understanding of executive power in the tradition of British parliamentary government. Within this inherited parliamentary tradition, there is a long-standing and fundamental commitment to the executive's subjection to the general system of law. Simply put, the executive requires positive prerogative or statutory authority for any decision purporting to alter rights or depart from the general condition of law. It lacks power over rights beyond those specific powers granted as common law prerogatives or by statute.

This underlying commitment to the conditionality of state power over subjects is expressed in a review to correct jurisdictional error in executive decisions. As set out above, the analytic of jurisdictional error is that it invalidates a purported decision in exercise of statutory (or prerogative) authority to determine rights so that it does not determine rights by force of statute or common law prerogative. The constitutional value of this analytic can be clarified by integrating it with the anterior common law commitment to inherent executive incapacity. Jurisdictional error identifies when statutory or prerogative authority for an executive act is removed, leaving the underlying inherent executive incapacity exposed. In this way, review of executive action for jurisdictional error serves one of the most vital foundational commitments to the conditionality of state power over subjects in our inherited parliamentary tradition.

It bears restating that the executive incapacity spoken of here is not a product of the strict separation rule in Chapter III. It is an anterior common law constitutional understanding that pertains to the nature of executive power rather than to any specific entrenched rules governing its allocation. As Groves might say, common law constitutionalism remains a dominant factor shaping Australian doctrine, and the doctrine is more complex than the Constitution alone can explain. Bearing this in mind, one is reminded not to oversell the impact of Chapter III's primary separation rule on Australian doctrine. The significance of Chapter III's primary separation rule lies in the attention it focuses on the distinctive characteristics of executive power – including the inherent incapacity that is a central tenet of the conditionality of state power over subjects in the common law tradition.[26]

[26] See L McDonald, K Rundle and E Hammond, *Principles of Administrative Law*, 4th edn (London, Oxford University Press, 2023) 58–63.

The primary separation rule in Chapter III, while not the *source* of the anterior commitment to executive subordination to law, does *centre* that commitment in the practice of entrenched review for jurisdictional error. In purely formal terms, the primary separation rule in Chapter III mandates judicial review for jurisdictional error in executive decisions with respect to identified subject matters (as described in sections 75 and 76 of the Constitution). But this is no mere formality because, in doing so, it also aligns jurisdictional error with the underlying commitment to a conditionality of state power over subjects, according to which an invalid executive act is constitutionally incapable of determining rights.

## B. Conditionality of State Power and Identification of Jurisdictional Error

This deep-rooted understanding of inherent executive incapacity can be traced through the method for identifying jurisdictional error. As noted earlier, jurisdictional error 'consists of a material breach of an express or implied condition on the valid exercise of a decision-making power conferred by that [a]ct'.[27] The field of potential jurisdictional errors is limited to errors of law, ie, non-compliance with an applicable legal requirement for decision-making. Within that field, 'jurisdictional' and 'non-jurisdictional' are distinguished by reference to two markers: whether compliance with the relevant legal requirement is a condition on valid decision-making and whether the non-compliance in the case was material. The inherent incapacity of the executive is reflected in both dimensions of this inquiry.

First, the underlying commitment to inherent executive incapacity is seen in the different starting points as to whether material legal error invalidates decisions of inferior courts (on the one hand) and decisions of tribunals as executive branch actors (on the other). As explained in *Craig v South Australia*[28] ('*Craig*'), there are distinct common law presumptions of statutory interpretation for decision-making by inferior courts and tribunals.[29] The basic distinction made in *Craig* is this: On the one hand, a statutory conferral of judicial power on a court will ordinarily encompass authority to determine questions of law, so errors of law are not presumed to be jurisdictional errors. On the other hand, the statutory conferral of power on an administrator will ordinarily be conditioned by an implied statutory requirement to exercise the power on a correct understanding of the applicable law, meaning that any legal error which affects the exercise of that power is presumed

[27] *Hossain v Minister for Immigration and Border Protection* (2018) 264 CLR 123, 135 [31] (Kiefel CJ, Gageler and Keane JJ).

[28] *Craig v South Australia* (1995) 184 CLR 163.

[29] Contrast the unified approach that emerged in British common law, when the approach applied to administrative decision-making in *Anisminic v Foreign Compensation Commission* [1969] 2 AC 147 was extended to inferior courts in *Re Racal Communications Ltd* [1984] AC 374.

to be a jurisdictional error.[30] As will be discussed further below, this distinction registers inherent executive incapacity as a factor in applying jurisdictional error.

Second, the axiom of executive inherent incapacity provides important context for the materiality precondition for jurisdictional error. As mentioned earlier, Australian authorities define jurisdictional error as a *material* breach of preconditions or conditions on valid decision-making. For a period from 2018, the materiality precondition for jurisdictional error was given controversial application in judgments on review of migration decisions reached under a procedurally unfair process.[31] The controversial aspect arose from the distinct onus placed on vulnerable applicants for judicial review to establish a counterfactual that looks backwards to the circumstances of decision-making within the government apparatus: namely that the decision may have been different had the procedural unfairness not occurred. This attracted strident criticism: it was considered unclear why a separate practical injustice inquiry is presumptively required for enacted conditions on power;[32] its coherence with existing authorities was challenged;[33] and it was considered to enmesh judicial review in a counter-factual analysis incompatible with the strict focus on legality that is the hallmark of judicial supervision of executive action.[34] Subsequently, the operation of the materiality precondition was clarified to be less demanding than it first appeared. It requires the applicant for review to prove *on the balance of probabilities* the historical facts necessary to enable a court to be satisfied *as a matter of reasonable conjecture* that the decision *could* have been different had the relevant condition on power been complied with.[35] Further, a separate inquiry would not be required in relation to certain errors: those the demonstration of which necessarily demonstrates materiality and those arising from breach of enacted requirements that define and delimit the power itself, such that *any* departure is material.[36]

To the extent that the Court has given a rationale for the materiality threshold, it has been a pragmatic one. The threshold has been described as a 'common sense'

[30] *Craig v South Australia* (1995) 184 CLR 163, 179.

[31] *Hossain v Minister for Immigration and Border Protection* (2018) 264 CLR 123; *Minister for Immigration and Border Protection v SZMTA* (2019) 264 CLR 421; *MZAPC v Minister for Immigration and Border Protection* (2021) 273 CLR 506; *Nathanson v Minister for Home Affairs* (2022) 276 CLR 80 103.

[32] See, eg, LB Crawford, 'Immaterial Errors, Jurisdictional Errors and the Presumptive Limits of Executive Power' (2019) 30(4) *Public Law Review* 281.

[33] See, eg, H Aniulis, 'Materiality: Marking the Metes and Bounds of Jurisdictional Error?' (2020) 27(2) *Australian Journal of Administrative Law* 88; N Carey, 'Presumptions Upon Presumptions: Problems with the Threshold of Materiality' (2021) 44(2) *University of New South Wales Law Journal* 548.

[34] *Minister for Immigration and Border Protection v SZMTA* (2019) 264 CLR 421, 460 [95] (Nettle and Gordon JJ).

[35] *Nathanson v Minister for Home Affairs* (2022) 276 CLR 80 103 [32]–[33] (Kiefel CJ, Keane and Gleeson JJ), 107–108 [46]–[47] (Gageler J).

[36] *MZAPC v Minister for Immigration and Border Protection* (2021) 273 CLR 506, 522 [33] (Kiefel CJ, Gageler, Keane and Gleeson JJ); *LPDT v Minister for Immigration, Citizenship, Migrant Services and Multicultural Affairs* [2024] HCA 12, [6] (Gageler CJ, Gordon, Edelman, Steward, Gleeson and Jagot JJ; Beech-Jones agreeing).

assumption as to what Parliament would intend when establishing a decision-making process as a 'function of the real world'.[37] There may also be a concern, in judicial review of judicial orders, to 'ensure, in the interests of making the best use of judicial resources, that [review] not result in a duplication of judicial process that cannot be justified by the demands of the rule of law'.[38]

However, it is difficult to shake the sense that there may also be features of the Australian constitutional context influencing the emphasis given by the Court to the materiality precondition for jurisdictional error. Plausibly, the materiality precondition can be understood as the logical corollary of constitutional values expressed in the application of jurisdictional error to executive decision-making. More specifically, the materiality precondition tracks the underlying commitment to the conditionality of state power expressed in the inherent executive incapacity to affect rights. Put simply, judicial review of executive action is not concerned with correcting legal error in administrative decisions as such. It is concerned with correcting legal errors that affect the administrative decision as a factum for a statutory (or prerogative) effect on rights. The focus is on whether the decision is the kind that statute (or prerogative) imbues with legal force. Logically, immaterial errors – understood as errors that have no possible effect on the decision – cannot affect whether a decision is or is not a specified kind of decision.

## III. Flexibility of State Constitutions as a Continuing Influence

The discussion in this Part turns to aspects of the Australian caselaw on jurisdictional error that do not co-exist as easily with the Chapter III context. Two such aspects are: (i) scepticism towards application of the *Craig* presumption that material legal errors invalidate state tribunal decision-making; and (ii) adherence to an orthodoxy that an invalid judicial order of an inferior court lacks legal force in the same way that an invalid executive decision lacks legal force.[39]

These aspects of jurisdictional error pull against the influence of executive inherent incapacity on the doctrine. They do this by deflecting attention from that distinctive characteristic of executive power. This can be seen to arise from an impulse to reflect the flexibility of state constitutional arrangements. The impulse is defensible at the level of principle. It is and remains an important feature of the Constitution that flexibility is afforded to the states to vest judicial power outside courts (subject to the *Burns* restriction). The problem, as will be discussed, is that

[37] See *MZAPC v Minister for Immigration and Border Protection* (2021) 273 CLR 506, 521–2 [32] (Kiefel CJ, Gageler, Keane and Gleeson JJ).

[38] *R (Cart) v Upper Tribunal* [2012] 1 AC 663, 698 [89], in observations that have drawn comparison to the Court's stated functionalist concerns.

[39] *State of Queensland v Mr Stradford (a pseudonym)* [2025] HCA 3, [51]–[53] (Gageler CJ, Gleeson, Jagot, Beech-Jones JJ).

the impulse has resulted in doctrine that lacks the nuance needed to best align the flexibility of state constitutions with the values that Chapter III protects.

Before proceeding, it might be wise to acknowledge that this discussion may be seen as an exercise in 'top-down' reasoning. Groves and co-authors have often remarked on the Court's strong aversion to 'top-down legal reasoning', in which an overarching theory is used to organise and explain caselaw principles.[40] This style of reasoning is thought to invite political, sociological or economic analysis that has no legitimacy or utility as a tool for adjudication of legal disputes. Perhaps then, the aspects of authority discussed in this part simply manifest this aversion on the part of Australian authorities. On the other hand, Groves and co-authors rightly emphasise that the judicial method of legal analysis evolves with reference to fundamental principles that lend coherence to an area of law. The expectation that jurisdictional error will be elaborated in reference to fundamental and enduring understandings of the conditionality of state power, reflected in the framework established by the Constitution, should not be contentious. To this extent, 'top-down reasoning' can be usefully applied to identify incremental adjustments that could bring jurisdictional error into a more productive alignment with Chapter III *and* the flexibility of state constitutions.

Of particular interest as candidates for adjustment by a 'top-down' account are aspects of Australian caselaw on jurisdictional error that do not overtly differentiate between judicial orders and executive decisions. Failing to draw a bright line between judicial and executive decision-making may seem relatively innocuous. It appears consistent with the flexibility of state constitutions. But the absence of a brightly drawn line also has a downside. It deflects attention from an important constitutional distinction between executive and judicial power. As such, it detracts from the clarity and coherence of review doctrine and the commitment to executive inherent incapacity that is a foundational principle of the inherited constitutional tradition for both the Commonwealth and the states.

With this in mind, the balance of this discussion will explore the two aspects of jurisdictional error identified, where doctrine seems to favour the flexibility of state constitutions at the expense of clear recognition of inherent executive incapacity.

## A. *Kirk* and Scepticism about the *Craig* Presumption for Non/Jurisdictional Errors

As has been mentioned earlier, *Craig* had recognised that there is a presumption of statutory interpretation that an administrative tribunal 'lacks authority to

[40] See, eg, M Groves and G Weeks, 'The Creation of Australian Administrative Law: The Constitution and its Judicial Gate-Keepers' in S Jhaveri and M Ramsden (eds), *Judicial Review of Administrative Action Across the Common Law World: Origins and Adaptation* (Cambridge, Cambridge University Press, 2021) 317–8.

authoritatively determine questions of law or to make an order or decision otherwise than in accordance with the law', with the consequence that any material legal error by an administrative tribunal is a jurisdictional error.[41] This presumption registers inherent executive incapacity as a factor in applying jurisdictional error. It does so by requiring clarity in legislation that operates on rights through executive decisions affected by legal error. The presumption that material legal errors by executive decision-makers are jurisdictional aligns with a presumption that it is a condition on the exercise of statutory executive powers that they be exercised on the basis of correct legal principles, correctly applied.[42]

In *Kirk*, the Court queried whether this approach was appropriate for state tribunal decisions:

> Behind these conclusions lies an assumption that a distinction can readily be made between a court and an administrative tribunal. At a State level that distinction may not always be drawn easily, for there is not, in the States' constitutional arrangements, that same separation of powers that is required at a federal level by Ch III of the Constitution. No less importantly, behind the conclusions expressed in *Craig* lie premises about what is meant by jurisdictional error. Unexpressed premises about what is meant by jurisdictional error give content to the notion of 'authoritative' when it is said, as it was in *Craig*, that tribunals cannot 'authoritatively' determine questions of law, but that courts can.[43]

*Kirk*'s scepticism about the *Craig* approach to jurisdictional error in state tribunals appears to be driven by consideration of the flexibility of state constitutional arrangements. Unfortunately, this was done in terms that detracted from recognition that the presumption reflects the inherent incapacity to affect rights and subordination to law that are essential features of state executive power, whether at state or federal level.

It is not surprising that the *Kirk* account of entrenched review by state Supreme Courts does not refer to inherent executive incapacity to determine rights. For one thing, at the time *Kirk* was handed down, it was not considered that Chapter III made any part of state judicial power exclusive to courts. This was to follow in *Burns*. Even following *Burns*, there is no specific reason that executive incapacity should be emphasised in judicial accounts of the entrenched review jurisdiction of state Supreme Courts. The restriction on state legislative power identified in *Burns* only affects the exercise of state judicial power on subject

[41] *Craig v South Australia* (1995) 184 CLR 163, 179.

[42] *Hossain v Minister for Immigration and Border Protection* (2018) 264 CLR 123, 134 [29] (Kiefel CJ, Gageler and Keane JJ). This is not to say all material legal errors by tribunals (or others) exercising executive power are jurisdictional errors. An empowering statute may be construed as authorising an executive decision-maker to have the last word on some questions of law, such that any errors a decision-maker may make on those questions will not affect the exercise of the power and will not prevent the statutory effect on rights being attracted to the decision. So, eg, the effect of *Coal & Allied Operations Pty Limited v Australian Industrial Relations Commission* (2000) 203 CLR 194 was that the full bench of the respondent federal industrial tribunal had considerable scope to make non-jurisdictional errors of law.

[43] *Kirk v Industrial Court (NSW)* (2010) 239 CLR 531, 573 [69].

matters falling within sections 75 and 76. Moreover, the *Burns* restriction is not made in service of separating state judicial from executive powers so as to preserve their distinct constitutional characteristics. Rather, the restriction is designed to bring every exercise of adjudicative authority on federal subject matters within the integrated national system of courts, subject to the system of appeals to the Court established by and under section 73 of the Constitution. With this as its primary motivation, the *Burns* ruling does not lend itself to centring executive incapacity in thinking about entrenched review of state executive powers.

Also relevant to an appraisal of the reasoning in *Kirk*, there is no 'gap' in the entrenched review described in that decision calling for recognition of a separation of powers mandate for review of state executive powers. Entrenched review by state Supreme Courts reaches any exercise of state judicial or executive power by persons or bodies other than the Supreme Court.[44] In contrast, at the Commonwealth level, the separation of powers mandate covers off a gap that otherwise appears in the express entrenchment of review. Among the direct grants of jurisdiction to the Court in section 75 of the Constitution, the two that support judicial review of executive action are section 75(iii) and (v). Of these two, only section 75(v) expressly references remedies associated with jurisdictional error. Yet section 75(v) only grants jurisdiction where the remedies are sought against an 'officer of the Commonwealth', a term that falls far short of covering all the various repositories of federal executive power. In this context, attention naturally shifts to the strict institutional separation of Commonwealth power. It provides an alternative mandate for judicial review of executive powers that can be accommodated under the terms of section 75(iii) in cases that are not covered by section 75(v). At the state level there is no comparable gap in the express creation and entrenchment of judicial review such as would drive attention to the separation of powers rationale.

So it is not particularly notable that *Kirk* did not emphasise executive incapacity as a basis for entrenched review of state executive powers. What is notable is that *Kirk* seems to downplay differences between executive and judicial powers by expressing scepticism about the *Craig* that there is a critical distinction to be made in relation to the presumptive jurisdiction of *courts* and *non-courts* at the state level.

## B. Clarifying the Basis for the *Craig* Presumption for State Tribunals?

The scepticism *Kirk* directed towards the *Craig* approach focused on the difficulty of drawing a line between courts and non-court tribunals in the states, where there was no strict institutional separation of powers. This specific, pragmatic objection

[44] *Kirk v Industrial Court (NSW)* (2010) 239 CLR 531, 580–1 [98].

to a differential application of jurisdictional error has fallen away following *Burns*, which requires a distinction to be drawn between state courts and tribunals and between state judicial and executive power. However, the underlying objection grounded in the flexibility of state constitutions has ongoing relevance. The question is what precisely the underlying objection is.

One possibility is that *Kirk* was emphasising that the states have an executive power to affect rights that is unaffected by the inherent incapacities that justify the *Craig* presumption at the Commonwealth level. Before *Burns*, there was relatively little need to consider whether the power exercised by a state tribunal was executive or judicial power. It was acceptable to refer to powers vested in a tribunal as 'executive power' according to the logic that it was power exercised by an executive branch institution. Reading the *Kirk* comments on *Craig* in this light, they may seem to be insisting that a state tribunal may be invested with *executive* power to render a determination of rights that has legal force even if its purported exercise of power is affected by legal error.

Another possibility is that *Kirk* is instead emphasising the scope for states to confer judicial power on non-court tribunals. It is this flexibility that warrants a qualification on the *Craig* presumption that material legal errors by tribunals are jurisdictional errors. This reading of *Kirk* was always available but is arguably supported by the greater attention that is being given, post-*Burns*, to the distinction between state executive and judicial powers. *Burns* prompts greater attention to whether the power exercised by a state tribunal is executive or judicial power. So prompted, there may be a straightforward way of explaining the *Kirk* emphasis on the possibility for state tribunals to make decisions that have legal force even though the exercise of power is affected by legal errors. The point is not that state executive power sustains this outcome, but that states can (subject to *Burns*) confer judicial power on non-courts.

This perspective would be consistent with the analysis in *Craig*. Specifically, it would align with the Court's observation in *Craig* on the impossibility of certain tribunals being empowered to authoritatively decide questions of law that affect the purported exercise of power – namely, those tribunals that are constitutionally incapable of exercising judicial power:

> where constitutional limitations arising from the doctrine of separation of judicial and executive powers … preclude legislative competence to confer judicial power upon an administrative tribunal. Where such an administrative tribunal falls into an error of law which causes it to identify a wrong issue, to ask itself a wrong question, to ignore relevant material, to rely on irrelevant material or, at least in some circumstances, to make an erroneous finding or to reach a mistaken conclusion, and the tribunal's exercise or purported exercise of power is thereby affected, it exceeds its authority or powers. Such an error of law is jurisdictional error which will invalidate any order or decision of the tribunal which reflects it.[45]

[45] *Craig v South Australia* (1990) 184 CLR 163, 179.

At the time *Craig* was handed down, it was not squarely contemplated that this observation would have any application to state executive decision-makers. Nevertheless, it was significant that this oriented jurisdictional error to a constitutional understanding of executive power (one which has practical application in the states following *Burns*). In this passage, *Craig* orients the different approaches to jurisdictional error to the basic doctrine of inherent executive incapacity and the contrast it creates between executive and judicial powers.

As Groves and co-authors emphasise, the Court in the *Craig* era had been receptive to a presumption that all legal errors affecting executive decisions are jurisdictional but reluctant to extend this presumption to judicial orders of inferior courts.[46] That this was the sticking point for the *Craig* era Court is telling. In this respect, the Court showed a keen appreciation that an approach to jurisdictional error for decision-making under executive power (which lacks any inherent authority to determine rights beyond that given by statute or prerogative) is not self-evidently apt for judicial decision-making. To this we might add: *Craig* confirms that the key presumption operating for state non-court tribunals is that the powers conferred on them are executive powers, for which there is a rebuttable presumption that material errors of law are jurisdictional. This understanding accommodates the flexibility of state constitutions without detracting from the constitutional commitment to executive inherent incapacity.

## C. The Inferiority of Inferior Court Orders

There is another aspect of jurisdictional error that blurs the bright line that exists between judicial and executive power. This is the orthodoxy that the effect of jurisdictional error on the legal force of a purported decision is the same for inferior court orders and executive decisions. Following *State of Queensland v Mr Stradford (a pseudonym)* ('*Stradford*'),[47] this remains the settled approach in Australian law.[48] The judicial orders of superior courts are recognised as binding unless and until set aside, even if impaired by jurisdictional error, whereas the judicial orders of inferior courts and executive decisions affected by jurisdictional error are said to lack legal force from the time they are made.[49] In *Kirk* this doctrine was invoked

[46] M Groves and G Weeks, 'The Creation of Australian Administrative Law: The Constitution and its Judicial Gate-Keepers' in S Jhaveri and M Ramsden (eds), *Judicial Review of Administrative Action Across the Common Law World: Origins and Adaptation* (Cambridge, Cambridge University Press, 2021) 309, 316.

[47] *State of Queensland v Mr Stradford (a pseudonym)* [2025] HCA 3.

[48] *State of Queensland v Mr Stradford (a pseudonym)* [2025] HCA 3, [51]–[53] (Gageler CJ, Gleeson, Jagot, Beech-Jones JJ).

[49] However, as the Court in *State of Queensland v Mr Stradford (a pseudonym)* [2025] HCA 3 went on to hold, this does not mean that the inferior court judge who makes an invalid order for imprisonment, or the court officers and police enforcing that invalid order, are tortiously liable. On the separate question of civil liability for detention under the invalid inferior court order, *Stradford* extends the judicial immunity of superior court justices to justices of inferior courts, and holds that officers who are under a

to challenge the notion that there is a constitutional difference between executive and judicial power to determine rights. If the only 'authoritative' judicial orders of inferior courts 'are those decisions which are not attended by jurisdictional error', how can it be said that there is a categorical distinction between judicial and executive powers to determine rights?[50]

One response to this provocation is to finesse the distinction between judicial and executive power to accommodate the inferiority of inferior court judicial orders. This inferiority does not contradict the underlying difference between judicial and executive power. It simply prompts a necessary refinement of the claim. The refined claim is that there is a categorical difference between the legal force that *can be* given to a judicial order in contrast to an executive decision. The specific inherent legal force attributed to even invalid superior court orders *can be* extended to invalid judicial orders of other institutions but *cannot* be extended to executive decisions. This would be consistent with the way the legal force of superior court orders has been analysed in the Court. For instance, in *New South Wales v Kable* (*'Kable 2'*),[51] the Court held that a superior court judicial order for the detention of Kable provided lawful authority for that detention until it was set aside on an appeal to the Court, despite being made under an unconstitutional statute. In their joint reasons, French CJ, Hayne, Crennan, Kiefel, Bell and Keane JJ explained that the 'roots of the doctrine, that the orders of a superior court of record are valid until set aside even if made in excess of jurisdiction, lie in the nature of judicial power'.[52] Giving the orders of a superior court these characteristics 'reflects the distinction between the exercise of judicial power (by the final quelling of controversies according to law) and the exercise of executive power (subject to law)'.[53] Gageler J, writing separately, endorsed the premise that a purported exercise of non-judicial power lacks legal force if made without jurisdiction.[54] His Honour also linked the status afforded to a judicial order of a superior court to the nature of judicial power – it has 'independent legal force as a judicial order', even if it is based on an invalid law or purported exercise of jurisdiction.[55] Thus, there is a clear recognition that there is a quality that *can* be present in an invalid purported exercise of judicial power but which is denied to any invalid purported exercise of executive power.

While the inferiority of inferior court orders can be reconciled with a separation of powers perspective on jurisdictional error in this way, it is an uncomfortable

legal duty to execute or enforce judicial orders are protected from liability if the order is invalid (unless an order is, on its face, beyond power).

[50] *Kirk v Industrial Court (NSW)* (2010) 239 CLR 531, 573 [69]–[70].

[51] *New South Wales v Kable* (2013) 252 CLR 118. See also *Re Macks; Ex parte Saint* (2000) 204 CLR 158.

[52] ibid 252 CLR 118, 133 [33].

[53] ibid 252 CLR 118, 134 [34].

[54] ibid 252 CLR 118, 144 [68], citing *Love v Attorney-General (NSW)* (1990) 169 CLR 307; *Ousley v The Queen* (1997) 192 CLR 69.

[55] *New South Wales v Kable* (2013) 252 CLR 118, 139 [53] (Gageler J).

fit. It would undeniably be neater if the judicial orders of all courts had the same legal force as exercises of judicial power. Notwithstanding the terse rejection by the plurality in *Stradford*, this would seem a modest and principled step to take. The United Kingdom Supreme Court held, in a 2021 judgment, that all court orders have, since 1846, had equivalent legal force unless and until set aside.[56] Retention of the inferiority of inferior court orders as a principle of Australian law has been criticised as an historical anachronism.[57]

## D. A Pragmatic Concession to Flexibility of State Constitutions?

It is odd that Australian authorities should insist on a difference in the legal force of superior and inferior court orders said to have been abandoned for the UK since 1846.[58] The distinction rests on anachronistic views of the inferior courts and judges. The public interest in finality and certainty in litigation applies equally to all courts. There is no overriding public interest in maintaining the current orthodoxy at the expense of finality and certainty. Abandoning the distinction between the legal force of inferior and superior court judicial court orders would not expand any inferior court's powers or jurisdiction. Nor would it erase all significance that may attach to a court being established as an 'inferior court'. That status could still convey certain parameters on a court's operation. For instance, the status could continue to be used as a legislative shorthand to indicate that conferral of jurisdiction will prima facie carry only those powers necessary to its exercise[59] or to indicate limited contempt jurisdiction.[60]

It might be speculated that a factor driving the Court to restrict the legal force of invalid judicial orders to superior courts is the flexibility of state constitutions, under which judicial powers can be vested entirely outside the courts. The Court has not spelled this out.[61] But one plausible hypothesis is that the distinction is considered important in the context of Australia's integrated national system of courts, where adjudication in tribunals appears as a potential disruptor or outlier that may give rise to distorted positions. That is, it may be considered that if the

[56] *R (on the application of Majera) v Secretary of State for the Home Department* [2021] UKSC 46. See The Hon Justice K Walker, 'When Can a Court's Decision be Ignored?' (2022) 46 *Melbourne University Law Review* 572, 583–6.

[57] *Queensland v Mr Stradford (a pseudonym)* [2025] HCA 3, [230]–[290] (Edelman J). See also E Campbell, 'Inferior and Superior Courts and Courts of Record' (1997) 6 *Journal of Judicial Administration* 249.

[58] An idea I expand on in E Hammond, 'Finality and Certainty in the Integrated National System of Chapter III Courts: Judge Vasta v Stradford' (2024) 46(2) *Sydney Law Review* 227. See now *Queensland v Mr Stradford (a pseudonym)* [2025] HCA 3, [230]–[290] (Edelman J).

[59] *Pelechowski v Registrar, Court of Appeal (NSW)* (1999) 198 CLR 435, 451–2 [50]–[51].

[60] Enid Campbell, 'Inferior and Superior Courts and Courts of Record' (1997) 6 *Journal of Judicial Administration* 249, 250, 258; 251–2; David Rolph, *Contempt* (Federation Press, 2023), 35.

[61] In *Queensland v Mr Stradford (a pseudonym)* [2025] HCA 3, the majority notes that the government parties did not challenge the distinction and says, without elaboration, that they 'were right not to do so' (at [52]).

'superior court effect' were extended as an attribute of judicial power, then it would have to be extended to *any* judicial order – including state judicial orders made outside courts, as is permitted under state constitutions (subject to the *Burns* restriction).

Here, it may be that the broader Chapter III scheme offers an appealing compromise position (although one that evidently did not appeal to the plurality in *Stradford*) – namely, to extend 'superior court effect' to the judicial orders of courts within the meaning of Chapter III (but not to the orders of any other non-court state bodies exercising state judicial power).[62] The relevant aspect of the Chapter III scheme is the complex of secondary rules that protect the essential characteristics of Chapter III courts. Extending superior court effect to judicial orders of Chapter III courts is justifiable precisely because all Chapter III courts must maintain, at the institutional level, the qualities that make them suitable repositories for separated judicial power. This means that any Chapter III court presents a suitable institutional context for the exercise of power to determine rights with legal force unless and until set aside.[63] Conversely, the Chapter III scheme supports a distinction between the judicial orders of Chapter III courts and others. The exercise of judicial power by repositories that are *not* Chapter III courts occurs in a distinct context, removed from the safeguards provided by the constitutional characteristics of Chapter III courts. Thus, it would seem defensible to draw a line between Chapter III courts and other repositories of judicial power when it comes to the legal force accorded to invalid judicial orders unless and until set aside.

That the plurality in *Stradford* preferred to maintain the established distinction between the legal force of superior and inferior court orders suggests that the flexibility of state constitutions is continuing to exert an influence on the application of jurisdictional error. Arguably this works against the development of a more nuanced position, one which can better reconcile state constitutional flexibility with separation of powers values.

## IV. Conclusion

In recent decades, significant judicial and scholarly attention has been directed to the impact of Chapter III of the Constitution on principles of judicial review.

[62] Compare Edelman J's approach in *Queensland v Mr Stradford (a pseudonym)* [2025] HCA 3, eg, at [262].

[63] Compare the influence of the Ch III scheme across the judgments in *Queensland v Mr Stradford (a pseudonym)* [2025] HCA 3, including in: the plurality holding that there is equivalent judicial immunity for judges across all courts (eg, at [2], [3], [74]–[76], [106], [113]); Gordon J's interpretation of the statutory power purportedly exercised by Vasta J (eg, at [179], [181], [183]) and ruling on judicial immunity (at [199]–[201], [204]–[208]); and throughout Edelman J's judgment holding that invalid inferior cout orders provide legal justification for execution/enforcement unless or until set aside, or altered by legislation, eg, [226].

Notably, the influence of Chapter III can be seen in the judicial elaboration of jurisdictional error as a central concept in entrenched judicial review. While recognising that Chapter III is a dominant force in relation to entrenched review, Matthew Groves has maintained a keen appreciation that Chapter III is not the sole influence, and constitutional principles reflected in Chapter III found earlier expression in state cases. This chapter has explored this idea with reference to the way jurisdictional error doctrine balances separation of powers principles and the flexibility of state constitutions. It has discussed first how the Chapter III lens emphasises an underlying constitutional understanding of executive power and next hypothesised that the impulse to reflect the flexibility in state arrangements lies behind certain aspects of jurisdictional error that blur the boundary between executive and judicial power. It is appropriate that Australian doctrine should reflect the latitude afforded to the states to confer judicial power on non-courts. However, the way this is reflected should not be at the expense of due recognition of constitutional differences between judicial and executive powers. As discussed in this chapter, some refinement may be necessary to strike the right balance. As Groves' work reminds us, there is a richer tradition of common law constitutionalism that influences the application of jurisdictional error. Recognising this is a crucial step towards integrating the flexibility of state constitutions with important long-standing commitments to the conditionality of state power over subjects.

# 10

# Negligence Law's Pure Omissions and Statutory Context

MARK ARONSON[1]

## I. Introduction

Despite its exponential growth over the last hundred or so years, negligence law's duty of care has retained what it has long regarded as a fundamental distinction[2] between positive conduct and pure omissions. The distinction results in the absence of a duty of care on the defendant's part to take steps, sometimes easy steps, to prevent plaintiffs from suffering harm or further harm from facts, circumstances or conditions that they (the defendants) neither created nor exacerbated. This is the 'pure omissions' rule, sometimes described as the absence of a common law duty to rescue. English courts now prefer to distinguish between *causing harm* (meaning to make matters worse) and *failing to confer a benefit* (meaning not making things better). However expressed, the result is the same: Good Samaritans act out of a sense of moral duty, not legal duty.[3]

The duty of care in negligence law therefore applies to the acts and some private individuals and organisations, but generally not to such of their omissions to act as are regarded as pure omissions. The same tort law principles that apply to private sector defendants apply also to public officers and statutory corporations. The duty of care therefore does not apply to the pure omissions of public sector defendants.

Each step in that syllogism is well-established, and on the face of it, the High Court's decision in *Electricity Networks Corporation (trading as Western Power) v Herridge*[4] (henceforth, *Western Power*) disclaimed any intention to rock the boat.

[1] I am grateful to the following for their comments and assistance: Chantal Bostock, Carol Harlow, Ellen Rock, Prue Vines and Greg Weeks.

[2] FH Bohlen, 'The Moral Duty to Aid Others as a Basis of Tort Liability' (1908) 56 *University of Pennsylvania Law Review* 217, 219; *Roadshow Films Pty Ltd v iiNet Ltd [No 2]* (2012) 248 CLR 42 at 79 [108]; and *Tindall v Thames Valley Police* [2024] 3 WLR 822 at [1].

[3] *Hargrave v Goldman* (1963) 110 CLR 40 at 66 (Windeyer J); and *Sutherland Shire Council v Heyman* (1985) 157 CLR 424 at 478 (Brennan J).

[4] *Electricity Networks Corporation (trading as Western Power) v Herridge* (2022) 276 CLR 271.

However, its reasons were unclear and raised questions as to why the defendant's public status and statutory status were regarded as central.

## II. Western Power and Brodie

*Western Power*'s facts can be summarised briefly.[5] A bushfire near Perth had destroyed 57 homes and damaged a number of others. It also destroyed or damaged vehicles, crops and other property. Viewed in the broad, three parties were sued in negligence: the electricity distributor (Western Power), its large contractor (Thiess Services), and Ms Campbell. She was blamed because the fire had started on her property when her wooden power pole collapsed. Either she herself should have noticed that it was rotten, or she should have had it regularly inspected. Thiess was blamed because their workers had replaced an ageing power pole standing outside the Campbell property and reconnected live wires from there to the Campbell pole. They, too, should have noticed the rot or tested for it. And Western Power was blamed because theirs were the live wires connected to a rotting pole whose collapse led to the fire. It was a government-owned, profit-making, statutory corporation acting as the regional electricity distributor. Its statutes were replete with obligations regarding safety and the delivery of electricity to its customers and (despite the distributor's arguments to the contrary) with ample statutory power to meet those obligations.

Western Power's public relations stance had been to deny any responsibility for the state of the roughly 150,000 private poles on private land to which their network connected.[6] That failed to win them any friends in the media, but its stance in the High Court was more nuanced. They conceded that they owed a duty of care but argued that it was limited to inspecting private poles only when they were working on their nearby assets and even then, perhaps only when (as in the Campbell case) their work would require them to use the private pole. The High Court said that that was an argument about breach, not duty, and that Western Power was mistaken for thinking otherwise.[7] The Court said that duty was the only question properly before it, and it therefore had no need to go into specifics, such as the timing of inspections or, one might assume, the possibility of temporary disconnection.[8] The Court imposed upon the distributor an extremely broad duty to take reasonable care to avoid or minimise a risk of fire arising from the

[5] My account of the facts comes not just from the High Court judgment, but also from the judgments of the courts below: *Herridge v Electricity Networks Corporation trading as Western Power [No 4]* [2019] WASC 94; and *Herridge Parties v Electricity Networks Corporation trading as Western Power* [2021] WASCA 111.

[6] M Ramsey, 'Western Power loses bushfire court appeal', *Australian Associated Press*, 8 December 2022.

[7] (2022) 276 CLR 271 at 281 [16].

[8] ibid at 294 [52].

operation of its network. The duty was owed to anyone in the vicinity of their live wires; it applied continuously, and it applied to wherever their wires went, even if that was on private land. In other words, it necessarily encompassed a duty to take reasonable care to *maintain* a safe system.[9]

It is interesting to compare *Western Power* with the High Court's majority decision in *Brodie v Singleton Shire Council*,[10] in which the Court had imposed a duty upon roads authorities to take reasonable care to inspect and maintain their infrastructure, including their bridges.[11] To get to that conclusion, the majority had to jettison a mass of complex cases that had ruled that the duty of care owed by roads authorites did not extend beyond misfeasance to nonfeasance. *Brodie*'s majority had pointed to the authority's power to control the source of risk and the inability of drivers to do anything about it, resulting in their 'dependence' or 'vulnerability'. *Western Power* disparaged that reasoning[12] and noted the absence of any evidence that the plaintiff driver had acted in 'reliance' upon an 'assumption of responsibility' on the part of the authority. An assumption of responsibility constitutes a classic exception to the pure omission rule, but *Western Power* doubted *Brodie*'s conclusion that there had been such an assumption. The Court found it unnecessary to delve deeper into *Brodie* because the defendant distributor before it had taken positive action, not just omissions. Crucially, however, it reached that conclusion by a close examination of the distributor's statutory functions, not the particular facts of the case.

The Court acknowledged that Western Power had no statutory choice but to act as the electricity distributor.[13] In fact, there had been nothing voluntary about the company's creation, functions, purposes, powers or duties, and one might therefore conclude that this could not be a case of a company voluntarily assuming a responsibility towards the plaintiffs. The Court reasoned that the fact that Western Power had acted as a distributor carried all before it. Western Power had *entered the field* (a statutory field) of distributing and supplying electricity.[14] It had *entered into the exercise of its statutory powers*.[15] Even though it had failed to *exercise* some of its statutory powers, it had *exercised* many others in such a way as to commit it to the wide-ranging duty of care.[16] It had *stepped into the arena* and

[9] ibid at 280–281 [14]–[16].

[10] *Brodie v Singleton Shire Council* (2001) 206 CLR 512.

[11] Most jurisdictions quickly legislated to narrow *Brodie*'s impact. Roads authorities are now liable for failing to inspect, warn or repair only if they have 'actual knowledge' of the 'particular risk': Civil Liability Act 2002 (NSW) s 45; Civil Liability Act 2003 (Qld) s 37; Civil Liability Act 2002 (Tas) s 42; Road Management Act 2004 (Vic) ss 40 and 102; and Civil Liability Act 2002 (WA) s 5Z. The ACT and South Australia are outliers; see: Civil Law (Wrongs) Act 2002 (ACT) s 113; Civil Liability Act 1936 (SA) s 42.

[12] (2022) 276 CLR 271 at 283–284 [24].

[13] ibid at 292 [48]: 'It had to enter the field …' (reference omitted).

[14] ibid at 285 [28] and 287 [32].

[15] ibid at 287 [32].

[16] ibid at 284–285 [25]–[28].

exercised its statutory functions.[17] The implication was that the statutes had set the scene, investing the defendant with a broad suite of powers, and that the defendant had taken positive action by exercising those powers. Further, it was because of the defendant's positive conduct that this was not a case of pure omission to act. The overall manner in which it had exercised some of its powers and failed to exercise other interconnected powers meant that it had 'created or increased the risk of harm'.[18]

With respect, however, it is difficult to avoid the impression that the defendant's duty of care flowed from nothing more than simply *being* an electricity distributor or, at least, of having been a distributor for some years. *Brodie*'s defendant, one might comment, had similarly *been* a roads authority for some considerable time.

## III. *Western Power*'s Use of Statute

The common law's duty of care is developed cautiously and incrementally. There is no overarching or all-encompassing test for determining the existence and extent of a common law duty of care.[19] Arguments for or against the recognition of novel duties of care and arguments for or against extending the boundaries of existing duties of care are developed incrementally by reference to multi-factorial elements called 'salient features'.[20] In Australia, as elsewhere, the principle of reasonable foreseeability is not and never could be the sole determinant. Incrementalism usually involves a comparison with past cases, but that appears to have been noticeably absent in *Western Power*. Instead, the Court focused *entirely* on the fact that the defendant was a public statutory authority and on the *minutiae* of the relevant statutes.

Almost exactly half of *Western Power*'s judgment consisted of a detailed analysis of the defendant's statutory regime. That would have been a massive overkill if its only purpose had been to conclude (as it did) that the common law duty of care could co-exist quite comfortably with its statutory context. It seems that there were further reasons for the Court's lengthy analysis of the defendant's statutes. Drawing on the statutory language, it repeatedly referenced the fact that Western Power had commenced exercising its many statutory functions as a distributor of undertaking, operating, managing and maintaining a regional electricity distribution

[17] ibid at 294 [53].
[18] ibid at 294 [51].
[19] *Perre v Apand Pty Ltd* (1999) 198 CLR 180. It is reasonably clear that Edelman J looks forward to the opportunity to ditch the 'salient features' theory, and prefers (at least in part) a negligence taxonomy that emphasises a plaintiff's rights or interests: *Mallonland Pty Ltd v Advanta Seeds Pty Ltd* (2024) 98 ALJR 956.
[20] *Perre v Apand Pty Ltd* (1999) 198 CLR 180 at 253 [198] and 254 [201]; *Sullivan v Moody* (2001) 207 CLR 562 at 579–580 [50]–[52]; *Graham Barclay Oysters Pty Ltd v Ryan* (2002) 211 CLR 540 at 597 [149], 620 [222], and 625 [236(2)]; and *Khul v Zurich Financial Services Australia Ltd* (2011) 243 CLR 361 at 371 [20].

network. On one level, that could be seen as no more than explaining why this was not a case of a pure omission, but the resort to the distributor's statutes went further than that.

The Court gave two more reasons for its focus on statute and used these to frame the bulk of its analysis. First:[21]

> There is no freestanding common law rule which fixes whether and when a common law duty of care upon a statutory authority might, or might not, arise. Statutory authorities take many forms and have different functions and powers. It is wrong to treat all statutory authorities alike.

Its second reason included a quotation (with emphasis added) from *Graham Barclay Oysters Pty Ltd v Ryan*[22] (*Graham Barclay*) and appeared in the next paragraph:[23]

> The starting point for analysis of any common law duty of care that might be owed by any statutory authority must always be the particular statutory framework within which the statutory authority operates:
>
>> The existence or otherwise of a common law duty of care allegedly owed by a statutory authority turns on a close examination of the terms, scope and purpose of the relevant statutory regime. The question is whether that regime *erects* or *facilitates* a relationship between the authority and a class of persons that, *in all the circumstances*, displays sufficient characteristics answering the criteria for intervention by the tort of negligence.

The Court's reference to the distributor's statutes *erecting or facilitating* a relevant negligence law *relationship* presents a number of challenges. The Court also spoke of a duty of care *arising from the statute*,[24] but all of its other references to how a duty of care *arises* took care to avoid giving the impression that this was in some way akin to an action for breach of statutory duty. To be clear, the Court was propounding a common law duty of care, albeit one that owed a lot to its statutory setting.[25] Why, then, did the Court look to the statutory regime to see if it erected or facilitated the necessary 'relationship'?

The passage quoted from *Graham Barclay* may have meant nothing more than saying that the issue was whether any statutes stood in the way of determining that a relevant relationship existed. On that interpretation, *Western Power*'s lengthy examination of the distributor's statutes resulted in nothing more than a conclusion that the statutes were found to be irrelevant. However, that minimalist interpretation is unconvincing for at least three reasons. It is at odds with the Court's repeated assertions of the importance of statutory context. It also fails to give any real meaning to the idea of a statute 'facilitating' a relationship, which surely means something more than 'not standing in the way' of a relationship.

[21] (2022) 276 CLR 271 at 282 [19], footnote omitted.
[22] (2002) 211 CLR 540 at 596–597 [146].
[23] (2022) 276 CLR 271 at 282 [20].
[24] ibid at 284 [26].
[25] ibid at 283 [22], 284–285 [27]–[28], 287 [32] and 294 [52].

Similarly, it would fail to give any meaning to the idea of a public authority's statutory regime *erecting* the necessary relationship.

## IV. Relationships and Starting Points

The passage quoted from *Graham Barclay* had spoken in terms of the Court determining whether there was a *relationship* between the defendant and a class of persons that warranted the imposition of tort law's duty of care. Negligence law's concept of a duty of care uses 'relationship' in a number of ways. At one level, it refers to types of circumstances in which the existence of a duty of care is uncontentious, such as the interactions between employers and their employees, occupiers of land and their entrants, and motorists and other road users. Used as a description of established categories in which there are duties of care, the term is reasonably clear. Where a plaintiff contends for recognition of a new category, however, the term is circular[26] or conclusory, and that is evidently how the Court used it in *Western Power* – a relationship that 'in all the circumstances' warrants the imposition of a duty of care. There is an inescapable element of unpredictability in arguing for or against the recognition of a duty of care in novel cases, but once affirmed, the duty question *should* become much easier in subsequent cases.

*Western Power*'s duty of care applies to the relationship between electricity distributors and people in the vicinity of their live wires. The questions which arise from the Court's analysis, however, are whether it applies to *all* electricity distributors or only to those which are publicly owned or only to those whose *statutes* positively create or advance a distributor/neighbour relationship. These questions are truly odd, but they arise because the Court treated the defendant's *statutes* as the primary factor and the defendant's *activities* as secondary.

Recall that two propositions framed the Court's entire analysis. Because statutory authorities come in all shapes and sizes, there can be no common law rule that fixes whether there is a duty of care. Statutes must therefore be the *starting point* for any search for a common law duty, the ultimate question being whether the statutory regime erects or facilitates a necessary relationship that has enough features to justify the imposition of the asserted duty. The Court's attention to the defendant's statutory powers was certainly not new, but treating it as the starting point was new.

The defendant council in *Gorringe v Calderdale Metropolitan Borough Council*[27] had a statutory duty to maintain a highway's safety, but that was a duty owed only to the public at large, meaning that judicial review was the only remedy for its breach. According to Lord Hoffmann:[28]

[26] *Graham Barclay* (2002) 211 CLR 540 at 623 [231] and 627 [24], Kirby J.
[27] *Gorringe v Calderdale Metropolitan Borough Council* [2004] 1 WLR 1057.
[28] ibid at [23], emphases added.

> If the statute does not create a private right of action, it would be, to say the least, unusual if the *mere* existence of the statutory *duty* could generate a common law duty of care.

A few paragraphs later, his Lordship added that it would be 'difficult to imagine' how a failure to exercise a statutory *power* might in itself be the basis for a common law duty of care.[29]

Because the common law duty of care is not a creature of statute, there is no need to look for a statutory 'intention' or 'permission' for it to exist alongside the statute.[30] The common law duty of care is not superimposed upon the statutory power,[31] because that would constitute an alteration to the statute itself.[32] As Gaudron J explained in *Crimmins v Stevedoring Industry Finance Committee*[33] (*Crimmins*):

> Rather, the statute pursuant to which the body is created and its powers conferred operates 'in the milieu of the common law'. And the common law applies to that body unless excluded.

In any inquiry into whether a public authority is under a common law duty of care, one would therefore have thought that the logical starting point lies in the common law's search for salient features. It is conceivable that *Western Power*'s insistence that the 'starting point' must *always* be an analysis of the statutory regime was not meant to be taken literally.[34] Perhaps the Court thought that statutes would no longer be the starting point as regards electricity distributors, because its decision has settled the law for that sort of 'relationship'. That would conflict, however, with the Court's equal insistence that no two statutory corporations are the same because each has a different statutory regime. On that footing, *Western Power* settles very little indeed, even as regards electricity distributors. That is just one reason why it would be a pity to take the Court's 'starting point' literally.

It is true that there is no freestanding common law tort rule fashioned just for statutory authorities, but that is because the same tort law usually applies to them as applies to private sector defendants. *That* should be the proper starting point. Statutes become relevant either when the defendant argues that they constitute a 'dispensation from the ordinary law of tort'[35] or (and much more interestingly because more novel) when the plaintiff contends for a public authority having more liability than a private defendant in similar circumstances. This is no mere technicality.

[29] ibid at [32], approved in *N v Poole Borough Council* [2020] AC 780 at 826 [32].
[30] *Graham Barclay* (2002) 211 CLR 540 at 597 [148].
[31] *Crimmins* (1999) 200 CLR 1 at 18 [26]; and *Western Power* (2022) 276 CLR 271 at 283 [22].
[32] *Graham Barclay* (2002) 211 CLR 540 at 574–575 [79]–[81].
[33] (1999) 200 CLR 1 at 18 [26], reference omitted.
[34] Gummow J said in *Crimmins* (1999) 200 CLR 1 at 59 [159] that the statutory setting will 'commonly' be the starting point if the relevant activity would not have occurred in the absence of statute.
[35] *Manchester Ship Canal Co Ltd v United Utilities Water Ltd (No 2)* [2024] 3 WLR 356 at [15].

## V. Level Playing Fields

Dicey wrote in 1885 that the starting point for assessing the liability of public entities and government officials was the same general law that applied to private sector defendants.[36] He was on safe ground.

The House of Lords had held in *Mersey Docks and Harbour Board v Gibbs*[37] that the general law in negligence cases against public authorities was to be no different from the law applying to private sector companies run for the benefit of their shareholders. It was said to be untenable to make liability turn on whether a company was a profit-making venture for its shareholders (as in the case of railway companies) or a company (such as that running the Liverpool docks) whose surplus revenue had to go towards improvements or a fee reduction. *Mersey Docks* was decided in 1866. Only 12 years later, the House of Lords held in *Geddis v Proprietors of the Bann Reservoir*[38] that the fact that a defendant was a statutory authority was no warrant for *implying* that it was immune from a negligence claim.

Australia's High Court adopted those principles in *Caledonian Collieries Ltd v Speirs*:[39]

> [W]hen statutory powers are conferred they must be exercised with reasonable care, so that if those who exercise them could by reasonable precaution have prevented an injury which has been occasioned, and was likely to be occasioned by their exercise, damages for negligence may be recovered …

It is sometimes plausible to imply statutory authority to act in ways that might otherwise have been actionable in torts such as nuisance or trespass. Implications to that effect arise only if the relevant infringement of the plaintiff's interest is an unavoidable or inevitable consequence of the particular Act.[40] That makes sense for authorised conduct that was indeed unavoidable, but by definition, conduct is negligent only if it was avoidable. Parliaments are relevantly omnipotent and could therefore explicitly authorise public or other actors to behave negligently, but it is highly unlikely. The closest that Parliaments have come to that position is to grant immunity from liability for acts or omissions taken in good faith, and 'good faith' clauses are usually interpreted restrictively.[41] Admittedly, Brennan J once suggested that one might be able to imply statutory authority to behave negligently where the statute allows or requires the defendant to engage in inherently

[36] AV Dicey, *The Law of the Constitution* (1885) 193.
[37] *Mersey Docks and Harbour Board v Gibbs* (1866) LR 1 HL 93.
[38] (1878) 3 App Cas 430.
[39] *Caledonian Collieries Ltd v Speirs* (1957) 97 CLR 202 at 220, Dixon CJ, McTiernan, Kitto and Taylor JJ.
[40] *Metropolitan Asylum District v Hill* (1881) 6 App Cas 193 (HL); *Fullarton v North Melbourne Electric Tramway and Lighting Co Ltd* (1916) 21 CLR 181, at 187–188; *Manchester Ship Canal Co Ltd v United Utilities Water Ltd (No 2)* [2024] 3 WLR 356; and *Transport for NSW v Hunt Leather Pty Ltd* [2024] NSWCA 227 at [128]–[129].
[41] *Board of Fire Commissioners (NSW) v Ardouin* (1961) 109 CLR 105.

dangerous activity.[42] However, one might counter that as the inherent danger increases, so, too, should the care with which the defendant conducts itself.

Dicey's level playing field will always be aspirational[43] and lacks constitutional status.[44] Legislation was needed to overturn the tort immunity of the Crown itself. Australia's Crown Proceedings Acts all require the same law to be applied in claims against the Crown as applies more generally. Some of them add that this shall be done 'as nearly as possible', while the remainder imply that qualification.[45] The general law has several policy-based exceptions, but they *are* exceptional. For example, the duty of care has no application to Australian military personnel engaged in combat.[46] Even prior to the turn of the last century, the starting point had become the level playing field, not the statutory context.

The joint judgment in *Western Power* briefly alluded to the Diceyan principle, but only to observe that the Court's conclusion was:[47]

> consistent with and required by the principles of negligence that apply more generally, whether to natural persons, bodies corporate or other commercial enterprises.

If the electricity distributor's duty of care was consistent with *and required by* the general law of negligence, then the starting point should have been the common law.

Leaving aside citations made to establish uncontroversial background doctrine about various features of negligence law, the most remarkable feature of the precedents on which the Court relied is their context. Even though the Court stated that it was not dealing with a problem of pure omission and any possible exceptions to that rule,[48] *all* of the precedents on which it relied had involved plaintiffs attempting to fix public authorities with duties of care to protect them from harm which the authorities neither created nor exacerbated. In other words, all of them had involved pure omissions.

Roughly 40 years ago, Mason J had proposed a 'general reliance' exception to the pure omissions rule as against public authorities whose raison d'être is to protect us from harm they have not caused.[49] He instanced public sector air traffic controllers and government inspectors of commercial aircraft design. His Honour's use of 'general reliance' bore similarities to his later use of 'legitimate expectations'

[42] *Sutherland Shire Council v Heyman* (1985) 157 CLR 424 at 485.

[43] *Graham Barclay* (2002) 211 CLR 540 at 556 [12], Gleeson CJ.

[44] *Palmer v Western Australia* (2021) 274 CLR 286 at 300–301 [24].

[45] See M Aronson, M Groves and G Weeks, *Judicial Review of Administrative Action and Government Liability*, 7th edn (Sydney, Thomson Reuters, 2022) 1188 [21.70] and 1213–1214 [21.250]–[21.260].

[46] *Shaw Savill and Albion Co Ltd v Commonwealth* (1940) 66 CLR 344; *Groves v Commonwealth* (1982) 150 CLR 113; and *Commonwealth v Verwayen* (1990) 170 CLR 394. England has a similar combat immunity, but allows negligence claims relating to inadequate procurement of equipment or inadequate training: *Smith v Ministry of Defence* [2014] AC 52.

[47] (2022) 276 CLR 271 at 287 [32].

[48] (2022) 276 CLR 271 at 284 [25]–[26].

[49] *Sutherland Shire Council v Heyman* (1985) 157 CLR 424 at 462–464.

as a basis for the imposition of procedural fairness duties,[50] each being subsequently killed off for much the same reasons.[51] The terminology assumed states of mind (reliance or expectations, respectively) that were usually fictitious, and there appeared to be no viable limits to the proposed extensions of the common law. It is notable that *Western Power* endorsed the rejection of 'general reliance'.[52]

Professor Stevens has another (and more substantive) criticism of 'reliance' tests at the duty stage of the negligence inquiry. He argues that reliance on a defendant's 'assumption of responsibility' makes sense in computing breach and loss, but that a necessarily exceptional duty to confer a benefit on the plaintiff flows from that assumption, not the reliance. On that view, unconscious patients admitted to the emergency wards of *public* hospitals (whose relevantly distinguishing feature is their assumption of responsibility to all-comers) cannot be said to have relied on the hospital's doctors rescuing them.[53]

*Western Power*'s disparagement of *Brodie* has already been noted,[54] but it bears repeating that one of the criticisms was that there had been 'little focus' on whether the roads 'authority had assumed responsibility for repair or whether the driver had relied upon that assumption of responsibility'.[55] With respect, however, it does seem peculiar to require specific reliance in addition to an assumption of responsibility. Perhaps *Western Power* saw that aspect of *Brodie* as nothing more than a disguised resuscitation of Mason J's 'general reliance'.

*Western Power* has multiple references to *Sutherland Shire Council v Heyman*,[56] but these are largely precedential ballast for its favoured passage from *Graham Barclay* quoted in Part III, and for its use of terminology such as 'control'. *Heyman*'s plaintiffs had bought a house that had been built some years before. After their purchase, the house manifested structural damage because its foundations were insufficient. Perhaps the Council had inspected the footings, perhaps not, but that was irrelevant because the purchasers had made no relevant inquiries of the Council.

*Western Power* also referenced *Stuart v Kirkland-Veenstra*[57] a number of times, but once again, not for its facts, nor for its most confronting aspect, which was that the police were under no common law duty of care to a potential suicide in respect of that act. Two police officers had talked with the man for some time and left under the impression that he was both sane and no longer contemplating suicide. There being nothing illegal, nor anything necessarily insane, in an apparently sane person killing themselves, the police had no relevant power of arrest or

[50] *Minister for Immigration and Ethnic Affairs v Teoh* (1995) 183 CLR 273 at 291.

[51] The Court rejected 'general reliance' in *Pyrenees Shire Council v Day* (1998) 192 CLR 330, and 'legitimate expectations' in *Re Minister for Immigration and Multicultural and Indigenous Affairs; Ex parte Lam* (2003) 214 CLR 1.

[52] (2022) 276 CLR 271 at 284 [25].

[53] R Stevens, *Torts and Rights* (Oxford, OUP, 2007) 9–15, cited by Edelman J in *Mallonland Pty Ltd v Advanta Seeds Pty Ltd* (2024) 98 ALJR 956 at [65].

[54] See above, text to notes 10–12.

[55] (2022) 276 CLR 271 at 284 [24].

[56] (1985) 157 CLR 424.

[57] *Stuart v Kirkland-Veenstra* (2009) 237 CLR 215.

civil detention. One is left wondering what the result would have been if they had been statutorily empowered to detain him.

Similarly, *Western Power* referenced *Pyrenees Shire Council v Day*[58] a number of times but gave no hint as to whether that case might now be doubted. Council officers in that case had extinguished a chimney fire and told the tenants not to use the fireplace until the chimney was repaired. However, they had failed to tell the owners and the adjacent neighbours. This was held to be negligent on the Council's part. Perhaps the case was easier than most cases of pure omission (if such it was),[59] because the whole point of the relevant statutory powers was to help avert damaging fires. Further, intervention would have been easy, and the class of potential claimants was determinate, as were the financial risks at stake. McHugh J had said in *Graham Barclay*[60] that this 'seems the best explanation' of the *Pyrenees* case. One should add, however, that his Honour was also an advocate of a 'general reliance' exception to the pure omissions rule.[61] That was in *Crimmins*, in which Gaudron J had also endorsed the concept of general reliance.

The successful claim in *Crimmins*[62] had been about the failure of a public authority to safeguard waterside workers from asbestos contamination over a number of years. The defendant had ample statutory power to protect the workers, who in law were all employed from day to day by different stevedore companies. The defendant had more power over the workers, including protective power, than the day-to-day succession of ship owners whose cargoes the workers loaded and unloaded, and more power than the various stevedore companies who were the relevant employers on any particular day. The stevedore companies had to pay their workers, but not directly; they paid the defendant, who then on-paid the workers. In addition, the defendant set the daily rosters for assigning individual workers to individual ships.

The majority in *Crimmins* appeared to explain the defendant's duty of care by reference to the authority's statute, rather than to a fact apparently overlooked by the plaintiff, namely, that the authority had actually ordered her since-deceased husband into the holds of ships laden with clouds of asbestos dust.[63] High Court

[58] *Pyrenees Shire Council v Day* (1988) 192 CLR 330.

[59] *Western Power* quoted from *Pyrenees* in support of a proposition that it might sometimes be difficult to characterise a case as one of pure omissions where a public authority has started to exercise a statutory power to protect others, but failed to complete the task: *Western Power* (2022) 276 CLR 271 at 286 [30]. However, the fact that the defendants had started to assist a person is not by itself sufficient for negligence law to require that assistance to continue: *East Suffolk Rivers Catchment Board v Kent* [1941] AC 74. The tort reform statutes seem to say the same thing: Civil Law (Wrongs) Act 2002 (ACT) s 114; Civil Liability Act 2002 (NSW) s 46; Civil Liability Act 2002 (Tas) s 43; Wrongs Act 1958 (Vic) s 85; and Civil Liability Act 2002 (WA) s 5AA; and *Doyle's Farm Produce Pty Ltd v Murray-Darling Basin Authority (No 2)* (2021) 106 NSWLR 41 at 51 [38].

[60] (2002) 211 CLR 540 at 576 [82].

[61] *Crimmins* (1999) 200 CLR 1 at 23–24 [42]–[43].

[62] (1999) 200 CLR 1.

[63] Callinan J took that view of *Crimmins* in *Graham Barclay* (2002) 211 CLR 540 at 663 [317]. Kirby J seemed to have the same view of *Crimmins*; see *British American Tobacco Australia Ltd v Western Australia* (2003) 217 CLR 30 at 75 [119].

explanations of *Crimmins* now tend to point to that and other factors, as if to say that the existence of a statutory power does not *by itself* translate into a common law duty of care that it be exercised where appropriate.[64] That would make the defendant's statutory regime a salient feature that might sometimes be necessary but never sufficient. In *Western Power* itself, the Court said that it would be a mistake to treat a statutory power of 'control' of a relevant risk 'as though it were the *sole criterion* of assumption of responsibility'.[65] As noted above, however, the Court did not pursue the possibility of Western Power having assumed responsibility because it said that this was not a case of pure omissions.

## VI. Four Hypotheticals

It is useful at this point to indulge in four thought experiments, in each of which I will delete Thiess from the equation.

First, imagine that Western Power was neither government-owned nor governed (let alone empowered) by statute. One would hope that its duty of care would have been the same.

Second, imagine that Western Power was a government-owned statutory corporation whose statutory powers, duties and assets all stopped at their own transmission poles standing outside the boundary lines of their customers' land. In other words, they did not even own the wire going from their pole to Ms Campbell's pole. Imagine further that the company nevertheless went on to her land (an act of trespass) and reconnected *her* wires to *her* rotting private pole. Albeit devoid of statutory power, one would hope that the company would still be liable for its conduct.

Third, imagine the same *statutory* scenario as in my second hypothetical but with different *facts*. In this version, the company's workers noticed the dangerous state of the pole but decided to do nothing. They saw Ms Campbell pottering around in her garden, frail and almost blind,[66] but they did not enter her property or even shout a warning to her. The ensuing bushfire wreaked the same destruction as in the actual litigation. An unyielding adherence to the pure omission rule might relieve the company of liability to Ms Campbell, but why should it make a difference to the claims of the other property owners?

[64] See: *Agar v Hyde* (2000) 201 CLR 552 at 581–582 [82]; *Graham Barclay* (2002) 211 CLR 540 at 581 [94], and 630 [249]; and *Stuart v Kirkland-Veenstra* (2009) 237 CLR 215 at 255 [115]–[116] and 260 [133].

[65] (2022) 276 CLR 271 at 283 [24], emphasis added.

[66] This may not be too much of a stretch. Ms Campbell was a pensioner in her mid-80s at the time of the fire. She had had her house inspected annually for termites, but not the pole, which she had thought to be immune from termite damage because it was made of jarrah: *Herridge v Electricity Networks Corporation trading as Western Power [No 4]* [2019] WASC 94 at [77]–[79].

Statute is entirely absent from the first hypothetical and must be ignored in the second, either because the defendant acted beyond its statutory powers (although that is irrelevant in my view) or because Australia[67] (and now England too)[68] have rejected the false allure of linking negligence liability to either the validity or invalidity of the public authority's conduct. If the reader accepts my arguments regarding the first two hypotheticals, then the defendant's statutory powers should also be irrelevant in the third hypothetical.

It is submitted that it is what electricity distributors *do* that should have been the basis of the Court's broad duty of care, rather than their statutory powers. Western Power's statutory regime was icing on the cake. The more intriguing question is whether the law should go further. Should electricity distributors have the same broad duty of care because of what they *are*, rather than what they *do*?

That leads to my fourth hypothetical, in which an electricity distributor (whether public or private) owns a shockingly maintained distribution network. It sells its assets to NewCo and then goes into liquidation with massive (and uninsured) net debts. Ms Campbell's pole collapses immediately after the sale, before NewCo has had a chance to *do* anything – a case of pure omission. The question then becomes whether NewCo's duty of care starts at the point of nothing more than owning a terrible network or only after it has started *doing* things to which negligence law's concept of fault can reasonably attach.

## VII. The Pure Omissions Rule

The pure omissions rule has a number of well-recognised categorical exceptions, imposing, for example, proactive duties of care upon teachers for their pupils,[69] but the rule's normative core has long excited criticism and even moral revulsion. Lord Hoffmann offered three rationales for the rule – political (because it maximises a defendant's freedom); moral (the 'why pick on me?' argument); and economic (pure inaction confers neither an economic benefit on the defendant nor extra cost on the plaintiff).[70] Those rationales appear to be least persuasive if the so-called rescue is easy, undemanding of the defendant's time, and risk-free – situations applying equally to public and private defendants alike. They are equally unpersuasive as applied to public actors whose principal rationale is to rescue others or help

[67] *Crimmins* (1999) 200 CLR 1 at 35–39 [81]–[94].

[68] *Robinson v Chief Constable of West Yorkshire* [2018] AC 736 at 748–750 [31]–[40]; and *N v Poole Borough Council* [2020] AC 780 at 825–826 [31]–[32].

[69] Eg, *Commonwealth v Introvigne* (1982) 150 CLR 258.

[70] *Stovin v Wise* [1996] AC 923 at 943–944. One suspects that the real economic consideration is something different, namely, the need to signal the doctrinal irrelevance of the depth of a defendant's pockets.

others stay out of harm's way. Lord Kerr's comment in *Michael v Chief Constable of South Wales* is apposite:[71]

> Whereas it is arguable that a private individual's freedom has an instrinsic value in its contribution to an autonomous life, the value of a state's freedom is instrumental and lies in the contribution that it makes to the fulfilment of its proper functions.

Public entities certainly have options as to the conduct they take, but it is hard to conceptualise that as 'autonomy'. Unlike private sector parties, government is constrained from doing anything unless it is legally permitted. 'Political' theory (in Lord Hoffmann's terms) demands recognition that governments do *not* have the freedom of natural persons.[72]

The pure omissions rule has proven to be remarkably durable, even where its theoretical rationales are unconvincing. The rule has explicit exceptions, of course, but they are all framed in terms of special relationships between the parties; they present as 'category' exceptions. They include a teacher's duty towards their pupils[73] and the duty of care owed by police[74] and prison[75] officers towards those in their custody. Sometimes these relationships are said to flow from the defendant's 'control' over the relevant risks or even over the plaintiffs themselves, the plaintiffs' particular 'vulnerability', or an explicit or imputed[76] 'assumption' of responsibility on the part of the defendant. *Western Power* went to some lengths, however, to emphasise that there are no sure-fire criteria; the labels might conceal more than they explain.[77]

Explicit inroads into the pure omissions rule have come nowhere close to questioning the rule itself, and this is best exemplified by cases involving negligence claims against the police. An officer's duty to care for those in their custody has long been clear,[78] but there is a level of doctrinal uncertainty about duties of care not based upon the safety of custodial conditions. Even when we are not in police custody, we expect police to keep us safe from violent criminals, but it has proven very difficult to translate that expectation into a common law duty to take care in the investigation and/or apprehension of such criminals before they harm us.

[71] [2015] AC 1732 at 1780–1781 [177].

[72] See: *Williams v Commonwealth* (2012) 248 CLR 156 at 186–187 [25]–[26], 191–193 [35]–[38], 236–239 [150]–[159], 254 [204], 343–344 [488] and 373–374 [595]; and *Williams v Commonwealth* (2014) 252 CLR 416 at 465 [69].

[73] *Commonwealth v Introvigne* (1982) 150 CLR 258.

[74] *Howard v Jarvis* (1958) 98 CLR 177.

[75] *New South Wales v Bujdoso* (2005) 227 CLR 1 at 9 [32].

[76] It is misleading to equate judicially *imposed* duties with express or implied assumptions of responsibility on the part of defendants: *Michael v Chief Constable of South Wales Police* [2015] AC 1732 at 1761 [100] (Lord Toulson); and *Mallonland Pty Ltd v Advanta Seeds Pty Ltd* (2024) 98 ALJR 956 at [60]–[65], Edelman J. See also: *Fuller-Wilson v New South Wales* (2018) Aust Torts Reports ¶82-413 at [40], Basten JA.

[77] (2022) 276 CLR 271 at 283–284 [23]–[25].

[78] *Howard v Jarvis* (1958) 98 CLR 177.

The much-debated decision of the House of Lords in *Hill v Chief Constable of West Yorkshire*[79] was that the police had owed no duty of care to all young women in Yorkshire in the course of their investigation of an ongoing series of attacks and murders in that district. The police eventually caught the so-called Yorkshire Ripper, but the plaintiff claimed that if only they had done a more careful job, he would have been apprehended before getting a chance to murder her daughter. The judgments spent a good deal of their time in demonstrating that there was no 'proximity' between the police and Ms Hill. Their Lordships thought that the class to which the *Hill* victim belonged was no different in substance from the public at large.

Although the proximity argument in *Hill* would have been sufficient to dispose of the appeal in that case, their Lordships then turned to policy reasons for creating what became a category exclusion from any duty of care towards potential crime victims. It would, they said, be difficult for a court to scrutinise the wisdom of detectives' work; it could lead the courts into policy and political issues; the threat of litigation could make police too cautious; and it would lead to a diversion of scarce resources from a police service that could usually be trusted to do their job conscientiously,[80] if not always well. That all led to a policy-based carve-out from the duty of care so far as it might have applied to police acts *or* omissions in the investigation or suppression of crime.[81]

The precise extent of *Hill*'s police immunity from negligence law's duty of care was hotly debated and has never been satisfactorily settled. That remains the case in Australia, where the debates seem to have morphed into whether the absence of a duty of care applies only to some categories of plaintiffs or whether the general rule or rules allow for exceptions.[82] However, in England, the UK Supreme Court has now walked away from the 'policy' basis for *Hill*'s result regarding police[83] and from similarly reasoned, policy-based immunities regarding public sector providers of social, educational and housing services.[84] That is not to say that the odds of winning a negligence claim against the English or Welsh police (or other public authorities) have increased; rather, direct engagement with the morass of policy factors has now been put to one side. The focus in those countries is now on the scope of the pure omissions rule itself and on its exceptions. The UK Supreme

[79] *Hill v Chief Constable of West Yorkshire* [1989] AC 53.

[80] Lord Steyn said in *Brooks v Commissioner of the Metropolitan Police* [2005] 1 WLR 1495 at [28] that the courts are more sceptical nowadays.

[81] *Hill v Chief Constable of West Yorkshire* [1989] AC 53 at 63–65.

[82] See, eg, *Cran v New South Wales* (2004) 62 NSWLR 95; *New South Wales v Klein* [2006] NSWCA 295; *Victoria v Richards* (2010) 27 VR 343; *Australian Capital Territory v Crowley* (2012) 273 FLR 370 at [273]–[287]; *Fuller-Wilson v New South Wales* (2018) Aust Torts Reports ¶82-413 at [86]; *Hannam v New South Wales (No 9)* [2022] NSWSC 648 at [174]–[175]; and *New South Wales v Cullen* (2024) Aust Torts Reports ¶83-148 at [71]–[79] and [181]–[213].

[83] *Robinson v Chief Constable of West Yorkshire Police* [2018] AC 736.

[84] The older cases from the House of Lords and the Supreme Court are too numerous to examine here. It must suffice to refer to the magisterial (and unanimous) analysis in *N v Poole Borough Council* [2020] AC 780.

Court now explains the actual results of the older cases solely in terms of the pure omissions rule and its limited exceptions.

Two sets of issues remained for some time after the Supreme Court's doctrinal revision. First, it remains as difficult as ever to set the dividing line between the causative acts or omissions of a defendant and their pure omission to prevent harm they neither caused nor worsened. The most that one can safely say is that acts and omissions are causative of plaintiffs' harms if the defendants created or worsened the initial risk of harm. The critical element here, of course, lies in determining exactly when the risk commenced.

Second, the Supreme Court initially endorsed[85] the following summary by Professors Tofaris and Steel of the types or categories of available exceptions to the pure omissions rule:[86]

> In the tort of negligence, a person *A* is not under a duty to take care to prevent harm occurring to person *B* through a source of danger not created by *A* unless (i) *A* has assumed a responsibility to protect *B* from that danger, (ii) *A* has done something which prevents another from protecting *B* from that danger, (iii) *A* has a special level of control over that source of danger, or (iv) *A*'s status creates an obligation to protect *B* from that danger.

The Court regarded those four categories as 'usually' or 'generally' to be 'helpful', but that is open to question. Category (i) does nothing to clarify the puzzle of when an assumption of responsibility is volunteered or imposed. The Supreme Court now acknowledges that category (ii) is not a case of pure omissions because it posits a defendant worsening a plaintiff's predicament.[87] Category (iii) would justify the result in *Brodie*. Category (iv) already accommodates those such as teachers and custodial officers whose jobs should obviously place them under positive duties of care.

Tofaris and Steel had argued for the police to be added to category (iv), but the Supreme Court rejects that option because it sees no reason for making public authorities liable unless private defendants would also be liable. 'However blameworthy' may be an authority's failure to exercise its statutory powers or its breach of its statutory duties; the level playing field henceforth rules the roost.[88] *Michael v Chief Constable of South Wales*[89] is now to be treated as a straightforward application of the pure omissions principle.[90] A police call centre had bungled a desperate call for help, as a result of which the police arrived too late to prevent her murder.

[85] In *Robinson v Chief Constable of West Yorkshire Police* [2018] AC 736 at 748 [34]; *N v Poole Borough Council* [2020] AC 780 at 840 [76]; and *HXA v Surrey County Council* [2024] 1 WLR 335 at [88].

[86] S Tofaris and S Steel, 'Negligence Liability for Omissions and the Police' (2016) 75 *Cambridge Law Journal* 128.

[87] *Tindall v Thames Valley Police* [2024] 3 WLR 822 at [49].

[88] ibid [2024] 3 WLR 822 at [1].

[89] *Michael v Chief Constable of South Wales* [2015] AC 1732.

[90] *Robinson v Chief Constable of West Yorkshire Police* [2018] AC 736 at 760 [69.7], 761 [72] and 763–764 [83]; *N v Poole Borough Council* [2020] AC 780 at 834 [61] and 840 [75]; and *Tindall v Thames Valley Police* [2024] 3 WLR 822 at [20] and [37]–[38].

The police were not liable because the call centre had not *expressly* told the victim to leave it all to the police, and there was no evidence of the police *actively* inducing the deceased to dispense with offers of help from third parties or flee the scene. One might comment that this should have been a case where an assumption of responsibility should have been inferred from the police status and the surrounding facts *unless* there was evidence of a disclaimer.

I would differentiate the merits of the claim in *Michael* from the claims in other Supreme Court cases involving public sector providers of social services such as housing and child support.[91] There is nothing counterintuitive in those cases ruling that the service providers had no affirmative common law duty of care to assist or to do better in the assistance that they did provide, where the providers did not worsen the claimants' predicaments. At our most optimistic, we would all hope for better results from these bodies. However, we all know that they are massively under-resourced, so that any win for one plaintiff must inevitably come at the cost of someone *equally* in need of assistance. Police protection from serious and imminent danger comes at the cost of *less* urgent matters.

England had dabbled with the idea of a statutory authority's liability in negligence for being *Wednesbury* unreasonable in failing to exercise (or to consider exercising) a statutory power (as opposed to a duty) to rescue or confer a benefit. This was essentially a new category exception to the pure omissions rule and would have applied only to public authorities. That was in *Anns v Merton London Borough Council*,[92] but a line of subsequent English decisions first reduced the scope of that aspect of *Anns*,[93] then strongly doubted it,[94] and finally rejected it.[95] It had never taken hold in Australian courts.[96] However, it did lead to an ill-advised provision in the tort reform legislation of three jurisdictions,[97] offering public authorities a complete defence for failing to exercise or even think about exercising their licensing or regulatory functions unless the plaintiff could have obtained a court order compelling action of some sort. The provision would be redundant in any circumstance where the common law's pure omissions rule would apply to the relevant authorities.[98]

The English position now appears to be rock-solid. Their exceptions to the pure omissions rule must be the same for all defendants, regardless of their powers,

[91] See *HXA v Surrey County Council* [2024] 1 WLR 335.

[92] *Anns v Merton London Borough Council* [1978] AC 728.

[93] *Stovin v Wise* [1996] AC 923 at 953.

[94] *Gorringe v Calderdale Metropolitan Borough Council* [2004] 1 WLR 1057 at 1065–1066 [26] and 1067 [32].

[95] *N v Poole Borough Council* [2020] AC 780 at 825–826 [34] and 835–836 [64]–[65]. See also *Chandler v Trinidad and Tobago* [2023] AC 285 at 325 [59].

[96] *Crimmins* (1999) 200 CLR 1 at 35–39 [81]–[94]; and *Queensland Bulk Water Supply Authority v Rodriguez & Sons Pty Ltd* (2021) 393 ALR 162 at [125]–[128].

[97] Civil Law (Wrongs) Act 2002 (ACT), s 112; Civil Liability Act 2002 (NSW), s 44; and Civil Liability Act 2002 (Tas), s 41.

[98] *Cf Meyers v Commissioner for Social Housing* [2019] ACTCA 19 at [127]–[139].

capacities, public status or their core job descriptions.[99] The 'assumption of responsibility' exception to the pure omission rule is as demanding for public defendants as it is for private defendants. This is Dicey's equality principle[100] and the second step in my Introduction's syllogism.

## VIII. When the Rationales Run Out

It would be a mistake for the common law to disapply the omissions rule to all cases where its rationales are absent. That approach is best left to the legislature, which would probably (and rightly, in my opinion) reject it on the grounds that it would replace a hard-edged rule with massive indeterminacy. There is a case, however, for the common law to be slightly more flexible regarding Category (iv) in Tofaris and Steel's list, at least with regard to public sector defendants that are funded, trained and resourced to undertake the duty in question.

Almost 30 years ago, Natalie Gray and James Edelman made a similar argument, framed in terms of classes of individuals performing specialist roles of providing affirmative assistance to others. They instanced doctors, fire fighters, life savers, police and coastguards – all people 'for whom rescue is the very thing for which they are trained'.[101] Their central aim was to bring doctrinal and normative concerns into greater alignment. They offered an interesting argument for the relevance of a public authority's statutory setting, which typically confers many public-facing powers but very few public-facing duties. They proposed a middle way, in which a statutory regime occasionally 'provides evidence of what seems clear' (in their example, that doctors voluntarily assume certain responsibilities).[102] Statutes *as evidence* are neither necessary nor sufficient but would, in today's terminology, be salient features.

Surely one of *Western Power*'s standout salient features was the fact that the distributor was free to recoup its costs from its customers *and* make a profit.[103] The market was inelastic, and the distributor could pass on the cost of inspecting the extra 150,000 private poles. That distinguishes the distributor from *Brodie*'s highway authorities, whose potential liabilities could well have been staggering had not the state Parliaments stepped in to narrow down their exposure to situations in which they have 'actual knowledge' of the 'particular risk'.[104]

[99] *Robinson v Chief Constable of West Yorkshire Police* [2018] AC 736 at 748–750 [31]–[40]; *N v Poole Borough Council* [2020] AC 780 at 835–836 [64]–[65]; *HXA v Surrey County Council* [2024] 1 WLR 335; and *Tindall v Thames Valley Police* [2024] 3 WLR 822.

[100] Invoked explicity in *Robinson v Chief Constable of West Yorkshire Police* [2018] AC 736 at 748 [32].

[101] N Gray and J Edelman, 'Developing the Law of Omissions: a Common Law Duty to Rescue?' (1986) 6 *Torts Law Journal* 240.

[102] ibid 250.

[103] The Court emphasised Western Power's obligations to run on prudent commercial principles and endeavour to make a profit: (2022) 276 CLR 271 at 287 [31], 288 [38] and 289 [40].

[104] Above, n 11.

If the reader accepts my reasoning regarding the first three hypothetical scenarios discussed above, the fact that Western Power's *statutes* allowed it to pass on the extra costs imposed by the High Court's broad-spectrum duty of care should be no more than an item of evidence. Monopolistic distributors would have had the same ability without having to look to statutes. The issue should be feasibility, not statutory feasibility. And if that is accepted, then at a high level of generality, Western Power's publicness (or statutory context) was a distraction. At a slightly lower level, and using its statutes as evidence in the manner advocated by Gray and Edelman, its publicness and statutory setting make it easier to see the argument for imposing a duty to act without having to engage the distinction between conduct and pure omission.

As for my fourth hypothetical, in which the Campbell pole collapsed moments after NewCo bought the ailing distribution network from a company that then folded, it is submitted that NewCo should be liable even though it has done nothing – a clear case of pure omission. The situation would be no different to that of a new company acquiring a run-down (and formerly public) hospital. *Western Power*'s repeated emphasis on the fact that the defendant had entered the field of electricity distribution could be construed that way, but it is unclear, and the Court had no need to take that step. Taking that extra step could be explained in a number of ways. In traditional terms, it could be framed as an example of an 'assumption of responsibility', but only if one were to extend that concept to circumstances in which the assumption is judicially imputed to the distributor.[105] It could be justified as flowing from the defendant's control of a risk that its victims (other than Ms Campbell) were wholly unable to avoid, or even Mason J's semantically incomplete but normatively attractive language of general reliance. The best justification, however, would also have been the simplest, namely, the creation of a new categorical exception to the pure omissions rule for electricity distributors. Ideally, the new exception would apply to public and private distributors alike, but if necessary, Dicey's equality principle could yield to competing considerations. We should not fetishise the level playing field.

## IX. Conclusion

The plaintiffs' win in *Western Power* was not only unexceptionable; it was surely obvious. No matter how narrow or broad one were to formulate the distributor's duty of care, on the facts, there was a clear case of breach. The difficulties were all self-inflicted by the company itself. First there was its public denial of any responsibility for the state of privately owned and located poles, and then there was its less bullish argument in court that any duty to test private poles for termite rot should arise only when they were working on them or after undemanding intervals of

[105] See above, n 76.

some years. Those were arguments designed to minimise the company's duty to take proactive steps for the protection of others, and one might have hoped for a new carve-out from the pure omissions rule.

Instead, the Court turned to the company's statutory regime to reason that any omissions were not 'pure' in the relevant sense because the company had started doing things in the exercise of its statutory functions. The things that it had started doing were not the incompetent reconnection of live wires to the private pole, because that went to 'breach', and 'duty' was the only issue before the Court. They were instead its exercise of statutory functions.

The writer believes that the turn to statute was a massive distraction. Statute can certainly be a salient feature, but its centrality in *Western Power* contradicts the principle that the duty of care should apply equally to private and public defendants. Worse, it raises the question of whether the same duty of care would apply to a private company or even to a government-owned company operating under a different statutory regime. There was no voluntary assumption of responsibility on the distributor's part, but none should have been needed. Malfunctioning live wires start bush fires, and all electricity distributors should have a duty to take reasonable care to minimise that risk, regardless of whether that requires acts or omissions, and regardless of their status as public or private.

# 11

# Brokering Public Trust and Confidence in Government Integrity

ELLEN ROCK*

## I. Introduction

Public trust is a key pillar supporting the legitimacy of government.[1] Without trust, government is said to lack the necessary social capital required for effective governance.[2] If true, there is good reason to be concerned by reports of declining levels of public trust in many countries around the world,[3] with Australia being no exception.[4] Public trust in government integrity is of particular concern, with surveys suggesting only around half of respondents would trust a government official to turn down a bribe.[5] As Bathurst CJ has observed extra-judicially, '[i]f there was ever a period where we expected the public to blindly trust institutions, it is long gone.'[6] Scholars point to complex causes of public trust issues, including some 'wicked problems'[7] that drive social and economic inequality.[8] Tackling those socio-political forces is beyond this author's more modest goal in this chapter.

* I would like to thank Professor Brian Opeskin as well as the editors of this collection for their helpful comments on earlier drafts. All errors of course remain my own.

[1] See, eg, O O'Neill, *A Question of Trust* (Cambridge, CUP, 2002) 3; RD Behn, *Rethinking Democratic Accountability* (Washington, Brookings Institution Press, 2001) 83; M Holzer, 'The Future of Public Administration' (2022) 24 *Public Integrity* 102, 102–03.

[2] S Vallentin, *Trust, Power and Public Sector Leadership: A Relational Approach* (Abingdon, Taylor & Francis, 2022) 1.

[3] Eg, Edelman Trust Institute, *2024 Edelman Trust Barometer: Global Report* (2024) tinyurl.com/yhyrupr2, 6.

[4] Edelman Trust Institute, *2024 Edelman Trust Barometer: Australia Report* (2024) tinyurl.com/ytnnbaxn. While overall trust within Australia increased compared with other countries, trust in government remains low: 6–7.

[5] OECD, *Building Trust to Reinforce Democracy: Main Findings from the 2021 OECD Survey on Drivers of Trust in Public Institutions* (July 2022) ch 5.

[6] Chief Justice Bathurst, 'Trust in the Judiciary', 2021 Opening of Law Term Address, 3 February 2021.

[7] HWJ Rittel and M Webber, 'Dilemmas in a General Theory of Planning' (1973) 4 *Policy Sciences* 155.

[8] See, eg, J Mansbridge, 'Social and Cultural Sources of Dissatisfaction with the US Government' in J Nye Jr, P Zelikow and D King (eds), *Why People Don't Trust Government* (Cambridge, MA, Harvard University Press, 1997) 133.

Inspired by Matthew Groves' enduring interest in public perception of the legitimacy and impartiality of government decision-making, this chapter evaluates the connection between administrative law and public trust in government integrity.

Part II begins with a brief survey of relevant literature on public trust, suggesting that the core of trust is acceptance of vulnerability, a willingness to rely on someone to do the 'right thing' without being forced. In James Madison's words, '[i]f angels were to govern men, neither external nor internal controls on government would be necessary'.[9] We are a long way from trusting government to that degree. Instead, we take Madison's advice to increase control with a view to engendering public confidence. Where we have control and *confidence*, we are less dependent on *trust*. Part III of this chapter outlines three promises of control via which administrative law theoretically supports public confidence in government integrity. The first is by setting expectations of impartiality, autonomy and altruism that apply to the exercise of public power; the second is by offering mechanisms that showcase enforcement of those standards; and the third is through institutional design that can ringfence officials against improper sources of influence. Working together, these controls ideally operate as a confidence-inducing 'security blanket' that can circumvent demands for the more vulnerable extension of trust.

In the face of rising public mistrust, it might seem intuitive to ratchet up levels of control over public power. We need *more* accountability bodies, tighter controls and increased surveillance of government activity. As Part IV of this chapter warns, however, this kneejerk reaction can potentially create more problems than it solves. Ever-increasing layers of control and scrutiny can sometimes distort the exercise of public power in unexpected ways that undermine, rather than support, public confidence. This is a particular risk where the government turns control mechanisms to its own advantage, applying them as a smokescreen to legitimise its activities rather than to genuinely hold itself to account, eroding trust even further.

## II. Perception, Trust and Confidence

Trust is a 'magic concept',[10] almost universally regarded as valuable but difficult to define.[11] In the political setting, it refers variously to the collective trust of citizens in the overall system of government, its institutions, or in specific individuals or groups within that system.[12] Trust is sometimes expressed as a rational calculation

[9] J Madison, 'The Federalist No. 51' in I Shapiro (ed), *The Federalist Papers* (New Haven, Yale University Press, 2009) 263, 264.

[10] Vallentin (n 2), 16.

[11] D Houston and L Harding, 'Public Trust in Government Administrators' (2013) 16 *Public Integrity* 53, 53; S-E Kim, 'The Role of Trust in the Modern Administrative State' (2005) 37 *Administration & Society* 611, 619–20.

[12] P Blind, 'Building Trust in Government: Linking Theory with Practice' in GS Cheema and V Popovski (eds), *Building Trust in Government* (Tokyo, UN University Press, 2010) 22, 23.

of the probability of being let down, while at other times it reflects a more general assessment of the moral character and values of the trustee.[13] At heart, trust is an exercise in risk-taking, an 'intention to accept vulnerability based on positive expectations of the intentions or behaviour of another'.[14] The required level of trust depends on how significant that leap of faith might be, referred to in this chapter as the distinction between *trust* and *confidence*:

> There is a large shaded area between the two categories but, in short, relations of confidence tend towards the side of objective information, external regulations over conduct, contractual agreements, rational and informed decisions; while relations of trust tend towards subjective perceptions, moral sanctions, gentleman's agreements, non-rational choices. *In the absence of mechanisms of confidence* (information, law, contracts), *one must fall back on trust* (perception, moral obligation, social bonds).[15]

The very nature of government means that there can be no absolute control. Accordingly, at a certain point, something must be left to trust.

The relationship between trust (risk) and confidence (control) is complex. On one view, trust is the *alternative* to confidence: we only need trust if we lack control and do not need control if we have strong trust. However, control is also a means of *brokering* trust: if we lack sufficient trust to take a large risk, increasing control (eg, by imposing transparency obligations) might 'bridge the difference by lowering the perceived risk to a level that can be managed by trust'.[16] There is a downside to pursuing that strategy too far, however, as excessive control can also potentially *undermine* trust. As noted in Part IV, the very suggestion that we need control implies that someone cannot be trusted without it, fostering 'institutionalised suspicion'.[17] The trust-confidence dynamic is therefore a delicate balancing act, relying on mechanisms of control that 'institutionalise distrust so we can enculturate trust'.[18]

Public trust is a complex construct of numerous factors, most of which are beyond the scope of this chapter.[19] It is beyond this author's expertise to address the broader forces that shape public perception of the trustworthiness of government institutions. This chapter explores the narrower contributions of administrative law to public trust, taking public perception of integrity as its focus. If trust is (at least in part) based on the 'leap of faith' between the known and unknown, how

[13] ibid 24.

[14] D Rousseau et al, 'Not so Different After All: A Cross-Discipline View of Trust' (1998) 23 *Academy of Management Review* 393, 395.

[15] F Tonkiss, 'Trust, Confidence and Economic Crisis' (2009) 44 *Intereconomics* 196, 199 (emphasis added). See also B Nooteboom, 'Trust' in C Ansell and J Torfing (eds), *Handbook on Theories of Governance*, 2nd edn (Cheltenham, Edward Elgar, 2022) 205.

[16] F David Schoorman et al, 'An Integrative Model of Organizational Trust' (2007) 32 *Academy of Management Review* 344, 346.

[17] Behn (n 1) 83.

[18] J Braithwaite, 'Institutionalizing Distrust, Enculturating Trust' in V Braithwaite and M Levi (eds), *Trust and Governance* (New York, Russell Sage Foundation, 1998) 343, 343.

[19] See S Grimmelikhuijsen, 'Do Transparent Government Agencies Strengthen Trust?' (2009) 14 *Information Polity* 173, 175 and sources cited therein.

effective is the machinery of administrative law in breaching that gap? In what ways does administrative law support public *confidence* in government integrity, reducing the amount left to the more difficult surrender of *trust*?

## III. Controlling Government Integrity

Integrity, like many other public governance catchcries, is a flexible concept put to a variety of different uses.[20] While it has potentially broader meanings,[21] this chapter focuses on the narrower integrity expectation that power will be exercised with an appropriate degree of impartiality that resists improper sources of influence. What might be thought 'improper' is obviously a context-specific inquiry. Conduct that is considered selfish, biased or subservient in one context might be entirely acceptable in another. Depending on context, it might be proper – or improper – for someone to act for personal gain,[22] to protect their position,[23] to avoid retaliation or sanction,[24] to further the interests of a third party,[25] or to give effect to the preferences of a superior.[26] 'Integrity' is not a one-size-fits-all code.

When it comes to government, the concept of integrity often refers to individual officials and their trustworthiness, impartiality, honesty and incorruptibility.[27] It also refers more broadly to the integrity of government *institutions*, which Creyke equates with the 'health' of the system and the degree to which it is 'functioning well'.[28] We can speak of the 'integrity' of the judicial system, for example, quite separately from the integrity of a particular judge. Individual and institutional integrity operate on a feedback loop that can reinforce or undermine public trust. When we clothe someone in the trappings of a particular institution, they take the benefit (or disbenefit) of generalised trust in that institution. Thus, a judge

[20] See, eg, AJ Brown, *Chaos or Coherence? Strengths, Opportunities and Challenges for Australia's Integrity Systems* (Final Report, 2005); R Creyke, 'An 'Integrity' Branch' (2012) 70 *AIAL Forum* 33.

[21] Eg encompassing obligations of fairness, to honour promises, or to act in the public interest: Schoorman et al (n 16) 345–46; Nooteboom (n 15) 212; N Nolan-Flecha, 'The Influence of Integrity on Public Trust' in OECD (ed), *Trust and Public Policy: How Better Governance Can Help Rebuild Public Trust* (OECD Public Governance Reviews, 2017) 27.

[22] A contrast is often drawn between permitted 'selfishness' in the private versus public spheres, though the split does not always run along those lines: M Aronson, 'Public Law Values in the Common Law' in M Elliott and D Feldman (eds), *The Cambridge Companion to Public Law* (Cambridge, CUP, 2015) 134, 144.

[23] Eg, a minister may be permitted to consider their political fortunes when making a decision: *Hot Holdings Pty Ltd v Creasy* (2002) 210 CLR 438, 455 [50] (Gaudron, Gummow and Hayne JJ) ('*Hot Holdings*').

[24] See discussion of judicial immunity in Part III.C.

[25] See discussion of the bias rules in Part III.A.

[26] See discussion of the rule against dictation in Part III.A.

[27] S Van de Walle and K Migchelbrink, 'Institutional Quality, Corruption, and Impartiality' (2022) 25 *Journal of Economic Policy Reform* 9.

[28] Creyke (n 20) 34. See also Justice JJ Spigelman, 'The Integrity Branch of Government' (2004) 78 *Australian Law Journal* 724.

may enjoy a 'positivity bias' due to public perception of the judiciary as an impartial and non-political decision-making forum,[29] while a politician may be saddled with the negative public perception of dishonesty in politics.[30] The more troubling part of the feedback loop is the impact of individual integrity problems on the perceived integrity of institutions: the dishonest or corrupt exercise of power by an individual can jeopardise the perceived integrity of their institution.[31]

Returning to the discussion above, public trust in government integrity involves an assessment of the degree to which a government trustee can be relied on to observe integrity expectations and resist improper forms of pressure or influence 'without the need for scrutiny'.[32] If trust is insufficient to take that leap of faith, the shortfall can potentially be ameliorated by adding measures that increase the sense of control. This chapter explores three styles of control mechanism: (A) setting integrity standards consistent with public expectations; (B) showcasing scrutiny and enforcement of those standards; and (C) designing institutions to secure against integrity risks.

## A. Setting Integrity Expectations

If we trusted government officials as we (hopefully) do our friends and family, we might be willing to rely on them simply to be guided by their own moral compass. That is not the case. Instead, we prescribe detailed standards that guide officials to act in a manner that is 'altruistic, honest, and impartial'.[33]

### *i. Defining Integrity*

Some integrity expectations are framed in positive terms, such as the statutory duty to exercise public powers 'honestly, in good faith and for a proper purpose'[34] and codes of conduct that anticipate officials will 'behave honestly and with integrity'.[35] Other expectations take a negative form, proscribing sources of temptation or influence an official ought to disregard. The following sections briefly outline a number of these integrity standards.

[29] S Grimmelikhuijsen and A Klijn, 'The Effects of Judicial Transparency on Public Trust' (2015) 93 *Public Administration* 995. *cf* MGroves, I Nielsen and R Smyth, 'Public Support for the Rule of Law' (2022) 51 *Australian Bar Review* 80, 92.

[30] Female politicians fared better than males in a study examining the effect of 'truth bias': K Mattes et al, 'Deception Detection in Politics: Can Voters Tell When Politicians Are Lying?' (2023) 45 *Political Behavior* 395.

[31] Creyke (n 20) 34.

[32] OECD, *Trust and Public Policy: How Better Governance Can Help Rebuild Public Trust* (OECD Public Governance Reviews, 2017). See also Grimmelikhuijsen (n 19) 183.

[33] Aronson (n 22) 151.

[34] Public Governance, Performance and Accountability Act 2013 (Cth) s 26 ('PGPA Act').

[35] Public Service Act 1999 (Cth) s 13(1) ('Public Service Act'). On the connection to public trust, see R Bacon, 'Values in the Australian Public Service' (2024) 111 *AIAL Forum* 43.

### a. Impartiality

According to the authors of the leading judicial review text, '[i]mpartiality and the confidence it engenders, are regarded as essential to the successful and proper operations of the public service, the tribunal system and the judiciary'.[36] Impartiality refers to an expectation of fair deliberation, implying detachment and a commitment to an open mind. It is often defined by its opposite: deliberation cannot be impartial if it is improperly influenced by personal interests, preferences, or loyalties.[37] The expectation of impartiality does not require decision-makers to bring a 'blank' mind to their task.[38] Indeed, experience and first-hand knowledge can be a good thing.[39] The expectation is instead directed towards excluding illegitimate sources of influence, making it a spectrum of ideas rather than a fixed ideal. Ministers are appointed to their positions precisely *because* of their alliance with their party's views, and it is generally accepted that (within legal limits) they will toe the party line when administering their portfolios.[40] By contrast, in its ideal form the public service is intended to be apolitical, with 'staffing decisions … independent of the party political system, free from political bias, and uninfluenced by individual employees' political beliefs'.[41] Further along the spectrum are bodies charged with independent functions to review or investigate government decisions and activity, such as merits review tribunals, anti-corruption commissions and courts. Expectations of impartiality here are far stronger, and perceived threats are potentially more damaging to public confidence.

Impartiality standards are sourced in a patchwork of legal and ethical rules, codes and policies. For some officials, the expectation is reflected in a formal oath of office. Judges, for example, must take an oath to 'do right to all manner of people according to law without fear or favour, affection or ill-will'.[42] Many other government officials take oaths of impartiality to similar effect.[43] Such oaths are a 'profound commitment' of 'moral significance',[44] a symbolic ritual that constitutes a 'social and moral bond between the oath taker and fellow citizens'.[45] Relevantly

[36] M Aronson, M Groves and G Weeks, *Judicial Review of Administrative Action and Government Liability*, 7th edn (London, Thomson Reuters, 2022), 608.

[37] G Cullity, 'Impartiality' in *The International Encyclopedia of Ethics* (Chichester, John Wiley & Sons, 2013).

[38] *Minister for Immigration and Multicultural Affairs v Jia Legeng* (2001) 205 CLR 507, 531 [71] (Gleeson CJ and Gummow J) ('*Jia*').

[39] See, eg, M Groves, 'Clarity and Complexity in the Bias Rule' (2020) 44 *Melbourne University Law Review* 565, 575; W Lucy, 'The Possibility of Impartiality' (2005) 25 *Oxford Journal of Legal Studies* 3, 15–16.

[40] As noted in Part III.A, the rule against bias accepts the political reality that a politician may act to further their party's interests.

[41] *Comcare v Banerji* (2019) 267 CLR 373, 401 [34] (Kiefel CJ, Bell, Keane and Nettle JJ).

[42] Eg, High Court of Australia Act 1979 (Cth) s 11, sch 1.

[43] Eg, tribunal members (Administrative Review Tribunal Act 2024 (Cth) s 213 ('ART Act')) and police (Police Regulation 2015 (NSW) cl 7).

[44] JA Rohr, *Public Service, Ethics, and Constitutional Practice* (Lawrence, University Press of Kansas, 1998) 71.

[45] M Rutgers, 'The Oath of Office as Public Value Guardian' (2010) 40 *The American Review of Public Administration* 428, 434–35.

for present purposes, it symbolises our trust in the oath-taker to act in accordance with their promise as a moral – rather than legal – constraint.[46]

Conflict of interest rules are another common form of impartiality standard. An interest represents a conflict if it has the potential to influence a decision-maker's evaluative process, and is problematic due to its tendency to cast doubt on the reliability of judgement.[47] Some conflict standards are simply prohibitive, instructing a person to avoid ending up in a situation that could give rise to a conflict in the first place. Other rules require a person to escape the conflict (eg, by recusal), or to disclose it, or to take steps to reduce its potential impact on the reliability of their judgement.[48] A variety of different conflict of interest standards feature in Australian government administration. Some take statutory form, such as the PGPA Act duty owed by officials to disclose 'material interests'[49] and the APS Code of Conduct requirement for public servants to take reasonable steps to avoid real or apparent conflicts of interest.[50] Other conflict rules take the form of agency-implemented codes of conduct, policies and guidelines,[51] and broader professional and ethical obligations.[52] In response to concerns about the compromised independence of its predecessor, the newly established Administrative Review Tribunal (ART) is governed by a Code of Conduct that explicitly contemplates its perceived independence and impartiality.[53] Citing public trust and confidence as a core concern, this Code imposes detailed conflict of interest requirements on members as well as restricting their public involvement in political activities.

The bias doctrine is perhaps the most obvious example of an impartiality standard. Originally developed as a constraint on judges, the rules have long been applied to other types of decision-makers exercising administrative power[54] and executive bodies charged with merits[55] and integrity[56] review functions. The more exacting ground of actual bias applies where a decision-maker is 'so committed to a conclusion already formed' that they are incapable of persuasion;[57] it is an allegation that a decision-maker's state of mind *in fact* reflects a 'concluded and unalterable view'.[58] The less demanding ground of apprehended bias puts the decision-maker's actual

[46] ibid 439–40.

[47] M Davis and A Stark (eds), *Conflict of Interest in the Professions* (Oxford, OUP, 2001) 9.

[48] A summary of approaches appears in ibid.

[49] PGPA Act (n 34) s 29.

[50] Public Service Act (n 35) s 13(7).

[51] Eg, Commonwealth Government, *Code of Conduct for Ministers* (June 2022).

[52] Eg, The Australasian Institute of Judicial Administration, *Guide to Judicial Conduct* (3rd edn, 2017); Hon J Thomas, *Judicial Ethics in Australia*, 3rd edn (London, LexisNexis, 2009).

[53] Administrative Review Tribunal, *Code of Conduct for Non-Judicial Members* (14 October 2024) ('ART Code of Conduct').

[54] Eg, *Isbester v Knox City Council* (2015) 255 CLR 135 ('*Isbester*').

[55] *Re Minister for Immigration and Multicultural Affairs and anor; Ex Parte Epeabaka* (2001) 206 CLR 128, 138 [27] (Gleeson CJ, McHugh, Gummow and Hayne JJ).

[56] *Duncan v Ipp* [2013] NSWSC 314.

[57] *Jia* (n 38) 532 [72] (Gleeson CJ and Gummow J).

[58] ibid 534 [81]. Gleeson CJ and Gummow J were speaking of the (incorrect) conclusion reached by the Full Court on this point.

state of mind to one side[59] and asks instead whether a 'hypothetical fair-minded lay observer' might perceive that decision-maker to be biased.[60] While not a closed list, sources of potential bias are commonly described as falling into four categories: interest, conduct, association and extraneous information.[61] The common thread running through those categories is the risk that an irrelevant factor might lead the decision-maker to reach a decision otherwise than on its merits.

### b. Improper Influence

A second category of integrity standards is those that demand an appropriate degree of autonomy and independence in the decision-making task. Sometimes styled 'decisional independence',[62] these standards indicate the extent to which an official is permitted to be influenced by the preferences of third parties or to bow to pressure or 'suggestions' from superiors.[63] As for impartiality, these expectations differ according to context, with some standards anticipating a high degree of autonomy.[64] The expectation of judicial independence is an obvious starting point. Jealously protected in the Australian system, it requires 'decisional independence from influences external to proceedings in the court, including, but not limited to, the influence of the executive government and its authorities'.[65] Another explicit example is the expected independence of the Auditor-General. That officer is designated by legislation as an 'independent officer of the Parliament' who has 'complete discretion in the performance of his or her functions or powers … [and] is not subject to direction'.[66]

In some contexts, there exists greater tension between expectations of autonomy and sensitivity to influence, such as political lobbying. Not all attempts at political influence are improper, and from a democratic perspective, there is good reason to support ongoing dialogue between politicians and public interest groups. The problematic aspect of lobbying is the risk that elected officials may be tempted to exercise power for the benefit of a particular group through direct 'quid pro quo' arrangements or more subtle 'clientelism'.[67] The patchwork of lobbying rules is not

[59] Apprehended bias may be an attractive doctrinal buffer that allows litigants and the courts to avoid confronting the 'murky and unpalatable' reality of actual bias: Justice D Mortimer, 'Whose Apprehension of Bias?' (2016) 84 *AIAL Forum* 45, 46. It is a 'polite fiction': *Johnson v Johnson* (2000) 201 CLR 488, 517 [79] (Callinan J).

[60] *Ebner v Official Trustee in Bankruptcy* (2000) 205 CLR 337, 344 [6] (Gleeson CJ, McHugh, Gummow and Hayne JJ).

[61] *Webb v The Queen* (1994) 181 CLR 41, 74 (Deane J) ('*Webb v The Queen*').

[62] *CNY17 v Minister for Immigration and Border Protection* (2019) 268 CLR 76, 87 [18] (Kiefel CJ and Gageler J) ('*CNY17*').

[63] Groves (n 39) fn 83.

[64] For discussion of a range of possible structures, see P Latimer, 'Ministerial Directions to Independent Statutory Commissions: Commissions Causing Trouble for Their Minister' (2004) 25 *Australian Bar Review* 29.

[65] *South Australia v Totani* (2010) 242 CLR 1, 43 [62].

[66] Auditor-General Act 1997 (Cth) s 8.

[67] *McCloy v New South Wales* (2015) 257 CLR 178, 204 [36].

always successful in promoting that balance.[68] The autonomy and independence of public servants is another area of potential tension between autonomy and subservience. The Public Service is intended to practice independence, with one of the legislated *APS Values* anticipating a public service that is 'apolitical and provides the Government with advice that is frank [and] honest'.[69] That aspiration does not mean a public servant is free to disregard the orders of superiors in favour of giving effect to their own views of what is right or proper. Indeed, that might expose them to disciplinary consequences.[70]

For public officials tasked with exercising discretionary power, the 'dictation' ground of judicial review reflects the relevant balancing act. That ground assumes that a decision-maker exercising discretionary power should give 'independent attention'[71] to that task and not abdicate that responsibility by acting at the direction or behest of another. That is only a starting point, however. As with the rules against bias, the expected degree of autonomy or independence is incredibly context-specific. It might be entirely appropriate, for example, for discretionary power conferred on a military officer to be exercised in accordance with the dictates of superiors – such power is conferred in the context of a pre-existing chain of command.[72] Sometimes the applicable legislative structure may attempt to make this position explicit by saddling an official who enjoys seemingly discretionary power with an overriding obligation to obey ministerial directions.[73] Generally, those types of provisions are read down in the expectation that the decision-maker will still deal with the merits of the matter.[74] This approach is consistent with the related rule that prohibits the inflexible application of government policy – a decision-maker is entitled to be guided by lawful government policy provided that they do not abdicate their overriding responsibility to determine a matter on its merits.[75]

### c. Breach of Public Trust

It has sometimes been said that officials hold power on 'public trust', akin to a fiduciary relationship.[76] While that idea has not been translated into an enforceable legal or equitable obligation, the courts have occasionally drawn on ideas of

[68] See generally Y-F Ng, 'Regulating the Influencers: The Evolution of Lobbying Regulation in Australia' (2020) 41 *Adelaide Law Review* 507. A Commonwealth Senate Committee has recently recommended modest reforms: Finance and Public Administration References Committee, *Access to Australian Parliament House by Lobbyists* (May 2024).

[69] Public Service Act (n 35) s 10(4).

[70] A recent example being *Azzi v State of NSW* [2024] NSWCA 169.

[71] *Telstra Corporation Ltd v Kendall* (1995) 55 FCR 221, 231.

[72] *CPCF v Minister for Immigration and Border Protection* (2015) 255 CLR 514, 541 [52] (French CJ).

[73] See examples in Aronson, Groves and Weeks (n 36) 310.

[74] ibid.

[75] *Green v Daniels* (1977) 13 ALR 1.

[76] Most famously by Paul Finn, eg, PD Finn, 'Public Trusts, Public Fiduciaries' (2010) 38(3) *Federal Law Review* 335. For recent discussion, see P Brereton, 'Values in the Public Service' (2024) 111 *AIAL Forum* 51, 53–54.

trust and public duty to describe the scope of government power.[77] In some jurisdictions, the terminology of 'breach of public trust' features in the definition of 'corrupt conduct' that can be investigated by anti-corruption bodies.[78] Interpreting the NSW provision, the NSW Court of Appeal in *Berejiklian v ICAC* agreed that a parliamentarian may breach public trust by placing themselves in a position where their private interests and public duty are in conflict.[79] The nature of that public duty is 'to serve, and in serving to act with fidelity and with a single-mindedness for the welfare of the community',[80] including 'an obligation to act according to good conscience, uninfluenced by other considerations'.[81]

More specific prohibitions on improper conduct reflect the most fundamental expectations of government integrity. The use of public power or position to advance private interests is a clear example, captured in various sources including PGPA Act duties,[82] the APS Code of Conduct,[83] Ministerial Codes of Conduct,[84] as well as various criminal offences such as bribery, corruption and misconduct in public office.[85] The latter of those offences has been described as capturing misconduct that is 'incompatible with the proper discharge of the responsibilities of [a public office] so as to amount to a breach of the confidence which the public has placed in the office'.[86] Other standards proscribe the 'dishonest' exercise of public power,[87] including improperly concealing or withholding information.[88] In the judicial review context, these types of conduct would satisfy the demanding ground of 'bad faith', a serious allegation involving a 'personal attack on the honesty of the decision-maker'.[89]

### *ii. Keeping Up Appearances*

One of the purposes of integrity standards is to promote the quality of government administration by insulating against the potential impact of illegitimate sources of

[77] Eg, *Porter v Magill* [2002] 2 AC 357, 463 [19]; *Hocking v Director-General of the National Archives of Australia* (2020) 271 CLR 1, 100–01 [243] (Edelman J).

[78] Eg, Independent Commission Against Corruption Act 1988 (NSW) s 8(1)(c) ('ICAC Act'); National Anti-Corruption Commission Act 2022 (Cth) s 8(1)(b).

[79] *Berejiklian v Independent Commission Against Corruption* [2024] NSWCA 177, [174] ('*Berejiklian v ICAC*').

[80] *R v Boston* (1923) 33 CLR 386, 400, cited in ibid [171].

[81] *Re Day [No 2]* (2017) 263 CLR 201, 221 [49], cited in *Berejiklian v ICAC* (n 79) [171].

[82] PGPA Act (n 34) ss 27–28.

[83] Public Service Act (n 35) s 13(10).

[84] Commonwealth: Code of Conduct for Ministers (n 51) [3.1]; NSW: Independent Commission Against Corruption Regulation 2017 (NSW), Appendix, item 6 ('NSW Ministerial Code of Conduct').

[85] Criminal Code Act 1995 (Cth) ('Criminal Code') ss 141.1(3), 142.1(3), 142.2. Misconduct in public office is a common law offence: *R v Obeid [No 12]* [2016] NSWSC 1815, [79].

[86] *R v Quach* (2010) 27 VR 310, 321 [40].

[87] ICAC Act (n 78) s 8(1)(b); NSW Ministerial Code of Conduct (n 84) item 6.

[88] Eg, an obligation to report potential corruption (ICAC Act (n 78) s s 11) or to provide information to the Ombudsman on request (Ombudsman Act 1976 (Cth) s 36).

[89] *SCAS v Minister for Immigration and Multicultural and Indigenous Affairs* [2002] FCAFC 397, [19].

influence.[90] A second rationale, explored here, is to support public confidence in the legitimacy of government.[91] Australia's public service legislation, for example, enshrines the value of a public service that is 'trustworthy' and requires public servants to uphold the 'integrity and good reputation' of the public service.[92] According to the High Court, this legislation serves constitutional purposes in securing 'integrity and the maintenance of public confidence in that integrity'.[93] Many Codes of Conduct include exhortations to similar effect.[94] In the judicial review context, the apprehended bias rule is firmly anchored to a public confidence rationale, being intended to 'foster public confidence in decision-makers and their institutions'.[95] As the Hon Robert French AC has observed:

> Fear or favour, affection or ill will or personal interest in the outcome … are pernicious irrelevant considerations because they deprive the judicial process and its outcomes of integrity. The mere appearance of those corrupting elements can deprive the process and outcome of legitimacy – in the eyes of the parties and of the public. So the authority of courts may be undermined.[96]

The above integrity standards demonstrate concern for 'keeping up appearances' in two ways. The first is the significant weight accorded to external appearances in the structure of many of these standards. The second is the exclusion of causal reasoning, in the sense that many integrity standards may be violated irrespective of whether the breach 'made a difference' to the outcome.

### a. Concern for Public Perception

Concern for appearances is baked into a number of integrity standards. To place a twist on Lord Hewart CJ's aphorism, these standards demand that integrity 'should not only be done, but should manifestly and undoubtedly be *seen to be done*'.[97] A number of jurisdictions recognise a particular species of corruption in the form of conduct that could 'impair public confidence in public administration',[98] being

[90] Eg, S Young, 'The Evolution of Bias: Spectrums, Species and the Weary Lay Observer' (2017) 41 *Melbourne University Law Review* 928, 955.

[91] Heydon J was particularly scathing of appeals to broad notions of 'public confidence' in *Moti v The Queen* (2011) 245 CLR 456, 494–96, [99]–[101].

[92] Public Service Act (n 35) ss 10(2) and 13.

[93] *Commissioner of Taxation v Day* (2008) 236 CLR 163, 181 [34] (Gummow, Hayne, Heydon and Kiefel JJ), referring to the previous iteration of the Public Service Act (n 35).

[94] Eg, Commonwealth Government, *Lobbying Code of Conduct* (November 2019), [4]; NSW Ministerial Code of Conduct (n 84), Preamble; NSW Public Service Commissioner, 'Behaving Ethically: A guide for NSW government sector employees' (Direction No. 2 of 2022) 13; ART Code of Conduct (n 53) parts 5–6 and 10.

[95] *CNY17* (n 62) 98 [55] (Nettle and Gordon JJ). Margaret Allars outlines the lineage of this rationale in 'Citizenship Theory and the Public Confidence Rationale for the Bias Rule' (2001) 18 *Law in Context* 12.

[96] R French AC, 'Preface' (2021) 28 *Australian Journal of Administrative Law* 61, 61.

[97] *R v Sussex Justices; Ex parte McCarthy* [1924] 1 KB 256, 259 (emphasis added).

[98] ICAC Act (n 78) s 8(2A); Crime and Corruption Act 2001 (Qld) s 15(2). Conduct only falls within this category if it amounts to a criminal or disciplinary offence, or, in NSW, a breach of an applicable code of conduct (ss 9 and 15 in the respective Acts).

conduct that might cause the public to question or lose trust in government.[99] Public perception issues also underpin conflict of interest rules, which by their nature are aimed at securing the reliability of judgment. A perceived conflict is a problem because 'it looks bad',[100] and for this reason many rules refer specifically to *apparent* sources of conflict, requiring officials to be mindful not only of situations in which their judgment is threatened but also to consider how it might appear to others.[101] As for other integrity issues, conflicts have the potential to impact public confidence in the integrity of both individual officials and the institutions of government, which is why the Commonwealth Ministerial Code of Conduct directs ministers to the risk that a conflict 'might contaminate not just their own decisions but also the decisions of the Cabinet to which they are a party'.[102]

The apprehended bias rule is a clear depiction of concern for external appearances, evidenced in the selection of the fair-minded lay observer as the gauge of partiality. As put by Mason CJ and McHugh J in *Webb v The Queen*:

> public confidence in the administration of justice is more likely to be maintained if the Court adopts a test that reflects the reaction of the ordinary reasonable member of the public to the irregularity in question.[103]

The bystander test 'tethers' the bias rule to its public confidence rationale.[104] The point cannot be taken too far, of course.[105] The bystander is not a direct proxy for public opinion, and the courts acknowledge that there will often be a disconnect between the two: the observer may sometimes be 'mistaken' because 'decision-makers will rarely be biased in the ways attributed to them'.[106] The bystander's intuition must be tempered by an understanding of institutional context and culture that does not always reflect public knowledge, in some instances even instructing the bystander to wave through practices that 'any sensible observer would be greatly troubled by'.[107]

Putting those concerns to one side, imbuing the bystander with an appreciation of real-world context permits the bias rule to be sensitive to higher and lower public expectations of different types of decision-makers. Thus, while a judge might be held to stringent expectations of impartiality, it would be 'unrealistic' to expect a politician to conform to those lofty standards.[108] As Groves observed,

[99] Queensland Crime and Corruption Commission, *Corruption in the Queensland Public Sector* (Prevention in Focus, 31 May 2019).
[100] D Luban, 'Law's Blindfold' in Davis and Stark (n 47) 23, 32.
[101] Eg, NSW Public Service Commissioner (n 94) 13.
[102] *Code of Conduct for Ministers* (n 51) [3.9].
[103] *Webb v The Queen* (n 61) 51.
[104] *QYFM v Minister for Immigration, Citizenship, Migrant Services and Multicultural Affairs* (2023) 409 ALR 65, 78 [45] (Kiefel CJ and Gageler J) ('*QYFM*').
[105] See, eg, M Groves, 'The Imaginary Observer of the Bias Rule' (2012) 19 *Australian Journal of Administrative Law* 188.
[106] *QYFM* (n 104) 83 [69].
[107] Groves (n 39) 585.
[108] *Isbester* (n 54) 147 [27] (Kiefel, Bell, Keane and Nettle JJ).

the courts are yet to provide clear guidance on the shape of the 'lesser … species of impartiality' applicable to non-adjudicatory bodies.[109] Taking politicians as an example, the fair-minded lay observer might be taken to accept that it is routine practice for politicians to participate in lobbying and donation activities,[110] to make partisan statements to the media,[111] and to weigh up 'the political fortunes of the government' when making decisions.[112] Provided that a decision-maker remains open to persuasion, these types of politicking do not undermine impartiality because this comes with the territory. Equally, however, the bias rules can be sensitive to differing levels of public trust (or 'scepticism')[113] that certain decision-makers will be willing and able to disregard improper sources of influence. In *CNY17*, for example, the High Court was called on to assess whether the bystander would trust a decision-maker to ignore irrelevant and prejudicial material.[114] Edelman J thought a 'more robust approach' could be taken to a judicial officer who enjoys greater 'independence and security of tenure' than an administrative official who does not.[115] The bystander might have greater confidence in impartiality where institutional arrangements reinforce a decision-maker's independence,[116] justifying a more vigorous application of the bias rule to a decision-maker who lacks those supports.

The applicable 'ground' of review might shift, but there is overlap between the bias rule's expected standard of impartiality and the expected degree of autonomy prescribed by the rule against dictation. In *CNY17*, Kiefel CJ and Gageler J pointed out that it may be difficult for a decision-making body to maintain its appearance of impartiality if it is on the receiving end of directions from a superior.[117] Their Honours dissented on the bias issue, finding that the bystander would not see the Secretary's transmission of prejudicial material to the Authority as undermining its impartiality. However, their Honours suggested that a different issue might arise if the Secretary's communication was interpreted as 'instruction, advice or opinion'.[118] That could be a problem of 'grave concern' due to the 'marked discrepancy in the hierarchical position' between the Secretary, as a more senior bureaucrat, and that of the more junior Authority reviewer.[119] Even if that falls short of 'dictation' in its traditional sense, the implication is that using inappropriate channels of communication to influence the exercise of power downstream in the bureaucratic hierarchy could undermine a decision-maker's apparent

[109] M Groves, 'Elected Officials and the Bias Rule' (2024) 35 *Public Law Review* 238, 242.
[110] *Austin BMI Pty Ltd v Deputy Premier* [2023] QSC 95, reasoning critiqued in ibid 247–48.
[111] Eg, *Jia* (n 38).
[112] Thus, a politician may legitimately act to maximise 'the political fortunes of the government': *Hot Holdings* (n 23) 455 [50] (Gaudron, Gummow and Hayne JJ).
[113] ibid 484 [141] (Kirby J), in dissent.
[114] *CNY17* (n 62) 119–20 [136] (Edelman J).
[115] ibid 119–20 [136] (Edelman J).
[116] Institutional arrangements are discussed in Part III.C below.
[117] *CNY17* (n 62).
[118] ibid 89 [26] (Kiefel CJ and Gageler J).
[119] ibid 89 [25] (Kiefel CJ and Gageler J).

impartiality. As Groves has noted, neither of these grounds is well-equipped to address the 'wider institutional pressures' that exert subtle forms of influence on administrative decision-making,[120] an issue to which I return in Part III.C below.

#### b. The Irrelevance of Causation

Some integrity standards demonstrate concern for appearances by treating causation as irrelevant. For these standards, a violation is problematic whether or not it can be said to have 'made a difference' to how power was exercised. Corruption standards that prohibit partiality in the exercise of public power are one example. A public official cannot defend a criminal charge of unlawful conspiracy by arguing that 'the same result might, or even would, have followed' in any event.[121] Similarly, a parliamentarian cannot dispute a corruption finding based on a conflict of interest by arguing that their decision 'would not have been different in absence of the private interest'.[122] Depending on the nature of the charge, it might be relevant to weigh competing motives in determining whether an official was, in fact, influenced by an improper motive.[123] After that question has been answered in the affirmative, however, a 'but for' test of causation has no further role to play.[124] It is 'wholly immaterial' that the exercise of power might have been otherwise beneficial to the public; the 'public mischief' arises at an anterior stage.[125]

This reasoning also explains why the public law 'materiality' principle[126] has limited application in judicial review claims involving breach of the bias rule. It is no response to a bias charge to argue that the alleged source of influence did not causally affect the decision-making process:

> Even though the decision-maker may in fact be scrupulously impartial, the appearance of bias can itself call into question the legitimacy of the decision-making process.[127]

For this reason, the bias ground can be taken to 'incorporate an element of materiality',[128] undermining jurisdiction 'irrespective of any effect that the error might or might not have had on the decision that was made in fact'.[129] The irrelevance of causal reasoning to these integrity standards is consistent with the public

[120] Groves (n 39) 581–82.

[121] *R v Boston* (n 80) 397 (Isaacs and Rich JJ). The same approach was followed in *Macdonald v The King* (2023) 112 NSWLR 402, 425.

[122] *Berejiklian v ICAC* (n 79) [256].

[123] The application of a 'but for' test in *Maitland v The Queen* (2019) 99 NSWLR 376 is better understood as directed at that question.

[124] *Macdonald v The King* (n 121) 425–26.

[125] *R v Boston* (n 80) 394 (Isaacs and Rich JJ).

[126] As recognised in *Hossain v Minister for Immigration and Border Protection* (2018) 264 CLR 123.

[127] *IW v City of Perth* (1997) 191 CLR 1, 51 (Gummow J).

[128] *MZAPC v Minister for Immigration and Border Protection* (2021) 273 CLR 506, 522 [33] (Kiefel CJ, Gageler, Keane and Gleeson JJ).

[129] *LPDT v Minister for Immigration, Citizenship, Migrant Services and Multicultural Affairs* (2024) 98 ALJR 610, [6].

confidence rationale. To ask whether a decision-maker 'would have made the same decision absent the appearance of bias' risks diminishing public confidence in government administration.[130]

## B. Enforcing Integrity Expectations

The vast majority of public servants are well-intentioned and conscientious individuals who can be relied on to comply with integrity expectations without the need for additional scrutiny. Our system of public law, however, assumes that trust is not sufficient for this leap of faith and is instead premised on the risk that 'every man … [might] be a knave'.[131] Many mechanisms exist to monitor and scrutinise government administration and to step in and deliver consequences when integrity standards are violated. Amongst others, these include political accountability processes (eg, parliamentary powers over the executive), legal accountability processes (eg, judicial review, criminal and tort law), and integrity bodies (eg, auditors-general, ombudsmen and anti-corruption commissions).[132]

Some of these mechanisms can intervene at an early stage to prevent an integrity problem from coming to fruition – court orders to prohibit or restrain a biased decision-maker are one example.[133] Other mechanisms are aimed at nullifying or delegitimising an exercise of power that falls foul of integrity requirements,[134] rectifying the causes of integrity problems,[135] or ameliorating the harm that they produce.[136] For more serious integrity breaches, punitive mechanisms can deliver public condemnation[137] and disciplinary[138] or criminal sanctions.[139] It is common to see reference to concerns about public trust and confidence in connection with these types of enforcement actions.[140] Thus, the bias rule is enforced to foster public confidence in decision-makers and their institutions, and misconduct in public office is punished (at least in part) to recognise that '[c]orruption by elected representatives consumes democracies [and] destroys public confidence in

[130] *Macdonald v The King* (n 121) 426.

[131] D Hume, 'Of the Independency of Parliament' in EF Miller (ed), *Essays, Moral, Political, and Literary* (Liberty Fund, 1987) 42, 42.

[132] See E Rock, *Measuring Accountability in Public Governance Regimes* (Cambridge, CUP, 2020).

[133] Eg, *Kalache v Local Government of NSW* [2017] NSWSC 1614.

[134] Eg, a writ of certiorari or declaration of invalidity in judicial review proceedings.

[135] Eg, recommendations by anti-corruption commissions to reduce opportunities for corruption: ICAC Act (n 78) s 13(1)(e)–(j).

[136] Eg, the award of damages for the tort of misfeasance in public office.

[137] A public finding of 'serious corrupt conduct' would fall into this category: ICAC Act (n 78) s 74BA.

[138] Eg, termination of employment for violation of PGPA Act duties: PGPA Act (n 34) s 30.

[139] Eg, fines and imprisonment following conviction for a criminal offence.

[140] Eg, the President of the ART can deal with a member's breach of the Code of Conduct by taking measures 'reasonably necessary to maintain public trust and confidence in the Tribunal': ART Act (n 43) s 203, described by Groves as an 'important innovation': M Groves, 'The Administrative Review Tribunal: A Big Step in Tribunal Justice, 50 years in the Making' (2024) 98 *Australian Law Journal* 902, 905.

democratic institutions'.[141] The enforcement of integrity standards can be seen to form part of a larger, longer-term project, stamping out small fires with a view to preventing a larger blaze from taking hold.

The very presence of these types of enforcement mechanisms can potentially bolster public confidence, serving as a safety net to reassure the public that wrongs will be rooted out and rectified. Not all accountability mechanisms are considered equal when it comes to supporting public confidence of this sort. A mechanism may potentially struggle to inspire confidence if it lacks robust enforcement powers or if its activities take place wholly 'behind closed doors'. Perceived independence is particularly important to public confidence in accountability bodies: a mechanism viewed as a government lapdog is unlikely to inspire the confidence afforded to a well-equipped watchdog. This might call for measures that enhance individual and structural independence from government pressure, including those directed at the quality of the appointments process and that insulate an official against influence and reprisal.[142] In the absence of structural supports that inspire confidence, we must trust an accountability body to practice independence of its own accord.

When it comes to public trust, the public may have a more positive perception of honesty and integrity where the government observes a high level of transparency.[143] Open government is said to promote confidence by showing that officials and institutions are in fact adhering to integrity expectations.[144] The assumption is that exposing the government to scrutiny is likely to improve integrity compliance. Transparency is framed as a means to 'alleviate moral hazard',[145] with sunlight being 'the best of disinfectants'.[146] Some transparency arrangements operate in the open, leaving an official with little doubt that their activities are being observed. Perhaps the most obvious examples are those aspects of government deliberation that take place in a public forum (eg, proceedings in Parliament, courts and tribunals) – these are the quintessential depiction of justice being 'seen to be done'. A related example would be those obligations that require officials to proactively offer information and explanations, such as a mandatory obligation to furnish reasons at the time of making a decision[147] or to publish certain agency information to the public.[148]

Other transparency structures warn officials that their activities *might* be exposed to scrutiny. Many officials make decisions in the knowledge that they may later need to prepare a statement of reasons on request, or see their internal

[141] *R v Obeid* (n 85) [137]–[138].

[142] See Part III.C.

[143] Grimmelikhuijsen (n 19) 183.

[144] J Wanna, 'Introduction' in J Wanna and S Vincent (eds), *Opening Government: Transparency and Engagement in the Information Age* (Acton, ANU Press, 2018) 3, 12.

[145] B Holmström, 'Moral Hazard and Observability' (1979) 10(1) *The Bell Journal of Economics* 74, 74.

[146] L Brandeis, *Other People's Money* (Frederick A Stokes Company, 1914) 62.

[147] Judges being the prime example: *Wainohu v New South Wales* (2011) 243 CLR 181, 215 [58] (French CJ and Kiefel J).

[148] Eg, proactive publication requirements under the Freedom of Information Act 1982 (Cth) s 8.

correspondence released pursuant to a freedom of information request, or be called to explain themselves before a parliamentary committee or an integrity body. Likewise, officials can be taken to be aware of the broad powers of integrity bodies that permit investigators to pore over the contents of internal documents and make demands for information. While perhaps discomforting, officials should also be aware of the possibility that their activities might be under general surveillance, either as part of increasingly routine arrangements that permit employers to monitor usage of company devices[149] or pursuant to more extreme covert surveillance powers available to anti-corruption and law enforcement agencies.

Returning to the central theme of this chapter, transparency arrangements such as these serve two related purposes. One is to incentivise the practice of integrity in the expectation that an official might be more cautious in their activities knowing that violations or missteps may be exposed. The second is to bolster public confidence. We do not need to depend on officials to do the right thing of their own accord because we can observe compliance in action – we see integrity 'being done'. For those areas of government activity that are concealed from public view, trust is therefore much more critical.

## C. Institutional Design

A third important means of controlling for potential integrity issues is through institutional design, including boosting confidence in the appointments process, and through measures to protect against influence. As for the other control measures discussed in this chapter, selecting the right settings for the 'structural and institutional framework' serves to reduce both the probability and perceived risk of integrity issues.[150]

### *i. Confidence in Appointments*

The appointment process by which officials are put in positions of power is a key part of the structural framework that informs public confidence in government integrity. Where appointments are controlled by a party who has a potential vested interest in the decision-maker's activities, the perception (if not reality)[151] may be that they will choose a sympathetic candidate whose ideological or political position is aligned with the outcomes the appointing party has in mind.[152] Politically

[149] Including arrangements governed by the Workplace Surveillance Act 2005 (NSW).

[150] *Gillies v Secretary of State for Work and Pensions* [2006] 1 WLR 781, 793 [38] (Baroness Hale).

[151] One study found politically-motivated appointments were more common for decision-making bodies with greater independence (and therefore less control) from government: LE-Jedenastik, 'The Politicization of Regulatory Agencies: Between Partisan Influence and Formal Independence' (2016) 26(3) *Journal of Public Administration Research and Theory* 507.

[152] Eg, G Stigler, 'The Theory of Economic Regulation' (1971) 2(1) *Bell Journal of Economics and Management Science* 3.

motivated appointees come with baggage that can breed concern that they are 'under pressure to reach decisions which are in the interests of their appointers and paymasters'.[153] The shift towards political control over public service staffing arrangements, for example, has been cited as undermining the capacity of public servants to provide '"frank and fearless advice" and public confidence in the non-partisanship of the APS'.[154] While many administrators appointed pursuant to questionable processes may turn out to be fair and impartial officials, the damage arising from the perceived risk of impartiality is not so easily undone.[155] The fate of the Administrative Appeals Tribunal (AAT) is an apt example. Allegations of 'stacking' and 'cronyism' were cited as a key driver for the decision to abolish and replace that 'fatally compromised' tribunal, with the Attorney-General claiming that its independence and standing had been 'irreversibly damaged' by partisan appointments made by the previous government.[156]

Eligibility criteria for appointment are one way to address potential integrity issues. Sometimes the criteria are set up to decrease the likelihood of appointing someone whose impartiality and autonomy might be in question. The Constitution offers a clear example. Section 44(v) prohibits a parliamentarian from holding a direct or indirect interest in an agreement with the Public Service. The purpose of that prohibition is twofold: preventing the Executive from being able to exert influence over members of the Parliament, and preventing the election of a member whose financial interests may give rise to a 'conflict of duty and interest'.[157] In some contexts, eligibility criteria might rule out the appointment of persons with particular political ties[158] or prohibit a decision-maker from wearing 'two hats' during their appointment.[159] Eligibility criteria can also be used to enhance the promise of impartiality by narrowing the field of candidates to those holding professional qualifications that anticipate impartiality – members of the auditing and legal profession, for example, can be expected to bring with them the integrity standards that are characteristic of those professions.[160] Narrowing

[153] K Malleson, 'Safeguarding Judicial Impartiality' (2002) 22 *Legal Studies* 53, 63–64. Paradoxically, political appointments may be a positive for public trust in contexts where populist views hold sway: C Harlow and R Rawlings, 'Populism and Administrative Law' in E Carolan, JNE Varuhas and S Fulham-McQuillan (eds), *The Making and Re-Making of Public Law* (Oxford, Hart Publishing, 2025) 271, 276–77.

[154] A Podger, *Report to the Royal Commission into the Robodebt Scheme* (20 February 2023), 2.

[155] See, eg, J Boughey, 'A Call for Ongoing Political Commitment to the Administrative Law Project' (2021) 28 *Australian Journal of Administrative Law* 242, 249; M Groves and G Weeks, 'Tribunal Justice and Politics in Australia: The Rise and Fall of the Administrative Appeals Tribunal' (2023) 97 *Australian Law Journal* 278, 288.

[156] The Hon M Dreyfus KC, 'Albanese Government to abolish Administrative Appeals Tribunal: Media Release' (16 December 2022).

[157] *Re Day [No 2]* (n 81), 218–29 [39] (Kiefel CJ, Bell and Edelman JJ).

[158] Eg, the exclusion of former MPs, public servants and members of political parties from appointment as the ACT Integrity Commissioner: Integrity Commission Act 2018 (ACT) s 26.

[159] An example being prohibitions on outside employment, eg, ART Act (n 43) s 216.

[160] See, eg, M Tushnet, *The New Fourth Branch: Institutions for Protecting Constitutional Democracy* (Cambridge, CUP, 2021) 46.

eligibility to current or former members of the judiciary takes that promise a step further.[161]

The appointment process is another means by which confidence concerns can be addressed, with the fate of the AAT again offering a neat example. While voluntary guidelines have been adopted at different times, the appointment of members to the AAT was primarily an unregulated process, placing a significant burden on public trust in the minister to make appointments aligned with the public interest. Following a steady stream of appointments of persons with apparent ties to the incumbent government, that trust was stretched to breaking point.[162] Legislation for the newly established ART is intended to counteract that problem, explicitly mandating a degree of transparency and requiring candidates to be assessed based on merit by an independent panel.[163] There is no intention here to exclude a person with political ties from appointment, but these procedural safeguards may offer reassurance that this was not the *reason* for a person's appointment, thereby increasing public confidence in the tribunal's independence and impartiality.

### *ii. Ringfencing against Influence*

A second category of structural arrangements is relevant 'on the job', bolstering the perception of integrity by ringfencing a decision-maker against the possibility of improper sources of influence, interference and reprisal. Some of these measures constrain the actions of third parties, prohibiting a person from engaging in activities that might amount to improper influence. To name just a few examples, it is a criminal offence for any person to attempt to dishonestly influence[164] or bribe a public official,[165] and in NSW it is a breach of the Ministerial Code of Conduct for a minister to issue directions to an agency with a view to requiring it to alter its advice or to act contrary to law.[166] Structural rules can also target otherwise 'innocent' actions that could potentially undermine the appearance of a decision-maker's impartiality, for example, by preventing certain parties from participating in an administrative or adjudicatory process.[167]

The terms and conditions of appointment, including security of tenure and remuneration, also have a role to play. We may be more confident, for example, that a judge who enjoys a career-length term in judicial office can safely disregard

[161] See, eg, sources cited above at n 29.

[162] See Groves and Weeks (n 155).

[163] ART Act (n 43) ss 205–209. The changes have not immunised the ART against allegations of questionable appointment decisions from some quarters: see K Barlow, 'Exclusive: Stacking claims at new tribunal' (*The Saturday Paper*, 19 October 2024).

[164] Criminal Code (n 85) s 135.1.

[165] ibid s 141.1.

[166] NSW Ministerial Code of Conduct (n 84) item 5.

[167] Eg. in *Lawal v Northern Spirit Ltd* [2004] 1 All ER 187, the House of Lords recommended institutional reform to prevent part-time judges from appearing before a tribunal containing lay members they had previously sat with: see generally Aronson, Groves and Weeks (n 36) 691.

government preferences than we would a tribunal member appointed for a limited term, who must front up and request reappointment from the very government whose decisions that member has been reviewing and potentially overturning.[168] We may also have greater confidence in the impartiality of a decision-maker who can only be removed from office on serious grounds (eg, misbehaviour or incapacity) compared to an official who can be removed at the pleasure of the executive. It would be understandable if an official in the latter category might have their own future in mind when making a decision that is inconvenient to, or critical of, their executive paymasters. Protections against liability are another structural method of ringfencing officials against potential sources of influence. Immunities from suit extend to a number of different categories of government officials.[169] For example, judicial immunity is intended to promote 'an independent judiciary whose members can be assumed with confidence to exercise authority without fear or favour'.[170]

As the above examples reveal, levels of institutional protection vary considerably for different categories of government officials, with some enjoying greater insulation against potential influence than others. To adopt Groves' terminology, many decision-makers continue to operate under the weight of 'institutional pressures'.[171] Whatever else we might say about the desirability of that state of affairs, if institutional arrangements are insufficient to bolster public confidence in government integrity, trust becomes much more important. Again, the AAT saga is illustrative. In his 2019 statutory review of the AAT, Callinan J doubted that political criticism of tribunal members was a realistic threat to the tribunal's integrity, and thought members capable of appreciating that the very nature of politics and merits review invites controversies in respect of which reasonable minds might disagree.[172] That may well be true. However, in the absence of structural supports of the types discussed above, there is less foundation for *confidence* that tribunal members can decide matters without fear or favour, and a greater need for *trust* in a member to put aside worries about their prospects of reappointment. This trust is implicit in Callinan J's remark that tribunal members 'should not be thin skinned'.[173] The sentiment is more colourfully depicted in an AAT decision published soon after the incumbent Minister for Immigration had levelled public criticism at the tribunal in 2017.[174] Acting President Logan urged that

[168] Groves (n 39) 581–82.

[169] Judges enjoy immunity at common law and pursuant to statute (eg, Judicial Officers Act 1986 (NSW) Pt 8A). Similar protections extend to tribunal members (eg, ART Act (n 43) s 293) and other integrity officers (eg, Ombudsman Act 1976 (Cth) s 33).

[170] *Fingleton v The Queen* (2005) 227 CLR 166, 186.

[171] Groves (n 39), 581–82.

[172] The Hon I Callinan, *Review: section 4 of the Tribunals Amalgamation Act 2015 (Cth)* (July 2019) [10.31]–[10.33].

[173] ibid [10.33].

[174] C Gribbin, 'Peter Dutton Blames "Politics" as Bid to Deport Six Refugees Fails', *ABC News Online*, 16 May 2017 tinyurl.com/64uh365e, referring to comments made by Mr Dutton in an interview with radio station 2GB.

> any member who allowed himself or herself to be persuaded as to an outcome by partisan or political rhetoric … would be unworthy of the trust and confidence placed in him or her by His Excellency the Governor-General and untrue to the oath or affirmation of office … For those members who do not enjoy the same security of tenure as judges, that may call at times for singular moral courage and depth of character.[175]

## IV. A Point of Diminishing Returns

If public trust in government integrity were sufficiently robust, the support structures discussed in this chapter might not be necessary. As for a trusted family member, we might have faith in government officials to be guided by their own moral compass in the exercise of public power, believing them capable of disregarding the irrelevant and prejudicial, ignoring opportunities for personal gain, and remaining staunch in the face of direct or indirect attempts to pressure or sway them. As expressed in the literature on trust, we would be willing to 'accept vulnerability'.[176] If the surveys are anything to go by, we are a long way from sufficiently trusting our government or its officials to take that leap of faith. Where trust is in short supply, traditional thinking is that we can turn to control mechanisms that reduce reliance on trust in government to do the 'right thing' of its own accord. We can carefully define integrity expectations with varying levels of precision (Part III.A). We can establish enforcement mechanisms to compel compliance with those standards (Part III.B), and we can implement structural arrangements that ringfence officials against potential integrity threats (Part III.C).

In theory, the more comprehensive and prescriptive our measures of control, the less dependent we would be on trust to bridge the gap that remains. There are, of course, some rather large holes in that theory. One is that it relies on the public having a relatively accurate understanding of these control mechanisms in order to appreciate their value and limitations, which is no small undertaking for the average citizen.[177] Another is that cultural shifts, such as rising populism, can breed scepticism regarding the value of control machinery. Rather than supporting public confidence, accountability controls may be disapproved of as evidence of unnecessary 'red tape'.[178] Even if we assume citizens both want and understand the range of control structures discussed here, this is no guarantee that their presence will support public confidence in government integrity. In the final Part of this chapter, I note a number of points at which efforts at greater control can produce diminishing returns.

[175] *Singh (Migration)* (2017) 850 AATA, [17]–[18].
[176] Rousseau et al (n 14) 395.
[177] Eg, Groves, Nielsen and Smyth (n 29) 91–92.
[178] See Harlow and Rawlings (n 153).

## A. Negative Impacts on Performance

It is a fact of life that control mechanisms cannot guarantee integrity. Rousseau's statement of doubt paints a colourful picture: 'books and auditing of accounts, instead of exposing frauds, only conceal them; for prudence is never so ready to conceive new precautions as knavery is to elude them'.[179] While some 'knaves' might be deliberately flouting integrity controls, a much larger majority of public servants are likely working hard to manage complex procedural checks and balances that can get in the way of doing their 'best work'.[180] Sometimes these mechanisms may even establish perverse incentives that distort performance. Take demands for greater transparency as an example – calls for greater openness and justification are often premised on the assumption that this will increase public confidence in government decision-making.[181] However, transparency can be a 'double-edged sword'.[182] Knowledge that your words will be subject to scrutiny can limit willingness to put pen to paper, potentially impacting the frankness of advice and compromising 'institutional memory'.[183]

The push towards an increased 'culture of justification' in which officials must explain themselves at every turn is also not necessarily conducive to public confidence in those explanations. In the modern administrative state, it is unrealistic – if not fanciful – to expect that ministers and senior officials are in a position to personally attend to all their decision-making duties. Many decisions are made by departmental officials rather than the more senior official on whom power was conferred,[184] and even decisions made personally are commonly informed by the 'collective knowledge and experience' of the department rather than the decision-maker's own research and reasoning process.[185] It is common and accepted practice for ministers to complete a 'tick and flick' of departmental summaries and recommendations before endorsing a draft statement of pre-prepared reasons.[186] Regardless of who does the drafting, there is also no guarantee that a formal statement reflects the 'real reasons' underlying a decision,[187] particularly if the statement is being prepared with a view to defending a legal challenge. Given the administrative burden and the incentive

[179] JJ Rousseau, *The Social Contract and Discourses* (EP Dutton & Co, 1950), 315.

[180] Kim (n 11) 613.

[181] In the context of a 'right to reasons', see, eg, PP Craig, 'The Common Law, Reasons and Administrative Justice' (1994) 53(2) *Cambridge Law Journal* 282, 283. Other justifications for reasons are discussed in J Boughey, 'The Culture of Justification in Administrative Law: Rationales and Consequences' (2021) 54(3) *University of British Columbia Law Review* 403.

[182] Wanna (n 144) 12.

[183] ibid 20.

[184] Eg, pursuant to formal delegation or based on the *Carltona* agency doctrine: *Minister for Immigration, Citizenship and Multicultural Affairs v McQueen* (2024) 418 ALR 133, 140 [18].

[185] ibid.

[186] As was the case in *McQueen*.

[187] See M Aronson, 'Ministers' Signatures – What Do They Prove?' (2023) 30 *Australian Journal of Administrative Law* 10, 16.

to produce a legally defensible explanation, an increased demand for reasons may encourage resort to those of a 'factory-made'[188] variety that, while meticulously composed, lack the authenticity that might otherwise engender public confidence.[189]

Similar difficulties can arise with other aspects of accountability processes designed to support public confidence. One of the key difficulties is that these processes commonly prioritise quantifiable aspects of performance, reducing expectations to measurable 'KPIs' that focus on procedure (eg, publishing policies and keeping records) over harder-to-measure matters of substance. For both agencies and officials, KPIs of this sort can potentially be distracting. It is no stretch to assume that many public servants are reliable and effective in their roles *in spite* of performance measures and 'box-ticking' exercises put in place to satisfy external scrutiny demands. As for other matters of institutional design, more accountability does not necessarily equate to better accountability.

## B. Breeding Suspicion and Mistrust

The idea that heightened scrutiny and control can encourage less rather than more trust is not a new one. Behn observed that the very separation of powers structure itself is built upon a foundation of mistrust and suspicion.[190] The implementation of an accountability system of checks and balances is predicated on the assumption that the government is liable to make mistakes, and (as for any organisation) this is inevitable. Unlike private enterprise, which is generally measured as successful based on its rate of getting it 'right', the government is more often judged based on occasions where it has gotten it wrong.[191] Instead of bolstering public confidence, an accountability system on the continuous hunt for scandals can feed a culture of public mistrust,[192] or, in O'Neill's words, a 'culture of suspicion'.[193] In short, the system we have set up to support our trust in government integrity may potentially be teaching us to look for problems that erode it. There is a delicate balance to be struck, then, in establishing a sufficient sense of control to 'enculturate trust'[194] but without leading us to believe that this is the only thing standing in the way of inevitable corruption.

[188] Aronson, Groves and Weeks (n 36) 712–13.

[189] For similar reasons, public confidence may be damaged where a decision-maker's reasons consist of extensive copying from one of the party's submissions: eg, *Ultimate Vision Inventions Pty Ltd v Innovation and Science Australia* [2023] FCAFC 23, [6].

[190] Behn (n 1) 83. For an empirical perspective see J Dyck, 'Initiated Distrust: Direct Democracy and Trust in Government' (2009) 37 *American Politics Research* 539.

[191] Behn (n 1) 85.

[192] This may go some way to explaining why increased use of police body cameras has not increased public trust in police: W Sousa et al, 'Inconsistencies in Public Opinion of Body-Worn Cameras on Police' (2018) 12 *Policing: A Journal of Policy and Practice* 100.

[193] O'Neill (n 1) 45.

[194] Braithwaite (n 18) 343.

A more insidious trust problem can arise when accountability processes are implemented without genuine commitment. In these circumstances, accountability is reduced to a 'ritual of comfort',[195] serving to deliver the *appearance* of accountability rather than its reality. It becomes 'simulated transparency'[196] or an 'institution of pacification rather than proof'.[197] If public confidence is our primary concern, we might wonder whether that type of hollow comfort and pacification is such a bad thing. I would argue that this type of 'security blanket' accountability may pose one of the most serious threats to public trust. Accountability is intended to serve the public as a sword, a potential threat that keeps government power in check. If the public realises that this sword has been overtaken by government and is being redeployed instead as a shield, this not only withdraws any comfort afforded by the accountability process but also reinforces that the government is unworthy of our trust.

Groves points to the application of the bias doctrine to elected officials as a potential example of this phenomenon.[198] As this chapter has outlined, the bias rules are intended to foster public confidence in the fairness and impartiality of government decision-making. That confidence, in theory, could act as a bridge that allows citizens to better accept the legitimacy of government decisions, even if they do not always agree with them. Groves notes, however, that this legitimacy effect may be stretched to breaking point if the bias rules travel too far from core expectations of impartiality, asking the fair-minded observer to accept patently questionable propositions under the guise of realism. For example, lobbying and donations may well be part and parcel of everyday politics, but does this justify asking the bystander to disregard the potential influence of these practices on government decision-making?[199] If we are asked to turn a blind eye to these types of politicking, Groves suggests there is a risk that the bias rules may end up being viewed as 'something of a doctrinal scam … [which] damages rather than enhances public confidence'.[200]

Another example of this type of risk is the Ombudsman's role in connection with the Robodebt scandal. Despite two investigations, the Ombudsman failed to uncover the unlawfulness of the automated debt recovery scheme that had been used to demand repayment of social security benefits. The 2023 Royal Commission into Robodebt exposed problematic issues regarding the Department's dealings with the Ombudsman's office, including withholding critical information from the investigation team.[201] The Commissioner levelled criticism at the Ombudsman for

[195] M Power, *The Audit Society: Rituals of Verification* (Oxford, Clarendon Press, 1997).

[196] Wanna (n 144) 13.

[197] J Braithwaite, *Regulatory Capitalism: How It Works, Ideas for Making It Work Better* (Cheltenham, Edward Elgar, 2008) 140.

[198] Groves (n 109) 250. See also K van den Bos, *Fair Process Effect: Overcoming Distrust, Polarization, and Conspiracy Thinking* (Cambridge, CUP, 2023).

[199] Groves points to the example of *Austin BMI* (n 110): Groves (n 109) 247.

[200] Groves (n 109) 250–51.

[201] *Royal Commission into the Robodebt Scheme* (Final Report, July 2023) 575–79.

failing to make more robust use of investigative powers that could have overcome the Department's reticence.[202] For present purposes, one of the most concerning aspects of this saga was the Department's use of the Ombudsman's softball investigation report to justify its unlawful debt mill: the report 'did more harm than good. It gave those wanting the Scheme to continue unexamined a shield against criticism'.[203] Rather than operating as an accountability safety net, the Ombudsman process was used by the government as a smokescreen that lent its actions a 'veneer of legitimacy'.[204] That result can only serve to shake public confidence in the Ombudsman's accountability role, as well as public trust in the government more generally.

## V. Conclusion

This chapter has examined various ways in which administrative law contributes to public trust and confidence in government integrity. It has described a number of standards that define expectations of government integrity, mechanisms that enforce those standards, and institutional arrangements that decrease the potential for integrity problems to arise. A common theme drawn throughout is that these arrangements can be understood to serve two interrelated functions – to borrow again from Lord Heward CJ, these arrangements both increase the likelihood that integrity will 'be done' while also ensuring that integrity is 'seen to be done' in the eyes of the public.[205] Both objectives are important in their own right because they are not always aligned. It is possible for an official to *in fact* act with integrity in circumstances where the external appearance of integrity is in doubt, and vice versa. Public confidence can sometimes be invested where it is not warranted or withheld in circumstances when it is justified. In theory, a healthy integrity structure can help iron out some of these problems, reducing our need to extend trust to officials to do the 'right thing' of their own accord. As Part IV of this chapter has warned, however, the antidote of 'more control' also has the potential to exacerbate underlying public trust problems when administered without due care. This is particularly so where there is a lack of government commitment to the values of integrity and accountability that the system is intended to reinforce.

[202] See generally ibid ch 21.
[203] ibid 593.
[204] ibid 594.
[205] *R v Sussex Justices; Ex parte McCarthy* (n 97) 259.

# 12

# Judicial Review and the Rule of Law(fare) in South Africa

CORA HOEXTER

## I. Introduction

South African administrative law has always been dominated by judicial review. In the era of white minority rule, judicial review on administrative-law grounds stood in for various rights and helped compensate for the paucity of non-curial constraints on the exercise of public power. After the introduction of constitutional democracy in 1994, there appeared to be no need for administrative justice to play this compensatory role, and it seemed likely that it would eventually be eclipsed by litigation invoking other constitutional rights.

But no such eclipse occurred. On the contrary, over the last 15 years, administrative-law review has become even more prominent than before. This is principally thanks to repeated failures of governance, endemic corruption, and ultimately state capture, a process facilitated by a wayward executive and a supine legislature in a context of one-party dominance. Almost every fight seems to have ended in court – or to have started there, for litigation has seldom been a matter of last resort even in the most political of cases. This barrage of litigation has been characterised as a type of lawfare: that is, lawfare in the specific sense of the judicialisation of politics in postcolonial societies.[1] And while much of it has been benign or 'good' lawfare, litigation brought to vindicate the rule of law rather than to abuse the legal process,[2] it has perhaps been too much of a good thing. Constant reliance on the courts has put pressure on public law in significant ways.

[1] See H Corder and C Hoexter, '"Lawfare" in South Africa and its Effects on the Judiciary' (2017) 10 *African Journal of Legal Studies* 105. This is the third sense of the term identified by these authors in the South African context, the first two being: (i) the state's use of law to conquer and suppress people; and (ii) the (admirable) use of litigation to resist state oppression, particularly during the apartheid era.

[2] On this distinction, see, eg, H Acton, 'Lawfare: How to Approach it in South Africa's Constitutional Democracy' (2022) 1 *The Africa Governance Papers* 48; T Roux, 'The Constitutional Court's 2018 Term: Lawfare or Window on the Struggle for Democratic Social Transformation?' (2020) 10 *Constitutional Court Review* 1.

The aim of this chapter is to pay tribute to the work of the honorand of this collection of essays, Professor Matthew Groves, by exploring this phenomenon and some of its effects. In publications too numerous to list here, Groves has not only shed brilliant light on the institution of judicial review itself. He has also engaged penetratingly with other themes raised in this chapter, including the concept of lawfare[3] and the beguiling tendency of judicial review to make one forget about the rest of administrative law.[4]

In South Africa the effects of continual reliance on judicial review in administrative law have been both positive and negative. On the positive side, the courts have risen to the challenge of defending the rule of law. We have seen great judicial inventiveness in the promotion of legality and accountability, including the creation of new pathways to review, new or expanded grounds of review, and the removal of procedural obstacles to review. But there have been costs too, and not merely in terms of adding to the workload of a seriously under-resourced and overstretched judiciary. Extreme use of the courts has also placed strain on the relationship between the judiciary and the other branches while perpetuating the unfortunate and longstanding lack of balance in our administrative law. As suggested by some of the contradictory case law emanating from the highest court during this period, the coherence of South Africa's administrative-law jurisprudence has also suffered.

Part II of this chapter outlines South Africa's abiding obsession with judicial review and accounts for the continuing dominance of this remedy today. Part III deals with some of the effects of the courts' interventions in administrative law, both beneficial and deleterious, and a conclusion follows in Part IV.

## II. The Rise and Rise of Judicial Review

### A. The Pre-democratic Era[5]

In 1910, four British colonies joined to form the Union[6] (later the Republic[7]) of South Africa under the rule of a white minority. In 1948 the National Party rose

[3] M Groves, 'Lawfare and the Enemy Within our Public Law' (2017) 90 *AIAL Forum* 32, criticising the tendency of politicians to characterise environmental and other litigation against the government as 'lawfare'.

[4] M Groves and G Weeks, 'The Iceberg of Australian Administrative Law: Justice Before and Beyond Judicial Review' in M Groves and G Weeks (eds), *Administrative Redress in and Out of the Courts* (Sydney, The Federation Press, 2019) 1.

[5] For more detail on this period, see C Hoexter, 'From Pale Reflection to Guiding Light: The Indigenisation of Judicial Review in South Africa' in S Jhaveri and M Ramsden (eds), *Judicial Review of Administrative Action Across the Common Law World: Origins and Adaptation* (Cambridge, CUP, 2021) 171, 174–77.

[6] South Africa Act 9 of 1909, also known as the Union Constitution.

[7] Republic of South Africa Constitution Act 32 of 1961.

to power and began officially to implement its policy of apartheid. Under the tricameral Constitution of 1983,[8] the franchise was extended to 'coloureds' (people of mixed race) and 'Indians' but still not to the black majority. This Kafkaesque situation lasted until April 1994, when constitutional democracy was famously achieved.[9]

These bald facts are well known. What is not obvious is that throughout this period the main safeguard against the abuse of public power was judicial review on administrative-law grounds. It was not always an effective safeguard, as the sovereign legislature tended to confer power very lavishly on public officials and the dominant judicial philosophy was executive-mindedness.[10] Still, the courts' common-law review powers helped compensate for the paucity and ineffectiveness of other controls, particularly under apartheid: a system that required Byzantine administration and that was predicated on the abuse of human rights. Extra-curial safeguards were feeble or non-existent. For instance, internal appeal tribunals were not known for their independence or fairness;[11] parliamentary oversight of the executive was notoriously weak;[12] and the law was directed at promoting secrecy rather than freedom of information.[13] Even an ombud created with fanfare in 1979, the Advocate-General,[14] was of limited use thanks to its constrained jurisdiction and difficulty of access.

In such circumstances it is not surprising that judicial review was relied on so heavily before 1994. An essential point is that pre-democratic South Africa was never simply an autocracy. Rather, it was a dual state that exhibited elements of legalism as well as of coercion and in which law operated as both sword and shield.[15] Paradoxically, then, judicial review sometimes allowed the rule of law to triumph. Indeed, review became a 'weapon of the weak',[16] a way of challenging unlawful and oppressive governmental action. This noble species of lawfare, in the second sense identified by Corder and Hoexter,[17] relied mainly on South Africa's closest approximation to a Bill of Rights: administrative law. Amongst

[8] Republic of South Africa Constitution Act 110 of 1983.

[9] Under a transitional constitution, the Constitution of the Republic of South Africa Act 200 of 1993 ('the interim Constitution'). This was replaced by the 'final' Constitution of the Republic of South Africa, 1996 ('the Constitution' or, to avoid confusion, 'the 1996 Constitution').

[10] See H Corder, *Judges at Work: The Role and Attitudes of the South African Appellate Judiciary, 1910–50* (Cape Town, Juta & Co Ltd, 1984) and C Forsyth, *In Danger for their Talents: A Study of the Appellate Division of the Supreme Court of South Africa, 1950–80* (Cape Town, Juta & Co Ltd, 1985).

[11] See H Corder, 'Administrative Tribunals in the Pursuit of Administrative Justice in South Africa' in S Thomson, M Groves and G Weeks (eds), *Administrative Tribunals in the Common Law World* (Oxford, Hart Publishing, 2024) 229.

[12] See L Baxter, *Administrative Law* (Cape Town, Juta & Co Ltd, 1984) 33.

[13] See A Mathews, *The Darker Reaches of Government* (Cape Town, Juta & Co Ltd, 1978) ch VII.

[14] Under the Advocate-General Act 118 of 1979.

[15] J Meierhenrich, *The Legacies of Law: Long-Run Consequences of Legal Development in South Africa, 1652–2000* (New York, CUP, 2008) 112, 129.

[16] J Comaroff, 'Colonialism, Culture and the Law: A Foreword' (2001) *Law and Social Inquiry* 305, 308.

[17] n 1, 108–10.

other things, principles of administrative law were deployed to promote freedom of movement, to impose limits on emergency powers, and to extend access to public amenities.[18] The courts used administrative law to resist or water down the effects of ouster or privative clauses, so contriving to protect people's access to court.[19] For half a century, the judicious application of Lord Russell's dictum in *Kruse v Johnson*[20] enabled the courts to undo some of the worst effects of discriminatory delegated legislation.[21] And, at a time when employees in the public sector were excluded from the protection of labour legislation (such as it was), principles of administrative law allowed the courts to insist on a hearing before dismissal.[22] As these examples suggest, in the pre-democratic era, lawyers who cared about human rights constantly sought to 'push the boundaries of administrative review' on behalf of their clients.[23]

## B. Judicial Review Since 1994

The year 1994 brought constitutional democracy to South Africa. At the time it may have seemed that while there might henceforth be more judicial review in general, considerably less of it would be based on administrative law. On one hand, the introduction of an actual Bill of Rights had brought about full-blown constitutional review on a wide range of guarantees: as many as 25 in the interim Constitution and 27 in the 1996 Constitution,[24] including rights to just administrative action.[25] The justiciability of all these rights seemed reason enough to anticipate increased resort to the courts. On the other hand, review on administrative-law grounds seemed bound to decrease precisely because this part of the law would no longer

[18] G Budlender, 'The Accessibility of Administrative Justice' [1993] *Acta Juridica* 128.

[19] An early example is *Union Government v Narainsamy* 1923 AD 673, 675 which upheld the court's right, notwithstanding an ouster clause, to interfere with a decision showing 'manifest absence of jurisdiction', fraud or 'a similar element'.

[20] *Kruse v Johnson* [1898] 1 QB 91, 99–100.

[21] See C Plasket and P Firman, 'Subordinate Legislation and Unreasonableness: The Application of *Kruse v Johnson* ([1898] 2 QB 91) by the South African Courts' (1984) 47 *Tyskrif vir Hedendaagse Romeins-Hollandse Reg* 416. The strategy became impracticable after *Minister of the Interior v Lockhat* 1961 (2) SA 587 (A) 602D–E, where the court admitted that Parliament must have contemplated 'substantial inequalities' when enacting apartheid statutes such as the Group Areas Act 77 of 1957.

[22] Most famously, in *Administrator, Transvaal v Zenzile* 1991 (1) SA 21 (A) the court held that temporary workers at a public hospital were entitled to be heard before being dismissed.

[23] K O'Regan, 'Breaking Ground: Some Thoughts on the Seismic Shift in Our Administrative Law' (2004) 121 *South African Law Journal* 424, 429.

[24] The 1996 Constitution protects a wider range of socio-economic rights, including access to housing (s 26) and health care, food, water and social security (s 27).

[25] Constitution, s 33: '(1) Everyone has a right to administrative action that is lawful, reasonable and procedurally fair. (2) Everyone whose rights have been adversely affected by administrative action has a right to be given written reasons. (3) National legislation must be enacted to give effect to these rights, and must – *(a)* provide for the review of administrative action by a court or, where appropriate, an independent or impartial tribunal; *(b)* impose a duty on the state to give effect to the rights in subsections (1) and (2); and *(c)* promote efficient administrative action.'

have to stand in for more specific guarantees such as equality, fair labour practices and access to court. As O'Regan explained ten years into the democratic dispensation, the 'social function' of administrative law had altered: it was 'no longer the legal remedy for challenging laws which infringe constitutional rights other than the right to administrative justice'.[26] Other factors, too, pointed in the direction of a reduced role for administrative law in the courts. Free and fair elections and other healthy political processes seemed bound to take over some of the work previously done by the courts' strategic use of administrative law. Furthermore, the democratic Constitution was replete with non-curial remedies and safeguards against the abuse of public power, including a range of institutions intended to support and strengthen constitutional democracy.[27] All this, one might have supposed, would ease the pressure on the courts – particularly in administrative law.

But this expectation was not realised. Judicial review on administrative-law grounds has actually burgeoned in the constitutional era. So has collateral challenge or indirect review, where the proceedings are not directed at the remedy of setting aside (quashing) but which still entails judicial review in the sense of scrutiny.

A decade ago I suggested a number of factors to explain the continuing prominence of judicial review after 1994.[28] These included the greatly enhanced constitutional role envisaged for the courts and the inspiring possibilities as well as the pressures of a consciously transformative Constitution. I also pointed to the problems of administrative incompetence and growing public corruption leading, in turn, to the increasing failure of non-curial safeguards. While none of these factors has lost its relevance, the constraints of a book chapter prevent their full rehearsal here. Two factors, however, have acquired additional significance since then.

The first is the extraordinary flourishing of the constitutional principle of legality. By no means all this judicial scrutiny has taken place under the Promotion of Administrative Justice Act 3 of 2000 (PAJA), the statute enacted to give effect to the constitutional rights to just administrative action. Rather, the burgeoning referred to above has coincided with the courts' discovery and swift elaboration of the principle of legality as an aspect of the rule of law, a founding value of the Republic.[29] The point of the principle was to ensure that non-administrative action did not go entirely uncontrolled, and initially it was held to encompass merely basic grounds of review associated with the right to lawful administrative action.[30] However, it

[26] O'Regan (n 23) 429.

[27] These 'Chapter 9' institutions ('Chapter 8' in the interim Constitution) include the Public Protector, the Auditor-General and the Human Rights Commission.

[28] C Hoexter, 'A Rainbow of One Colour? Review on Substantive Grounds in South African law' in H Wilberg and M Elliott (eds), *The Scope and Intensity of Substantive Review: Traversing Taggart's Rainbow* (Oxford, Hart Publishing, 2015) 163, 187–93.

[29] Constitution, s 1*(c)*. As to the development of the principle, see Hoexter (n 28) 175–84.

[30] *Fedsure v Greater Johannesburg Metropolitan Council* 1999 (1) SA 374 (CC) ('*Fedsure*') [56]–[59]; *President of the Republic of South Africa v South African Rugby Football Union* 2000 (1) SA 1 (CC) ('*SARFU*') [148].

was soon developed to require a minimum level of rationality in the form of a link between any exercise of public power and the purposes for which that power was conferred.[31] Since then, rationality has expanded into something far more demanding. Today the courts deploy not only substantive or decisional rationality, which is concerned with a decision itself, but also procedural rationality, which allows scrutiny of every step taken in the process of arriving at that decision.[32] In appropriate cases, ingredients ordinarily associated with procedural fairness[33] and the giving of reasons[34] may also be required as a matter of procedural rationality. All in all, the only ground of review not (yet) encompassed in some manner by the legality principle is full-blown reasonableness, of which proportionality is a significant element.

This expansive reach is not the only advantage of the legality principle. Because it is not confined to the realm of 'administrative action', the application of the principle does not depend on compliance with every element of the daunting definition of that concept in the PAJA. Rather, it applies to all exercises of public power. Furthermore, 'legality review' attracts a weaker duty to exhaust internal remedies than 'PAJA review', is likewise more indulgent of a delayed review application, and is more flexible when it comes to remedies.

The user-friendliness of the principle and its apparently infinite ability to mimic ordinary administrative law (represented by the PAJA) have made legality review enormously attractive to litigants and courts alike, so much so that the PAJA is now in real danger of becoming redundant as an avenue to judicial review. Both these propositions have been endorsed judicially,[35] and that is hardly surprising. Even in the absence of official statistics, it is evident to all who work in the area that the principle of legality has greatly facilitated applications for judicial review. There is also no doubt that such applications are essentially for *administrative-law* review. After all, the rule of law is understood to be administrative law under another name,[36] and the principle of legality was conceived as the more general counterpart of the right to lawful administrative action found in section 33(1).[37]

A second significant factor has been the many failures of governance and threats to the rule of law experienced during and since the presidency of Jacob

[31] *Pharmaceutical Manufacturers Association of SA: In re Ex parte President of the Republic of South Africa* 2000 (2) SA 674 (CC) [85].

[32] *Democratic Alliance v President of the Republic of South Africa* 2013 (1) SA 248 (CC) [37] and [39], better known as the *Simelane* case.

[33] *Albutt v Centre for the Study of Violence and Reconciliation* 2010 (3) SA 293 (CC) ('*Albutt*') [68], [72]. However, in *Law Society of South Africa v President of the Republic of South Africa* 2019 (3) SA 30 (CC) ('*Law Society*') [64] the court insisted on the term 'procedural rationality' and defined 'procedural fairness' narrowly, so as to exclude fairness for the sake of rationality; see Part III.C.i below.

[34] *Judicial Service Commission v Cape Bar Council* 2013 (1) SA 170 (SCA) [44]–[45].

[35] See especially *State Information Technology Agency Soc Ltd v Gijima Holdings (Pty) Ltd* 2017 (2) SA 63 (SCA) ('*Gijima* SCA') [34]–[37].

[36] C Plasket, 'The Fundamental Right to Just Administrative Action: Judicial Review of Administrative Action in the Democratic South Africa' (PhD thesis, Rhodes University, 2002) 164.

[37] *Fedsure* (n 30) [59].

Zuma (2009–18).[38] By the time Zuma was 'recalled' by his party, the African National Congress (ANC), and forced to resign in February 2018, the country had become thoroughly enmeshed in corruption, looting and the politics of patronage. The rot extended to state capture, a form of 'systematic corruption' in which political elites or other interest groups manipulate public institutions and functions to serve their own interests rather than the public interest.[39]

It is ironic that one of Zuma's last actions as President was to appoint, albeit reluctantly,[40] a commission of inquiry into state capture. For more than four years the Zondo Commission[41] investigated and recorded how, by whom and to what extent the South African state was in fact captured. Significantly, it found that state capture was facilitated by a supine legislature that repeatedly failed to hold the dominant executive to account.[42] The resulting accountability vacuum was filled by the courts, which had largely managed to retain their independence despite persistent efforts to suborn them: for instance, by packing the Judicial Service Commission with ANC 'cadres'.[43] Tellingly, too, this vacuum-filling role was acknowledged by the ruling party itself. In March 2017, almost a year before the party forced Zuma's resignation, the Secretary-General of the ANC admitted in an unusually candid public statement: '[T]hat the courts are playing a more interventionist role in governance is reflective of our role in abdicating our governance responsibilities to the judiciary.'[44]

To be sure, judicial review of politically fraught disputes predated the ascendancy of Jacob Zuma. Indeed, some degree of judicial involvement in politics is

[38] For detail, see Corder and Hoexter (n 1) 111–20.

[39] E Dávid-Barrett, 'State Capture and Development: A Conceptual Framework' (2023) 25 *Journal of International Relations and Development* 224, 224. On the South African experience, see, eg, ME Martin and H Solomon, 'Understanding the Phenomenon of "State Capture" in South Africa' (2016) 5 *Southern African Peace and Security Studies* 21; I Chipkin and M Swilling, *Shadow State: The Politics of State Capture* (Johannesburg, Wits University Press, 2018); M Buthelezi and P Vale (eds), *State Capture in South Africa: How and Why it Happened* (Johannesburg, Wits University Press, 2023).

[40] After being ordered by the Public Protector to appoint such an inquiry (see Public Protector, *State of Capture* (Report No 6 of 2016/17)), Zuma sought unsuccessfully to have that order set aside in *President of the Republic of South Africa v Office of the Public Protector* 2018 (2) SA 100 (GP).

[41] The *Judicial Commission of Inquiry into Allegations of State Capture, Corruption and Fraud in the Public Sector Including Organs of State* under Acting Chief Justice Raymond Zondo. The Zondo Commission was appointed in January 2018 and released the final part of its very extensive report in June 2022.

[42] See the discussion of parliamentary oversight in Zondo Commission, *Report* Part VI, vol 2 statecapture.org.za/site/information/reports, accessed 28 September 2023. See also M Doyle, J Rault-Smith and R Alli, *'Where Was Parliament?' A PMG Review of Parliamentary Oversight in Light of State Capture and the Zondo Report* (Cape Town, Parliamentary Monitoring Group, August 2022).

[43] See M Olivier and C Hoexter, 'The Judicial Service Commission' in C Hoexter and M Olivier (contributing eds), *The Judiciary in South Africa* (Cape Town, Juta & Co Ltd, 2014) 154, 171–72. This and other aspects of the ANC's 'cadre deployment' policy were laid bare by the publication of records of the party's Deployment Committee download.da.org.za/ANC-cadre-documents-20240220.pdf, accessed 16 May 2024.

[44] Gwede Mantashe, Secretary-General, 'Statement of the African National Congress following the National Executive Committee meeting held 24–26 March 2017' www.anc.org.za, accessed 29 January 2018.

unavoidable under our Constitution. This is apparent from the unequivocal language of provisions such as sections 7[45] and 172[46] and is encouraged also by the courts' liberal attitude to justiciability; for 20 years ago the Constitutional Court confirmed in *Kaunda*,[47] a case about diplomatic protection, that it did not regard any exercise of public power as beyond judicial scrutiny. Two of the most essential conditions for the judicialisation of politics were thus satisfied: a conducive constitutional framework and an active and engaged judiciary.[48] However, the political environment is the most crucial factor of all;[49] and, as Dent explains in her doctoral study of the topic,[50] the failure of political branches to fulfil their assigned constitutional roles is a primary cause of the judicialisation of politics. In their quest for accountability, opposition parties and other civil-society organisations have (or feel they have) no option but to turn to the courts, and the courts feel compelled to assist. One might say that the government's abdication from governance and its leaving a political vacuum for the judiciary to fill guaranteed the migration of politics to the courts – including 'pure' politics, or contentious issues of an outright political nature[51] – and the rise of lawfare in the third sense.

This type of lawfare has often been waged in the arena of administrative law, whether under the PAJA or, more frequently, the legality principle. To give just a few examples, administrative law has featured prominently in the scrutiny of controversial appointments to key public positions such as National Director of Public Prosecutions[52] and head of the Directorate of Priority Crime Investigation;[53] in any number of cases concerning public procurement, that perfect vehicle for looting and plunder;[54] and in waves of litigation concerning the Public Protector, whether it be enforcing the orders of one effective incumbent against a recalcitrant government[55] or challenging the many irrational reports of her successor.[56]

[45] Section 7 provides: 'The state must respect, protect, promote and fulfil the rights in the Bill of Rights.'

[46] In terms of s 172(1)*(a)*, when deciding a constitutional matter within its power 'a court … must declare that any law or conduct that is inconsistent with the Constitution is invalid to the extent of its inconsistency'. Section 172(1)*(b)* then empowers the court to make any order that is 'just and equitable'.

[47] *Kaunda v President of the Republic of South Africa* 2005 (4) SA 235 (CC) [244].

[48] R Hirschl, 'The Judicialization of Politics' in AG Caldeira, D Kelemen and KE Whittington (eds), *The Oxford Handbook of Law and Politics* (Oxford, OUP, 2008) 119.

[49] ibid 134.

[50] KJ Dent, 'Lawfare and Legitimacy: The Wicked Problem of Judicial Resilience at a Time of Judicialisation of Politics in South Africa' (PhD thesis, University of Cape Town, 2021) 82–83.

[51] Hirschl (n 48) 120.

[52] *Simelane* (n 32).

[53] *Helen Suzman Foundation v Minister of Police* 2017 (1) SACR 683 (GP).

[54] Over 30% of the Zondo Commission's report relates to public procurement abuses, a fact acknowledged by the President in his State of the Nation Address in 2024, stateofthenation.gov.za, accessed 21 May 2024.

[55] See especially *Economic Freedom Fighters v Speaker, National Assembly* 2016 (3) SA 580 (CC), handed down during the tenure of Thuli Madonsela (2009–2016), which affirmed the binding nature of the Public Protector's orders.

[56] Busisiwe Mkhwebane was ultimately removed from office in 2023 for incompetence and misconduct. Prominent cases in which her reports were set aside as irrational include *South African Reserve Bank v Public Protector* 2017 (6) SA 198 (GP), *Absa Bank Ltd v Public Protector* [2018] 2 All SA 1 (GP) and *President of the Republic of South Africa v Public Protector* [2020] 2 All SA 865 (GP).

Another area of litigious growth has been 'self-review', where organs of state seek judicial review of their own unlawful decisions on administrative-law grounds. Their motives range from the innocent (a genuine desire to sweep clean) to the shameless, such as the wish to avoid paying for services rendered in good faith under a procurement contract.[57] Administrative law also featured in a slew of cases concerning the general election of 29 May 2024,[58] which lost the ANC its majority for the first time since 1994 and necessitated the formation of a coalition government.

Some of this has clearly been 'bad' lawfare: self-reviews brought cynically to resist a claim for payment or cases launched to toy with the legal process or to score political points. (An example of the latter is the case launched by an opposition party to have the entire national election of May 2024 set aside for vote-rigging and fraud, seemingly without a shred of evidence to back these allegations.[59]) Most of it has probably been 'good' lawfare, even if that is a contradiction in terms for some.[60] The moral quality of the cases may be less important than the sheer number of them, however, for it seems that if there is enough of it, even well-intentioned litigation can have deleterious effects.

## III. Responses and Reverberations

Broadly speaking, over the last 15 years the highest courts[61] have responded to this barrage of litigation by prioritising legality and accountability over certainty and coherence and by making it ever easier for applicants to obtain judicial scrutiny and redress in administrative law.

A significant part of this project has been the expansion of existing grounds of review and the creation of new ones. Early examples are the expansive interpretation of the *Wednesbury* clone, section 6(2)*(h)* of the PAJA, by the Constitutional Court in *Bato Star*[62] and the SCA's development of 'material mistake of fact', aka non-jurisdictional mistake of fact, as a ground of review despite its absence

[57] Boonzaier has drawn attention to the government's 'opportunistic and self-interested' use of judicial review to 'evade, rather than assert, its obligations' by pointing out that those obligations were incurred by its own unlawful conduct: L Boonzaier, 'Good Reviews, Bad Actors: The Constitutional Court's Procedural Drama' (2015) 7 *Constitutional Court Review* 1, 4.

[58] Cases that reached the Constitutional Court were *Electoral Commission of South Africa v Umkhonto Wesizwe Political Party* 2024 (7) BCLR 869 (CC) and *African Congress for Transformation v Electoral Commission of South Africa* [2024] ZACC 7 (20 May 2024).

[59] Having made its point in the court of public opinion, the uMkhonto weSizwe Party withdrew its case in mid-2024. At the time of writing, however, it had mounted another such challenge.

[60] Roux (n 2) is amongst those for whom the term essentially evokes 'an idea of the law being *improperly* used in pursuit of political ends' (at 3).

[61] The Constitutional Court is now the highest court in all matters, while the Supreme Court of Appeal (SCA) is an intermediate court of appeal situated between the High Court and the Constitutional Court.

[62] *Bato Star Fishing (Pty) Ltd v Minister of Environmental Affairs* 2004 (4) SA 490 (CC) ('*Bato Star*'), described more fully in Hoexter (n 28) 169–70.

from the PAJA.[63] In the context of jurisdictional facts, the Constitutional Court unequivocally rejected ipsedixitism more than 15 years ago.[64] More recently, it boldly expanded the scope of error of law, section 6(2)*(d)* of the PAJA, holding this ground to be applicable not only within its traditional remit, the misinterpretation of legislative provisions, but also where the offending decision was based on the judgment of a court, fully binding on the decision-maker at the time, but now seen as wrongly decided.[65]

The highest court has been equally intrepid in the area of procedural fairness. For instance, in *Joseph*[66] it identified a new species of 'public-law right' capable of triggering procedural fairness under section 3(1) of the PAJA, and in *AllPay*[67] it relaxed the requirement of that same provision from 'adversely affected rights' to the mere *capacity* to affect rights. It has also pushed the boundaries of the legitimate expectation doctrine by departing sometimes from the well-established requirements of a promise or a past practice and adopting a much more flexible approach based on the duty to act fairly.[68] And while the court has not yet embraced substantive enforcement of legitimate expectations, it has pioneered an alternative method of enforcing public promises.[69]

That method of enforcement has subsequently been developed into nothing less than a new pathway to judicial review, the public-law claim of unconscionable state conduct, which is said to be based on constitutional rights other than those in section 33.[70] As explained below, the effect is to rescue claims that might otherwise fail on procedural grounds.[71] Other procedural obstacles have been diminished as well. For example, standing in administrative law has been reformed by reading the generous provisions of section 38 of the Constitution[72] into the PAJA.[73] Self-review has burgeoned as a result of the courts' insistence that organs of state are duty-bound to go to court to correct their own unlawful decisions in the public

[63] In a line of cases starting with *Pepcor Retirement Fund v Financial Services Board* 2003 (6) SA 38 (SCA).

[64] *Walele v City of Cape Town* 2008 (1) SA 126 (CC) [60].

[65] *Genesis Medical Aid Scheme v Registrar, Medical Schemes* 2017 (6) SA 1 (CC) [20]–[22].

[66] *Joseph v City of Johannesburg* 2010 (4) SA 55 (CC) [40], [47].

[67] *Allpay Consolidated Investment Holdings (Pty) Ltd v Chief Executive Officer of the South African Social Security Agency (No 1)* 2014 (1) SA 604 (CC) [60].

[68] See especially *SARFU* (n 30) and *MEC for Education, Gauteng Province v Governing Body, Rivonia Primary School* 2013 (6) SA 582 (CC), discussed in C Hoexter, 'The Unruly Horse and the Gordian knot: Legitimate Expectations in South Africa' in M Groves and G Weeks (eds), *Legitimate Expectations in the Common Law World* (Oxford, Hart Publishing, 2017) 165, 173–77.

[69] *KwaZulu-Natal Joint Liaison Committee v MEC for Education, KwaZulu-Natal* 2013 (4) SA 262 (CC) ('*KZN Joint Liaison Committee*') [30]–[33], enforcing a promise of subsidy in approximate amounts. See Hoexter (n 68) 177–87.

[70] *KZN Joint Liaison Committee* (n 69) as explained and elaborated in *Pretorius v Transport Pension Fund* 2019 (2) SA 37 (CC).

[71] See at C.ii below.

[72] Section 38, which governs enforcement of the Bill of Rights, allows inter alia for class actions and public-interest standing.

[73] *Giant Concerts CC v Rinaldo Investments (Pty) Ltd* 2013 (1) BCLR 251 (CC) [29].

interest.[74] In a similar vein, collateral challenge (or indirect review) is now available to organs of state as well as private parties, and indeed 'where justice requires it to be'.[75]

This explosion of administrative law has been exhilarating and sometimes even thrilling. However, there have also been costs attached to all this litigation – quite apart from the burden it must have imposed on courts known to be seriously under-resourced[76] and on judges exhausted by 'crushing workloads' in some divisions.[77] In what follows, three distinct costs are identified of constant lawfare waged in administrative law, whether it be of the 'good' or 'bad' variety. First, and most generally, it has placed unwelcome strain on the courts' relationship with the political branches. Second, it has reinforced and helped to perpetuate the long-standing lack of balance in administrative law, by which is meant the traditional focus of the discipline on court-based relief and the relative neglect of other safeguards and remedies. Third, the coherence of the case law has suffered when the highest court has seemingly pursued the values of legality and accountability at any price.

## A. Strained Relationships

In a pattern familiar enough in adolescent democracies in post-colonial Africa, the courts' constant filling of the accountability vacuum has caused tension in the relationship between the judiciary and the political branches. When judgments have gone against the government in high-profile cases with a strong political flavour, as has frequently happened, there have been cries of 'judicial overreach': the courts have been accused of violating the separation of powers by encroaching on the

[74] See, eg, *Municipal Manager: Qaukeni Local Municipality v FV General Trading CC* 2010 (1) SA 356 (SCA) [23]; *MEC for Health, Eastern Cape v Kirland Investments (Pty) Ltd t/a Eye & Lazer Institute* 2014 (3) SA 481 (CC) [82]. For remarks on the burgeoning of self-review, see *Buffalo City Metropolitan Municipality v Asla Construction (Pty) Ltd* 2019 (4) SA 331 (CC) [111].

[75] *Merafong City v AngloGold Ashanti Ltd* 2017 (2) SA 211 (CC) ('*Merafong*') [55].

[76] See, eg, M Benjamin, 'We Are Woefully Short of Judges' *Groundup* 7 August 2023, www.groundup.org.za and *Interim Report of the Committee on the Rationalisation of Areas Under the Jurisdiction of the Divisions of the High Court of South Africa and Judicial Establishments*, www.justice.gov.za, accessed 18 June 2024. The two divisions of the Gauteng High Court are reported to be especially badly affected by high volumes and a shortage of judges: see R Cokayne, 'Gauteng Civil Justice System in Crisis' *Moneyweb* 25 July 2024, www.moneyweb.co.za, accessed 26 July 2024. The Constitutional Court, too, seems to be struggling with an unmanageable workload. Ally and Boonzaier record that the Court's average processing time almost doubled in the 12-year period 2010–21, a problem they attribute mainly to the increased workload of the Court (which became the highest court in all matters a decade ago) as well as vacancies and absenteeism; see N Ally and L Boonzaier, 'The Constitutional Court's Efficiency: Statistics from the Mogoeng Era, 2010–2021' (2022) 12 *Constitutional Court Review* 317, 322. Nor do conditions seem to have improved since then, for in 2024 the Court set an alarming precedent by handing down its first judgment of the year only in mid-April.

[77] See E Rossouw and S Rothman, 'Job Demands and Job Resources and Well-being of Judges in South Africa' (2020) 46 *SA Journal of Industrial Psychology* 1, 12.

preserve of the political branches.[78] The courts, and sometimes individual judges, have been subjected to extravagant criticism and have been accused of bias and even tyranny against the government.[79]

Of course, reason tells us that finding against the government does not necessarily imply overreach. In the South African context, cases of actual overreach are probably quite rare when one considers the amplitude of the courts' powers in terms of the Constitution.[80] A court would indeed be in breach of an express constitutional duty if, in a proper case, it refused or failed to declare unlawful any law or conduct found to be inconsistent with the Constitution.[81] Accordingly, where judicial overreach does occur, it is more likely to take the form of an order that is vague, overly broad, or that has budgetary implications.[82]

But reasoned responses along these lines seem to have little effect. In most instances one suspects that whether overreach has really occurred in a particular case is immaterial and that the point of the criticism is to make political capital or to discredit and thus delegitimise the judiciary. As Dent describes it, the judicialisation of politics forces an adversarial relationship between the government and the judiciary, and when that relationship breaks down, the courts may be 'exposed to political attack framed in the narrative of judicial aggrandisement and democratic usurpation'.[83] The essential problem is that mud need not be flung in good faith in order to stick, so even unjustified political attacks tend to reduce public faith in the judiciary and detract from its legitimacy. In this way, as has been argued more fully elsewhere,[84] the judiciary inevitably becomes the casualty of a larger political battle.

## B. Perpetuating Lack of Balance in Administrative Law

One of the most notable features of pre-1994 South African administrative law was its incompleteness or lack of balance. As already observed, judicial review operated as almost the sole check on maladministration owing to the paucity of other effective controls on administrative power. In the pre-democratic era, this position became thoroughly entrenched, a given. One indication of this is that when reporting in 1992 on the possibility of the reform of administrative or internal

[78] For a catalogue of such accusations, see C Ramsden *Judicial Overreach* 8 June 2017, a brief written for the Helen Suzman Foundation, www.hsf.org.za, accessed 8 June 2017.

[79] For a detailed account see Dent (n 50) ch 4.

[80] See, eg, W Andrew-Befeld, 'South African Courts: Are They Guilty of Judicial Overreach or Merely Upholding the Rule of Law?' *IOL* 7 September 2021, www.iol.co.za, accessed 25 June 2024.

[81] Constitution, s 172(1)*(a)*: see n 46 above.

[82] For recent illustrations of such orders, see Professor Balthazar, 'In Times of Government Failure, the Danger of Judicial Overreach is Ever Present' *Daily Maverick* 7 December 2023, www.dailymaverick.co.za, accessed 27 May 2024.

[83] n 50, 138–39.

[84] See Corder and Hoexter (n 1) 120–25; Dent (n 50) ch 4; M le Roux and D Davis, *Lawfare: Judging Politics in South Africa* (Johannesburg & Cape Town, Jonathan Ball Publishers, 2019) ch 1.

appeals – reform as badly needed then as it is today[85] – the Law Commission contented itself with proposing the extension and codification of the *grounds of review*.[86] To be fair, considerations such as cost and the likelihood of imminent constitutional change also featured in the Law Commission's reasoning, and the grounds of review could certainly have done with extension; but even so, the proposed solution speaks volumes.

The overreliance on judicial review and the need for additional methods of control were both acknowledged at the Breakwater Workshop of February 1993. This remains the most seminal gathering in the history of South African administrative law, and the manifesto produced by participants at the workshop served almost as an agenda for subsequent reform. 'The Breakwater Declaration: Administrative Law for a Future South Africa' recorded that our administrative law suffered from a 'retrospective focus' as a result of its almost exclusive focus on court-based remedies and called for the creation of 'procedures and structures which will foster good decision-making'.[87] It recommended safeguards such as effective parliamentary control over delegated power, participatory rulemaking and decision-making procedures, reason-giving, access to official information, and the proper training of public officials.[88] The 'need for and the design of administrative appeals, internal or external' also featured, if only at the top of a list of 'Areas requiring further consideration'.

In short, the Breakwater Declaration saw clearly what the Law Commission did not: that administrative accountability was unlikely to be achieved by reliance on judicial review alone. A range of other devices, including political and administrative safeguards, was needed to complement judicial review and to make up for its inherent limitations (its focus on legality rather than the merits) and disadvantages. Amongst other drawbacks, review is undeniably backward-looking, unsystematic, slow and expensive.[89]

While there has unfortunately been no methodical reform of internal appeals, most of the other Breakwater recommendations became a reality after 1994 – at least on paper. The problem has been the implementation of the non-curial safeguards that form part of our integrity and accountability system. Some devices, such as ministerial responsibility and parliamentary scrutiny of delegated legislation, have proved weak in practice;[90] and one of the most promising, the office of Public Protector, has too often failed to exhibit independence and impartiality. So

[85] See Corder (n 11) 337.

[86] South African Law Commission, *Report* (Project 24) (1992) 50, and for a full account see Corder ibid 334–37.

[87] Item (ii) of the 'Points of departure'. Together with papers from the workshop, the Breakwater Declaration was reproduced in [1993] *Acta Juridica* 18–20 and republished in TW Bennett and H Corder (eds), *Administrative Law Reform* (Cape Town, Juta & Co, Ltd, 1993) 18–20.

[88] Breakwater Declaration, ibid 18.

[89] See C Hoexter, 'The Future of Judicial Review in South African Administrative Law' (2000) 117 *South African Law Journal* 484, 488–94.

[90] See C Hoexter and G Penfold, *Administrative Law in South Africa*, 3rd edn (Cape Town, Juta & Co Ltd, 2021) 97–100.

far the only really effective incumbent has been the unflinching Thuli Madonsela, whose seven-year term of office ended in October 2016. Her successor was ignominiously removed from office in 2023, shortly before the end of her term, on the grounds of misconduct and incompetence.

But even Madonsela's recommendations were sometimes ignored and had to be enforced by the courts.[91] Other mechanisms, too, have continued to depend on the courts for their effectiveness, thus reinforcing and perpetuating the tradition of reliance mainly on court-based remedies. For instance, widespread non-compliance with the Promotion of Access to Information Act 2 of 2000 (PAIA) meant that judicial intervention was constantly required to enforce its provisions against incapable or recalcitrant information officers. In the hope of addressing this problem, recent amendments to the PAIA confer a range of functions on a new Information Regulator and empower it to deal with complaints against information officers.[92] The effectiveness of this reform has yet to be assessed.

What does seem clear is that in the space of 30 years, the presence of a wide range of alternative public-law safeguards has done little to change the South African reflex of turning to the courts. As Corder puts it, judicial review 'has, if anything, gained a greater share of the administrative justice field than before'.[93] And, like Corder, I wonder whether the Constitutional Court's constant 'pushing [of] the boundaries of judicial review' has had something to do with it.[94]

## C. Legality at Any Price?

Judicial lawmaking is best undertaken slowly and cautiously, in small increments over long periods, to allow plenty of time for reflection and for making slight adjustments along the way.[95] Operating under extreme pressure and with constrained human resources, as the South African courts have been doing for years, is bound to tell in the case law. As illustrated above, in their determination to defend the rule of law, the two highest courts have expanded the reach of administrative law in bursts of remarkable judicial creativity, with some invigorating results. However, in the Constitutional Court at least, this pressure seems also to have encouraged an increasingly ad-hoc style of adjudication and a somewhat more erratic and contradictory jurisprudence in which principle and precedent, and even the PAJA, have sometimes been sacrificed to expediency. The examples below indicate that the tendency has been especially noticeable in the court's engagement with legality review. This is hardly surprising, as the procedural advantages and infinitely

[91] See especially *EFF v Speaker, NA* (n 55).

[92] Chapter 1A, inserted by the Protection of Personal Information Act 4 of 2013, s 110 with effect from 30 June 2021.

[93] Corder (n 11) 331.

[94] ibid.

[95] See, eg, D Gibson, 'Judges as Legislators: Not Whether but How' (1987) 25 *Alberta Law Review* 249.

flexible content of the judge-made principle of legality would be a temptation to any court – let alone one that is said to have a predilection for outcomes-based[96] and result-driven[97] reasoning.

## *i. Scope and Content of Rationality*

The legality principle can easily be made to mean whatever the court wants it to mean in a particular case. This plasticity has been a boon, especially to a result-driven court, but in recent years it has not necessarily served to enhance the coherence of the highest court's jurisprudence. While the early development of the principle of legality was unproblematic, the later elaboration of 'legality rationality' by the Constitutional Court has given rise to some sharply divergent and even contradictory judgments in the context of powers of an 'executive' nature.

Today it is very difficult to predict what level and form of rationality will be required, as the guidance given by the highest court ranges from the highly interventionist approach of the *Simelane* case[98] to the highly deferential majority judgment in *Electronic Media Network Ltd v e.tv*.[99] Both cases deal with policy-laden powers of an executive nature, but one tells us that rationality in that context demands the same standard as rationality applied to administrative action (rationality 'does not conceive of different thresholds' in different contexts),[100] while the other says repressively that rationality is not a 'master key that opens every and any door' and that it is to be applied 'cautiously'.[101] Even more confusing is the contradiction within the *Simelane* judgment itself, for the Court's assertion that 'a rationality standard by its very nature prescribes the lowest possible threshold for the validity of executive decisions'[102] seems incongruent with the notion that rationality 'does not conceive of different thresholds' – and with the Court's daring expansion of rationality doctrine in that case.[103]

A related issue is the inclusion of aspects of procedural fairness under the banner of 'legality rationality'. This is a theme on which the Constitutional Court executed several about-turns in its treatment of powers of an executive nature, and without ever acknowledging contradictions in its jurisprudence. In *Masetlha*,[104] a

[96] S Woolman, 'The Amazing, Vanishing Bill of Rights' (2007) 124 *South African Law Journal* 762.

[97] H Scott, 'The Death of Doctrine? Private Law Scholarship in South Africa Today' in J Basedow, H Fleischer and R Zimmermann (eds), *Legislators, Judges, and Professors* (Tübingen, Mohr Siebeck, 2016) 223. The case of *Chirwa v Transnet Ltd* 2008 (4) SA 367 (CC) offers a striking example of such reasoning in relation to s 33 and the PAJA. See C Hoexter, 'The Importance of Dissent: Two Judgments in Administrative Law' [2015] *Acta Juridica* 120, 123–33.

[98] n 32.

[99] *Electronic Media Network Ltd v e.tv* 2017 (9) BCLR 1108 (CC).

[100] *Simelane* (n 32) [44].

[101] *Electronic Media Network v e.tv* (n 99) [6].

[102] *Simelane* (n 32) [42].

[103] See L Kohn, 'The Burgeoning Constitutional Requirement of Rationality and the Separation of Powers: Has Rationality Review Gone Too Far?' (2013) 130 *South African Law Journal* 810, 835.

[104] *Masetlha v President of the Republic of South Africa* 2008 (1) SA 566 (CC) ('*Masetlha*') [77].

case concerning the 'executive' dismissal of the head of the National Intelligence Agency, the Court said unequivocally that it would be inappropriate to constrain executive power to requirements of procedural fairness. A couple of years later, in *Albutt*,[105] the Court performed a volte-face by subjecting a pre-eminently 'executive' pardoning power to procedural fairness – briefly footnoting *Masetlha* but making no attempt to distinguish that case. Not long afterwards, in *ARMSA*,[106] the Court was concerned with an executive decision about the remuneration of magistrates. Here the Court reverted to the *Masetlha* approach to executive powers, adding that a procedural fairness challenge was 'not competent' under the principle of legality.[107] Even more remarkably, while it referred to *Albutt* on other points, the court in *ARMSA* omitted to mention that a procedural fairness challenge had succeeded in that very case under the selfsame principle. In *Motau*[108] the court admitted that procedural fairness might indeed apply to executive powers under the legality principle and reproached commentators for taking the statement in *Masetlha* too literally.

These contradictions were eventually resolved in *Law Society*,[109] another politically fraught case in which the Court set aside decisions of President Zuma that undermined the functioning of the SADC Tribunal.[110] Here the Court distinguished between 'procedural rationality' and 'procedural fairness' and defined the latter narrowly to exclude consultation or hearings directed at enhancing the rationality of a decision. The distinction is an unfortunate one, however, to the extent that it classifies decisions attracting hearings or consultation in an either/or manner as having to do primarily or exclusively with either procedural rationality or procedural fairness. In practice, these ingredients tend to enhance *both* rationality and fairness.[111] What is worse, the distinction made in *Law Society* contradicts the Court's own previous dicta that established rationality as one of the two main rationales for procedural fairness.[112]

[105] n 33; *Masetlha* (n 104) is footnoted at [73] fn 59.

[106] *Association of Regional Magistrates of Southern Africa v President of the Republic of South Africa* 2013 (7) BCLR 762 (CC) ('*ARMSA*').

[107] ibid [59].

[108] *Minister of Defence and Military Veterans v Motau* 2014 (5) SA 69 (CC) ('*Motau*') [81].

[109] n 33, [64].

[110] The Tribunal of the Southern African Development Community was rendered dysfunctional by the refusal of leaders in the region, including Zuma, to appoint or reappoint Tribunal members; and by Zuma's signing of a 2014 Protocol that stripped the Tribunal of its jurisdiction over individual disputes, including human rights violations.

[111] Hoexter and Penfold (n 90) 575. For further criticism see W Freedman and N Mzolo, 'The Principle of Legality and the Requirements of Lawfulness and Procedural Rationality: *Law Society of South Africa v President of the RSA* (2019 (3) SA 30 (CC))' (2021) 42 *Obiter* 421, 429–30. *Cf* N Ally and MJ Murcott, 'Beyond Labels: Executive Action and the Duty to Consult' (2023) 27 *Law, Democracy and Development* 93, 103–104, who offer a partial defence of the Court's approach.

[112] See *De Lange v Smuts NO* 1998 (3) SA 785 (CC) [131]; *Janse van Rensburg NO v Minister of Trade and Industry NO* 2001 (1) SA 29 (CC) [24]; *Masetlha* (n 104) [184]; *Psychological Society of South Africa v Qwelane* 2017 (8) BCLR 1039 (CC) [24].

### *ii. Promotion of Other Pathways at the Expense of the PAJA*

The judge-made legality principle is attractive on account of the flexibility of its content as well as the more indulgent procedures associated with it. The PAJA, a statute, is far less manipulable. However, the PAJA is the main avenue to judicial review in administrative law because it was enacted in response to a constitutional mandate to give effect to the administrative-justice rights in section 33 of the Constitution.

Two decades ago, at a time of greater jurisprudential stability, the Constitutional Court sought to protect the PAJA and uphold its status. In particular, the Court made it clear that where the PAJA was of application, the statute could not legitimately be sidestepped by purported reliance on the common law or on section 33 itself as pathways to review.[113] It was not entirely clear, however, whether this also ruled out reliance on the principle of legality *where the PAJA was or might be applicable*, which is to say in cases involving administrative action or conduct not yet classified as non-administrative action. This lack of clarity led to widespread avoidance of the PAJA for several years, during which the Constitutional Court kept silent about the practice and seemed to ignore its dangers – effectively leaving the courts free to sidestep the PAJA when it suited them. Then, in its unanimous 2010 judgment in *Albutt*,[114] the Court engaged in the most blatant and unashamed kind of PAJA-avoidance. Given that the case could be resolved on the legality principle, Ngcobo CJ characterised the administrative action inquiry as 'ancillary' and went so far as to criticise the High Court for having 'reached' this liminal question unnecessarily.[115]

The PAJA would soon have become redundant on this extreme approach, and the Court seemed eventually to repent it. A few years later it mentioned briefly, by way of a footnote, that the correct order of inquiry is to consider first whether the PAJA is applicable and only then to consider what is required by more general principles such as the rule of law.[116] This unobtrusive bit of guidance had little effect, however: litigants continued to sidestep the PAJA and most courts continued to allow it. More prominent statements of the orthodoxy have appeared since,[117] perhaps in response to commentary pointing out that PAJA-avoidance offends against the logic of constitutional subsidiarity and that neither the legislature nor the drafters of the Constitution could possibly have contemplated the

[113] In *Bato Star* (n 62) [20]–[27] and *Minister of Health v New Clicks South Africa (Pty) Ltd* 2006 (2) SA 311 (CC) [92]–[97].

[114] n 33.

[115] ibid [80]–[84].

[116] *Motau* (n 108) [27] fn 28.

[117] See, eg, *Hunter v Financial Sector Conduct Authority* 2018 (6) SA 348 (CC) [38]; *Notyawa v Makana Municipality* (2020) 41 *ILJ* 1069 (CC) [38].

redundancy of constitutionally mandated legislation.[118] But orthodoxy was abandoned in *Gijima*[119] in the context of self-review.

In this case the State Information Technology Agency (SITA) had awarded a contract to the respondent company, Gijima, outside of the authorised public procurement framework. About 22 months later, a dispute about payment inspired SITA to go to court to have its own decision reviewed for unlawfulness. Though the decision was clearly a piece of administrative action, SITA argued that it was entitled to proceed by way of the legality principle, a pathway more forgiving of delay than the PAJA. The issue of PAJA-avoidance thus arose squarely and was argued fully. Both the High Court[120] and a majority of the SCA[121] held that litigants are not entitled to bypass the PAJA in favour of a more general safety net or measure of last resort. Indeed, SITA's unreasonable and unexplained delay meant that it would have been non-suited even on legality review.[122]

On further appeal, however, the Constitutional Court found a way around the applicability of the PAJA in a case of self-review (and, as will be seen, the delay problem). It reasoned unanimously that since human beings are the beneficiaries of the section 33 rights and organs of state are the duty-bearers, the PAJA is not ordinarily available to organs of state when seeking review of their own decisions[123] – notwithstanding the clear legislative intention to bring under section 6(1) of the statute 'any person' seeking judicial review. The result was that organs of state seeking self-review were now *obliged* to proceed by way of the (procedurally more indulgent) principle of legality. Two possible exceptions were suggested:[124] where the organ purported to be acting in the public interest or where it was challenging the decision of another organ of state and thus in a position 'akin to' a beneficiary.

The reasoning in *Gijima* has been subjected to considerable criticism. Apart from the contrariness of making the appropriate pathway to review depend on the identity of the applicant, critics have also pointed out that section 38 of the Constitution makes it unnecessary for the applicant to be the beneficiary or right-holder;[125] that organs of state will almost inevitably be acting in the public interest

[118] See, eg, M Murcott and W Van der Westhuizen, 'The Ebb and Flow of the Application of the Principle of Subsidiarity: Critical Reflections on *Motau* and *My Vote Counts*' (2015) 7 *Constitutional Court Review* 43; R Henrico, 'Subverting the Promotion of Administrative Justice Act in Judicial Review: The Cause of Much Uncertainty in South African Administrative Law' [2018] *Journal of South African Law* 288. Remarkably, however, in *South African Human Rights Commission obo South African Jewish Board of Deputies v Masuku* 2022 (4) SA 1 (CC) ('*Masuku*') [114] the Court defended its approach in *Albutt* (n 33) as 'entirely sagacious'.

[119] *State Information Technology Agency Soc Ltd v Gijima Holdings (Pty) Ltd (Gijima)* 2018 (2) SA 23 (CC) ('*Gijima*').

[120] *State Information Technology Agency Soc Ltd v Gijima Holdings (Pty) Ltd* [2015] ZAGPPHC 1079 (18 May 2015) [28].

[121] *Gijima* SCA (n 35) [44]. The minority saw this as 'slavish adherence to formalism': ibid [55].

[122] ibid [44].

[123] *Gijima* (n 119) [35] and [38]–[40].

[124] ibid [2].

[125] L Boonzaier, 'A Decision to Undo' (2018) 135 *South African Law Journal* 642, 644–65.

when they seek self-review;[126] and that on the Court's own logic, organs of state can never be in a position 'akin to' that of a beneficiary.[127] It need hardly be added that the judgment's promotion of the legality principle detracts from the PAJA, which was constitutionally envisaged as governing the review of *all* administrative action and which had up to then been used for self-reviews of such action.

Another such detraction, though perhaps a more defensible one, occurred in the *Ledla* case,[128] in which the Constitutional Court found that an anti-corruption court, the Special Tribunal, enjoyed review jurisdiction – not under the PAJA, but under the legality principle. The PAJA could not apply, the Court found, because the Special Tribunal did not fall within the PAJA's definition of 'tribunal': 'any independent and impartial tribunal established by national legislation for the purposes of judicially reviewing an administrative action in terms of this Act'. Adopting an entirely literal approach, the Court did not pause to consider whether the Special Tribunal might be brought under that definition; it was enough that the Special Tribunal had been established under legislation that predated the PAJA.

The Court's earlier creation of a public-law claim of unconscionable state conduct also detracts from the PAJA, even though the public-law claim is said to be based on constitutional rights other than those in section 33.[129] In truth, the claim invites avoidance of the PAJA more obviously than the legality principle does. Whereas legality review was originally conceived as a safety net for cases in which the PAJA was not applicable, the public-law claim was conceived in a case that ought to have been but was not argued under the PAJA: a point made by the Court itself.[130] To be blunt, the successful outcome effectively rewarded the applicant's PAJA-avoidance.[131] Confusingly, too, the public-law claim closely resembles administrative-law review and is based on concepts that resonate with the legality principle as well as with administrative law more generally: reliance, accountability and rationality.[132] As for the notion that section 33 rights are not implicated, that is easily said. Even in cases that plainly do implicate administrative justice, one or more of the other 26 constitutional guarantees almost always feature alongside the section 33 rights, so it is temptingly simple to characterise any case of administrative justice as a claim based on another right.[133]

[126] Hoexter and Penfold (n 90) 693–94; R Cachalia, 'Resuscitating the PAJA in State Self-Reviews?' (2022) 38 *South African Journal on Human Rights* 70.

[127] This exception was indeed ruled out as illogical in *Mapholisa NO v Phetoe NO* 2023 (3) SA 149 (SCA) [18]–[19].

[128] *Ledla Structural Development (Pty) Ltd v Special Investigating Unit* 2023 (2) SACR 1 (CC) [53]–[70].

[129] *KZN Joint Liaison Committee* (n 69) as elaborated in *Pretorius v Transport Pension Fund* (n 70).

[130] *KZN Joint Liaison Committee*, ibid [30]–[33].

[131] In *Masuku* (n 118) [115] the Court denied having ignored the PAJA in *KZN Joint Liaison Committee* and explained that it had merely opted 'to dispose of the matter before deciding whether [PAJA] even applied'. While that description is not quite accurate, it does seem a useful definition of PAJA-avoidance.

[132] *KZN Joint Liaison Committee* (n 69) [62]–[66].

[133] See further C Hoexter, 'Courageous Creativity and Anti-Formalism in Administrative Law: Notable Contributions from the Jurisprudence of Johan Froneman' (2022) 12 *Constitutional Court Review* 121, 128.

These episodes seem to demonstrate an increasing willingness on the part of the highest court to undermine the PAJA in the course of upholding lawfulness and dispensing justice. To say the least, the Court seems uncertain whether administrative justice will be best served by 'embracing' the PAJA or 'sidelining' it.[134]

## *iii. The Volte-Face on Delay*

The *Gijima* matter, discussed above, also featured an abrupt about-turn in the doctrine governing the consequences of undue delay. Up to then, even in a legality review, an unreasonably tardy application would be refused in the absence of factors allowing condonation of the delay, and the impugned decision would stand. In the leading case on delay in legality review, *Khumalo*,[135] the Court found that an unexplained delay of about 20 months could not be condoned, and it ruled that the self-review ought not to have been entertained by the court a quo.

The judgment of the Constitutional Court in *Gijima*[136] broke this pattern too. The applicant, SITA, had allowed 22 months to elapse before it sought review of its own decision to award a contract to Gijima. This was found to be an unreasonably long delay, and the Court could find 'no possible basis' on which to exercise its discretion to overlook or condone it.[137] That ought to have been the end of the matter. However, the Court had already accepted[138] that in the absence of a competitive bidding process, the award of the contract must have been unconstitutional; and it went ahead and declared SITA's decision invalid. It reasoned simply that, delay or no, section 172(1)*(a)* of the Constitution *obliges* a court to declare invalid any law or conduct that it finds to be inconsistent with the Constitution.[139] The Court thus treated this constitutional duty as absolute even though it had, just a year earlier, confirmed in *Tasima*[140] that undue delay effectively barred the application of 172(1)*(a)*.

In short, the normal and well-established consequences of unreasonable delay did not follow. Instead of non-suiting the applicant, in *Gijima* the Court entertained the merits and granted the applicant relief in the form of a declaration of invalidity. It was at the point of remedy that the delay became relevant, together with the fact that SITA had repeatedly assured Gijima that it had not breached procurement law when awarding it the contract. The Court pointed out that section 172(1)*(b)* of the Constitution grants remedial discretion 'bounded only by considerations of justice

[134] G Quinot and E van der Sijde, 'Opening at the Close: Clarity from the Constitutional Court on the Legal Cause of Action and Regulatory Framework for an Organ of State Seeking to Review its Own Decisions?' 2019 *Journal of South African Law* 324, 333.

[135] *Khumalo v MEC for Education, KwaZulu-Natal* 2014 (5) SA 579 (CC) [69].

[136] n 119.

[137] ibid [49], particularly given the higher duty on the state to comply with the law and follow due process: see *Kirland* (n 74) [82].

[138] This, too, was unusual, as the applicant did very little to discharge the burden of establishing unlawfulness.

[139] *Gijima* (n 119) [52].

[140] *Department of Transport v Tasima (Pty) Ltd* 2017 (2) SA 622 (CC) [144]. See also *Merafong* (n 75) [37].

and equity'.[141] Taking the delay and the false assurances into account, the Court stipulated that the invalidity of the contract would not divest Gijima of any of the rights it would otherwise have been entitled to under the contract; and it awarded Gijima all its costs, including the costs of two counsel.[142]

This unprecedented treatment of delay was heralded by the Court's leaving the issue, a quintessentially liminal one, to a late stage in its judgment. At that point it asked: 'What impact, if any, should this delay have?'[143] More than anything else in *Gijima*, that question – a wholly novel one at the time – suggested a whatever-it-takes approach. In its determination to do justice, the Court seemed to claim what Woolman had earlier described as 'licence to decide [any] case as it pleases, unmoored from its own precedent', and to 'sit as a court of equity'.[144]

# IV. Conclusion

This chapter, written in honour of Professor Matthew Groves, resonates with themes in his published work. It has explored the long South African tradition of over-reliance on administrative-law review. A way of compensating for the paucity of other safeguards and of vindicating the rule of law in the pre-democratic era, judicial review in administrative law confounded expectations by becoming even more prominent after 1994 – and still more so with the migration of politics to the courts after 2009. As illustrated in this chapter, the courts have pushed the boundaries of South African administrative law in remarkable ways over the last decade and a half. Some of the effects of the orgy of judicial lawmaking have been exhilarating, for inventive judicial elaboration of grounds of review and many other reforms have served to promote the rule of law and advance the accountability of public actors.

However, the courts' constant filling of an accountability vacuum has had negative effects as well. It has placed strain on the relationship between the judiciary and the other branches of government while perpetuating the longstanding lack of balance in South African administrative law. Finally, as illustrated by examples drawn from the jurisprudence of the Constitutional Court, its prioritising of legality and accountability over other values has encouraged a more erratic and contradictory jurisprudence and has detracted from the coherence of administrative-law doctrine. This is especially obvious in the highest court's engagement with its own creation, the constitutional principle of legality. Here the temptations of indulgent procedures and malleable content seem to have been irresistible, increasingly leading the court to undermine a constitutionally mandated statute that it once sought to protect.

[141] *Gijima* (n 119) [53].
[142] ibid [54]–[55].
[143] ibid [42].
[144] Woolman (n 96) 763.

# 13

# Civilian or Military Justice? Dealing with Criminal Offences of Defence Force Members

ALISON DUXBURY AND RAIN LIIVOJA*

## I. Introduction

In November 2020, the Inspector-General of the Australian Defence Force released the report of a four-year inquiry into allegations of war crimes committed by members of the Australian Defence Force (ADF) in Afghanistan.[1] The inquiry found that there was 'credible information' to substantiate the unlawful killing of 39 people by Australian Special Forces, including the Special Air Service (SAS), while deployed as part of the International Security Assistance Force.[2] Notably, Major General Paul Brereton, a judge of the Supreme Court of New South Wales who led the inquiry, recommended that any criminal investigation and prosecution of these alleged war crimes should be undertaken by the Australian Federal Police and the Commonwealth Director of Public Prosecutions, rather than by military authorities.[3] The reasons for this preference included the fact that some alleged perpetrators were no longer serving in the ADF, that a single agency should be responsible for any criminal investigations, and that it would potentially avoid 'any arguable constitutional complication', such as the requirement for trial by jury under section 80 of the Commonwealth Constitution.[4]

* We presented an earlier version of this chapter at the International Military Justice Forum organised by the Saint-Cyr Military Academy on 18–19 November 2021. We are grateful to Associate Professor Rebecca Ananian-Welsh, Professor Jeremy Gans, Air Commodore Ian Henderson and Wing Commander Joshua Liddy for discussing different aspects of this chapter with us. Any opinions and inaccuracies are our own.

[1] Inspector-General of the Australian Defence Force, 'Inspector-General of the Australian Defence Force Afghanistan Inquiry Report' (November 2020), available at www.defence.gov.au/about/reviews-inquiries/afghanistan-inquiry ('Brereton Report').

[2] ibid 28–29.

[3] ibid 171 (Recommendation 20).

[4] ibid.

Australia is not the only state that has faced difficult choices regarding the appropriate avenue for dealing with well-publicised allegations of criminal activity by members of defence forces. In November 2021, following damning reports of sexual abuse in the Canadian Armed Forces (CAF), Anita Anand, the (then) Canadian Defence Minister, announced that allegations of sexual assault and sexual misconduct involving CAF members would be moved to the civilian justice system, at least on an interim basis.[5] Following this announcement, Louise Arbour, a prominent human rights lawyer and a former justice of the Supreme Court of Canada, concluded her review of the Canadian Department of National Defence and CAF, and recommended that 'sexual offences should be removed from the jurisdiction of the CAF'.[6] Arbour favoured civilian prosecution in all cases, with investigations led by the civilian police where the offence takes place in Canada, while maintaining a role for the military police in safeguarding evidence and commencing an investigation where the offence occurs outside Canada.[7] Arbour's recommendation to favour civilian investigations and prosecutions was the result of concerns regarding the independence of the Canadian Forces National Investigation Service and the Canadian Military Police in relation to sexual offences.[8] These two examples suffice to make the point that, in some instances, states have a choice as to whether to investigate and prosecute a defence force member through the civilian justice system or the military justice system.

The aim of this chapter is to identify and analyse the key factors that contribute to this choice. As is the case with much of Matthew Groves' work on military justice,[9] this chapter will draw mainly on the Australian experience while also highlighting relevant factors in other states where there are separate military justice systems. The specific question under consideration in this chapter – 'should a particular allegation be investigated and tried within the military or civilian justice system?' – only arises where a choice is available. Where a distinct military justice system exists, a conflict of jurisdiction can arise: the military may claim jurisdiction over a matter that would otherwise be dealt with by the civilian system, or the civilian

[5] P Zimonjic, 'Defence Minister Anand moving military sexual misconduct cases into civilian justice system', *CBC News*, 4 November 2021, available at www.cbc.ca/news/politics/anita-anand-arbour-justice-1.6236969.

[6] L Arbour, *Report of the Independent External Comprehensive Review of the Department of National Defence and the Canadian Armed Forces* (20 May 2022), 103 (Recommendation 5), available at www.canada.ca/en/department-national-defence/corporate/reports-publications/report-of-the-independent-external-comprehensive-review.html.

[7] ibid.

[8] ibid 84–87. In 2024, legislation was introduced into the Canadian Parliament to implement the Arbour Report's recommendations: M Brewster, 'Ottawa moves to strip military of power to investigate sexual offences', 21 March 2024, *CBC News*, available at www.cbc.ca/news/politics/canadian-armed-forces-sexual-misconduct-assault-1.7151080.

[9] See, eg, M Groves, 'The Use of Criminal Law Principles in Military Discipline: *Chief of General Staff v Stuart* (1995) 133 ALR 523' (1997) 23 *Monash Law Review* 456; M Groves, 'The Civilianisation of Australian Military Law' (2005) 28 *University of New South Wales Law Journal* 264; M Groves, 'Military Justice, its Punishments and the Constitution' (2011) 35 *Criminal Law Journal* 265.

justice system may claim authority over a crime committed in the military context (for example, a war crime). However, separate military courts and tribunals are not without their critics. Part II will examine some of the debates about the design and legitimacy of military justice systems. Part III of this chapter articulates, by reference to the nature of offences and the ambit of the law, when a conflict of jurisdiction with the civilian system arises and, conversely, when it does not arise. The last substantive parts of the chapter consider how a conflict of jurisdiction is resolved. Part IV identifies the procedural mechanisms, in particular formalised protocols or arrangements between civilian and military law enforcement authorities. Part V considers the factors that contribute to the choice of avenue for investigation and prosecution of offences in the military context, including the perceived public interest in a matter and allocation of resources between military and civilian authorities.

## II. Separate Military Justice Systems

States take different approaches to addressing the misconduct of defence force members rising to the level of criminal behaviour. As Matthew Groves and one of the authors of this chapter noted in their co-edited book, *Military Justice in the Modern Age*:

> In some states, separate regimes (including distinct courts or courts martial) have been established to deal with violations committed by members of the armed forces and civilians who are associated with the military. Such violations may include offences against the ordinary criminal law as well as specific offences known only to the military (eg disobeying a superior order). In other situations, states deal these offences within their ordinary civilian criminal justice systems.[10]

Separate military justice systems, in particular military courts and courts martial, have their defenders and detractors. Those who support the existence of a parallel military justice system highlight the unique purpose of military justice (to maintain discipline and morale in the defence force) as well as the practicalities (for example, the need for the justice system to be deployable when the military is on operations abroad).[11] They also point to commanders' obligations to ensure compliance with the law of armed conflict.[12] Critics raise concerns regarding the independence and impartiality of military courts and tribunals from the executive branch of government and query their compliance with the right to a fair trial in

[10] M Groves and A Duxbury, 'The Reform of Military Justice' in A Duxbury and M Groves (eds), *Military Justice in the Modern Age* (Cambridge, Cambridge University Press, 2016) 1, 2.

[11] See, eg, MR Gibson, 'International Human Rights Law and the Administration of Justice through Military Tribunals: Preserving Utility while Precluding Impunity' (2008) 4 *Journal of International Law and International Relations* 1, 8–13.

[12] V Hansen, 'The Impact of Military Justice Reforms on the Law of Armed Conflict: How to Avoid Unintended Consequences' in Duxbury and Groves (n 10) 106.

human rights law in individual states.[13] Some of these concerns relate to particular aspects of the system, for example, if jurisdiction over civilians is asserted by a military court or tribunal,[14] or they emanate from the perception that military judicial institutions are not independent or impartial from the executive branch of government.[15]

Such concerns have driven international efforts to articulate basic standards of military justice. Two sets of principles have been drafted: one by Emmanuel Decaux, as a Special Rapporteur of the Sub-Commission on the Promotion and Protection of Human Rights (the 'Decaux Principles'),[16] and the other by an expert group convened by the Commonwealth Secretariat (the 'Draft Commonwealth Principles').[17] Both sets of principles emphasise that military tribunals ('when they exist') should be a part of the 'general judicial system'.[18] Both also highlight the need for personnel within the system to be impartial: the Draft Commonwealth Principles state that judges (and prosecutors) must be free from command interference and perceived or actual bias, while the Decaux Principles require military judges to have 'a status guaranteeing their independence and impartiality'.[19] The Decaux Principles also state that military judges should have received the same legal training as other judges.[20] According to both sets of Principles, defendants must be accorded rights of due process, including the presumption of innocence.[21] These Principles reinforce the findings of national and regional courts charged with hearing cases that have challenged the legality of military justice systems on the basis of human rights standards, including the right to a fair trial.[22]

[13] See, eg, R Naluwairo, 'Military Courts and Human Rights: A Critical Analysis of the Compliance of Uganda's Military Justice with the Right to an Independent and Impartial Tribunal' (2012) 12 *African Human Rights Law Journal* 448; *Report of the Special Rapporteur on the Independence of Judges and Lawyers*, UN Doc A/68/285 (7 August 2013).

[14] See, eg, DE Stigall, 'An Unnecessary Convenience: The Assertion of the Uniform Code of Military Justice ("UCMJ") over Civilians and the Implications of International Human Rights Law' (2009) 17 *Cardozo Journal of International and Comparative Law* 39; R Liivoja, 'Trying Civilian Contractors in Military Courts: A Necessary Evil?' in Duxbury and Groves (n 10) 81.

[15] In 2024, arguments about the independence and impartiality of military judges were raised in the highest courts of two countries: *R v Edwards* [2024] SCC 15 ('*Edwards*') (Supreme Court of Canada) and *Lieutenant Colonel K O'Brien N.O v Minister of Defence and Military Affairs (and others)* Case CCT 14/23 (20 December 2024) ('*O'Brien*) (Constitutional Court of South Africa).

[16] Civil and Political Rights, including the Question of Independence of the Judiciary, Administration of Justice, Impunity: Issue of the Administration of Justice through Military Tribunals, Report submitted by the Special Rapporteur of the Sub-Commission on the Promotion and Protection of Human Rights, Emmanual Decaux, 13 January 2006, E/CN.4/2006/58 ('Decaux Principles').

[17] Commonwealth Military Justice Principles: The Stellenbosch Draft, 7 November 2023 ('Draft Commonwealth Principles'), Principle 1, available at thecommonwealth.org/news/transformative-military-justice-principles-envisioned-experts-across-commonwealth.

[18] 'Decaux Principles' (n 16) Principle 1; 'Draft Commonwealth Principles' (n 17) Principle 1.

[19] 'Draft Commonwealth Principles' (n 17) Principles 2 and 5; 'Decaux Principles' (n 16) Principle 13.

[20] 'Decaux Principles' (n 16) Principle 13 [47].

[21] 'Decaux Principles' (n 16) Principle 15; 'Draft Commonwealth Principles' (n 17) Principle 7.

[22] Such cases have been very prominent in Canada and the European Court of Human Rights. They include *R v Généreux* [1992] 1 SCR 259 ('*Généreux*'); *Edwards* (n 15); *Findlay v United Kingdom* (1977) 24 EHRR 221 ('*Findlay*'); *Hood v United Kingdom* (2000) 29 EHRR 365; *Morris v United Kingdom* (2002) 34 EHRR 52; *Martin v United Kingdom* (2007) 44 EHRR 31 ('*Martin*'). Recent cases

International efforts to reform military justice reflect a growing push to 'civilianise' military law – a process that Groves has described as 'the incorporation of the institutions and norms of the civilian legal system into military law.'[23] In Australia, the move to reduce command influence on prosecutorial discretion and increase the level of expertise in the military trial process led to the creation of the offices of the Director of Military Prosecutions (DMP) and the Registrar of Military Justice (RMJ).[24] These 2005 changes to the Australian military justice system reflected the recommendations of a 2001 inquiry into military justice in the ADF led by James Burchett.[25] While acknowledging that there is no federal Bill of Rights in Australia, Burchett's report refers to cases in the Supreme Court of Canada and the European Court of Human Rights where arguments were raised in terms of the right to fair trial in the Canadian Charter of Rights and Freedoms and the European Convention on Human Rights respectively, to bolster his conclusion that 'the essential principles are no less important in Australia than they are overseas'.[26]

In addition to the introduction of these roles, another reform designed to increase the independence and impartiality of Australia's military justice system was the establishment, in 2007, of a new permanent military court, the Australian Military Court (AMC), to replace the system of courts martial and Defence Force magistrates in the Defence Force Discipline Act 1982 (Cth) (DFDA).[27] The AMC was created outside the federal judicial system in Chapter III of the Australian Constitution and was staffed by judges with military knowledge but without the security of tenure afforded to federal judges in section 72 of the Australian Constitution.[28] However, the AMC had a limited lifespan – by August 2009, in the case of *Lane v Morrison*, the High Court of Australia had declared it

in other jurisdictions include *O'Brien*, above n 15; *Attorney-General v Hon Michael A Kabaziguruka* Constitutional Appeal No 02 of 2021 (31 January 2025) (Supreme Court of Uganda).

[23] Groves, 'The Civilianisation of Australian Military Law' (n 9) 366–367. See also CP Waters, 'Is the Military Legally Encircled?' (2008) 8 *Defence Studies* 26; GR Rubin, 'United Kingdom Military Law: Autonomy, Civilianisation, Juridification' (2002) 65 *Modern Law Review* 36.

[24] Defence Legislation Amendment Act (No 2) 2005 (Cth).

[25] J Burchett, *Report of an Inquiry into Military Justice in the Australian Defence Force Conducted by Mr J.C.S Burchett, QC, An Investigating Officer Appointed by the Chief of the Defence Force under the* Defence Inquiry (Regulations) 1985 (July 2001).

[26] ibid 128.

[27] The AMC was introduced via the Defence Legislation Amendment Act 2006 (Cth). It did not replace the lower tier of the system comprising summary authorities and discipline officers (dealing with minor disciplinary infringements): see Defence Force Discipline Act 1982 (Australia), ss 106–08; Part IA (Disciplinary infringements) (DFDA). As demonstrated by the statistics in the Judge Advocate General's annual reports, the majority of cases under the DFDA are heard in the lower tiers of the system, rather than by court martial or Defence Force magistrate: see, eg, Judge Advocate General, *Defence Force Discipline Act 1982 – Report for the Period 1 January to 31 December 2023* (2024), Annexes F (Summary Authorities), G, H and I (disciplinary infringements), M (Courts Martial and Defence Force magistrates) ('DFDA Report 2023').

[28] Section 72 of the Australian Constitution provides that judges are appointed until retirement age (that is, 70 years). For a discussion of the features of the AMC see A Duxbury, 'The Curious Case of the Australian Military Court' (2010) 10 *Oxford University Journal of Commonwealth Law* 156.

unconstitutional.[29] In the eyes of the High Court, the AMC was neither fish nor fowl.[30] Unlike the system of courts martial created under the defence power in section 51(vi) of the Constitution, it could not be said that the AMC was directed to 'the maintenance of discipline of the forces' rather than 'the exercise of the judicial power of the Commonwealth'.[31] However, it was also not a court for the purposes of Chapter III of the Constitution given that the appointment of military judges did not comply with section 72. Following *Lane*, the Federal Parliament rapidly reintroduced the system of courts martial and Defence Force magistrates.[32] Subsequent efforts to replace the AMC with a permanent military court in Australia, fully integrated with the (civilian) federal judicial system, have also been unsuccessful.[33] As a result, courts martial (general and restricted) and Defence Force magistrates under the DFDA, as well as the summary authority system for more minor disciplinary offences, are still in operation in Australia.

This discussion of the recent history of Australia's approach highlights two points that are important when considering the choice of jurisdiction. First, while a separate military justice system with jurisdiction over ADF members and defence civilians still operates in Australia, its role has been subject to debate. In this respect, Australia joins other states where questions surrounding the administration of military justice have been raised by civil society, the legislature, military personnel, or national and international courts. These perceptions of the legitimacy, or otherwise, of military justice in a particular state may, beyond the specific factors identified later in this chapter, subtly influence the choice of military or civilian jurisdiction in individual cases.

Second, states that maintain a separate military justice system have recognised the need for reform. Many of those reform efforts have been directed at ensuring that military justice more closely replicates features of civilian justice and is distanced from command influence. Some have been driven by the requirements of human rights law. For example, in both New Zealand and the United Kingdom, reforms have resulted in military courts being staffed with civilian judges and becoming permanent, instead of ad hoc, institutions.[34] In Canada, reforms introduced after the leading Supreme Court of Canada decision in *Généreux* in 1992

[29] *Lane v Morrison* (2009) 239 CLR 230 ('*Lane*').

[30] In a paper published in the Australian Institute of Administrative Law Forum one of the counsel in *Lane* described this as the 'looks like a duck, quacks like a duck' argument: K Cochrane, 'Lane v Morrison [2009] HCA 29' (2010) 61 *AIAL Forum* 62, 69.

[31] *Lane* (n 29) 257.

[32] This was accomplished via the Military Justice (Interim Measures) Act (No 1) 2009 (Cth).

[33] See The Senate Legal and Constitutional Affairs Legislation Committee, Military Court of Australia Bill 2012 [Provisions]; Military Court of Australia (Transitional Provisions and Consequential Amendments) Bill 2012 [Provisions], (October, 2012), vii (recommendation 2), available at www.aph.gov.au/Parliamentary_Business/Committees/Senate/Legal_and_Constitutional_Affairs/Completed_inquiries/2010-13/militarycourt2012/report/index.

[34] See 'National Reports' in S Horvat, I Van Hespen and V Can Gijsegem (eds), *Military Jurisdiction – La Jurisdiction Militaire* (International Society for Military Law and the Law of War, 2013) 366 (New Zealand), 428 (United Kingdom).

gave military judges greater security of tenure by removing fixed renewable terms.[35] The extent to which a military justice system has been 'civilianised' may influence the choice to pursue a case in the civilian or military justice system.

## III. Choice between Military and Civilian Justice Systems

While the need for reform has been recognised in a number of states, many of these efforts have been directed at amending the existing military justice system, rather than abolishing the system and transferring its jurisdiction to civilian institutions. Consequently, there will be a choice as to where an alleged offender will be prosecuted. This part examines the question, 'when' does a conflict of jurisdiction arise?

### A. Nature of the Offence

Defence force members may commit offences that are purely military in character (for example, absence without leave or insubordination) or that would also constitute offences under the ordinary criminal law (for example, theft, rape or fraud). When an offence is only known to the military justice system, the sole option for its prosecution and trial is within that system. In other words, the kind of choice contemplated in this chapter does not arise. But many military criminal codes are broad in nature and aim to capture military offences as well as offences under the ordinary criminal law. The rationale for this coverage is linked to the need to maintain 'discipline and morale' in the defence forces and to ensure that members abide by the criminal law to assist in fulfilling their primary purpose of defending the nation.[36]

In Australia, for example, the DFDA provides a 'comprehensive system of criminal law'[37] that applies to ADF members and defence civilians.[38] Three types of offences are recognised in the DFDA: those that can only be committed in the military context (for example, mutiny and desertion); offences that are known to ordinary criminal law but have a particular relationship to military discipline (for example, assault on a superior officer); and those offences where the only connection with the military is that the alleged offender is a 'Defence member' (a member

[35] For a summary of reforms in the Canadian system see *R v Stillman* [2019] 3 SCR 144, 173–8; *Edwards* (n 15) [101]–102].

[36] See the argument of the Commonwealth of Australia in *Private R v Cowen* (2020) 271 CLR 316, 321.

[37] *Re Tracey; Ex parte Ryan* (1989) 166 CLR 518, 586 ('*Re Tracey*').

[38] A defence civilian is defined as a person who is outside Australia or on enemy operations and has 'consented, in writing, to subject himself or herself to Defence Force discipline while so accompanying that part of the Defence Force': DFDA, s 3.

of the ADF) or a 'Defence civilian'.[39] The incorporation of ordinary criminal offences into military law occurs via section 61 of the DFDA whereby the criminal law of the Australian Capital Territory (ACT) applies in the Jervis Bay Territory.[40] A Defence member or Defence civilian commits an offence under the DFDA when engaging in conduct that would be a civilian offence if committed in the Jervis Bay Territory.[41]

A similar mechanism to incorporate civilian criminal law into military law is also used in other common law jurisdictions, including the United Kingdom, Canada, and New Zealand.[42] Another option for including ordinary crimes within the ambit of military justice is to broadly define military offences so that they effectively cover most, if not all, civilian offences. For example, in the United States, the offence of prejudicial conduct in section 134 of the Uniform Code of Military Justice (UCMJ) captures 'all disorders and neglects to the prejudice of good order and discipline in the armed forces, all conduct of a nature to bring discredit upon the armed forces, and crimes and offenses not capital'.[43]

Even when such a broad incorporation of civilian offences into military law occurs, the state may specifically deny the military justice system jurisdiction over specific civilian offences. For example, even though civilian offences are incorporated into Canadian military law and defence force members accused of such offences are subject to the jurisdiction of courts-martial,[44] a court martial does not have jurisdiction to try any person charged with murder, manslaughter or child abduction committed in Canada.[45] In her 2022 report, Arbour quotes from the 1997 *Report of the Special Advisory Group on Military Justice and Military Police Investigation Services* by Chief Justice Dickson, who suggested that the rationale for excluding these offences was 'presumably because Parliament has determined that such offences have repercussions in society which transcend the interest of the [Canadian Forces] in maintaining military discipline'.[46]

## B. Place where the Offence was Committed

A second factor that will resolve the jurisdictional question is the place where the alleged offence was committed. While civil law countries tend to apply their civilian criminal law to a wide range of extraterritorial offences when committed by

[39] This description of the division of offences in the DFDA is found in *Re Tracey* (n 37) 586–7.
[40] See also definition of a 'Territory Offence' in s 3 of the DFDA.
[41] Jervis Bay is administered directly by the Federal government where the criminal law of the ACT applies.
[42] Armed Forces Act 2006 (UK) s 42: National Defence Act 1985 (Canada) s 130; Armed Forces Discipline Act 1971 (NZ) s 74.
[43] UCMJ art 134.
[44] See above n 42.
[45] National Defence Act 1985 (Canada) s 70.
[46] Quoted in Arbour (n 6) 61.

their nationals, the extraterritorial ambit of the civilian criminal law of common law countries is often more limited.[47] However, military criminal law is normally applicable to all offences committed by defence force members, whether at home or abroad.[48] Accordingly, prosecution under military criminal law in a military court or tribunal may be the only available option when a defence force member commits an offence abroad.

This is illustrated by a 2004 High Court of Australia case, *Re Colonel Aird; Ex parte Alpert*, involving an ADF member stationed at the Royal Malaysian Air Force Base at Butterworth, who was alleged to have raped a British tourist while both were on holiday in Thailand.[49] The complainant went to the Australian military authorities, who intended to try the defence force member in a general court martial. The question for the High Court was whether 'it is beyond the power of the Australian Parliament to make it an offence, punishable by a military tribunal, for a member of the Regular Army, who is on overseas service, but who is on recreation leave at the time, to engage in an act of rape'.[50] The majority of the High Court rejected the constitutional challenge on the basis that the matter 'pertains directly to the discipline, efficiency and morale of the military'.[51] Significantly, proceedings in the military justice system were the only option, as an alleged rape committed by an Australian national in Thailand is generally not punishable under Australian civilian criminal law.

## IV. Mechanisms for Determining the Exercise of Military or Civilian Jurisdiction

Where statutory restrictions on the jurisdiction of military courts or the limitations to the ambit of civilian criminal law are not applicable, the jurisdiction of civilian courts and military tribunals is concurrent. In such situations, law enforcement authorities have a degree of discretion as to where proceedings will be launched.

There are multiple mechanisms through which the exercise of such discretion may be coordinated. One option would be the appointment of a decision-maker who can resolve competition between military and civilian authorities in particular scenarios. Under Australian law, for example, proceedings for treason, murder, manslaughter, bigamy and certain other offences allegedly committed in Australia can only be instituted in the military justice system with the consent of the

[47] See R Liivoja, *Criminal Jurisdiction over Armed Forces Abroad* (Cambridge, Cambridge University Press, 2017) 32.

[48] See DFDA, s 9, for the extra-territorial reach of the Act to Defence members and Defence civilians outside Australia.

[49] *Re Colonel Aird; Ex parte Alpert* (2004) 220 CLR 308 ('*Alpert*').

[50] ibid 311.

[51] ibid 313 (per Gleeson CJ).

Commonwealth Director of Public Prosecutions.[52] In New Zealand, a trial by their Court Martial of a person for treason, murder, manslaughter, sexual violation or bigamy can only occur with the consent of the Attorney-General.[53]

Indeed, this appears to be a common feature of many military justice systems that trace their origins to British military law. Interestingly, the United Kingdom itself has recently become an exception. Until 2009, UK courts-martial were not able to deal with a small number of serious civilian offences – principally murder, manslaughter and rape – when committed in the United Kingdom.[54] The entry into force of the Armed Forces Act 2006 removed this constraint. This development has proven to be controversial.[55] In the lead-up to the adoption of the Armed Forces Act 2006, it was assumed that the newly-established permanent Court Martial would only sparingly exercise jurisdiction over serious civilian offences committed in the United Kingdom.[56] Civil society organisations subsequently raised concerns about multiple issues: the level of coordination between military and civilian authorities, the substantial number of sexual offences dealt with by the military justice system, the number of convictions obtained in that system, and the option of downgrading allegations of sexual assault from indictable-equivalent offences to summary offences (where they would be dealt with by military summary authorities).[57] Shaun Lyons, a retired senior Crown Court judge, recommended in his 2018 review of the UK service justice system that Court Martial jurisdiction should no longer include murder, manslaughter and rape when these offences are committed in the United Kingdom, except with the consent of the Attorney General.[58] In other words, the review recommended adopting the New Zealand approach. While the UK government did not accept this recommendation, the Armed Forces Act 2006 was subsequently amended so as to direct military and civilian prosecutors to agree on protocols regarding the exercise of concurrent jurisdiction.[59]

This leads to the other coordinating mechanism, namely prosecutorial guidelines or express agreements between military and civilian prosecutors. In the

[52] DFDA, s 63.

[53] Armed Forces Discipline Act 1971 (New Zealand) s 74.

[54] Naval Discipline Act 1957, s 48(2); Army Act 1955, s 70(4); and Air Force Act 1955, s 70(4).

[55] See initial concerns reflected in, eg, C Taylor, *The Armed Forces Bill: Bill 94 of Session 2005-2006* (House of Commons Library Research Paper 05/86, 7 December 2005) 15, available at researchbriefings.files.parliament.uk/documents/RP05-86/RP05-86.pdf.

[56] See UK House of Commons, Select Committee on the Armed Forces Bill, *Armed Forces Bill: Special Report of Session 2005–06* (25 April 2006) vol 1, paras 93–94, available at publications.parliament.uk/pa/cm200506/cmselect/cmarmed/828/828i.pdf; HL Deb (6 November 2006) col. 597 (Lord Drayson), available at publications.parliament.uk/pa/ld199697/ldhansrd/pdvn/lds06/text/61106-0002.htm.

[57] See, eg, Liberty, *Military Justice, Second-Rate Justice: Criminal Justice, Complaints and Human Rights Myths in the Armed Forces* (January 2019), pt 1, available at www.libertyhumanrights.org.uk/wp-content/uploads/2020/01/LIB-10-Military-Justice-Report-20_01_19.pdf.

[58] See S Lyons, *Service Justice System Review (Part 1)* (29 March 2018) recommendation 1, available at assets.publishing.service.gov.uk/media/5f636c83e90e0759fdaaba37/SJS_Review_Part_1_Report_for_publication__accessible_.pdf.

[59] See Armed Forces Act 2006, pt 13, ch 3A (ss 320A, 320B and 320C), inserted by Armed Forces Act 2021, s 7.

United Kingdom, as now required by the Armed Forces Act 2006, there are protocols between the Director of Public Prosecutions and the Director of Service Prosecutions regarding the exercise of criminal jurisdiction in England and Wales and Northern Ireland, respectively.[60] The UK protocols are divided into sections on 'principles governing decisions regarding jurisdiction' and 'factors' relevant to determining jurisdiction. In Australia, the Director of Military Prosecutions has signed a Memorandum of Understanding with the Commonwealth Director of Public Prosecutions and the Directors of Public Prosecutions of each of the Australian states and territories.[61] While in Australia such a memorandum is neither required nor specifically authorised by statute, in *Private R v Cowen*, the plurality of the High Court acknowledged that policies between the military and civilian authorities may govern questions of whether the jurisdiction of service tribunals 'should' be exercised.[62] In Canada, the exercise of concurrent jurisdiction is governed by the 2023 Statement of Principles and Presumptions for the Exercise of Concurrent Jurisdiction by Canadian Prosecuting Authorities.[63] And in New Zealand, the Commander's Handbook on Armed Forces Law outlines the principles that govern concurrent jurisdiction.[64]

## V. Factors Influencing the Choice of Jurisdiction

As well as the mechanisms discussed above, there are a range of other factors that impact the choice between civilian and military justice systems, including those that have been identified in the relevant prosecutorial protocols, agreements, or guidelines, as well as those that operate independently of such guidelines. The

[60] Protocol Regarding the Exercise of Criminal Jurisdiction in England and Wales between the Director of Public Prosecutions and the Director of Service Prosecutions, 25 October 2023 ('England and Wales Protocol'); Protocol Regarding the Exercise of Criminal Jurisdiction in Northern Ireland between the Director of Public Prosecutions for Northern Ireland and the Director of Service Prosecutions, 4 November 2024 ('Northern Ireland Protocol'), available at www.gov.uk/guidance/service-prosecuting-authority#protocols-relating-to-concurrent-jurisdiction-in-the-uk. At the time of writing, it was reported that a protocol regarding jurisdiction in Scotland was still being negotiated.

[61] Memorandum of Understanding between the Australian Directors of Public Prosecutions and Director of Military Prosecutions (22 May 2007), Annex B to Director of Military Prosecutions, *Report for the Period 12 June 2006 to 31 December 2007* (Department of Defence 2008). This Memorandum of Understanding is complemented by the Director of Military Prosecutions Prosecution Policy, 23 December 2021, Annex A to Director of Military Prosecutions, *Report for the Period 01 January to 31 December 2021* (Commonwealth of Australia 2022).

[62] *Private R v Cowen* (n 36) 344.

[63] Federal-Provincial-Territorial Heads of Prosecution Committee, Statement of Principles and Presumptions for the Exercise of Concurrent Jurisdiction by Canadian Prosecuting Authorities, 1 November 2023, available at www.canada.ca/en/department-national-defence/corporate/reports-publications/military-law/statement-principles-presumptions-concurrent-jurisdiction.html ('Canadian Statement').

[64] 'Section 7 – Concurrent Jurisdiction in New Zealand', in New Zealand Defence Force, *Manual of Armed Forces Law – Commander's Handbook on Military Law* (DM 69 2ed Vol 1), 2–15 ('NZ Manual of Armed Forces Law').

significance and the compelling force of these factors will differ from jurisdiction to jurisdiction. The factors listed here fall into two broad groups. The first group – promoting fair and efficient justice, maintaining or enforcing discipline, and promoting public interest – amount to overarching principles that broadly guide the decision-making process. The second group – seriousness of the offence, national security, resourcing, and other considerations – are more specific factors that flow from the overarching principles.

## A. Promoting Fair and Efficient Justice

In the United Kingdom, the Armed Forces Act provides that the guidance contained in protocols agreed between military and civilian prosecutors 'must be designed to promote fair and efficient justice.'[65] The two UK protocols likewise include a provision stating that 'the overriding principle is to promote fair and efficient justice', including 'support for the effective participation of the victims, witnesses, suspects and defendants, to ensure public confidence in both the civilian justice system and the service justice system.'[66] Neither the Canadian nor the Australian policies include a similar express statement – instead, both focus on the purpose of service discipline – that is, to maintain discipline and morale in the respective defence forces.[67] However, various factors outlined below (for example, those relating to alleged crimes involving civilian victims) are based on perceptions as to the fairness and efficiency of the system to both the accused and the victims of offences.

## B. Maintaining or Enforcing Discipline

Maintaining the discipline of the defence forces is a foundational objective of military justice systems.[68] The centrality of this consideration arises in some instances from the constitutional provisions that enable the creation and functioning of the military justice system. For example, in Australia, the federal Parliament has competence to legislate in certain constitutionally enumerated areas, including 'naval and military defence'.[69] The federal Parliament can only legislate with respect to this power if a measure 'does tend or might reasonably be considered to conduce to or to promote or to advance the defence of the Commonwealth'.[70] The question of military discipline and the Constitution is more oblique when certain

[65] Armed Force Act 2006 (UK), s 320A(4), 320B(5) and 320C(5).
[66] England and Wales Protocol (n 60) [3.2]; Northern Ireland Protocol (n 60) [3.2].
[67] Australian Memorandum of Understanding (n 61) [12]; Canadian Statement (n 63) [1].
[68] *Généreux*' (n 22) 293 ; *Private R v Cowen* (n 36) 338, 343.
[69] Australian Constitution, s 51(vi).
[70] *Marcus Clark & Co Ltd v The Commonwealth* (1952) 87 CLR 177, 216 (Dixon CJ).

due process rights are denied in the military justice system. In the United States, the Fifth Amendment to the Constitution creates a right to a jury trial, 'except in cases arising in the land or naval forces'.[71] Similarly, section 11(f) of the Canadian Charter of Rights and Freedoms guarantees the right to a jury trial for any offence where the maximum punishment is five years imprisonment (or more), 'except in the case of an offence under military law tried before a military tribunal'.[72] In Australia, section 80 of the Constitution requires a jury for 'the trial on indictment of any offence against the law of the Commonwealth'. However, trials in the military justice system are not 'on indictment' and therefore are excluded from the constitutional guarantee.[73]

Of course, whether these provisions place limitations on the jurisdiction of military courts in practice depends on the way in which they are interpreted. It has been argued in the United States, Canada and Australia that the constitutionality of military justice depends on there being a substantial connection between the matter under consideration and the defence forces, beyond the status of the accused as a defence force member. The Canadian context was described by Karakatsanis and Rowe JJ of the Supreme Court of Canada in their dissenting judgment in *R v Stillman* as follows:

> Military court jurisdiction has historically been subject to important limits. Initially, the types of offences that could be tried by military courts were limited to offences that were specific to the military, such as desertion, mutiny and sedition. As the jurisdiction of military courts expanded to include civilian offences, civilian courts maintained primary jurisdiction where offences were triable in either court .... Over the last four decades, the development of a military connection test in Canada has limited military court jurisdiction to offences that are military in nature or take place in military circumstances.[74]

While Karakatsanis and Rowe JJ favoured the military connection requirement,[75] the majority held that the accused's military status was sufficient for an offence to be tried by a military tribunal.[76] Similarly, the US Supreme Court in 1987[77] and the High Court of Australia in 2020[78] rejected the so-called 'service connection' test and acknowledged the constitutionality of a military trial of a currently serving defence force member for any civilian offence.

As a result, even crimes that have only a small connection with military service can be tried in a military court – this includes the trial of a defence force member who commits sexual assault against a civilian while off duty, off base and where

[71] United States Constitution, amend V.
[72] See *Stillman* (n 35).
[73] See discussion in Duxbury, 'The Curious Case of the Australian Military Court' (n 28) 172, 180–1.
[74] *Stillman* (n 35) 206.
[75] ibid 207.
[76] ibid 203.
[77] *Solorio v US*, 483 US 435 (1987).
[78] *Private R v Cowen* (n 36).

there is no connection to the military.[79] In *Private R v Cowen*, the plaintiff, in arguing for the service connection test, suggested that a defence force member who drives at excessive speed while on holiday or chops down a protected tree in his or her own backyard should be dealt with by the civilian system.[80] However, the plurality of the High Court rejected these examples on the basis that 'it is essential to the discipline and morale of the ADF that its members are required to abide by the law of the land'.[81] While the judges recognised that there may be policy reasons for favouring one jurisdiction over the other for minor offences, such policies of the civil and military authorities did not impact on the valid conferral of jurisdiction on the military.[82]

These decisions mean that there are few constitutional limits on the power of military courts or tribunals to hear cases involving defence force personnel. This is particularly important where constitutional guarantees, for example, trial by jury, for serious offences are not required in the military justice system. In the US context, Eugene Fidell has suggested that '[t]he use of the military justice system to prosecute non-service-connected offenses is undesirable because it tends to buttress the unfortunate notion that the military is a separate society'.[83] His concern focuses on the impact of 'diluting constitutional rights relating to the trial of criminal cases'.[84] Groves, in a submission co-authored with the authors of this chapter to the Senate Legal and Constitutional Affairs Legislation Committee, expressed concern that if a permanent military court, governed by Chapter III of the Australian Constitution, was to be established, then any attempt to exclude trial by jury in section 80 of the Constitution should be interrogated carefully lest it give rise to a future constitutional challenge.[85] However, currently there are few constitutional principles that restrict the choice of the military over the civilian system for crimes under civilian criminal law.

Although a broad reading of the relevant constitutional provisions has resulted in an extensive concurrent jurisdiction between military and civilian courts, that does not mean that law enforcement authorities cannot consider the extent to which military discipline is furthered by proceedings in a specific case. The opposite is true. Notably, the Australian Memorandum of Understanding provides that '[j]urisdiction under [the DFDA] may be only be exercised where proceedings

[79] Recall the facts of *Ex parte Alpert* (2004) 220 CLR 308, as discussed in the text accompanying notes 49–51 above.

[80] *Private R v Cowen* (n 36) 344.

[81] ibid (per Kiefel CJ, Bell and Keane JJ). See also 355 (per Gageler J).

[82] ibid 344.

[83] ER Fidell, 'The Service-Connection Story – From O'Callahan to Solorio' in N Singh and FD Rosenblatt, *March to Justice: Global Military Justice Landmarks* (Noida, OCCAM, 2022) 23, 32.

[84] ibid 33.

[85] See A Duxbury, R Liivoja and M Groves, *Submission to the Senate Standing Committee on Legal and Constitutional Affairs: Inquiry into the Military Court of Australia Bill 2012 and the Military Court of Australia (Transitional Provisions and Consequential Amendments) Bill 2012* (13 July 2012), available at www.aph.gov.au/Parliamentary_Business/Committees/Senate/Legal_and_Constitutional_Affairs/Completed_inquiries/2010-13/militarycourt2012/submissions.

under the Act can reasonably be regarded as serving the purpose of maintaining or enforcing service discipline.'[86] The Canadian Statement includes a similar presumption while noting that this is not limited to actions 'occurring in military circumstances'.[87] The Australian Memorandum of Understanding is more explicit in listing a number of circumstances relevant to determining a connection with service discipline, including whether the defence member was on duty at the time of the alleged conduct and whether it involved 'an abuse of rank, or position or military authority, or of privilege or trust'.[88] In New Zealand, in determining whether to refer an allegation to the civilian authority, the commanding officer can take into account whether 'the alleged offence is of a type which is of particular concern to the discipline or efficiency of the Armed Forces'.[89] Certain offences, including serious sexual assault, committed in New Zealand in peacetime should 'normally be investigated by the civil authority'.[90] In other words, although the military justice system may not be precluded from exercising jurisdiction over a matter where the disciplinary aspect is secondary compared to the overall criminality of the conduct, the arrangements between law enforcement authorities may favour proceedings in the civilian justice system.

## C. Public Interest

The 'public interest' is explicitly mentioned as a relevant factor in the Australian Memorandum of Understanding and the Canadian Statement of Principles and Presumptions. In the Australian Memorandum of Understanding, serious crimes are linked to the concept of 'public interest', pointing to prosecution in a civilian criminal court.[91] In addition, the Australian Memorandum of Understanding refers to matters that 'have a high public profile or are likely to attract substantial public interest' – indicating that these are more likely to be tried in a civilian court.[92] In this way, the Australian Memorandum of Understanding recognises two forms of public interest: that commonly used in the public law context (referring to '"community", "common" good or welfare, "general" welfare, "society", public" or the "nation"')[93] as well as the prospect of the public (and media) being 'interested' in a matter. In Canada, the 'degree of public interest in a potential prosecution' is to be assessed by both the civilian and military prosecution authorities to determine

[86] Australian Memorandum of Understanding (n 61) [21].
[87] Canadian Statement (n 63) [12] and note 3.
[88] Australian Memorandum of Understanding (n 61) [23].
[89] NZ Manual of Armed Forces Law (n 64) [2.7.3(b)].
[90] ibid [2.7.4(b)].
[91] Australian Memorandum of Understanding (n 61) [36].
[92] ibid.
[93] C Wheeler, 'The Public Interest: We know it is important, but do we know what it means' (2006) 48 *AIAL Forum* 12, 16.

jurisdiction.[94] In the UK protocols, the term 'public interest' is not used; instead, reference is made to maintaining 'public confidence'[95] in the two justice systems. The importance of maintaining public confidence in military tribunals has also been affirmed repeatedly in the European Court of Human Rights case law considering the United Kingdom military justice system.[96]

The concept of 'public interest' is notoriously difficult to define – a point that has been highlighted by both scholars and courts.[97] The Australian Memorandum of Understanding links the public interest to the 'serious nature' of the alleged conduct. In determining whether either a civilian or military justice system is appropriate, there could be a range of other relevant factors, including the public interest in open justice (which would arguably be enhanced by civilian trials over military trials)[98] and the public interest in ensuring that serious matters are heard before a jury (to ensure parity between the treatment of civilians and service members). In the military justice context, the European Court of Human Rights has referred to the concept when considering whether the decision by a British soldier to waive his right to trial by court martial in favour of summary trial would 'run counter to any important public interest'.[99] Thus, the Court recognised that the public had an interest in ensuring that an individual's rights are protected in any trial process.

The public interest could also include wider considerations. In the case of the war crimes allegations against Australia Special Forces and, indeed, where such offences have been alleged in other countries, there is also an implicit understanding that a state's national interests have been damaged by these allegations. This may lead to a perception that the military will be reluctant to investigate and prosecute its own – hence the need to establish civilian processes with a degree of transparency, outside the military justice system.[100] The public interest could also include the effect on operational effectiveness and morale of the military. In Canada, Morris Fish, a former Justice of the Supreme Court of Canada, recognised in his report as the Third Independent Review Authority to the Minister of National Defence (the 'Fish Report') that 'impact on unit morale and cohesion' and 'military exigency', as articulated in the Military Police Group Orders, are

[94] Canadian Statement (n 63) [20(a); (b)].

[95] England and Wales Protocol (n 60) [3.2]; Northern Ireland Protocol (n 60) [3.2].

[96] *Cooper v United Kingdom* (2004) 39 EHRR 8, [104]; *Grieves v United Kingdom* (2004) 39 EHRR 2 [69]; *Martin* (n 22) [41].

[97] The difficulty in defining the 'public interest' is succinctly explained in J Johnston, 'Whose interests? Why defining the 'public interest' is such a challenge', *The Conversation* (23 January 2017), theconversation.com/whose-interests-why-defining-the-public-interest-is-such-a-challenge-84278.

[98] In Australia, proceedings by way of court martial or Defence Force magistrate 'shall be in public' unless there are reasons to exclude members of the public: DFDA, s 140.

[99] *Bell v United Kingdom* (2007) 45 EHRR 24, [45].

[100] The UK's decision to launch an independent statutory inquiry, led by Justice Haddon Cave, to investigate alleged war crimes committed by members of the British SAS follows an investigation by the Royal Military Police which resulted in no charges being laid: see 'Revised Terms of Reference for the Independent Inquiry Relating to Afghanistan' (September 2023), available at www.iia.independent-inquiry.uk/.

relevant factors in determining whether military police will pursue an investigation or whether the civilian police should deal with a complaint.[101] This could work in two ways: is the morale of the military enhanced by having military personnel treated in the same way as other citizens when faced with serious offences (the 'citizens in uniform' concept)? Or is morale enhanced by having offences on operational service dealt with by those with an understanding of the unique 'characteristics' of military life?[102]

## D. Seriousness of the Offence

As already discussed, some states exclude the exercise of military jurisdiction over certain serious offences altogether or require the concurrence of civilian authorities.[103] But even beyond those enumerated offences, some states prefer dealing with serious offences committed in the territory of the state through the civilian justice system. Thus, the Australian Memorandum of Understanding specifies that the public interest 'may be best served' by the prosecution of certain serious offences, terrorism, trafficking in weapons or arms, or those affected by Australia's international obligations, including war crimes, in the civilian system.[104] In the case of the allegations of war crimes mentioned at the beginning of this chapter, investigation by the Federal Police and prosecution through the (civilian) Commonwealth Director of Prosecutions was preferred.[105] A new body, the Office of the Special Investigator (OSI), was established to work with the Australian Federal Police to investigate allegations of offences against Australian criminal law that arose out of the Brereton Report.[106] At the time of writing, despite 19 people having been referred to the OSI, only one ADF member has been charged (with the war crime of murder) under this process.[107] There may be many reasons for the slow progress, including the difficulty in engaging with people in Afghanistan following the return to power of the Taliban.[108]

[101] MJ Fish, *Report of the Third Independent Review Authority to the Minister of National Defence Pursuant to subsection 273.601(1) of the National Defence Act, RSC 1985, c N-5* (30 April 2021), [222]–[223] ('Fish Report'), available at www.canada.ca/en/department-national-defence/corporate/policies-standards/acts-regulations/third-independent-reviews-nda.html.

[102] See *Engel v Netherlands* (1979-80) 1 EHRR 647, 688.

[103] See Part IV above.

[104] Australian Memorandum of Understanding (n 61) [36].

[105] Brereton Report (n 1) 284–5, [61].

[106] See 'Office of the Special Investigator', available at www.osi.gov.au/.

[107] S Rubensztein-Dunlop and M Willacy, 'SAS veteran Oliver Schulz charged with war crime of murder over killing of Afghan man in field', *The Age* (20 March 2023), available at www.abc.net.au/news/2023-03-20/former-sas-soldier-arrested-over-afghanistan-killing/102119554; L Tingle, 'Why allegations of war crimes against Australian Defence Force soldiers may never result in charges', *ABC News* (9 October), available at www.abc.net.au/news/2024-10-09/australian-soliders-more-war-crime-charges-unlikely-brereton/104450080.

[108] See discussion in Tingle (n 107).

The decision to prefer civilian prosecution in relation to allegations raised in the Brereton Report appears to be for (at least) two reasons: first, to ensure that there was no question that Australia would fulfil its obligations under the Rome Statute of the International Criminal Court given requirements of complementarity,[109] and second, so that the defendants would be tried by a jury.[110] While the military justice system operates without a civilian jury, there is clearly some discomfort about the possibility of a war crimes trial for murder being held without a jury. Despite the ease with which the requirement in section 80 of the Australian Constitution may be circumvented, many would regard a jury trial for a serious offence in Australia as a fundamental constitutional guarantee. This also raises the question of the 'public interest' in a jury trial and public perceptions about the 'guarantee' of such a trial, despite the limited ambit of section 80.

## E. National Security

Considerations of national security may impact whether a matter proceeds to the military or civilian justice system. This could be seen in two ways: first, it may be considered that crimes involving matters of national security should be heard in a civilian criminal court on the basis that they are of a serious nature and this would best serve the public interest. Second, it could be argued that matters involving national security should be heard in military courts or tribunals where the personnel have security clearances. For example, if the matter relates to the conduct of a military operation overseas and the alleged conduct amounts to a war crime – thereby activating the possibility of concurrent jurisdiction – there may be a need to protect classified and security-sensitive information in the course of investigations and proceedings. The ability of the military or civilian justice systems to protect such information (without compromising the integrity of the proceedings) may differ. In support of the first approach, pursuant to the Australian Memorandum of Understanding, the preference is for serious alleged offences involving 'espionage or a threat or potential threat to Australia's national security, other than provided in the [DFDA]' to be heard in a civilian court on the basis that this best serves the public interest.[111] Consequently, the seriousness of these offences favours civilian trials.

While there is a presumption in favour of open justice in both civilian and military courts, proceedings can be closed in certain circumstances, including for national security reasons.[112] An example in the military context is provided by a

[109] Brereton Report (n 1) 284, [59].
[110] ibid 284–5, [61].
[111] Australian Memorandum of Understanding (n 61) [36].
[112] See above n 98. Section 140(2) of the DFDA provides that in proceedings before a court martial or Defence Force magistrate members of the public can be excluded, or an order preventing report of the whole or part of proceedings can be made, if it is considered 'necessary in the interest of the security or defence of Australia'. In the civilian context, courts can also be closed: see, eg, the Open Courts Act 2013

trial of a New Zealand defence force member facing multiple counts relating to espionage in the Court Martial of New Zealand.[113] In March 2023, it was reported that the Chief Judge closed proceedings on the basis that the processes for recording and retention of the transcript did not comply with security requirements.[114] However, there may be additional complications when a civilian jury is present. Civilian justice systems increasingly allow for the admission into evidence of material containing classified information without a change in the classification status of such material. In Australia, the National Security Information (Criminal and Civil Proceedings) Act 2004 (Cth) provides a framework for how such information is disclosed and protected in criminal proceedings, although an independent review has found that the framework suffers from multiple shortcomings.[115] Any such framework is bound to have limitations, especially when it comes to civilian trials by jury. In a case before a military tribunal, ensuring that all participants, including members of a court martial panel, hold appropriate security clearances may be easier than in a civilian court.

## F. Resources

Another factor that will assist in determining the appropriate jurisdiction is the effective use of resources. The England and Wales Protocol suggests that capacity and resources 'may make it more efficient to bring proceedings in either the service or civilian jurisdiction'.[116] Similarly, the Fish Report highlights the 'respective expertise and resources of the military and civilian justice systems' as being a relevant factor.[117] Issues involving resources can include questions as to whether a military investigatory and prosecution service is adequately resourced to deal with certain types of offences. The Fish Report points to the existence of 'specialized resources' in the Canadian civilian justice system for dealing with matters such as domestic violence, child assault and driving offences.[118] However, resourcing concerns may also be felt by the civilian police. For example, in response to the proposal to move sexual offences in the CAF to the civilian authorities, in 2022 the

(Vic), which enables a court to be closed or a suppression order to be made where it is 'necessary to prevent prejudice to the interests of the Commonwealth or a State or Territory in relation to national or international security': ss 18(1)(b), 30(2)(b).

[113] J Wilkinson, 'Proceedings relating to New Zealand's first military case of espionage to recommence in private', *The New Zealand Herald* (30 March 2023), available at www.nzherald.co.nz/nz/proceedings-relating-to-new-zealands-first-military-case-of-espionage-to-recommence-in-private/MT76QKKICZAUPJCC5T77LIIO6A/.

[114] ibid.

[115] G Donaldson, *Independent National Security Legislation Monitor (INSLM) Report: Review into the operation and effectiveness of the National Security Information (Criminal and Civil Proceedings) Act 2004* (October 2023), available at www.inslm.gov.au/publications/national-security-information-criminal-and-civil-proceedings-act-2004.

[116] England and Wales Protocol (n 60) [3.5.4].

[117] Fish Report (n 101) [245].

[118] ibid [225].

Ontario Association of Chiefs of Police wrote to the Solicitor-General of Ontario expressing concerns regarding resources, particularly for 'smaller police forces'.[119]

Another resourcing type 'concern' relates to the need for an investigation to take place wholly in the territory of the relevant defence force or whether an investigation must take place overseas. Additionally, if part of the proceedings needs to be heard overseas because of witness availability, it may be that the deployability of a military justice system and its ability to hear cases outside a state's jurisdiction suggest that it is the more appropriate forum. Interestingly, in Australia, even though courts martial, as provided for in Australian law, can sit overseas, this seldom occurs. There are at least two reasons: first, the security situation in places where the Defence Force is deployed is often not conducive to holding trials; and second, the time taken to investigate serious offences may mean that the accused has already been posted back to Australia by the time proceedings get to the trial stage.

## G. Other Considerations

There are a range of other factors that may give rise to a preference for commencing proceedings in either the military or the civilian justice system – some of these are explicitly related to the public interest or the seriousness of the offence; others may be considered more broadly. For example, the location of witnesses may be a relevant consideration in determining 'who' should assume prosecutorial jurisdiction. The two UK protocols highlight the ability of 'service police to deploy rapidly' where witnesses are outside the UK.[120] The list of factors that favour civilian jurisdiction in Australia, Canada, the United Kingdom and New Zealand includes whether the offence impacted on civilian persons or property.[121] In Australia, this is seen as relevant to the public interest (as discussed above);[122] in the United Kingdom, it is listed as 'a principle' that points to proceedings being 'ordinarily … brought in the civilian jurisdiction'.[123] If the alleged offences involve family violence[124] or civilian co-accused,[125] then civilian prosecution and trial may also be favoured. Amongst other provisions, the UK protocols specifically point to the

[119] See Arbour (n 6) 97.

[120] England and Wales Protocol (n 60) [3.7.4]; Northern Ireland Protocol (n 60) [3.7.4]. See also Canadian Statement on 'geographic considerations' (n 63) [20(e)].

[121] Australian Memorandum of Understanding (n 61) [36]; Canadian Statement (n 63) [13]; England and Wales Protocol (n 60) [3.3.1]; Northern Ireland Protocol (n 60) [3.3.1]; NZ Manual of Armed Forces Law (n 64) [2.7.4(d)].

[122] Australian Memorandum of Understanding (n 61) [36].

[123] England and Wales Protocol (n 60) [3.3.1]; Northern Ireland Protocol (n 60) [3.3.1].

[124] Eg, England and Wales Protocol (n 60) [3.6.2]; Northern Ireland Protocol (n 60) [3.6.2]; Canadian Statement (n 63) [15(c)].

[125] Eg, Australian Memorandum of Understanding (n 61) [36]; Canadian Statement (n 63) [15(d)]; England and Wales Protocol (n 60) [3.3.3]; Northern Ireland Protocol (n 60) [3.3.3]; NZ Manual of Armed Forces Law (n 64) [2.7.4(e)].

UK's obligation under the United Nations Convention on the Rights of the Child to treat the best interests of the child as a primary consideration as favouring civilian jurisdiction where the accused, victim or witness is a child.[126] The recognition of this factor is pertinent in the military context given that persons under 18 can be recruited into many defence forces.

A final factor that may be relevant in determining whether to investigate and prosecute via the military or civilian justice system may be the wishes of the complainant.[127] While the wishes of the complainant may not determine whether and where a matter is investigated and prosecuted, it is unlikely that prosecution authorities would act contrary to the wishes of a complainant.

## VI. Concluding Remarks

The aim of this chapter was to demonstrate that a potential clash between military and civilian justice systems arising from the incorporation of civilian offences into military law can be resolved in several different ways. At the highest level, constraints on the subject matter jurisdiction of military courts and limitations on the geographical ambit of civilian criminal law may preclude such clashes altogether. Where competition or conflict arises, the solution may lie with formal coordination mechanisms and a complex mix of factors. The question may well arise whether this situation is appropriate. Indeed, it could be suggested that the factors analysed in Part V of this chapter introduce a degree of uncertainty for an alleged offender.

We suggest that this is not as problematic as it may seem.

First, considering the complexities of military offences, it is difficult to provide hard and fast rules that would provide a solution in all instances. For example, Australian practice suggests that the more serious the crime, the more likely it is to be tried in the civilian justice system. This appears to be the case because the criminal dimension of such offences is more significant than the disciplinary dimension. Thus, the public interest demands civilian prosecution and a civilian trial. Such a calculation has clearly driven the decision to prosecute alleged war crimes by Australian defence force members in Afghanistan through the civilian system. The opposite may also be true: an offence that in the civilian context would be relatively minor (for example, petty theft) may be so corrosive to trust and discipline in the defence forces as to be treated as a serious matter. In any event, it would be very difficult to stipulate in the abstract that, for example, murder should only be prosecuted in the civilian system whereas a case involving the causing of bodily injury should be brought in the military system. The degree of discretion

[126] England and Wales Protocol (n 60) [3.6.1]; Northern Ireland Protocol (n 60) [3.6.1].

[127] Eg, Canadian Statement (n 63) [20(c)]; England and Wales Protocol (n 60) [3.5.5]; Northern Ireland Protocol (n 60) [3.5.4].

afforded to prosecutors in the relevant guidelines of all four countries discussed in this chapter allows for a finer balancing of competing interests than a one-size-fits-all regulation.

Second, provided that both the military and civilian systems comply with principles of independence and impartiality and the requirements for a fair trial, the uncertainty about the prospects of a military or civilian prosecution does not necessarily result in a serious injustice to the defendant. In this respect the Australian Judge Advocate General (JAG), Rear Admiral John Rush, in his 2023 report to Parliament, listed several recommendations for amendments to the DFDA, some of which are relevant to ensuring fairness for the accused. For example, he highlighted the need for courts martial panels to provide reasons for sentence as Australia is 'the only Five eyes military retaining the historic system of a court martial panel determining guilt and determining penalty without providing reasons'.[128] Rush was also critical of the failure to give a defence member the ability to choose between trial before a court martial or a Defence Force magistrate.[129] He compares this to the civilian system, where an accused has the right to choose trial by jury, and suggests legislative reform to remedy this issue.[130]

Leaving aside these concerns, defence force members must assume that their actions are governed by military and civilian law. Defence members, at least in Australia, are informed on enlistment that they are subject to discipline law. Defence force members know – or at least ought to know – what kind of behaviour is prohibited and punishable. Not knowing definitively which justice system will address their wrongdoing does not seem to offend against the principle of legality under criminal law. Having said this, it is important to be upfront and explicit about the factors that prosecutors and investigators consider when allocating cases between military and civilian justice systems. The guidelines governing Australian, Canadian, New Zealand and United Kingdom prosecutorial authorities are significant in enhancing transparency and accountability in decision-making.

[128] DFDA Report 2023 (n 27) 8 [44(a)]. Rush describes the failure to provide such reasons as 'anachronistic and contrary to fundamental principles of open justice and fairness'. The Royal Commission into Defence and Veteran Suicide also recommended that the 'current provisions relating to court martial panels not being required to provide reasons for punishments' should be reviewed: see Royal Commission into Defence and Veteran Suicide, *Executive Summary, Recommendations and the Fundamentals – Final Report (Vol 1)* (2024), 115 (Recommendation 34).

[129] DFDA Report 2023 (n 27) 9 [g].

[130] ibid 10.

# INDEX

www.ingramcontent.com/pod-product-compliance
Ingram Content Group UK Ltd.
Pitfield, Milton Keynes, MK11 3LW, UK
UKHW020241290926
15470UKWH00002B/660